The Empire of Things

Publication of the Advanced Seminar Series is made possible by generous support from The Brown Foundation, Inc., of Houston, Texas.

School of American Research
Advanced Seminar Series

Douglas W. Schwartz
General Editor

The Empire of Things

Contributors

Annie E. Coombes
Department of History of Art, Birbeck College, University of London

Webb Keane
Department of Anthropology, University of Michigan

Barbara Kirshenblatt-Gimblett
Department of Performance Studies, New York University

Claudio Lomnitz
Department of History, University of Chicago

Daniel Miller
Department of Anthropology, University College–London

Fred R. Myers
Department of Anthropology, New York University

Christopher B. Steiner
Department of Art History and Museum Studies, Connecticut College

Nicholas Thomas
Department of Anthropology
Goldsmith College, University of London

Annette B. Weiner
Department of Anthropology, New York University

To the memory of Annette Weiner,
an inspiring friend and colleague

The Empire of Things

Regimes of Value and Material Culture

Edited by Fred R. Myers

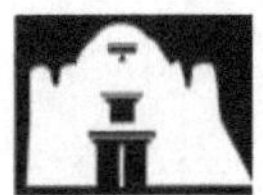

School of American Research Press
Santa Fe

School of American Research Press
Post Office Box 2188
Santa Fe, New Mexico 87504-2188
www.sarpress.sarweb.org

Editors: Joan K. O'Donnell and Jane Kepp
Production Manager: Cynthia Welch
Series Design: Context, Inc.
Indexer: Jan Wright

Library of Congress Cataloging-in-Publication Data:
The empire of things : regimes of value and material culture / edited by Fred R. Myers.— 1st ed.

p. cm. — (School of American Research advanced seminar series)

Essays from an advanced seminar held at the School of American Research, Nov. 3-7, 1996.

Includes bibliographical references and index.

ISBN 1-930618-05-0 (cloth)—1-930618-06-9 (paper)

1. Material culture—Social aspects—Congresses. 2. Group identity—Congresses. 3. Values—Congresses. 4. Art and society—Congresses. 5. Ceremonial exchange—Congresses. I. Myers, Fred R., 1948- II. Series.

GN406 .E56 2001
306—dc21 2001032038

Library of Congress Catalog Card Number 2001032038.
International Standard Book Numbers 0-930618-05-0 (cloth) and 0-930618-06-9 (paper). Fourth paperback printing 2009.

Cover illustration: Foreign loans to the exhibition *Cubism and Abstract Art,* refused admission to the United States as "works of art" by customs inspectors, 1936. Photograph by Beaumont Newhall, courtesy of the Museum of Modern Art, New York.

Contents

Illustrations

Preface

The essays in this volume are a product of an advanced seminar at the School of American Research titled "Material Culture: Habitats and Values." Originally organized by Annette Weiner and me, the seminar met from Sunday, 3 November 1996, through Thursday, 7 November 1996. Thanks are due to the staff of the School of American Research for their hospitality and patience.

I would like to thank Annette Weiner for her inspiration to have the conference and for the many discussions we had about these issues. Because of illness, Annette was unable to attend, but the spirit of her work remained a major inspiration for the papers and the discussion. Her untimely death on 7 December 1997 delayed the publication of these papers, which we now offer as a *festschrift* to her memory. An extended interview with Annette is included as part of the volume's particular rethinking of material culture.

Fred R. Myers

The Empire of Things

1

Introduction

The Empire of Things

Fred R. Myers

The conditions of transnationalism under which most people in the world now live have created new and often contradictory cultural and economic values and meanings in objects—that is, in material culture—as those objects travel in an accelerated fashion through local, national, and international markets and other regimes of value production. These emerging conditions, or "predicaments of culture," to borrow a phrase from James Clifford (1988), offer a critical moment in which to reexamine the ways objects come to convey and condense value and, in doing so, are used to construct social identities and communicate cultural differences between individuals and groups. The renewed interest in material culture created by this situation has defined the two major concerns of this volume.

One concern is to reevaluate the relationship between material culture and exchange theory. The traditional opposition between "gift" and "commodity" has been displaced, in part, by approaches emphasizing the materiality of exchange valuables rather than their social function in reciprocity or their purely symbolic meanings. This is helping to make the classic topic of exchange more relevant to other discussions in anthropology (see Keane 1997: chs. 1, 3, and 8).

The second concern is to examine the ways in which art objects particularly are used to construct or deny identity and cultural difference. We hope to link the production of "art" as a category of objects (and practices) to questions about local identities, globalization, and the peculiar nature of art objects as "commodities."

The discourses surrounding these two areas should not be dissociated from each other. Rather, discussions of art and its appropriation or circulation should be explicitly combined with a more general theorizing of material culture. One warrant for this position is that the valorization of "art" and material culture in the West has often been based on the object's resistance to, or transcendence of, global processes involving commodification, markets, money, and mass culture. Anthropologists have also long described the "gift," like art, as lying outside the domain of commodity production and circulation. Whereas some art critics have asked what it means to define oppositions such as those between "art" and "non-art" (Clifford 1988; Foster 1983; Lippard 1991; McEvilley 1985; see also Danto 1986), and some anthropologists question the division between the "gift" and the "commodity" (Appadurai 1986; Miller 1987; Thomas 1991; Weiner 1992), the goal of our seminar was to bring these two areas together in a more coherent fashion, to reformulate a more comprehensive role for material culture studies in anthropology and other disciplines.

Ultimately, we see that role to lie in the recognition that what is at stake (as Webb Keane argues in chapter 2) is the relationship between persons and things. We are exploring distinctions among kinds of objects and the ways in which they circulate. These distinctions matter, as Keane shows, "in part, because they have profound implications for the character of the humans who possess the objects and carry out transactions with them." Therefore, combined discussion of gifts and art provides a significant set of essays clustering around two different kinds of limiting cases that help define the core problems of objectification, value, and identity. As Annette Weiner's (1985, 1992) conceptualization of "inalienability" began to show us, the sustaining intuition is that "art" and "gift" are both examples of things that have a special relationship to the human subject, and therefore their merely "material" aspect has tended to be played down or even denied.

The chapters in this book are part of the new wave of work developing in what has been repeatedly and eloquently traced as a trajectory of "material culture studies" (Appadurai, ed., 1986; Miller 1987, 1995; Miller, ed., 1998; Thomas 1991; Weiner 1992, 1994). The promise of recent material culture studies lies in their concern with the way "things" are actually used by people, but the pathway of such studies has also involved a critical reexamination of some of the principal theoretical bases of earlier work in the field. Insofar as something called "material culture studies" is emerging as a distinct field, it will be useful to outline the histories through which its considerations and conceptualizations have passed.

TRAJECTORIES

Historically, material culture studies held a stable if unchallenged place in American anthropology, receiving little sustained theoretical attention other than that of materialist and evolutionary approaches, on the one hand, or considerations of style, form, and technique, on the other. A more prominent aspect of material culture studies was located in exchange theory, which, building on the work of Durkheim (1984 [1893]), Mauss (1990 [1925]), and Malinowski (1922), maintained a vital trajectory throughout the twentieth century (see especially Lévi-Strauss 1949; Sahlins 1965, 1972, 1976).

Considerations of exchange have provided important insights into the significancc of cultural objects. The study of exchange has highlighted the importance of categories of objects in maintaining social life—either through giving and reciprocity (Sahlins 1965) or through keeping (Weiner 1985, 1992, 1994)—and in producing identity. In the fullest Maussian framework, the consideration of the gift (usually in contrast to the commodity) drew attention to varied notions of the person, especially to variations from the Western monadic, rationalizing individual.

Unfortunately and ironically, as Weiner has argued (1992, and ch. 10, this volume), much of this work gave decidedly Western economic and political readings to "gifts," reciprocity, authority, ownership, and gender. The question of how objects come to be invested with what she called "dense" sociocultural meaning and value (Weiner 1994) was substantially evaded by recourse to categories that themselves needed scrutiny. In the absence of such scrutiny, exchange practices in "primitive" or "archaic" societies were all too easily seen as based on laws of reciprocity—as opposed to exchange in the marketplace, where self-interest rather than reciprocity was thought to predominate.

Value

It is not surprising that this socially constructed but nonetheless deep divide between gift-exchange and capitalist economies has dominated anthropologists' discussions of material culture and social life. In many places in the world, people see money and markets as challenges to the values or qualitative distinctions embodied in exchange. Exchange has seemed, consequently, to be an alternative to capitalism's reduction of humanity to use-value. Critical theory in and of itself has seemed insufficient to grasp these processes of change. Even when critical theorists have drawn on anthropological work (for example, Bataille [see Richman 1982]; Baudrillard 1972) to find some "alternative" to the commodity form, their work has lacked a comparative and sociologically informed perspective as well as institutional specificity.

The recent work of several scholars has insistently deconstructed the gift/commodity opposition as not necessarily (or usefully) representing broad differences in whole societies (archaic vs. modern). Appadurai's edited volume *The Social Life of Things* (1986)—the central point of which is that there is some capitalism in the gift and vice versa—offered the beginning of a dialogue on the tensions between productions of value based on differentiations of objects and the options of economic gain that threaten to destabilize those differences (but see also Miller 1987; Weiner 1992). Our volume looks instead to the existence of multiple, coexisting, and variously related "regimes of value" (Appadurai 1986; Thomas 1991; Weiner 1992),[1] and even to the embedding of exchange in more encompassing systems of value production (see Fajans 1993; Myers 1993; Turner 1989). In either case, the value possessed by objects is subject to slippage and therefore is problematic. It must be sustained or reproduced through the complex work of production. Indeed, the contrast between value as produced in organizations of difference ("qualitative" value) and value as a measure of relative price in transaction ("quantitative" value) may underlie significant dynamics within structures of social action.

Keane's essay (this volume) shows the Sumbanese people of eastern Indonesia as "involved in a classic confrontation between an elaborate, costly, and socially potent system of ceremonial exchange and the growing importance of money." This dialectical potential is evoked in the notion of alternative regimes of value, as evidenced in the essays by Keane and Miller, which make up part one of this volume and which display the strongest emphasis on exchange and on the complex relationship between "the gift" and money (see also Myers, this volume). The potential contribution of anthropology to these problems of value is revealed here, I believe, as twofold. On the one hand, as Beidelman brilliantly showed in his 1989 essay on Homeric exchange, the making of equivalence—between different objects, between objects or wealth and a human life—is hardly a given; equivalence is, rather, commonly *imposed* through the application of social power.[2] On the other hand, this slippage from natural value and equivalence at the level of practice should allow us to see the operation of what I will describe as value produced in organizations of difference—in which exchange itself, as an institution, may be part of a larger totality of social action (see Turner 1989:264). Anthropology should see these particular dialectical organizations of value in a broader, comparative light and in relation to sites of cultural production.

Categories of Value

If discussions of "exchange" and "gifts" challenged the imputed universality of quantitative value, then historical conceptualizations of "art" have tended (in parallel course) to challenge the priority of simple rationalization. In the dominant discussions of art in the West, art objects were conceived typically as transcending simple utility; they were the limiting case for the reduction of all value to that of utility in capitalist exchange. They stood against the corrosive effects of capitalism and money.

"Art" has been situated in the West as a category of redemptive value, distinct from money and discrete from other sociocultural values (see Coombes's and Steiner's chapters, this volume).[3] More recently, the taken-for-grantedness of this cultural construction has changed as critics have seen the value of particular classes or categories of objects to be deeply implicated in the relationship both to money and also to other forms of material culture through which people fashion themselves (Marcus and Myers, eds., 1995). This is often delineated in the conversion of what Bourdieu (1984) called "economic capital" into "cultural capital." Bourdieu is not, however, the only connection. For example, Marcus (1992) delineated the complex relationship between art and money as part of the strategies of dynastic families in the United States to consolidate their wealth for future generations. And Sullivan (1995) demonstrated the linkage between inflation and the inflated rhetoric of the postmodern art boom of the 1980s. The rhetoric of art's redemptive autonomy can displace other features of the practices involved with its cultural production.

It is not only the relationship between art and money that is destabilized, however. The destabilization of the category "art" and its neutral universality has been particularly visible in the arena of cultural politics and class hierarchy within the West (see Bourdieu 1984; Wallis 1984). It is also visible in the problems surrounding its extension beyond the West, where the relationships between art, politics, and identity have been much discussed (Coombes, Myers, Thomas, this volume). As I describe more substantially later, an emerging canon of writings now challenges the label "primitivism" in art, the Western appropriations of cultural meanings in critics' own assessments of artifacts as "art," and the ethnocentric representations in museum displays defined through colonial domination (Appadurai 1990; Clifford 1988; Coombes 1994; Errington 1998; Foster 1985a; Manning 1985; Price 1989; Root 1996; Torgovnick 1990). Clearly, the complexities of a global economy are shattering the conceit of art's autonomy from other spheres of social life, the supposed neutrality of its classification. There is no longer a shock in the revelation that the value of an art object—or class of objects—is linked to other political and social values (see, for example, Karp and Lavine 1991; Price 1989).

Commodity/Treasure

For these reasons, a general reformulation of material culture studies should consider the dynamics surrounding objects, rather than their more static moments of definition and secure classification. In her contribution to the planning statement for the advanced seminar, for example, Weiner pointed out that

> individuals resist the marketplace to keep certain objects as treasures, or in other cases sell them with impunity as commodities, or even approach the marketplace in an effort to translate their value into new forms. Some objects become so symbolically "dense" with cultural meaning that people covet them as prized collectibles, "art," or ancestral relics. Such density accrues through an object's association with its owner's fame, ancestral histories, secrecy, sacredness, and aesthetic and economic values. These especially dense objects circulate in exchange or in the marketplace exceedingly slowly in comparison with less dense ones that are easily reduced to commodities. The most highly prized are those "inalienable possessions"—such as a sacred heirloom, ancestral valuables, or a ruler's regalia—that cannot easily be replaced by any other object. Such inalienable possessions are more than "art" as traditionally defined because they acquire unique value through the personal importance they have to someone—be it a curator, antique dealer, patron, chief, or queen.

Weiner insisted that we focus on how individuals or groups create value in objects, using them as commodities or treasures in fortifying or reconstructing their cultural identities. Because of the instability of our systems of classification (rooted in practice), we recognize that the categories "commodity" and "treasure" are not mutually exclusive. An object's value may shift through time as individuals or groups are forced or elect to enter treasures into the marketplace or as an ordinary commodity becomes revered by a collector or family members and takes on the value of an inalienable possession (one that cannot be replaced by another). Similarly, Keane has pointed out how money itself may be caught up in such diversions—how coins, for example, may become jewelry. The persistence of objects such as cloth as valuables—in Sumba and elsewhere—should be understood within the dynamics of inalienability "as a continual refusal to allow them to return to their original state" (Keane, this volume). This project involves not only the work and tactics of keeping, as Weiner envisioned, but also the broader ideological production of ritualization that maintains a boundary between the semiotics of exchange valuables and possible alternative meanings and uses. Such questions about "art" and "artifact" are now being asked with great frequency in the art world, where non-Western artifacts and cultural property loosed from their ethnographic moorings are reclassified as "art" in a Western context.

Art/Culture

Clifford (1988:222) identified another dynamic of value production in what he analyzed as the "modern art-culture system," the cultural machinery through which "objects collected from non-Western sources are classified into two major categories: as (scientific) cultural artifacts or as (aesthetic) works of art" (see also Phillips and Steiner 1999). He argued that "the system classifies objects and assigns them relative value. It establishes the 'contexts' in which they properly belong and between which they circulate" (1988:223).[4] In this model, Clifford described how regular movements ("traffic") toward positive value can occur: "These movements select artifacts of enduring worth or rarity, their value normally guaranteed by a 'vanishing' cultural status or by the selection and pricing mechanisms of the art market" (1988:223).

An area of frequent traffic in the system, he writes, is that linking "art" (distinguished by connoisseurship, the art museum, the art market) with "culture" (history and folklore, the ethnographic museum, material culture, craft). Indeed, "things of cultural or historical value may be promoted to the status of fine art...from ethnographic 'culture' to fine art" (Clifford 1988:223–24). This movement within the system involves the representation of works as original and singular, as masterpieces—and the meanings or values embedded in such distinctions (Beidelman 1997a; Myers, this volume). I should point out that this "art-culture system" might be distinguished from the rather Simmelian understanding of value articulated in Weiner's conception of inalienable possessions (see Simmel 1990 [1907]). Furthermore, the historically specific (Clifford 1988:226) art-culture system is actually a structure or schema of value-producing activities that organizes or mediates (see Fajans 1997; Turner 1973) the relationships between distinct fields of material culture (art/culture or art/artifact), "mutually reinforcing domains of human value" and the institutional contexts or activities in which they are embedded (Clifford 1988:234).[5] As Clifford implies, the classifications "art" and "culture" are rooted in or linked to the distinct institutions and practices they mediate. (Concrete examples of the practices and institutions underlying the process of classification are explored in Beidelman 1997b and George 1999; see also Myers, this volume).

The current situation is one in which—as a recent collection (George 1999) named the predicament—objects are "on the loose." As in Christopher Steiner's discussion (this volume) of abstract modern art objects being subject to customs duties as raw materials (they are not "art" because they are nonrepresentational), objects may not fit the same category of classification for everyone. In the art law case he describes, the placement of "art" in distinction to ordinary utility and commerce was contested. Steiner draws attention to the role of international borders as sites of negotiation and transaction over the definition of things, indicating the human agency and knowledge involved in acts of classification (see also Steiner 1994). "At each point in its movement through space and time," he notes, "an object has the potential to shift from one category to another, and in doing so, to slide along the slippery line that divides art from artifact from commodity." These border sites are also, then, potentially sites of anxiety, where definitions are contested, subverted, and threatened.

Movement, destabilization, and dynamics are highly visible processes in the social life of things. But the argument of this volume is that changes in the intersections of different levels of circulation cannot be studied simply as "breakdowns"—either from art into commodity or from "culturally authentic" to inauthentic—or as simple appropriations. The recent case of Aboriginal Australian acrylic painting (Myers 1989, 1991, 1994, 1998, and this volume; see also Dussart 1988, 1993; Morphy 1992, 1995) illustrates a transformation (not a breakdown) of what are essentially Aboriginal inalienable possessions—sacred designs. As they circulate through the state, where they are perceived as having the economic and cultural potential for addressing its "Aboriginal problem," they are transformed into commodities and then into fine art, supposedly emptied of ethnicity. Curators elevate their value in Western terms into that of a museum's inalienable possessions. The different levels of circulation and different forms of inalienability are articulated through the connection of distinct institutional contexts.

Our interest is in exploring these new intersections as both culturally productive and dynamic. One tension at the center of such cases is that between inalienable possessions and the social and political (hierarchical) differences they are employed to define. The postmodern blurring of boundaries between "high" and "low" art—illustrated in the auction Weiner mentions in chapter 10 of Andy Warhol's collectibles, a vast jumble of masterpieces and junk, in which the junk took on great value—shows the increasing scale of attempts to make commodities into inalienable possessions while inalienable possessions themselves are at times reduced to commodities. Provenance and fame enable antiques and art to provide storage for economic value, with their futures already imagined by collectors, auction houses, and museums (see Beidelman 1997b:12; Freund 1993). The world markets have always been and remain today deeply implicated in the relocation between inalienable possessions as sites for the storage of value and the way such possessions resist exchange in the face of more immediate economic gain. As Webb Keane argued during the seminar, art and antiques do store economic value, but they are capable of doing so only because they also promise the collector something else—some value that cannot be reduced to economics.[6] The delineation of this alternative value as "transcendence" (see Keane 1997) marks the relationship between regimes of value as potentially a weighted, marked, or encompassing one, while Annie Coombes's delineation (this volume) of a "(relative) autonomy" for art objects imagines "a space to comment on life."

Thus, rather than accepting any simple opposition between "art" and "money" or between "gift" and "commodity," this collection of essays explores cultural, economic, and political forms of resistance to these categories. The relocation of material culture demands understanding that value is never simply defined but is always involved in global as well as local circuits of exchange, display, and storage. This is especially important as objects move through space and time with greater rapidity than ever before, breaking down the analytical categories that for so long have been used to contain and define them theoretically.

INALIENABLE OBJECTS

A central link is Weiner's critique of exchange theory (1980, 1985, 1992)—a critique summarized in her development of the notion of "inalienable possessions" and in her increasing emphasis on the role of material properties in making sense of objects. In Weiner's work one can see most clearly the transition from classical exchange theory and its models toward an object-oriented consideration of material culture. Theories of exchange, Weiner argued, had been too much identified with the problems of reciprocity and equivalence, a position articulated, for example, in a classic essay of Sahlins (1965). Instead of this reduction to economics, she insisted, exchange—or "giving"—should be related to reproduction, to politics, and to the production of hierarchies, recognizing the significance of political manipulation and strategies (see also Bourdieu 1977; Strathern 1988).

Focusing on cycles beyond the immediate moment of exchange itself, in which equivalence is often central, Weiner recognized the embeddedness of such moments of exchange in larger projects of social life—projects in which, for example, a Trobriand man's gifts to his sons are, after his death, reclaimed by his sisters as property of his matrilineal descent group. This moment of exchange might be understood, she wrote in 1980, as "replacement." The longer cycle of such exchange processes expanded the range of persons identified through the circulation (so to speak) of identity-bearing objects, while delaying the inevitable delineation of societal cleavages. The concept of "keeping-while-giving" became her key insight, marking exchange as always dynamic and contradictory and always embedded in a process beyond the establishment of equivalence (see also Turner 1989:263). Subtly but significantly, Weiner's formulation shifted attention from the mechanics of exchange to the movement of objects into or out of different circuits of exchange and control—where value accrued through the objects' capacity to resist exchange (see Simmel 1990 [1907]) or through their exposure to risk (see Douglas and Wildavsky 1982).

Moreover, drawing heavily on the indigenous metaphors of Pacific societies, Weiner was among those whose theorizing followed Mauss's intuitions in expanding the range of giving activities that might be conceived of as exchange (see also Munn 1986; Strathern 1988). This led her to a concern with the ways in which the properties of various media (objects) entered into the expansion or contraction of the cycles of social reproduction (see ch. 10, this volume). Names, food, cloth, sexuality, words, and places, along with pigs, pearl shells, and women, could all become media of exchange. One of the significant insights of anthropology has been the recognition of distinct cultural categories of objects (Bohannon 1955; Malinowski 1922; Mauss 1990 [1925]; Weiner 1976) and of the "spheres of exchange" appropriate to them—a recognition that the capacity of objects to be simple equivalents for one another was highly restricted. Weiner's work drew attention again to the different spheres of exchange in which *kula* objects, banana leaves, women's grass skirts, and yams moved and of the links between them—the links through which value could be converted.

Weiner recognized that the different kinds of materiality were important to the value and effectiveness of objects as media of social life. It was her insight, then, that the different qualities of the objects exchanged were significant—that different kinds of objects ("hard" or "durable" versus "soft," "perishable," "scarce," "transportable," and so on) mattered or were differently appropriated to the circumstances of human social life (see also Munn 1986). Moreover, she pointed out that different kinds of objectifications (words, objects, magic) were absorbed into different processes within a society (Weiner 1984). Objects are an important medium of social activity precisely because they have properties—because they are vulnerable, fragile, and losable, because they rot or endure.

Equally significantly, her appreciation of the subtlety of exchange shows the achievement of equality between objects to be exceptional—such an achievement of reciprocity, far from being a given, must be carefully managed. Unlike currencies, objects are very difficult to make the same. When Weiner later became interested in hierarchy, she found great significance in the fact that the objects involved in exchange, whatever they might be, usually had properties that made their equivalence problematical. Consequently, hierarchy was always a potential property of any exchange. Rather than reciprocity or equivalence's being a natural state or a background of hierarchy, she argued, people worked to keep hierarchy out—so the reciprocity was the result of exchange, a means of making people equal. Rather than there being an expectation of reciprocity among equal persons, exchange acted to produce equality, at least for a moment. If objects, like people, were never entirely or perfectly identical, then objects could metonymically and metaphorically objectify the relational properties of persons in complex ways—with some kinds of objects (e.g., fine mats) being particularly capable of embodying these relationships in a different medium. Thus, as she saw it, the production of social identity was closely connected to exchange as a process of symbolic action. This is why material culture matters—because it provides a register for these differentia and similarities.

Pursuing the subtlest intimations of the field imagined by Mauss, Weiner challenged the simple gift/commodity dichotomy for exchange and argued that exchange should be understood as having the capacity to express identity and to produce hierarchy—ranked or valued difference. Hierarchy is produced or sustained in the ongoing political struggle of social agents to claim their identity by holding onto valued objects or forms of property, such as those claimed by Trobriand subclans in mortuary rituals. This is a theory that recognizes not a class of objects called "inalienable" but rather a set of social processes in which the capacity to exchange or withhold can become a marker of social strength and identity. In recent years, the insights deriving from Weiner's theorizing of what she called "inalienability" have become significant not only in Oceanic ethnography but also in many other areas of work on material culture and consumption.

Annette Weiner's critique of exchange theory was obviously one of our starting points in imagining the seminar. Although she was unable to participate in the seminar, she commented extensively on its issues in two interviews that Barbara Kirshenblatt-Gimblett and I held with her shortly afterward (see ch. 10, this volume). Her influential theorizing attempted to move toward the object and social relations and away from reifications of exchange that focused on reciprocity (see also Strathern 1988). Her interest turned toward the social (or relational) need for inalienability and toward the "material" (e.g., names, women's skirts, green jade valuables, sacred land) available to produce the "inalienable," or, more literally, the "immovable" (Mauss's *immeuble* [1990 (1925)]). Despite the many uses to which Weiner's work has been put, her focus was generally less on things' being inalienable and more on the production of inalienability and on the strategies and work of keeping or resisting exchange. The classic form of the inalienable, from which Mauss derived the concept *immeuble*, was, after all, land—precisely an object that is not movable in itself.

EXCHANGE THEORY AS CULTURAL CRITICISM

Most anthropologists agree that the prevailing economic approaches to material culture and its consumption are problematical. They have attempted, therefore, to reject or question the priority of markets in thinking about value and the significance of objects. Some—those whom Daniel Miller (1987) identified as "Romantics"—have been concerned to trace the existence (or production) of cultural value beyond the utilitarian, beyond that established through pricing in exchange. Often those developing this critical stance have sought support in positing the giving of gifts—or, if you will, in reifying the gift—as a form of social action that cannot be reduced to economic imperatives, one in which people matter more than things. They have equally reified the counterpart of the gift, the commodity (see Appadurai 1986; Miller, this volume). For this enterprise, however, the distinction between gifts and commodities—and between "gift economies" and "commodity economies"—has often provided a basis on which to develop a critique of contemporary capitalism or modern social life.

Recent work on "primitivism," as Thomas (1991) pointed out, fundamentally questions this critical enterprise and its theoretical products, especially its portrayal of societies as stable, bounded entities. Inspired, apparently, as much by work on problems of representation arising from museum exhibitions and collecting as by substantive analyses of exchange practices themselves, Thomas (1991:3) claimed that most such writing "conceives of tribal societies and even places such as Indonesia and India as authentic, meaningfully stable domains which differ fundamentally from Western social regimes and which resist interpretation on the basis of Western categories." The semiotic (or typological) work of "primitivism," moreover, has suppressed recognition of the variable ranges of exchange practices and forms found in historically known societies. The mature study of material culture, it would seem, has followed from criticism of the criticisms themselves to pursue more complex understandings of the relationships between persons and things.

Thomas made the point eloquently in his critical rejection of the common and simple differentiation of societies into those characterized by gift exchange and those characterized by commodity exchange.

He demonstrated, in contrast, the range of exchange forms that coexisted historically in Fiji. "The point," he wrote,

> is rather that while alienation, commoditization, and abstract exchange media are most pronounced in capitalist economies, they are not peculiar to those systems. Capitalism is characterized by social relations which bind worker to capitalist in exploitative transactions, rather than the facts of alienation and commoditization, which predated capitalism historically and which now exist in some forms in all societies. The identification of these social relations in societies which are or were supposedly dominated by "the gift" permits one to recognize the forms of inequality and domination that exist in such systems and to understand the particular kinds of material culture that take the form of "valuables" and exchange items in various contexts. The transformations and contextual mutations of objects cannot be appreciated if it is presumed that gifts are invariably gifts and commodities invariably commodities. (Thomas 1991:38–39)

The work of both Appadurai and Thomas aims at dissolving the centrality of the gift/commodity distinction and accompanying debates. Thomas particularly argues against the typological thinking involved in subordinating actual ranges of transactions to the constraints of the critically produced emphasis on the gift's difference from the commodity. Although these critical trajectories—Appadurai's, Miller's, and Thomas's—vary in their articulation of the project of material culture study, collectively they delineate the specificities of previous work and challenge the reification of exchange and exchange types in thinking about material culture.

CRACKING THE GIFT/COMMODITY OPPOSITION: RECONTEXTUALIZATION

The expansion in theorizing exchange corresponds to a recognition of the many contexts—beyond those once imagined for supposedly stable simple societies—in which material culture moves, and of the way value is transformed through movement between contexts (Appadurai 1986; see also Thomas 1991). This emphasis on movement underlies Appadurai's insights into the social life of things as they move between "regimes of value," as well as Thomas's ideas on "contexts." Arguing that it is an oversimplification to understand the movement of indigenous objects out of their societies as an inconceivable rupture with prior local practices, Thomas articulated an emphasis on context in recognition of diverse economic regimes within a society and of the movement of objects into and out of different categories of relationship to persons.[7]

Drawing on Appadurai and on his own critique of the apparent immutability of the gift, Thomas (1991) pointed to the more general question of the movement of objects through contexts—what he called "recontextualizations." That such recontextualizations necessarily include colonial relations (and appropriations) within their purview, rather than excluding them as external to the question of precolonial gift economies, recognizes the growing empirical interest in collecting, museum exhibition, and transnational circulation.

Envisioning the way objects might move in and out of a commodity status, Appadurai (1986:15) had argued that "commoditization lies at the complex intersection of temporal, cultural, and social factors" and is not, therefore, an immutable state of any object. Rather, the "commodity situation" of a thing is a phase in its longer history or "social life," in which "its exchangeability (past, present, or future) for some other thing is its socially relevant feature" (Appadurai 1986:13). This "can be disaggregated into (1) the commodity phase in the social life of any thing; (2) the commodity candidacy of any thing; and (3) the commodity context in which any thing may be placed" (Appadurai 1986:13). In pace with Appadurai's rethinking of cultural movement in terms of global disjunctures and connections, Thomas turned these insights into a reformulation of the problem of material culture as one of recontextualization: "Although certain influential theorists of material culture have stressed the objectivity of the artifact, I can only recognize the reverse: the mutability of things in recontextualization. Axes, old cars, striped condoms—they are never things embodying pure or original templates or intentions....What we are confronted with is thus never more or less than a succession of uses and recontextualizations" (Thomas 1991:28–29). What might be required, then, is a theorizing of such contexts and classifications as objects move through them (see Steiner, this volume).

For Weiner, similarly, movement was central. Circulation was the counterpoint, often the context, of efforts at inalienability—for which the much-discussed Trobriand institution of *kula* (Leach and Leach 1983; Malinowski 1922; Weiner 1976, 1983, 1988) clearly provided a model. Underlying such movement, however, there must remain some existing structures of value, some contexts or regimes whose relationships to one another are always being worked out or contested. The movement of objects ("recontextualization"), as Steiner (this volume) shows, necessarily makes visible these frequently contradictory structures and schemas.

The cases in this volume represent principally one distinctive historical vector of such recontextualization and contestation: the intrusion of the market and its effect of destabilizing the meanings and values of money and material things. This is a complex nexus, but the essays emphasize that this vector is not different in kind from other processes. The effect is not a replacement of regimes of value. In Aboriginal Australia, as in Sumba, the destabilization is experienced in the context of efforts at "modernization," and in both places what Keane (this volume) describes as "government officials and development experts" tend to see "money and markets as an incipient challenge to the values supposedly embodied in exchange." In my own chapter I delineate the struggle by painters and their advisers to sustain the authenticity of Aboriginal acrylic paintings—which emanate from and are valued for their source in the domain of religion—despite the engagement of these newly portable objects in the commercial market that is also necessary for the material survival of contemporary Aboriginal producers. In this case, the attempts to make qualitative value commensurate with monetary value represent an effort to mediate these value regimes, one in which some participants can imagine that monetary value will reinforce (rather than destroy) indigenous distinctions. Nonetheless, the new destination makes acrylic paintings subject to shifting physical, economic, and semiotic contexts. The market, in this sense, is a site of symbolic transformation. It puts Aboriginal culture into an arena of value in which it is comparable with other signs and vehicles—in which designs are "stolen" and used in commercial carpeting, only to be reconsidered legally as intellectual property and subject to copyright. In the context of "fine art," curators also explain how this market strips (or suppresses) the paintings of "Aboriginality" itself.

As Keane (this volume) writes, "market economies...do not do away with inalienables so much as they reorder the regimes of value in which they function." The excess of meanings in exchange and in objects themselves, as Keane demonstrates, is exemplary of this problem. And these contradictory schemas are brought into renewed relationships to each other, not in abstract terms but in specific historical arenas where their relative value is worked out. This truism of legal anthropology is observed not only in the case of modern art's becoming taxed (Steiner, this volume)—the eruption of the boundary between art and economic value—or in the appropriation of Western Desert acrylic painting by Australia's nativizing but cosmopolitan new professional class (Myers, this volume), but even more provocatively in the case of art's cultural "autonomy" in an exhibition of African art analyzed by Coombes (this volume; see also Beidelman 1997b). At the Royal Academy of Arts, controversy over sponsorship deals and the problem of displaying stolen antiquities threatened to overcome the exhibition and was met by a set of justifications made in terms of art's "autonomy." That these recontextualizations might need to be analyzed further, either with a theory of value or semiotically, is discussed later.

OBJECTIFICATION

Miller (1987, 1995) has offered a distinguishably different—non-Romantic—challenge to the dominance of the market approach to objects, thereby avoiding some of the difficulties of the exchange paradigm. He has attempted to make a theory of "objectification" into the framework for considering material culture because of its potential to refuse a prevailing "reductionism or privileging of something called society" (Miller, ed., 1998:10; see also Strathern 1988). Critical of economics for its lack of attention to the *constitutive* role and value of things, Miller takes objectification to be one of the principal vectors of material culture. In objectification, cultural objects externalize values and meanings embedded in social processes, making them available, visible, or negotiable for further action by subjects (see Miller 1987). Material culture as objectification provides the basis on which subjects come into being, rather than simply answering their preexisting needs. The subject can become aware that it actually is, he writes, only "by its becoming aware that there is something that it actually is not. Awareness of the self is predicated on awareness of the 'other,' and it is the process of creation and acknowledgment of the other which is the key to the achievement of self-awareness" (Miller 1987:22). The subject realizes that this apparently alien other is in fact a product of itself, created as a mirror by means of which the subject might further his or her own self-awareness.

As an exemplar of this approach, Munn's work (1970, 1983, 1986) on the construction and use of the external world of objects is praised for discrediting "the idea that the relationship between people and the things they construct in the physical world is separable from some prior form of social relation" (Miller 1987:13). Instead, objectification points toward some kind of dialectical relationship between subjects and objects, persons and things, but not one that privileges the boundaries of personhood as understood in the West. This places material culture in a processual and relational position with respect to human subjects, a position in which objects and their capacity to give form may further the development of the subject: "Objectification describes the inevitable process by which all expression, conscious or unconscious, social or individual, takes specific form. It is only through the giving of form that something can be conceived of. The term objectification, however, always implies that form is part of a larger process of becoming" (Miller 1987:81).

Miller's most productive insight has been his (populist) challenge to elitist framings of consumption, to the view that commodity consumption necessarily means an erosion of people's capacity to produce or sustain complex subjectivities or identities. Whereas the typological generalities that have been inferred from the commodity form have often presumed loss of specificity to be an effect of commodity consumption (erasing difference, producing homogeneity), Miller's emphasis on the actualities of the consumption of material culture combines with the insights of exchange theory to recognize the continuing significance of material culture in constituting ("objectifying") diverse identities.

The Materiality of Signs

There is a Maussian subtheme that can be further connected to Miller's elaboration of objectification and its subsequent moment of reappropriation and subjectification. That material forms (or cultural objects) have been regularly used in human social life to classify persons is a well-established understanding in anthropology. Emanating from the work of Mauss (Durkheim and Mauss 1963 [1904]; Mauss 1979 [1904]), this insight was projected into anthropology most forcefully by Lévi-Strauss in *Totemism* (1962) and *The Savage Mind* (1966). Lévi-Strauss's insight lay in recognizing the capacity of a range of entities (concrete objects) to represent—or embody—similarity and difference. From Lévi-Strauss we learn that music (or musical form), landscape, names, dialects, what have you, can be used homologously as media through which to classify people as similar or different. That is, they provide a substance whose properties allow for the expression of sameness and difference. This brilliant recognition was limited by the Saussurian attempt to use language as the model of analysis, a model in which the substance of articulation was regarded as irrelevant to the effect of objectification. The doctrine of the arbitrariness of signs led people to overlook the material properties of things, but these properties were not simply metaphorical materials, not simply media for transparently offering a "message," as a synchronic structuralism had it.

Keane's essay cogently explores the properties of objects as social media, distinguishing between the materiality of objects and their semiotic deployment—with the latter requiring extensive work (formality in exchange, ritualization in speech) to contain the possible diversions of their "natural meanings." Unlike words, he shows, objects cannot be produced at will but must be sought from somewhere. They are, therefore, subject to scarcity and are easy to quantify. Objects also have durability—they persist over time, across multiple transactions, and they pass through the hands of many people. In these ways, they "bear physical properties in excess of their purely conventional attributes." Such properties contribute to objects' potential for diversion into use or into alternative kinds of transactions. Another example from this book that can be compared with the case presented by Keane is the transformation of Aboriginal ritual body decoration or cave painting designs, whose deployment is involved in value production in persons (see Myers 1986, 1993), into acrylic paintings. The multiple uses, mobility, and durability of objects allows them to extend the agency of their producers and original transactors. But the same properties entail the possibility that they will become detached from their transactors altogether.

One implication of Keane's concern with the materiality of things, rather than their simple value as coded signs, is that greater attention needs to be given to the substances or media through which people have objectified themselves. This is a significant point in Nicholas Thomas's essay (this volume), in his consideration of the failure of Margaret Preston, an Australian artist working in the mid-twentieth century, to produce—in her "flower works" and her combination of Aboriginal influences with the still life—an indigenized national culture. "The idea of national art," he writes, "is not easily reconciled with diminutive and decorative works, which have more obvious affiliations with craft and design than with the landscapes and history paintings that were the more conventional vehicles for the expression of national spirit and historical purpose." Thomas's essay draws closely on an understanding of the materiality of objectification, seeing these objectifications as having to mediate not through material properties simply taken but through historically existing hierarchies of cultural creativity and genre.

Things are objectifications in a more complex sense than the doctrines of the arbitrary sign would have it; their materiality is overdetermined as they genuinely mediate—indexically—social processes. This involves not only the temporal dimension of the processes into which objects enter but also the reorganizations of value consequent on processes of recontextualization. Such processes are—as Kapferer (1979) argued for ritual—reorganizations of context that depend on the full materiality, indexical and iconic, of the sign-vehicles they deploy.

A dramatic example of this approach is Munn's ground-breaking work (1970) on subjects and objects in Aboriginal Australia, showing how subjects come into being through their relationships to the land, itself an objectification of ancestral action and potency. As I have tried to show in my own work on Western Desert Aboriginal relationships to named places, or "country" *(ngurra)*, as they call it, named places mediate and objectify a complex set of geographical and social relations (spatial, generational, temporal) that are formulated in exchange, the ultimate value product of which is social persons. This provides an example of the combination of structure, objectification, and subjectification—how objectifications of social life are appropriated by the subjects they recursively produce. Insofar as this "landscape" is itself the objectification from which are derived the acrylic paintings I discuss in chapter 6, that case helps us grasp some of the subtler dimensions of the connections between objectification and alienation.

My earlier accounts (Myers 1986, 1993) emphasized exchange as a process of value production in which similarities and differences are constructed among persons by virtue of their positions in the activities of exchange. And land is an enduring objectification or mediation of these practices. Where nurturance is the principal "template" (Munn 1986) or "schema" (Fajans 1997) of value production, "country" or named places can be objectified as forms that are necessary for the completion of one's personhood. Country in these situations is an entity that brings with it the capacity for subjective agency, for power, understood as the ability to participate in exchange and in the nurturance of others. Named places, then, are an exemplary case of the inalienable possession, the "dense" cultural object, its meaning generated through its engagement with a complex set of ongoing practices that constitute persons as similar and different in various ways and in different contexts.

The point is that objectifications must also be regarded as tokens of value, raising the question of how exchanges of such tokens—representing such complex and distinct formulations of value—can take place. It has been something of a conundrum to commentators that in Australia, the most significant tokens or objectifications of this value—the ritual objects known as *tjurunga* in Central Australia and the acrylic paintings which, to some extent, are held to be simulacra of them—have been sold, given, or exchanged with whites (see Jones 1995). If *tjurunga* are, as many commentators have said, a kind of inalienable title deed to land—representations of an individual's personal and family group relationship with the Dreaming—and if humans are not involved in their production, then the question remains, why were they "given," traded, bartered, sold, or exchanged? It would be convenient to regard this circulation only as expropriation by dominant whites, and often this was the case. It appears, however, that Aboriginal people also sometimes participated actively and willingly in this exchange. It should be noted that the *tjurunga's* material properties as objectifications—as one medium of identity—have made them available for circulation in a way different from "land." Yet the question of their alienation is more complex. It goes to the heart of the relationship between regimes of value and the question of recontextualization. One argument that Pannell has made, drawing on Weiner (1992), is that *tjurunga* are to be considered as themselves alienable representations of a more central objectification—the land:

> If...we view *tjurunga* as alienable representations of what is inalienable, namely the Dreaming and its objectification as both cultural geography and social memory, then the movement of these objects out of the domain of Aboriginal control and into the sphere of European control still ensures the permanence and continuity of the cosmological order.... If this is the case, the ritual objects which Europeans acquired, divested of their cosmological importance and sacred power by the very acts of acquisition, are, from one perspective, merely empty and dead things; shadows of their former selves. (Pannell 1995:117)

In other words, Aboriginals may have, in Weiner's terms, "kept while giving."

A second argument Pannell makes follows Thomas's (1991:184) insistence on the capacity of indigenous people to appropriate value. How might Aboriginal people understand divesting themselves of what are fundamental objectifications of their own identity? She argues that "if *tjurunga* represent Aboriginal society for Europeans, then why is it not possible for commodities to signify European society for Aboriginal people?" (Pannell 1995:117). This scenario can be extended from the consideration of the *tjurunga* artifact to the acrylic painting—as occurred during the discussion of my paper at the seminar—when one considers that for Aboriginals the desired commodity of inestimable or socially productive value is the four-wheel-drive Toyota.

Nationalism

Turning in this direction suggests that objectifications must be conceived as various within a society and not as transparent transformations of a single process. Objectifications should be regarded, first, as mediations of specific processes. Claudio Lomnitz's chapter in this volume is important in this regard, because it delineates three distinct objectifications of Mexican national sovereignty. Addressing the problem of how national identity has been differently embodied in the ideological figuration of the Mexican president over time, Lomnitz's case is relevant to the other essays that attempt to understand how art or other manifestations of material culture come to be meaningful within a national project. These manifestations relate not just to identity in a general sense but also to the mediation of contradictory relations within the state (in the case of Mexico, the relationship of the state to regionally fragmented local powers—family, bureaucracy, rural estates—and to foreign powers who must variously be seduced or frightened off).

At the heart of Lomnitz's analysis is a consideration of objectification in a person's performance—a consideration of the ways in which "sovereignty" has been embodied in the persona of the national president. The figurations of the presidency in post-independence Mexico have been threefold: the form of the martyr (selfless sacrifice embodied or enshrined in body parts lost in the service of the nation), the exemplary citizen (racial identification with the land in the figure of the Indian), and the spiritual guide for nationalizing modernity. The national project in this case has been "to free Mexico from [colonial] subservience" and make it the equal of every other great nation. The material objectifications of Mexican nationalism, whatever their debts to earlier Catholic discourse (as relics and/or communitarian ideals for a Christian utopia), address specifiable contradictions in the formation of sovereignty in a postcolonial nation. These objectifications are cultural constructs and artifacts that embody the mediation between imperial powers, local power interests, and the interests of the political class. They represent the ideal types of legitimacy that must be performed by those aspiring to be president. These objectifications, however, are also themselves the nation's inalienable possessions—revealing, as in the case of the war hero Santa Anna's amputated leg, the degree to which Mexico is "vulnerable to foreign appropriation and internal desecration."

As in Australia, where the ANZAC War Memorial (see Kapferer 1988) can coexist with the enshrinement of Aboriginal art—or the wildflower still life (Thomas, this volume)—as an objectification of national identity, so in other nationalisms one should anticipate the coexistence of objectifications and the different constituencies whose presence they project. In projecting this presence, however, the objectifications are also brought into relationship with each other—or "coordinated" (Turner 1973)—and their relative value is asserted. Thus are mediations also forms of symbolic transformation, reorganizing regimes of value.

In Australia, the circulation of Aboriginal acrylic paintings has recombined national constituencies and forms of value in ways that Margaret Preston's wildflower still lifes and Aboriginal appropriations in domestic genres did not. Whereas Preston's combinations failed as objectifications of a national identity, the capacity of portable and purchasable indigenous acrylic paintings to mark Australia as a significant tourist destination in the 1980s and 1990s combined successfully with their ability to represent a distinctive national identity for the emerging fraction of the modernizing but postcolonial professional managerial class.

Lomnitz's essay provides insights that we can apply to this processual case: the project of Aboriginal acrylic painting itself grew out of an Australian project of modernization (intended to deal with the "Aboriginal problem") that reflexively produced a new Australian national identity (as an agent of modernity and fairness) in a world of such identities. The success of this new production is reflected in the appreciation that connoisseurs have for "Aboriginal art" and in the distribution of value back to Aboriginal producers. This transformation of a broader structure of contexts, I want to argue, does actively reposition the Aboriginal culture that the producers represent.

ART, CIRCULATION, AND RECONTEXTUALIZATION

The preceding discussion provides a basis for moving into the final area of consideration in our seminar: an attempt to bring together the specificities of "art" and its exhibition with general considerations of material culture. The interest in art was multiple, emphasizing (1) the art-versus-commodity problem, namely, the complexity of the relationship of the category "art" and its practices as a regime of value to rational, utilitarian values (see Marcus and Myers, eds., 1995); (2) the cultural hierarchy (art-versus-artifact) problem, or the problems raised by the materiality of art objects as collectible and distinguishable from artifacts; and (3) the problems of intercultural appropriation and identity production.

Art enters into more than a single regime of value or value production, as can be seen from the range of concerns in recently published scholarly work. Writings on art come out of a concern for the ways in which such objects have been used to represent or signify identity in a range of contexts—personal, local, and national. In this capacity, art can valorize or exclude minority identities. Another range of work explores how art acquires value in the institutions of what might be called the "art world," a situation in which inalienability can be considered an issue. Finally, a good deal of thinking about art as a category of cultural activity approaches it in terms of its value as a potential alterity to commodity-value, or kitsch. How these components of value, emanating potential from distinguishable regimes of value, enter into the biographies of such things helps illuminate one of the significant elaborations of material culture and its properties.

The movement of art objects within the market—and the production of value in paintings—was a point of fundamental convergence for Weiner and me, which led to the planning of the seminar. We anticipated that it would be productive to consider art as a significant and illuminating dimension of material culture studies. Weiner's thinking about art followed closely her understanding of the implications of the circulation and value of *kula* valuables for other processes of value production and personhood. This extension of her thinking has proved very productive, but notions of inalienability, objectification, and recontextualization are not historically specific enough to account for the workings of "art."

Earlier I reviewed the work of some scholars who have tried to extend exchange theory in the direction of understanding how objects acquire value through movement between points—or through not moving. This understanding involves the transnational, intercultural movements—the circulation—of objects across value systems (Appadurai 1990; Price 1989; Steiner 1994; Thomas 1991), movements that have formed the substance of significant debates about public culture, modernity, and national identity. Although these debates about the intercultural are deeply involved with the circulation of art, it is important to recognize another dimension of movement and context. In this dimension, the category "art," as a context for objects, is a particular example of material culture and the signifying practices in which such forms might be involved. Indeed, movement "between cultures" is movement between contexts, not entirely different from (and also frequently including) the movement or transformation of objects in a cultural hierarchy, such as transformations of objects into the category "fine art."

Despite her linkage of art with its capacity to objectify identity, Weiner's conception of art's value (essentially Simmelian) was not tied closely to the problem that has dominated much anthropological consideration—that of intercultural movement and the representation of local or indigenous identities. Indeed, the postcolonial emergence of an emphasis on cultural difference has been strongly registered in the arena of art. Whether the concepts appropriate for other kinds of recontextualizations were applicable to the circulation of art objects was a central question for the seminar. It was here in particular that the concern for specific institutional locations proved essential as a method of consideration—necessitating discussion of what is involved in "art."

Art, Politics, Identity

Art is not just another example of material culture. The position taken in this volume is that "art" is a historically specific cultural classification, a distinct category whose historical meanings (see Danto 1986; Kristeller 1965 [1951]; Williams 1977)—whose oppositions to or differences from other categories of objects and activities—are vital to the contexts it establishes for objects and activities.[8] Further, the category "art" is imbricated in a range of distinct institutions—museums, art galleries, critical writing, art education—that are not themselves all of a piece. Indeed, the discursive formation of "modern art," situated in metropolitan centers such as Paris and New York and representing itself hegemonically as encompassing the history of human artistic activity, may be one of the strongest exemplars of the emerging transnational or international institutions of global flow—framed as cosmopolitanism. Art is an institution that purports to judge, place, and define a range of differences within its own hierarchy of value. As a medium of objectification, the materiality of art and its meanings have made it particularly productive, in the context of modernity, as an arena for constituting and considering human difference and value.

The discourses of art engage two of the principal foci of contemporary concern about cultural difference: ethnic or cultural identity and class. Four central themes occupy most of the contemporary writing about art and difference relevant to our reconsideration. (1) *Art and kitsch:* Modern art is an arena of cultural claims especially about mass culture, industrialization, commodification and use-value—a context in which fine art has come to signify an alternative value (human spirit). (2) *Distinction:* Embodying higher forms of taste, the potential of material culture, when consumed, to signify or produce "distinction" presents a different ideological function, that of classifying persons. The capacity of material forms to be distinguished as "art" allows them to become valuable in differentiating—and producing—persons or classes of persons in processes of subjectification (see Bourdieu 1984). (3) *The family of man:* In response to the growing numbers of exhibitions and other appropriations of non-Western objects and cultural forms, critics have pointed out the ideological functioning of the category "art" (see Foster 1983, 1985a) and the power (or perhaps hegemonic capacity) involved in the exhibitionary complex (see especially Mitchell 1989). In this critique, the discourses of orientalism or primitivism are understood as artifacts of the expansion of Western capitalism, as part of its production of a modern, or Western, identity through constructing an other. (4) *The nation:* Art's incorporation into projects of nation building and national identity has drawn on a Romantic nationalism that posited a characteristic national spirit or ethos, objectified materially in the cultural forms of the national subject. In a sense, the so-called global art market and the movement of artworks through space and time constitute an objectification that contributes to the production of nations.

As Webb Keane pointed out during the seminar, while discussing Christopher Steiner's essay on the movement of art objects across national boundaries, one ought not to take space and time for granted. They are socially constructed—or rather, they are constructed very much through the circulation of objects, in ways similar to the way in which exchange elsewhere constitutes a sociocultural framework. The very existence of the international art market constitutes yet another medium in which nation-states may produce themselves. I quote his remarks at some length:

> One of the things that seems to be going on when we talk about "motion" of works of art through space and time is a twofold relationship among metropoles, a relationship among metropoles (places where art galleries and art critics are located, art collectors, art producers tend to congregate) and the hinterlands. There is a way in which the art world sharpens something we see in other respects: the ways in which metropoles are often closer in sociopolitical terms to other metropoles than to their own hinterlands. Elite art collectors in Jakarta are closer to art collectors in Hong Kong and New York than they are to the average Javanese village a few miles down the road. But when we raise the question of the nationality of art, we can say that each metropole, to the extent that it wants to make a claim over and against other metropoles as having a certain specificity, brings tokens of its hinterland to market in order to circulate them among other metropoles. So that New York really starts to distinguish itself against Paris hegemony when it is able to circulate John Marins and Georgia O'Keeffes (drawing on hinterlands of Maine and New Mexico). But they had to be tokens that are detachable enough from the hinterland to then be recognizable and circulable among other metropoles. The circulation of artworks is creating an imaginary space-time, something that is not identifiable with physical space-time. (4 November 1996)

In our discussions (and in this volume), we observed two specific regimes of value, one delineated in the art/commodity opposition, which we might refer to as a market framing, and the other delineated around ethnic and national identity. Interestingly, the concept of "inalienability" appeared useful in discussing both of them.

Art and the Modern

No less than was the case for the "gift," the historical specificity of the discourse about art and its baggage requires that the category "art" be made an object of inquiry rather than taken for granted as a basis of explanation. The workings of art objects and exhibitions are dependent on art's historical construction as an autonomous sphere of cultural activity. It is a sphere distinguished by its separation from (or transcendence of) considerations of utility or rationality, and it is formulated in the notion of an aesthetic experience constituted through the disinterested contemplation of objects as art objects, removed from instrumental associations (see Bourdieu 1984). The American lawyer John Quinn's plea for art's freedom from taxation, quoted by Steiner (this volume), expresses the ideal neatly: "It is an absurdity to argue that art is merely a luxury. It is a degradation to treat it as though it were something like opium or a drug or an adulterated food,... and it is ...reactionary to consider it merely a means of raising a little revenue, as if it were leather or wool" (Quinn 1913:16).

The scaffolding for this modern doctrine of art is historical and specific, formulating a distinctive place for art on which many kinds of cultural production have been based. These have been illuminated, or exposed, in recent discussions and debates that have questioned art's supposed isolation (autonomy) from other spheres of activity and placed modern art and aesthetic activities more complexly within the specific historical nexus of modernity.

The processes of modernity and modernization have a significant linkage to this formulation of art as an autonomous domain of value, and the historically prevailing ideologies of artistic practice were born in precisely this context. Max Weber, for example, recognized the cultural project of art in the West to have been assumed increasingly with the growing autonomy of art as a category of activity separated from the rational, utilitarian, everyday world but with the possibility of "enriching" it. The particularity of the discourse itself, however, can be traced to the emergence of "cultural modernity" and broadly to modernization in France.

The linkage between "modern" art and modernization crystallized in mid-nineteenth-century France, where Haussmann's project of transforming Paris, the exemplary moment of modernization, was the subject of Baudelaire's (1964 [1863]) ruminations about art's role in managing what he recognized as the contradictory dislocations—the fragmentation—of the processes of social planning, rationalization, and so on. It might even be said that "artistic modernism" is one of the ideologies of modernization. Modernization is a process of self-fashioning, of directed transformation that makes culture the object of its planning and evaluation. The cultural hierarchy distinguishing between "high" and "low"—"high culture" versus "popular culture" or "mass culture"—represents an organization of difference that attempts to install qualitative judgments and notions of directions of cultural flow around the value of particular cultural forms. In this process of modernization, the category "art" came to stand redemptively against kitsch, the mass-produced, the "inauthentic." Its autonomy implies that art must be nonutilitarian (art for art's sake), "authentic," handmade, expressive of other qualities of the human spirit, and of high quality. At the same time, the subject matter of painting was equally engaged with these circumstances. Social historians of art have demonstrated how paintings in this period were objects whose value or significance was defined in circuits of meaning related to the evaluation of modernity or responding to the processes of modernization (as Clark [1984] argued for Manet), or related more distantly to discourses produced in the context of earlier European experiences of modernity.

One must argue, therefore, that there is a connection between the historical emergence of art as a domain of value and one of the pressing issues or predicaments of material culture—the existence and effects of changing patterns of cultural flow and the registration of cultural difference. The evaluation of these changes is undertaken in terms established in the development of the category "art." How we feel about or judge cultural change, cultural homogenization, even the process of assimilation to Western patterns has been set by terms such as "authenticity" (see Errington 1998; Phillips and Steiner 1999) established within modernist discourses about art. This has involved many complex issues, and I can summarize them only briefly here.

A qualification is needed first. For analytical purposes, I suggest we understand the lowercase "modernism" as embracing a range of artistic doctrines and practices that address the contradictory qualities of modernity. Uppercase "Modernism" in art should refer to the specific doctrine of an autonomous art domain in which the appropriate problem for each art form is the investigation of the formal properties of its own medium (Blake and Frascina 1993:127). Neither Baudelaire's call for a "modern" art, though it addresses the contradictory conditions of "modern life," nor the advent of various doctrines of modern art should be confused with the particular aesthetic doctrine of Modernism.

The capacity of some objects, as "art," to operate in a critical relationship within the cultural formation of modernity has resonances in other, contemporaneous inflections of material culture. Formulations of a "primitive" otherness have provided a parallel critique, similarly deployed to attest to the existence of forms of humanity that are integral, cohesive, working as a totality. "Difference," in this form of Romantic atavism, was harnessed to function as a critical opposite to modernity's fragmented life-world, reversing the more common nineteenth-century placement of this "difference" as an inferior state of human development that needed to be replaced or overcome. A figure such as the "positive primitive" and its represented reality—like the positive value sometimes ascribed to the handcrafted object—permits the very characterization of the "modern" as fragmented and a sense of contemporary mass culture as "spurious" and somehow inauthentic. This has made the collection and domestic display of native baskets (Cohodas 1999), pottery (Babcock 1995; Mullin 1995), masks, and other goods into a meaningful distinction, representing the presence or coexistence of other values—even of an alternative regime of value.

A Hierarchy of Value?

It is widely perceived that the category of art posits a hierarchy of cultural value and constitutes an arena of cultural evaluation. A significant effect of postmodern criticism has been to articulate a more relativist position about cultural value. Formalist definitions, it has been argued, are projected and circulated partly as defensive responses to a surrounding context—to the threat to "art," for example, of theatricality (Fried 1967), kitsch (Greenberg 1961 [1939]), entertainment, and mass culture (Adorno 1983 [1970]). Critically oriented postmodern theorists such as Rosalind Krauss, Hal Foster, Craig Owens, and others identified with the journal *October,* as well as more straightforward sociological critics such as Pierre Bourdieu (1984), see art's defensive strategy of self-definition not merely as a neutral fact but as a form of cultural production itself, an exclusionary, boundary-maintaining activity, a hegemonic exercise of power through knowledge. Bourdieu asked why cultural forms that were distanced from use (and utility)—as in the disinterested contemplation of objects as art objects removed from instrumental associations—were inherently more valuable than others, recognizing that the taste and capacity for these kinds of differences depended on class position. It is the dominant class's position that allows its members to make their tastes appear to be the universal ideal.

Thus, claims to the universality of these values is suspect; conversely, access—both in taste and in material possession—to the objects instantiating this ideal is limited, allowing only the economically leisured to acquire cultural value. Disinterested aesthetic contemplation, as imagined in Kantian philosophy,[9] is a bourgeois class position or *habitus* and therefore one exclusive of other classes, and the supposed hierarchy of value is an objectification of social relations into the world of objects. In fact, as critics have pointed out, not only do constructions of taste seem to represent different class and ethnic groups and to exclude or subordinate some tastes or styles as of lesser value under the guise of an objective, universal judgment, but also the hierarchy itself is produced in hegemonic struggles among classes or class fractions to produce their own domination.

Clearly, then, a central issue involved with such modernisms and with the aesthetic theorizations of "art" that drew on the Kantian ideal of disinterested judgment has come to be the problem of cultural difference, homogenization, and heterogeneity. The sense of hierarchy and exclusion as defensive strategies underlies much of the critical work of the late twentieth century

Culture has not remained comfortably within the classifications of value constructed in art discourse. Some critical awareness emerged directly from confronting the commodity status of fine art objects and their inability to remain external to other spheres of value, such as the market. A related series of debates, under the sign of "anti-aesthetics" (Foster 1983), recognized the disingenuous quality of art's purported separateness and the involvement of aesthetics in the world of utility, politics, and commodities. These debates partially drew on the positioning of art's historical avant-garde, their suspicions of aestheticization, and their movement toward performance and dematerialization of the art object as a counter to the commoditization of what was supposed to be transcendent and redemptive (see Kirshenblatt-Gimblett 1995 and this volume).

It is not only the participation of objects as art in such formations that is a matter of ambivalence. Whether the issue is mass consumption (as a degraded form of cultural value) or the problem of cultural homogenization or heterogeneity (high/low, popular, folk), hierarchies of judgment place ethnic differences within a universalizing judgment. Thus is art more than accidentally an arena in which discourses about cultural values are produced and in which identities are circulated.

Such doctrines continue to operate, albeit in changing contexts, and these contexts may reveal the constructedness of the mediating categories. In this sense, the objects are now loosened from what might have been more secure anchorings within the discourse of modern art, and notions of "art's autonomy" can be variously used as parts of emerging contexts. To Nicholas Thomas, as he emphasized in his comments during the seminar (7 November 1996), the notion of "autonomy" itself constitutes simply another context, another way of valorizing objects. Annie Coombes, in her chapter in this volume, analyzes the translation of objects from Africa as they moved to a new context in the exhibition *Africa: Art of a Continent* at London's Royal Academy of Arts. Her focus is on the exhibitors' recourse to universalistic models of art and its autonomy from other spheres of activity. The claim that the Royal Academy exhibition was an aesthetic activity, Coombes argues, and therefore not responsible for the political concerns confronting it, did not fully hide the provenance of these objects in colonial (and subsequent) expropriation. The alternate regime of value imagined in the discourse of art as redemptive did not here serve to "enrich the life-world." The discourse of art's autonomy was deployed instead to displace criticisms of the academy's display of what one might regard, in the light of international conventions for cultural property, as uncomfortably loosened (looted) objects from Africa, as well as to displace concerns about restitution and the suspect economic and political motivations of the show's sponsors. The exhibition's mediation of different contexts and schemas for classifying objects, Coombes argues, failed (see Beidelman also 1997b, esp. p. 18).

For all this, however, many consider that there is still significance in the redemptive value of art as an autonomous sphere of value—but this sphere exists less as an abstract or self-subsisting one than in situational deployments. In our seminar, Ivan Karp (who was unable to contribute a chapter to this volume) suggested the necessity of locating these categories (art, autonomy) more clearly in institutional settings: it might be useful, he pointed out, to differentiate autonomy at the point of production (for the producer) from autonomy at the destination (the exhibition, the curation). Coombes, during the seminar, argued that there is more than one model of autonomy. She tried to retain the critical (and redemptive) value of "art"—drawing on Adorno's insights—in discussing the value of what she called a "relative autonomy," as distinct from the autonomy imagined in certain kinds of Modernism that deny the significance of social relations. This relative autonomy—"that is, a recognition of certain kinds of principles and practices which are inherent to that particular way of working and also [to] the spaces in which it operates" (Coombes, 6 November 1996)—draws on the "irreducibility" of material culture and its manufacture to other processes and is vital for its critical potential. Perhaps, she suggested, "it's healthy to think about it in the ways in which the role of the intellectual has been theorized—as somebody who necessarily operates within a particular kind of isolated or rarefied sphere and is productive and necessary."

In the aftermath of such critiques, we might view the emergence of the very doctrines of art as autonomous from other domains of social life (such as in High Modernism), as historically specific, and as linked organically to the same processes of modernization that they protest. Modernism in the very broad sense—within the arts, then, varied as they are—may be seen as addressing the contradictory qualities of modernity. Primitives and avant-gardes, separately and conjoined, occupy this discursive space. This is the Janus-faced quality of modernity, the dialectical regimes of values—a dialectic in which ideologies of material culture are deeply imbricated.

The "Primitivism" Debate

The discourses of art have come into illumination partly through the watershed debates about "primitivism" occasioned especially by the Museum of Modern Art's 1984 exhibition *"Primitivism" in Twentieth-*

Century Art: Affinities of the Tribal and the Modern (see Rubin 1984). Although these debates now extend to the broader question of cultural representation and postcoloniality (see Coombes 1994, and this volume), they must be understood as having initially manifested criticism of the hegemonic position of the Museum of Modern Art (MOMA) in New York and its ideological construction of Modernism. Inevitably, they also raised the question of what it means to to collect or exhibit the artifacts of cultures. In this volume, part three particularly examines what I have called the "border zones," meaning thereby to draw attention to points where the limits of the frames of classification and regimes of value in which objects are circulated come to be exposed. In this chapter, however, I want to maintain continuity with the particular history of exhibition that produced vital critical insight. When critics approached the MOMA show on grounds of the inapplicability of the Modernist, formal concept of "art" (as a universal interpretive-evaluative category), they saw their criticism to be aimed at a broader ideological structure. They identified exhibitions as moments of cultural production and power—as objectifications into material form of a range of interests and positions, imposing a hierarchy of values that legitimated a hierarchy of persons.

The debate has made it clear that exhibitions (and related textual constructions) are not only media of representation but also forms of cultural (or ideological) production. What was collected, selected, and exhibited constructs a framework for the representation of people, their culture, their history. Critics have pointed out how such representation "traps" or subjectifies others and has defining power (as dominant knowledge) over their identities (Said 1978), arguing the concern of those represented in exhibitions (but also in texts) for their own voice, for control over their representation. Critics have also delineated how the structures and codes of Modernism contribute to subordinating or managing a "difference" that is threatening (Clifford 1988; Foster 1985a) to Modernism's own cultural assumptions—in this case, of a universal humanity defined by creativity and formal innovation. Thus "primitivism," as Foster argued, is an instrumentality of modernist cultural formation, in the service of sustaining and producing a Western identity. This identity is confirmed in the articulation of what Clifford (1985:166) called the "Modernist Family of Art" (following

Barthes's [1957] famous essay on the ideology of MOMA's *Family of Man* photographic exhibition). The "Family of Art" allegorized in the *"Primitivism" in Twentieth-Century Art* exhibition at MOMA, Clifford argued, emphasized creativity and formal innovation as the gist of "art" everywhere, as a basic human impulse. Thus, so-called primitive artists were represented as having the same formal motivations and interests said to be central to the modern avant-garde. The deconstructionist view is suspicious of the "naturalization" of what is historically specific, and it regards the construction "primitive art" as an attempt to legitimate current formations of power. Far from being autonomous and transcendent, therefore, art is shown to be complicit with forms of power.

Addressing the poetics of exhibition and exhibitionary practices, Clifford (and others) have questioned what we are supposed to "see" in the objects displayed—and what we are not supposed to see. In the course of representing art as a human universal (and legitimating specifically Western notions of art), the Modernist exhibition effaces the specific meanings, values, and histories of the makers. Producing ourselves or objectifying ourselves through their objects produces them as reflexes of our desires (Clifford 1985). The critique, then, is of Modernism's claim to universality and its suppression of "difference" in constructing itself. "Primitivist" exhibitions select that which sustains Modernism's insistent identification of art with formal, artistic invention. "Difference," which might challenge the security of Western assumptions about humanity and the world, is acknowledged only insofar as it conforms to this hegemony (see Clifford 1988; McEvilley 1984:59, 60).

This defensiveness at the heart of Modernism's hegemony comes into view in Steiner's essay in this volume. If the doctrine of art seems to fuel or legitimate itself by its successful application to the non-Western, then the international border is where the question of the spatial extensiveness of Modern Art is adjudicated, where it is decided whether this art is capable of circulating without limits. During the seminar, Keane commented on precisely this question:

> Thus, the border reinforces the presuppositions of the art-system as a claim to spatiotemporal transcendence, and this

> transcendence is part of what the connoisseurs and collectors are trying to buy into. So where is the politics? There is the obvious Bourdieuian class struggle going on here, and there is also the collector versus the state. The collectors at the border are in a struggle with the state over who has the authority and the judgment, over which is the ultimate authority. And the Modernist collector is in part trying to escape confinement to a national location. These are people who are asserting the cosmopolitanism at the border.
>
> What's the threat? The anxiety? Part of the threat is that the border is the point at which it might turn out that art is not transcendent and universal, because different systems of value meet at the border. Here, what is supposed to be universal faces the threat of being relativized. It might turn out that these are not universal values after all.
>
> The second threat is that art might turn out not to be transcendent....it might turn out to be just a bunch of bronze after all, just so much stuff. (4 November 1996)

Suspicion about the uses of primitivism has not been aimed only at the supposedly transcendent, autonomous aesthetic domain postulated by High Modernism. It has equally significant implications for the way in which local identities might lose their integrity or have their distinctiveness subsumed within a grand narrative that does not engage their own histories (see Coombes, this volume; Burn et al. [1988] discuss the problem of art at the periphery of the world system). Thus, exhibitions of what is called "primitive art," while they emphasize form—by displaying objects on the usual white walls with little information other than general date and probable "tribal identity"—deny to these works the history and authorship that would be part of the Western context (see Price 1989).

This has led to the considerable irony that the valorized "primitive" usable in critique is nonetheless presumed to be ahistorical, timeless, unchanging, authorless. These qualities seem to preserve the capacity of this formation to provide an alterity to the West. On the one hand, primitive art is authentic, expressive of the truly different other, only when it originates outside of Western contact, when it is precolonial. On the other hand, such modes of exhibition efface the specific histories and power relations through which non-Western objects became parts of Western collections, available for display. Indeed, they typically exclude the contemporary representatives of these cultural traditions as "inauthentic." Yet, as deconstruction provides, these very meanings are available in the presence of the objects and their exhibition, and they offer evidence of the cultural work (through recontextualization itself) in which objects have often been deployed—the work of remembering, forgetting, dismembering, obviating, and displacing histories and relationships (see Battaglia 1990; Wagner 1978). Coombes (this volume) goes a step further in relating the construction of exhibitions to contradictions that, while general, are more specific and distinctive in the historical and geographical relationships mediated.

For Aboriginal Australian and First Nations people, "primitivism" has a particular salience for the production and circulation of political and cultural identities (see Ziff and Rao 1997). Clifford (1988, 1991) and some of the essayists in Karp and Lavine 1991 have eloquently made this point about museums particularly, but they have done so in recognition of the active political projects of indigenous people and their representatives. Repeatedly, those represented have engaged the obstacles of the binding doctrines of "authenticity" and cultural purity with their own insistence that "we are not dead, nor less 'Indian.'"

FROM GAZE TO ARENA: THE INTERCULTURAL FIELD

To be sure, the recognition that non-Western peoples "had art" did result, and not inconsequentially, in their inclusion in the authorized "family of man." They were "creative," "humane," "spiritual." But the exhibitions promoting this inclusion—and the success of the intensified circulation of the products and images of non-Western others—comprise a complex for recontextualizing objects that has drawn considerable attention. They are sites of cultural production (Bourdieu 1993a).

Returning to the theme of recontextualization offers an opportunity for some suggestions beyond those imagined in the first round of primitivism debates. In this volume, the larger frame for grasping "primitivism" is that of intercultural exchange and transaction. This is a frame that can include the sort of "appropriations" that have concerned critics, but the weight is placed not on the boundaries but on the charged social field that encompasses the actors. Although critics of the paradigmatic "primitivist fantasy" have commonly drawn on the Foucauldian association of power with knowledge to give theoretical shape to their efforts to discern the imposition of meaning and values on native peoples, the emphasis on "appropriation" and the primitivizing "gaze" is insufficient to enable an understanding of what happens when such objects circulate in an international art world. In this volume, we attempt to ask what actually does happen in circulation, at the sites of exhibition—to ask how objects, identities, and discourses are produced, inflected, and invoked in actual institutional settings. These "fields of cultural production" (Bourdieu 1993a) have distinct histories, purposes, and structures of their own. Research and writing on the nation and the native offer considerable insight into the problem.

In pursuit of this sort of specificity, it is clearly necessary to break down the very generalized notion of the "primitive" that analysts have tended to deploy. In part, this involves recognizing that the processes of modernization are mediated through a range of institutions. In nation building, for example, distinct and varying values may be conveyed to the "native." We cannot assume we know what these values will be, as Lomnitz (this volume) shows in his discussion of Benito Juárez's embodiment of the native in Mexico, but we can imagine that their conveyance occurs in an institutionally specific field of cultural production. Three of the chapters in this volume (those by Lomnitz, Thomas, and me) track the figure of the "indigenous other" through particular circuits of artistic, regional, and national institutions and identity.

The focus on distinct cases, however, does not mean an absence of comparison. There has been a general context for revaluing indigenous people and their products in the English-speaking settler states. One is struck, for example, by the importance of World War I, in the United States, Canada, and Australia, in leading these settler nations more actively to pursue an identity distinct from that of Europe. Often, this effort to escape the anxiety of European influence and to express a unique experience has resulted in an appropriation of the "native," the "indigene," as a component of an authentic national culture. The workings here seem to differ from the ideological function of "primitivism" in the MOMA exhibition of 1984, which was concerned with using the other to legitimate the Western construction of "art." MOMA's primitivism seems to have derived from a cosmopolitan modernity of tasteful international subjects, rather than from a national hybridity in pursuit of geographical distinction.

The appropriation of the indigenous other by nationalist culture represents different temporal and spatial juxtapositions. The differentiation of national identity could combine, as Lomnitz (this volume) shows for Mexico, with a critical stance toward modernity, against what Lears (1983) described as "the modern ethic of instrumental rationality that desanctified the outer world of nature and the inner world of self." National and class-organized differences could be conflated in particularly powerful circuits of value.

The recuperation of indigenous culture in such appropriations may, however, value it only in ways defined by the dominant culture—that is, in terms of a hegemony that does not really accept "difference" or that organizes difference in the service of another set of values. This is the effect of the effort at appropriation of the indigenous—the *indio*—by Mexican fine arts in the service of the revolution's ideology of hybridization (Bakewell 1995). For such work to be "fine art," however, it could not be made by those regarded as artisans, and certainly not by *indios* themselves. Similarly, the re-significations of the Australian Aboriginal relationship to land embodied in their paintings may be resisted within the immediate region where they live (where settlers compete for control of land), or by immigrant minorities (who are threatened by a special Aboriginal status), but have a different meaning when they are "re-placed" in the context of emerging Australian nationalism, international tourism, and the new professional class that seeks to define itself. While Aboriginal producers of the paintings—living in dilapidated and impoverished communities—may be stripped of their historical specificity and their images converted to signifiers in Australian national myth, their insistence of a return of value for their paintings also resists this incorporation.

The language of "objectification"—rather than "appropriation"—may provide greater leverage in teasing out the complicated and subtle intersections of relative value and interests. If the appropriations of Aboriginal paintings or decorations are objectifications of national identity, they are also objectifications of their Aboriginal makers, and we need to follow out the implications of their movement through a new system of value. The essays in this volume suggest that we must recognize that the media in which these objectifications occur are a problem to be considered. As Kirshenblatt-Gimblett (1991a) has maintained, the seeking for something distinctive is central to modernity/nationalism.

The requirements for the expression of a nation-state's "identity" are not simply cognitive (see Lomnitz, this volume). Rather, mimicry seems to be an operative principle through which nation-states produce—objectify—themselves as equal and equivalent entities, both as politically sovereign and as distinctive tourist destinations with something of value to see and consume. Australia's policy of developing the arts (Myers, this volume) offers a good example of why cultural policy—policy concerning the production of culture—has become an important domain of state intervention.

Moreover, objectifications of national identity are both variable and contextually limited in their stability. Aboriginal art's status as a commodity of consumption involves forms of commercial value that are potentially at odds with its capacity to articulate national identity as something spiritual, authentic, and attached to the land. It was nothing short of a scandal when an Aboriginal bark painting in the prime minister's collection was discovered to be a forgery, painted by a white person! Furthermore, these paintings are not the only media in which national identity may be objectified. War memorials, automobiles, heritage sites, archaeological formations, heroes, battlefields, natural history museums, symphony orchestras, and so on may offer very different, even competing, representations of the national self, representations that may circulate within different contexts and social formations.

Objectification, Mediation, and Value

The implications of what Thomas (this volume) calls "settler primitivism" are very different from the implications of a more general primitivism such as that represented in European modernist art. Critics of the latter sort of primitivism have emphasized its inability to represent the primitive as coexisting with the modern, in the same time (see Fabian 1983). The whole significance of settler primitivism, on the other hand, is that the "native" and the "settler" are coeval. The instabilities and tensions come from the fact that indigenous communities are not only contemporaneous but also to some extent recognizably in the same space with so-called modern ones. While it draws on many tropes that are familiar, settler primitivism has a special problem of context: the indigenous people cannot be fully relegated to prehistory as the predecessors of the settlers. There is a basic situation of copresence, even of competing claims to the land.

During the seminar discussion, Daniel Miller pointed out this distinct formulation of value in settler primitivism. Acknowledgment of the "natives" and their incorporation as part of the whole may constitute a recontextualization, a symbolic transformation. The "uplifting upward," as Miller characterized it, may mark a particular and new hybrid formulation of the indigenous and the native, a "hierarchy in the making." The result of this transformation is to shift "the interpretation of these art movements from a question of 'appropriation'—of two distinctly defined groups and no relation of one to the other—to an understanding of increasing 'acknowledgment' of something that is happening in cultural identity and nationalism. This is being acknowledged through the transformations in these materials" (Miller, 5 November 1996).

Whereas Margaret Preston's juxtaposition of Aboriginal motifs and modernist renderings, as presented by Thomas, drew attention only to their difference and to the specificity of the Aboriginal, the kind of self-fashioning currently being achieved through Aboriginal acrylic paintings has a different effect: There is a production of value in the native.

These recontextualizations—in this case of a hybrid formation of settler primitivism—are not just surprising or ironic juxtapositions but reorganizations of value. Such reorganizations, insofar as they have the properties of symbolic transformation—relating contexts in new structures of relationship—might usefully be compared with ritual (see Kapferer 1979), which comprises another medium of objectification. The gain in value for native cultural forms should be conceptualized in terms that are relevant for anthropological theory more generally, and indeed such recontextualizations are increasingly common in the world (see Turner n.d.). What might it mean for Aboriginal cultural products to be accepted in the full terms of the international art market? Terence Turner (personal communication, 15 July 1999) has suggested that the appropriation of indigenous forms by the "national types"—in Australia, the professional-managerial class—as an aspect of national identity has several implications. One is that the evolutionary classification of indigenous people as less fully integrated or more peripheral in various hierarchical and linear rankings of difference becomes repudiated in favor of a pluralistic, multicultural formulation. Here the ability of the nation to embrace qualitatively different modes of cultural life—a symbolic transformation—gets registered as a measure of its strength and vitality. A second and equally important implication, from the point of view of indigenous people, is that they are recognized as having value in an equal way—as having art, for example. Because they are implicated in a system of the same order, in which each component has art, they are given an equivalent claim on that order; they are given a stronger claim on the other goods of the nation, legal and economic. In part, what is observed here, at the broadest level, is a framework in which monetary success, a form of quantitative value, is converted into qualitative value (in a structure that combines, nonetheless, several distinct regimes of value) (see Graeber n.d.: ch. 2).

A similar process, interestingly, is delineated in Daniel Miller's presentation (this volume) of British "provisioning" in North London, which moves beyond the simple irony of the calculated "gift" and the selfless shopping toward a recognition of the effects of the objectification of the ideal of "thrift" and its mediation of the relations between regimes of value. Miller shows provisioning to be a practice of expending cash in a structure of sacrifice that "creates through the domestic arena the fundamental microcosm of all that most people in this area understand as value" (that is, "love" as a transcendent ideal). Just as nationalisms and primitivisms might vary, there is a distinctiveness to this North London formulation of the expenditure of cash in shopping. As a practice, provisioning defines family members in terms of persons' abilities to recognize and satisfy the desires of the other—quite differently from practices on the Indonesian island of Sumba, for which

Keane shows a concern about money's capacity to unleash individual desire, a bad thing. Ultimately, the practices of spending must be seen as caught up, or embedded, in broader systems of value, systems of relations in which even use-value can be transformed into something more permanent as a token of relationship. The story of shopping, here, is the story of reproducing (in practice) family relations as part of "the daily dynamics through which such relations are objectified" (indeed created). "It is the very alienability and diversity of the commodity," Miller argues, deployed within the structure of North London households, "that allows it to play a role equivalent to that of the inalienable possession as portrayed by Weiner." The inalienable object of this system, however, is the person—constructed, by the effort of shopping and its constant reconsiderations and reevaluations, as the source of desire. In this case, alienable and highly flexible forms of material culture provide the means to create and sustain the sanctified "person."

In the North London case, too, the issue of the material properties of objects and their effects on the functioning of exchange may be relevant. During the seminar discussion, Lomnitz raised a question about "whether the fact that provisioning involves perishable goods doesn't subject the relationships constructed to more intense politics of memory than the inalienable possessions that Annette [Weiner] was talking about." In provisioning, he suggested, "there is a built-in tension between short-term and long-term goals. So the mother can talk about her shopping as self-sacrificing and as concern and thoughtfulness for her daughter or for her son, but the daughter or son can construct that as manipulation, self-seeking, whatever—all kinds of ulterior motives, which are harder to attribute to a thing that is inherited from a more abstract past" (3 November 1996).

The Problem of Museum Display

Debates about the globalizing processes in which many kinds of things are caught up have often lacked a grounded understanding of how processes work in contexts that are the local end points or transition points in movement. One of the principal arenas for which discussions of material culture and recontextualization have taken place has been that of museums and exhibitions (see Clifford 1988, 1991; Karp and Lavine 1991).

Today it may be taken for granted that objects or material culture is exhibited, that meaning is produced from their presentation to viewers, but it was not always so (see Hooper-Greenhill 1992). Many writers have noted the growing significance of visual representation and exhibition in the West from the late eighteenth century onward. Museums, for example, are a distinctively nineteenth-century form of making knowledge available.

Museums have been known as places, or institutions, that are "object-centered" (Conn 1998), but in recent years the meaning of museum practice has been a lively subject of inquiry (Hooper-Greenhill 1992; Kaplan 1994; Root 1996). Such reconsiderations of exhibition as a practice have been strongly oriented around the critical question of what it means to represent people and cultures. Curators, deeply involved in the problem of exhibition and display of material culture, recognize this as a central issue. In this area, analyses are often historically and discursively very specific, and one of the goals of our seminar was to bring them into association with the broader and usually less specific framework of inalienability.

Barbara Kirshenblatt-Gimblett's much-cited essay "Objects of Ethnography" (1991b) is particularly concerned with this dominant contemporary example of recontextualization—the exhibition. Kirshenblatt-Gimblett's writing on what some have described as "the exhibitionary complex" (Bennett 1995) has made a significant contribution to the poetics and politics of display, asking, "What does it mean to show?"

From a deep concern with the practice of display—with the aesthetic and/or poetic effects of different display techniques—she takes the problem of "showing" as a mode of knowledge into its deep ontological commitments, questioning some of the tacit assumptions of what should be called "material ideologies" (after the term "language ideologies"; see Schieffelin, Woolard, and Kroskrity 1998; Silverstein 1979; also Keane, this volume). The very notion that objects are more real than other media of representation, Kirshenblatt-Gimblett points out, has complex roots in Renaissance attitudes about representations of the "true cross." Her complex and careful delineation of the effects (the poetics [Jakobson 1960], as it were) of various techniques of display (in situ, in context, panoramic, and panoptic) demonstrates the power of considering practices of exhibition—of making visible—as performances. This approach (see also Kirshenblatt-Gimblett 1998) draws not on exchange theory (concerned with gifts and commodities) but on art and performance theory (concerned with the effects of detaching and reframing and the relationship between "art" and "artifact" or the "everyday"). Thus she brings the critical insights of the historical avant-garde—suspicious of the rational, seeking after the unsettling, relying on the senses—into contact with other theorizations of representation.

The avant-gardists' historical concern about the separation of art from everyday life often turns them toward the quotidian itself, which they frame or display as "art/not art." This is evident in attempts to perform the "everyday." Kirshenblatt-Gimblett's study of the Los Angeles Arts Festival, organized by Peter Brooks, shows how this avant-garde framing can have bewildering effects when it is applied to performance practices from other cultural traditions that are exhibited, without any contextualization but essentially as artworks, for their capacity to "shock" or "defamiliarize" (see Kirshenblatt-Gimblett 1995). Anthropological exhibitions, which typically emphasize the everyday, therefore share a substantial and representational problem with the arts—a sharing marked by their involvement with similar genres of performance.

The blurring of genres that Kirshenblatt-Gimblett notes is provocative and productive of the circuits through which objects can move, the circuits through which the practices of making visible are themselves meaningful. Slumming, tourism, and ethnography share, partially, a meaningful frame with the museum effect—a frame of the power to view. This is not accidental. Historically, it has been the poor, the mad, children, animals, and the "lower" order of humankind who are revealed by being exposed to view. The effect she describes for early-twentieth-century "slumming" (in which one can "see" humankind, in which the city becomes the recipient of the habits of museum viewing) encapsulates the moral discomfort that some recent critiques of ethnography itself have articulated, a discomfort that arises from ethnography's verging on "what might be termed social pornography—the private made public." This recontextualization, as much as any of the objects themselves, generates a voyeuristic excitement: "Not surprisingly...in a convergence of moral adventure, social exploration, and sensation seeking, the inner city is constructed as a socially distant but physically proximate exotic—and erotic—territory" (Kirshenblatt-Gimblett 1991b:413).

To understand differences between the varying effects of genres of performance and of things on display, Kirshenblatt-Gimblett points to the relevance of the sensory and material properties of the objects. The question is, how do displays have an effect? The question is provocative in the context of exhibitions that attempt to display daily life—exhibitions in which objects might be found. In an argument that resonates with Moore and Myerhoff's (1977) insights into ritual, Kirshenblatt-Gimblett writes that exhibitions of the quotidian "force us to make comparisons that pierce the membrane of our own quotidian world, allowing us for a brief moment to be spectacles of ourselves, an effect that is also experienced by those on display" (Kirshenblatt-Gimblett 1991b:409). Their effect is to make the taken-for-granted available for contemplation, but it also "propels the fascination with penetrating the life space of others, getting inside, burrowing deep into the most intimate places, whether the interiors of lives or the innermost recesses of bodies" (Kirshenblatt-Gimblett 1991b:408).

In this way, Kirshenblatt-Gimblett's discussion of "objects of ethnography," fragments detached from their original context and reproduced under the sign of academic discipline and historically available exhibitionary practices, is valuable for its deconstruction of the apparent singularity of the museum. She examines various practices of display for their "effects," very much aware of the problems faced by curators and the choices available to make objects meaningful. By showing the links between museum practices and other performance activities and the arts—as in theatrical scene painting—Kirshenblatt-Gimblett delineates the instability of genres and their boundaries. Her awareness of the emergence of distinct discursive formations and institutions, or ways of seeing, out of specific histories of display (e.g., the zoological or theatrical option for displaying live people [1991b:402]), preexisting frames, and familiar genres allows us to see the active process of convergence through which objects are made to signify. At the same time, her analysis offers the deconstructive sense that objects and practices have properties other than those of transparent or rational design.

What is the museum, then, in which so many objects are recontextualized? The practices and conceits of display that govern or constitute the museum have a history themselves, ranging from the museum as a "form of interment" (burial) to the museum as a live display. The difference between these forms is expressed in the sensory organization of display. Kirshenblatt-Gimblett notes that the European tendency has been to split up the senses and parcel them out, one at a time, to the appropriate art form. Conventional museum exhibitions follow a pattern of partiality, of fragmentation in sensory apprehension, by prioritizing the visual—a display practice that inevitably draws them toward classifying objects as "art": "When reclassified as 'primitive art' and exhibited as painting and sculpture, as singular objects for visual apprehension, ethnographic artifacts are elevated, for in the hierarchy of material manifestations, the fine arts reign supreme. To the degree that objects are identified with their makers, the cultures represented by works of art also rise in the hierarchy" (Kirshenblatt-Gimblett 1991b:416).

Kirshenblatt-Gimblett has provided a cogent introduction to the specificities of "seeing" and the recontextualization of objects for display. In doing so, she has outlined a range of techniques and their effects, especially in relationship to the dangers of depoliticizing the oppositional potential of the cultural differences being represented. Her genuine understanding of the aesthetics of display and the problems of curation represents a careful approach—even a typology—to understanding how objects may be, and have been, "made to signify" in one of the distinctive and prevalent institutional contexts of recontextualization.

Intercultural Performance and Culture Making

Kirshenblatt-Gimblett's point of reference has been principally that of curation and display. It has remained for others to engage the frameworks and experiences of those engaging globalizing processes from peripheral locations. The intensified circulation, exhibition, and commodification of cultures and their objects does constitute a new regime—one that presents analysts and critics with the difficult problem of moving beyond complacent assumptions about "culture," its subjects, its products, and the processes of commoditization.

Considering that "culture" as a concept originated in evaluative discourses (see Stocking 1968; Williams 1977), it has proved difficult to engage analytically with questions of cultural circulation, power, and inequality without resorting to simple judgments. This is similar to the problem Daniel Miller has repeatedly articulated with regard to academic discussions of commodities.

The collapse of the boundaries that might once have separated indigenous art worlds and the West has forced a sea change, with a declining emphasis on the problem of authenticity (see Phillips and Steiner 1999). This is a change with numerous theoretical implications. It has led to a movement (Myers 1998) beyond the focus on ethnoaesthetics (local categories through which the formal qualities of objects and practices are engaged) to a different point of departure. Following the implications of Thomas (1991), scholars now foreground something like the hybrid, the crossing of traditions. The stability of the ethnoaesthetic conventions is disrupted when objects move between and among participants who obviously do not share a framework of evaluation. The emphasis on recontextualization requires that we focus not on supposed boundaries but on the activities of social agents, on the processes (for example) by which categories of evaluation and comprehension were brought into use, stabilized, or contested.

As we have seen, the construction of "primitivism" has a particular salience for the production and circulation of political and cultural identities. Concerns with representation and its capacity to define have been popular in the world of art criticism and art history, where they sprang up beyond the shadow of anthropology. Indeed, one wonders whether the very figuration of subjectification and resistance (see Abu-Lughod 1991)—a figuration that is highly evaluative—holds a suspicious family resemblance to art's nineteenth-century arrogation of responsibility for the human spirit in the face of the oppression of modernization, capitalism, and industrialization.

Most analyses of intercultural performances, consequently, have not addressed such events as forms of social action. Instead, the prevailing discourse about such performances, emerging from discussions by many analysts, revolves around a view that indigenous people (natives) should present themselves. This position developed through an opposition to previous representational frames that had ignored the power of the exhibitionary gaze to impose identity, and the resulting stance still tends to dismiss intercultural productions of identity as complicitous. The case that Phillips (n.d.) presents of First Nations performers at the end of the nineteenth century and their willingness to participate has many correspondences elsewhere. Critics seem ambivalent about just such practices, reflecting a continuing view of colonialism as absolutely determinative and of native peoples as merely victims or passive recipients of the actions of others. This corresponds to Clifford's (1988) discussion of the valorization of cultural "purity" as an essential prerequisite for authenticity. As Phillips argues, such judgments erase from our sight the ways in which aboriginal peoples use these discourses and opportunities to define and gain value from the circumstances that confront them.

If one dispenses temporarily with the wish to evaluate (good/bad, authentic/inauthentic), then one can recognize powerful forces of culture making in Native American performance, in Aboriginal acrylic painting's movement into the category of fine art, and in the New Zealand artist's appropriation of Maori design. As representations and objects move into new contexts, changing the relationships between those contexts, they are also connecting regimes of value.

UNSETTLED OBJECTS: REGIMES OF VALUE AND MODERNITY

As Ken George recently put it (1999), we are coming to recognize a series of dilemmas, or problems, attached to the signification of fine art objects. We now devote more attention to objects whose trajectories are less easily fixed in the familiar categories of classification. George has pointed out the range of discourses in which such objects can be (and have been) inscribed: discourses about modernity, taste, authenticity, artistic genius, historicity, and cultural heritage. Further, these discourses are mingled in a "thoroughly commodified and globalized art market." In other words, paintings, textiles—what have you—are collected, bought, sold, and displayed as valuable because of the ways in which they are understood to represent or embody or instantiate varying regimes of value (Appadurai 1986).

We have usually come to recognize these discourses, these regimes of value, because of the way they have been discussed and critically articulated in the field of Western art practice and cultural criticism. The big question that has been problematical for theories of value is, surely, why people place so much value on particular objects that are essentially nonutilitarian. Phrased so grandly, this narrative has given way to more varied and partial considerations. Sometimes the awareness of complexity—such as the relationship of art and money, taste and class—by analyst or participant is framed in the language of scandal, representing the mixture of supposedly distinct categories. Taste is not, supposedly, a capacity that money can buy. Often the scandal is that art and money are in fact linked, even though they are culturally constructed as contrasting forms of value; sometimes the scandal is that certain styles or categories of objects are valued not because they represent transcendent value but because they embody the tastes of a particular class. The sense of outrage or discomfort is presumably not unlike the discomfort Douglas (1966) reported the Lele to feel regarding the pangolin, an animal whose characteristics mysteriously represent those of two different categories of animal. As in the case of such classificatory confusion elsewhere, the discomfort may be a clue to the nature of value construction. Therefore, critical confrontation may in fact contribute to our understanding and reveal underlying structures, recognizing the historicity of the category "art."

Analysts should not, however, remain content with criticism or judgment. Objectively, the contradictions and crossings, the commodifications and appropriations, are simply social facts, and this insistently nonevaluative stance is recognized in the choice of "recontextualization" as a reigning concept. However we arrive at the point, I believe these insights offer us the opportunity to place that which we are inclined to know as "art" in a less positivistic framework—one in which the life of cultural objects is unrelentingly and unquestionably social, located in specific, historically constituted worlds.

The language of scandal (represented also by Bourdieu's notion of "misrecognition") does articulate the existence of tension or contradiction in the location of "art," categorically and institutionally. The notion of the movement of objects (or practices) through differing regimes of value or different contexts, and the sense of the meanings of things as "unsettled" or "contested," has a distinguished and developing history. It draws not only on Victor Turner's work (1974) and that of the Manchester school of social anthropology in the 1950s and 1960s but also on the rediscovery of Bakhtin's (1983) and Volosinov's (1973) focus on the dialogical—and I have tried to reinstate this orientation.

These issues overlap with the concerns expressed by the contributors to Appadurai's *The Social Life of Things* (1986), and they show the need for an elucidation of the often untheorized concept of "regimes of value." Modifying as it does the formulation of material culture as moving through distinct spheres of exchange, the notion of "regimes of value" has been used in a rather qualitative way, as more or less equivalent to "context." Because the concept is still relatively untheorized, there remains a need for a more direct consideration of a theory of value—a need largely neglected in many current considerations of the global, the postcolonial, and the national.

Far from beginning with intercultural movement as the boundary condition, I suggest, one should begin with a focus on "intercultural" objects and activities, on cultural forms and practices that circulate across boundaries. And those boundaries are not only of cultural difference conceived of in ethnic terms but also of "difference" conceived of under the sign of cultural hierarchy. Both types of difference involve the movement of objects through diverse institutions and social fields that classify them, that give them their meaning and value. The needed framework is one that focuses on circulation (or movement), on institutions, and on culture making rather than on relatively static cultural categories. The emphasis on circulation and recontextualization that we have taken up in this volume avoids reifying supposed "boundaries"—between reified cultures, for example—but leaves open the possibility of their construction in signifying practices around "difference."

Thus, "art" defines a hierarchy in which objects take part. Objects participate in systems of taste, or distinction, built around the market, connoisseurship, and hierarchies of value. Very commonly, objects—in the form of cultural property, heritage, and art—are also subsumed in projects of nationalism, in which indigenous cultural production and identities are engaged with the state's ideological dynamics. These two sorts of arenas are well known, of course, to those who write about art, and there are various quite distinct institutions that comprise them—mediating, thereby, the representation of, for example, Aboriginal painting.

The way in which Aboriginal products are circulating through new spaces and institutional linkages, building new audiences as well as meanings, argues against the imposition of boundaries and in favor of a framework of recontextualization. This framework has the potential for articulating the productive effect of culture making. The circulation of indigenous art may formulate distinct, if context-specific, new sociopolitical alliances, such as those between Aboriginal people and Australia's new professional-managerial class or, in the American Southwest, between Native American artists and a disenchanted eastern female elite (Mullin 1995). Because the imposition of identity in exchange may be something less than actual equivalence, so also does this kind of culture making leave its own ironies and loose threads. Many writers have noted the irony in the way in which Aboriginal acrylic paintings—objects whose significance lies partly in their asserting Aboriginal presence and rights over the land—are organized as significant components of an Australian "national imaginary." The consequent identity they construct is one produced by the very state that has subordinated Aboriginals in the first place.

The argument I am making is that the analysis of these new forms of cultural production needs to be more than semiotic, more linking of the practices and contexts in and through which value is established. This is the potential of the focus on activities of cultural production, particularly those that transform or link previous contexts. The case of Aboriginal acrylic paintings seems useful in exploring other histories in which regimes of value have become linked. When the settler state, Australia, is concerned with the problems presented by the existence of different categories of people (Aboriginal, Anglo-Celtic), the economic support of Aboriginals and the question of national identity may become linked. Ginsburg (1993) has drawn attention to the role of the state and its interests in such formations of cultural production. In the contemporary context, she argues, the state has been concerned to promulgate the image and production of the "high-tech primitive."

Roughly speaking, what should be observed in the case of Aboriginal paintings is a complex indexical convergence between the values of the two different regimes: there is not only the economic value of Aboriginal painting, which operates as a solution to the poverty of Aboriginal people, but there is also the indexical relationship of acrylic paintings as an indigenous form within Australian national space. The movement between regimes is a movement between contexts, reorganizing the values of each. In other nation-states, of course, art's capacity to mediate or reorganize internal differences and similarities is regulated by the specific interests and values involved there, but the parallels are cogent.

To pursue cultural production in this fashion is to acknowledge the importance of grounding any analysis of discourse within the specificity of institutional locations and their broader fields of cultural production. Ivan Karp discussed this matter eloquently at the seminar in terms of "institutional specificity." Aboriginal acrylic paintings, for example, are constructed as meaningful not only through museums and fine arts galleries but also within the funding practices and policies of bureaucracies that are concerned with the quite different discourses of Aboriginal employment, economy, and the market. They are also constructed as meaningful through the concerns of national and state educational establishments and even through the agencies of the state that are intended to "help" Aborigines. Thus the sociocultural significance, or value, of these paintings is surely composite and varied.

As anthropologists struggle against the pervasive framework of value drawn from Western economic theory, and with the historical placement of art and heritage at odds with this system of value, "inalienability" seems too static a framework. Perhaps this is the moment to return to Bourdieu's (1993a) "fields of cultural production," a concept itself concerned with brokering different kinds of resources for entering into social action. Such a reconsideration of regimes of value might delineate rather limited productions of commensurability, emphasizing the shallow connections they might produce between existing differences. This represents a move that should be noted as a way of treating material culture in a less static frame, less connected to concerns about authenticity.

It is clear that consumer utility and choice cannot explain the circulation and value of objects. Some objects are clearly valued for their link to identity and the past, for representing alternate regimes of value. The materiality of objects and their endurance through time make them particularly susceptible to such shiftings of trajectory, to being switched from one regime of value to another, and they seem singularly available for such processes of construction as take place in the organization of identities and temporalities. Indeed, can we not recognize the multivocality in objects—the oversupply of meaning—that Lévi-Strauss's (1966) *bricoleur* perceived, and not simply in *la pensée sauvage?* But objects are not just "good to think." The nostalgia of former East German citizens for the functionally deficient products of the old regime (Berdahl 1999) shows with great clarity the dialectic between capitalism and historical identity, and these objects embody this dialectic as mediations. While East German products are recuperated in the project of fashioning a distinctive historical identity for those who treasure them, their marketing and consumption simultaneously represent and "affirm the new order of the consumer market economy" (Berdahl 1999:206). This is what it means to say that such objects circulate in gravitational fields of force. The work of tracing these fields of force must also follow.

FIELDS OF FORCE

I have traced a number of trajectories and problems in material culture studies, especially those that represent intersections of the essays in this volume. To my mind, two very significant problems should be traced further. One of these concerns the rise of autonomous spheres or fields of cultural production—as delineated sociologically by Bourdieu (1993a), as represented concretely in the cases here by the growth of Aboriginal painting into "fine art," and as represented elsewhere by the development of the Southwest Indian art market (see McChesney 1992; Mullin 1995). In such processes, it should be noted, standards and conventions are created that allow producers and consumers/collectors to evaluate the quality of work. The direction of such standards in autonomous art worlds is toward self-referentiality—away from the utility value of objects and toward what emerges from the comparison of objects, what makes one different from another. This is a feature of a special kind of market, no doubt, but it shares with other markets the significance of the circulation of information between consumers, producers, and dealers. This canon, to call it by its name, is established within a specific history and privileges innovation, development, and stylistic novelty rather than immediate use-value. What needs to be understood about this process is that the market regime does not replace other regimes of value so much as it reorganizes them. Here, the development of a fine art market, focused on quality, transforms the relationship between ordinary production and that aimed at the luxury consumer. With that, as well, one must recognize that the production of the artist (as a constructed social person) is linked to the production of the new subject, distinguished by the consumption of these new products.

Objects such as Aboriginal paintings or Hopi pottery instantiate the dilemma of how one translates the value of heritage, memory, tradition, and the like into exchangeable value. That this conversion takes place is certain: people buy and sell these objects for money. And yet the producers complain that the buyers need to be "educated" in order to give the producers appropriate value in return. This allows us to engage the second problem I want to outline: what is going on with what is called "commoditization"? Perhaps we understand "commodity" and "commoditization" less well than we have presumed. Appadurai (1986) recognized how difficult this was and chose to expand the framework of commoditization to include many more circumstances of circulation—so that even *kula* exchange could be conceptualized in his terms as a kind of commodity in a tournament of value. The importance of this shift is that boundaries are not placed around different kinds of exchange, and it recognizes—as has been argued here—that different types of exchange may coexist within a social space.

What needs to be recognized and explored further is the market, not as a separated domain but as a structure of symbolic transformation. It does not necessarily erase all the distinctions embodied in objects: Hopi ceramics are still valued for their connection to a tribal past, to authentic producers, and the like. It is not always the case that the market's domination is complete: other systems of value may coexist, and their meaning may be reconstructed in relation to the presence of market practices. Just as "provisioning," as a practice—mere shopping, as it were—may come to be the totalizing practice constitutive of the higher (indeed, transcendent) ideals of North London British families (Miller, this volume), so we must imagine that commodities and commoditization practices are themselves embedded in more encompassing spheres or systems of value production. Such systems not only recognize the existence of distinct regimes of value but also combine and reorganize the activity from these various contexts into more complex mediations as what Annette Weiner might have articulated as "hierarchies-in-the making"—in a word, culture making.

Notes

I am grateful to Barbara Kirshenblatt-Gimblett for her comments during the seminar and for subsequent discussions, and to T. O. Beidelman, Faye Ginsburg, Webb Keane, Ken George, Don Brenneis, and Joan O'Donnell for their critical comments on various phases of the writing of this introduction. Jane Kepp deserves special thanks for her editorial suggestions. None of these people is responsible, of course, for the positions taken here. My discussion draws heavily on the contributions and wide-ranging comments of the participants in the seminar, and I hope I have not misrepresented them. Indeed, I have borrowed freely on language and analysis from the various discussions we had, and I understand this introduction to be a product of that collaboration.

1. "Regimes of value" is Appadurai's usage (1986). He draws on a well-known history involving the recognition of different categories of objects that should be exchanged within distinct and separate spheres of exchange (Bohannon 1955) and the notion that objects can be converted in value transactions between these spheres.

2. In exploring the agonistic quality of Greek exchange—its value in constructing personhood through risk and challenge—Beidelman (1989:236) wrote that "Greeks, like Nuer, observe that bloodwealth is necessary; but like Nuer they also recognize that compensation never actually makes up fully for losses such as death, suffering, and shame. Payment is all that is culturally available if one rejects violence and seeks deliberate agreement *(euboulia)*." Beidelman took a position on the problem of equivalence that he adopted explicitly from Simmel, recognizing the "sense of pathos characterizing problematic relationships between persons and the objects which they exchange" (1989:228) and the tension and struggle involved in social interaction.

3. To "redeem" is literally to take or buy back, but it is extended to notions of repurchasing, clearing, and restoring—of freeing from what distresses or harms, to change for the better, to free from the consequences of sin, to offset the bad effect of, and so on. An interesting discussion of one formulation of this redemptive quality in art emerged at the seminar after Kirshenblatt-Gimblett's summing up. This discussion is now represented in Coombes's essay (this vol-

ume), which points out how this cultural evaluation is brought into signifying practice rhetorically.

4. Clifford's "contexts" should be understood as the "commodity context" envisioned by Appadurai (1986).

5. It should be noted that what is described here might be considered a framework of objectification, through which a new subject ("humanist man") is constructed. See Miller (1987), as discussed below, but the point would be that the value-producing structure is generated in the process of objectification. Recently, Phillips and Steiner (1999) have criticized the enduring binary schema of "art" and "artifact"—a schema that, they argue, has masked the key third term that since the nineteenth century has become central: commodity.

6. "What rich collectors are really worried about," he points out, "is not getting richer but finding a way to translate money into something meaningful, e.g., social recognition" (Keane, personal communication, 22 June 1999).

7. Thomas's practical definitions are helpful: "Commodities are here understood as objects, persons, or elements of persons which are placed in a context in which they have exchange value and can be alienated. The alienation of a thing is its dissociation from producers, former users, or prior context. Prior context may refer to a commoditized person's kin associations; these terms are deliberately vague in order to allow scope for the nuances of particular movements" (Thomas 1991:39).

8. Critical work on art theory and philosophy—such as that by Danto (1964, 1986), Hadjinicolauo (1978), and Carrier (1987), among others—shows that the construction of an object or activity as "art," its differentiation from an ordinary object that might look the same, is a social process and not simply equivalent to the subjective recognition of its aesthetic value. The Marxist art historian Hadjinicolaou stated this point clearly in emphasizing that his study "is devoted to the theory and practice of the discipline of art history and not to aesthetics" (1978:6). "Art" in this sense has a history distinct from that of "aesthetics" and is not identical to it.

9. In the recent round of critiques to which I am referring, Kant's formulations of art and aesthetics have been most influential. Nietzsche has also been understood as extremely influential in the understanding of modern art—especially because of his engagement with the Platonic view of art/poetry and his endorsement of the body as the site of understanding (T. O. Beidelman, personal communication, 16 July 1999).

Part One

Dialectical Regimes

2

Money Is No Object

Materiality, Desire, and Modernity in an Indonesian Society

Webb Keane

The distinction between what should and what should not have a price—between the alienable and the inalienable—is crucial to the ordering of relations among what Appadurai (1986) has called regimes of value, and it is central to Weiner's (1992) postulate about the creation of political hierarchies. Although often discussed with reference to so-called traditional exchange, the power and value of inalienables and of their supposed antitheses, commodities and money, are hardly restricted to "traditional" or "precapitalist" social or economic arrangements. In the contemporary United States, for instance, amid the efflorescence of free-market ideologies, the problem of confining the scope of alienability is evident in everything from debates over patenting genes and the question of child labor to the nervousness that often attends the circulation of money within the household.

As Miller (this volume) cogently argues, inalienable value need not be restricted to elite or rare activities. What is at stake, rather, is the relationship between persons and things. Distinctions among kinds of objects and the ways they circulate matter, in part, because they have profound implications for the character of the humans who possess the objects and carry out transactions with them. After all, to be without a price is often taken, as it was by Kant (1956 [1785]), to define the human subject. Late in the twentieth century, most inhabitants of even the "freest" of market economies were still likely to feel that cash value stopped, or should stop, where the truly human began.[1] Market economies, then, do not do away with inalienables so much as they reorder the regimes of value in which they function (Carrier 1995; Miller 1994; Zelizer 1994). And contestations over these reorderings are not simply economic matters but are deeply concerned with the nature of persons as it is defined at the shifting boundaries between subjects and objects, boundaries whose particular configurations may define a historical epoch (Latour 1993).

In this chapter I address the unstable meanings of money and material objects at the margins of twentieth-century capitalism. In the process, I raise some general questions about the relations among materiality and abstraction, the values of persons and things, and the imagining of "modernity." For the last few generations, people in Sumba, an island of eastern Indonesia, have been involved in a classic confrontation between an elaborate, costly, and socially potent system of ceremonial exchange and the growing importance of money. We can no longer assume, as an earlier generation of anthropologists did, that people who practice ceremonial exchange will simply perceive money to be a threat to social values. It has become clear both that the advent of money may be welcomed even in so-called exchange societies and that it is not necessarily seen as inimical to the persistence of exchange (Akin and Robbins 1999). But certainly the growing availability of alternative regimes of value can give heightened visibility to certain cultural assumptions. Faced with money and its attendant discourses about modernity, freedom, and economic rationality, Sumbanese must try to account for the value things hold for people.

Their efforts to do so, I argue, often involve a certain dematerialization of the human world, a denial of the ways in which human subjects are enmeshed with material objects. But in an increasingly abstract world, where could value come from? One common site in which to locate the sources of value is the desires of the individual person. And it is money, issued by the state and linked to state discourses about modernity, that seems most to promote these desires. Thus, in dealing with money, people find themselves wrestling with a host of dilemmas raised by the tensions between the promises and threats of modernity.[2]

These tensions are especially prominent in local talk about "materialism." As their long-term interests, immediate concerns, and discursive circumstances variously incline them, Sumbanese may portray "the modern age" (I. *masa moderen*)[3] in terms of an increasing materialism in people's needs and economic activities—or in terms of disenchantment, as people lose their primitive and fetishistic overinvestment in things such as ancestral valuables or bridewealth. New forms of production and circulation may be celebrated as bringing with them rationality and enlightenment. Conversely, money and commodities may be portrayed as corrosive agents that attack kinship, amity, spirituality, sociality, and virtue on all fronts. The relationship between modernity and "the materialist" (I. *materialis*) is a topic of anxious concern across Indonesia, whose ruling regime from 1966 until its fall in 1998 combined an aggressive emphasis on economic development with social conservatism and political authoritarianism. By conventional measures, until the crisis of 1997 the regime fostered rapid economic progress, although this progress may have seemed distant and of questionable value for many who lived at the geographical and political margins of the nation.

On the island of Sumba, modernity, markets, and money appear in the context of a subsistence economy and a thriving system of ceremonial exchange.[4] Since Mauss's *The Gift* (1990 [1925]), scholars have tended to see money and ceremonial exchange as fundamentally opposed. The latter is distinguished from the former by the obligations between people that bind one moment of exchange to others, and by the spiritual links between people and the things that circulate between and, in marriage, along with them. Similar views on markets and exchange are found in local talk in many places like late-twentieth-century Sumba. Many Sumbanese tend to see money and markets as incipient challenges to the values supposedly embodied in exchange. Government officials and development experts worry, on the one hand, that ceremonial exchange is hindering economic development and, on the other, that the demise of exchange systems will have destructive consequences for social cohesion (Iskandar and Djoeroemana 1994).

Nor are such worries new; in 1952 a Dutch missionary forecast that once Sumbanese came to see their traditional valuables in economic terms, possessions would "become a dangerous and threatening power" (Onvlee 1973:26). But the distinction between inalienable and alienable may not be so clear-cut. On examination, both money and ceremonial exchange present certain difficulties to any effort to explain the value of objects solely by appeal to their conventional sign value, mode of production, or innate ties to persons.

MEANING AND THE MOTION OF THINGS

Consider the following episode from a marriage negotiation I attended in 1986 in the Sumbanese district of Anakalang. Early in the initial stages of negotiation, trouble arose because the principals on the bride's side were from a neighboring district and thus unfamiliar with local procedural nuances. The bride's side initiated the exchange in the conventional way by sending over a dish on which they had placed a cloth, in order formally "to ask the purpose" of their guests' visit. The groom's side replied in an equally conventional manner by sending the dish back with a 100-rupiah note (a trivial sum even on Sumba—the smallest sum available in paper form, worth less than the price of a pack of cigarettes). The proper reciprocal to cloth is a gold ornament or its substitute, money. In either case, the object in the offering dish is an obligatory token that serves as a "base" to make the spoken words formal and binding. But the mother of the bride loudly rejected the note, saying the use of money in a formal exchange was inappropriate. After some discussion, the bride's party asked that the Rp 100 note be replaced with Rp 500. At this, the spokesman from the groom's side sharply berated them, explaining that when money is placed in the dish, it must not be treated as money. It is a token, just like a gold ornament. With a certain amount of grumbling, the bride's side was persuaded to accept this, on the condition that it was a proper procedure and not an insult, and the negotiation proceeded.

This incident took place at the highly fraught border between money and exchange, but are the two positions really clear-cut? The bride's side seems at first to be defending moral boundaries in a way familiar from received descriptions of spheres of exchange. From this point of view, they recognize the threat that money and the marketplace pose to traditional moral values and the solidarity of precapitalist society. But when they retreat, they ask for an increase in the face value of the money, as if the insult had not been the intrusion of money after all, but rather the low price. In this, they reveal a possibility that always exists in exchange—that symbolic tokens might slip into alternative regimes of value. For, on the one hand, exchange valuables do not necessarily possess all the properties (inalienability, personality, morality) attributed to them by the model of the gift a priori (see Keane 1997). And on the other, the status of money itself is not entirely stable: in this case it serves as a formal token whose referent is confined to ceremonial exchange, yet it retains the potential for reinterpretation as cash value. In either case it is "symbolic," but its vulnerability to slippage is a function in part of its irreducible materiality. Even money shares with other objects the property of taking objectual form. Thus it can cross contexts and, being semiotically underdetermined, is subject to reinterpretation. To make sense of the materiality and semiotics of money, however, first requires a look at the meaning and value of other objects that circulate in Sumba.

In Sumba, objects come most prominently into their own in formal exchanges between individuals or groups of people. Formal exchanges are the binding transactions at the heart of virtually all events of any importance; in the 1980s and 1990s the most prominent were marriage alliances. I have discussed these exchanges in detail in Keane 1997. Here, in order to compare the semiotics and materiality of valuables and money, I want briefly to return to one incident recounted in that book.

Ubu Tara had a large stone tomb carved for himself. By convention, when the capstone was dragged from the quarry to his village, his wife's kin provided two valuable textiles that were carried on top of it as banners. When Ama Koda, an important affine, was leaving the concluding feast, one of Ubu Tara's sons gave him one of the "banners," which by now were neatly folded up, to placate him in the wake of earlier hurt feelings. On arriving home, Ama Koda opened it up and discovered that he had only half a textile. On inquiry, it turned out that during the tomb dragging, the banner had snagged on a tree branch, and someone had cut off the tangled half. Once folded in the village, this was no longer apparent. Furious, Ama Koda sent the cloth back to Ubu Tara with the message, "I'm not yet so poor that I need a bit of cloth to cover my loins!" Great efforts were required to heal the rupture.

This episode shows some of vicissitudes to which material signs are prone. Ama Koda correctly placed great semiotic weight on the physical condition of the cloth, but that physical condition was subject to happenstance. Note the rapid series of roles through which the piece of cloth moved: by turns, it was a conventional obligation between affines, a figurative banner, a physical encumbrance tangled in a tree, a token of regard meant to placate an irate guest, a vehicle of insult, a metaphoric rag of poverty, and finally a rejected gift. In practical terms, this sequence of roles illuminates three things about objects as social media: that they are readily separated from the transactors and the context of the transaction; that they are available for multiple interpretations; and that throughout, they remain material objects and thus vulnerable to all that can happen to things.

These roles illustrate how both the value and possible meanings of objects are underdetermined. They call for speech, interpretive practices, and political strategies. This means they are necessarily caught up in the uncertainties of social action. Being material, objects are always subject to the forces of what Grice (1957) called "natural meaning" (signs based on causality, as a tear means the cloth was snagged in a tree). But as tokens within social action, they are also always subject to transformation into bearers of "non-natural meaning" (intentional signs, as a torn cloth means an insult). And this means the latter is always intertwined with the former. The meanings of things cannot be sharply disengaged from the ways in which they are embedded in the physical world. Thus the very materiality of objects means they are not merely arbitrary signs. Their materiality makes a difference both in the sources of their meanings and in their destinations, such that they are subject to shifting physical, economic, and semiotic contexts. Finally, insofar as objects often *seem* to carry their values and meanings on their sleeves, as it were, they can play critical roles at the intersections among these shifting contexts.[5] Their power and value emerge at the intersection of their character as conventional signs and their potential roles in a possibly unlimited range of contexts.

AMBIGUOUS ATTACHMENTS

In practice, Sumbanese formal exchanges stress the representative functions of objects, play down utility, and rigorously exclude money except as a symbolic piece of metal. Nonetheless, formal exchanges are embedded within a larger political economy of both social signs and usable things, and they take some of their meaning from the way in which they articulate with other "regimes of value." Explicit talk about "the real tradition" is one of the ways in which the barriers between exchange and its alternatives are regulated. Sumbanese can point to the coexistence of exchange with markets, barter, usurious lending, and theft in order to insist on its distinctive moral value. For example, when Ubu Kura tried to impress upon me the superior morality of exchange, he said that the same pig that would get you five buffalo and five horses in marriage exchange would be worth the price of only one middling buffalo and a small horse if sold. In saying this, he was drawing on market values as a way to measure the heavy weight of the obligations imposed by proper exchange. (The claims of rational calculation cut both ways: the early Christian converts sought to discredit ancestral ritual for its wastefulness. As one proselytizer put it, the offerings "just use up chickens." Of course, by some understandings of sacrifice [e.g., Bataille 1988a], that would be precisely the point.)

As elsewhere (Akin and Robbins 1999; Thomas 1991), such comparisons are part of the background against which exchange has long been carried out. They simultaneously represent formal exchange as morally elevated by virtue of its supposed exemption from the calculation and rationality of other transactions and as a difficult burden. The point of explicit comparisons between formal exchange and alternative regimes of value is usually to affirm the status and compulsory nature of "real custom" as a discrete domain of social action. Sumbanese who make this case may draw on the discourse of contemporary Indonesian national culture in order to contrast "real" and "politicized" custom. In reference to exchange, "politicized custom" denotes competition, calculation, and profit and confines these to the disorderly present. These are familiar themes in talk about capitalist relations (Bloch and Parry 1989; Hugh-Jones 1990). But I argue that they also manifest pervasive concerns about the potential detachment of objects from persons and thus about the boundaries of the subject and the ability to locate value in persons or in things.

One aspect of the comparison of exchange and its alternatives is an implicit claim about rank. Sumbanese frequently assert that market thinking is purely a recent development and (depending on the case they want to make) usually a deplorable one—that in the past, no one calculated the value of what they gave you. This is a part of the logic in talk about custom, which explicitly portrays both donors and recipients as acting not out of their own desires or willfulness but only because they are obligated by ancestral requirements. But, people say, now we live in a selfish era whose slogan is "as long as I (get mine)" *(mali nyuwa)*, an era in which people are driven by personal desires.[6] As a way of expressing and historicizing the difference between formal exchange and its alternatives, people sometimes talk about the economic irrationality of the past. For example, one man told me that people used to trade like quantities for like, regardless of the actual substance: one sack of rice would go for one much more expensive sack of coffee. He was suggesting that the folly of his forebears consisted in being taken in by the very materiality of things. They were unable to perform the symbolic operations embodied in money: exchange value in those days was inseparable from the things themselves (see Keane 1996). Part of the subtext here is that the ancestors' apparent folly is inseparable from their aristocratic disdain for haggling and calculation. The hierarchical implications of alternative regimes of value become explicit when some people observe that Sumbanese who engage in trade are usually of low rank, because, they claim, such people are naturally more clever at calculation. This is supposedly because they are unconstrained by the sense of honor, having little to lose.

Calculation implies a play on the relations between the object as a sign of something other than itself and as a source of value in itself, which is most evident at the boundaries between formal exchange and other kinds of transactions. The boundaries among kinds of transactions are permeable—if not conceptually then practically, for there are few exchange valuables that do not have some value in other contexts. For example, a horse received from Christian affines in marriage exchange can be sacrificed to "pagan" spirits or sold for cash. This permeability is both a resource and a threat, insofar as a skillful or simply powerful player can take advantage of it, but the existence of alternative schemes of value bears the increasingly real potential to undermine the status claims that are sustained by exchange, a threat at once logical, political, and economic.

Despite the traditionalist tendency to claim for the past the high values of ceremonial exchange and to confine less exalted alternatives to the present, all sorts of transactions have been available to Sumbanese, even before the introduction of markets and shops (compare Barnes and Barnes 1989). The most formal kinds of exchange impose the greatest constraints on potential interpretations. They do so in part by drawing on the social authority of elders to limit the kinds of objects involved and the functions they may serve, and by emphasizing the properties by which they serve as representations (signs) and representatives (of agents).

Material objects contrast in several ways to the familiar Saussurean model of the arbitrary sign, which signifies only by virtue of a social convention, and whose phenomenal qualities (such as color or sound) are relevant only as marks of difference from other signs. Objects cannot be produced at will but must be sought from somewhere—they are subject to scarcity and are relatively easy to quantify. Moreover, even exchange valuables bear physical properties in excess of their purely conventional attributes, which contributes to their potential for diversion into use or to alternative kinds of transactions. Finally, they have durability. Nonconsumables persist over time, across multiple transactions, passing through the hands of many people and taking on a range of possible functions. The materiality of objects is a condition of possibility for their movement across social and semiotic domains. For example, the charisma of the Thai monk, once it has been objectified in the form of an amulet, is able to enter into the mundane realm of distinctly nonascetic purposes, such as good luck in the lottery (Tambiah 1984:336). The multiple uses, mobility, and durability of objects allows them to extend the agency of their producers and original transactors. But the same properties entail the possibility that they will become detached from their transactors altogether.

One effect of the high formality of exchange events in Sumba is to help separate signification and utility, emphasizing the semiotic character of objects that also bear use and market values. Such formality is part of the ongoing effort it takes to keep gift and commodity distinct. It is reinforced by the ritual speech, which states explicitly that neither party desires the objects in question, but rather, each is compelled only by ancestral mandate. Acknowledging the possibility of misconstrual, people often say that marriage is not like going to the market. They insist that they seek objects not for the value or utility of the things themselves, as in purchase and sale, but as expressions of each party's value for the other. Underlining this insistence is the great attention they pay to the proper forms of transaction.

The insistent attentiveness given to tokens in offerings implies a latent alternative. People are aware of the possibility that the gift will become detached from the giver and the intent. Objects require the reflexive capacity of language if they are to serve as fully efficacious media of social relations. One pig, horse, or piece of cloth is pretty much like another of its kind: it is words that specify what kind of action is being performed, from whom the prestations come, to whom they are directed, and what kind of act they perform. As a result, the capacity of objects to serve semiotically as representations and economically as representatives of persons is unstable and requires constant effort to sustain. Recall the quarrel between Ama Koda and Ubu Tara over the torn banner. The conventional meanings that material signs convey are vulnerable to the accidents to which objects are prone. The insult is made possible in part by the way in which material signs expose semantics to objective circumstances, and in part by the way in which people's manipulation of objects constantly works to transform natural qualities into signs of persons. If a cloth really represents its transactors, how could a torn cloth fail to do so as well? If objects are parts of larger projects, then could the giving of a torn cloth be only an isolated incident?

Mauss's great insight was to challenge the Cartesian obviousness of the distinction between possessing subject and possessed object. But the very workings of exchange depend on the fact that the identity between the two is not seamless: their relation has a double character. For objects to be able to exteriorize and represent their possessors in circulation, they also must in some way be detachable from them. Like Mauss, Simmel saw possessions as extensions of the self: when a person acquires property, "the sphere of the individual extends beyond its original limits, and extends into another self which, however, is still 'his'" (1990 [1907]:323). This capacity for "extension" exists only to the degree that the object is *not* fully identified with the subject. It follows from this double character of objects that the subject must engage actively with them, that possession is a form of action (Simmel 1990 [1907]:302–5).

The relentless work—and the formality, the politics, the talk, the attentiveness—demanded by Sumbanese exchange seems to be one way of responding to these circumstances. Exteriorization and objectification (see Miller 1987) work hand in hand with detachability and mobility. Therein lies both the promise and the risk posed by things, as vehicles of representation. Sent into circulation, they can extend the identity and agency of their transactors. By the same token, they may become lost to those whom they would serve, or be diverted into other regimes of value. The capacity of the prestation to stand for its owner over the course of its travels is not an inherent property of objects themselves but requires human efforts and interactions to sustain.

ENTER MONEY

Since Mauss, systems of exchange like those in Sumba have come to stand for everything that the economic character of "modernity" supposedly lacks. The contrast is not restricted to Western scholars; for people in Sumba, as in many other places, the concept of "modernity" and the experience of the state that attends it are inseparable from the ubiquity of money. Sumbanese often experience modernity, strive for its promises, and resist its threats by way of their dealings with money. Like many of those who have written about modernity, Sumbanese often treat money as something with its own dynamic, something that, once introduced into society, has a rapid corrosive effect. The classic expression of this perspective remains that given by Marx (1976 [1867]:229), for whom money was a radical leveler, extinguishing all distinctions, because it never revealed which commodities had been transformed into it: "Circulation becomes the great social retort into which everything is thrown, to come out again as the money crystal." In this context, Sumbanese practices and discourses surrounding formal exchange are not simply remnants from an archaic past but are developing into strenuous and self-conscious responses to the world of money and markets. This response is both discursive, a vision of an alternative regime of value, and practical, an effort to control the circulation of value's objectified forms (compare Akin and Robbins 1999; Comaroff and Comaroff 1990; Ferguson 1985; Hutchinson 1996).

Here I focus on three aspects of money: its relations to abstraction, alienation, and production. I look at money not primarily as a component of an established system of commodity circulation but rather as currency in its phenomenal and imagined forms, ways in which it appears even in the absence of a full-fledged monetary economy. I am interested, that is, in local experiences of and ideas about money. For whatever the larger political economic context, as Guyer (1995:6) points out, money "is a vastly important reality to vast numbers of people, all but an infinitesimal number of whom have absolutely no idea of the official doctrines under which it 'makes sense,' but whose own constructions...are a necessary component of that 'sense' as it works out in practice." People, that is, cannot *not* have ideas about why and how money is valuable. Both money's fluidity and its limits—including the extent to which people trust it—are functions of those ideas.

Sumba is a useful place from which to look at money, because, being a relatively recent arrival and still scarce, money is far less taken for granted there than in more thoroughly monetized places. Until the twentieth century, the few coins that made it to Sumba were either treated like other inalienable valuables or melted down as raw materials for ornaments.[7] It was not until the 1920s and 1930s, with Dutch encouragement, that regular markets appeared, but trade was still carried out largely by barter (Versluys 1941:463–64). In Anakalang, the first petty traders, none of them Sumbanese, seem to have set up more permanent kiosks in the 1930s (Riekerk 1934). Beginning in 1911, the colonial government imposed a head tax, to be paid in cash (Couvreur 1914). But by the end of Dutch rule, just before the Japanese occupation, one study found that money had made little impact on local society, being used largely as a unit of value for things of small worth (Versluys 1941:481).

Under the Indonesian state, monetization of Sumba lagged behind the rest of the nation, and large-scale government expenditure, the most important source of cash there, began only in the 1970s (Corner 1989:184; Iskandar and Djoeroemana 1994:67).[8] In the 1980s and 1990s, most Sumbanese still lacked a regular cash income.

Everyday subsistence and most ceremonial needs were largely met by local production, barter, and other forms of exchange. Cash was required primarily for taxes, school fees, church offerings, and purchase of items such as medicine, kerosene, cooking oil, salt, sugar, coffee, tobacco, shirts, sandals, dishware, and bus fares. Only in the most recent decade or so have the most ambitious and well-heeled families begun to send children off the island for higher education, in the hope that they will land positions in the civil service. Funds for this are usually raised piecemeal by pooling the resources of many kinfolk—usually along links built through past ceremonial exchanges. In the 1990s, off-island schooling constituted perhaps the single greatest incentive for Sumbanese to sell cattle.

Money thus plays a limited and highly marked role on Sumba. Although the Indonesian rupiah is trusted, or at least was until the crisis of 1997 (in contrast to money in highly inflationary economies or weak states), in Sumba it does not flow freely or pervasively. Money's purchasing power is highly constrained; labor, land, and cattle, for instance, are more easily and legitimately acquired through kinship, patronage, or exchange.[9] Many people obtain money only for specific purposes (Vel 1994:70) such as paying taxes or school fees, and thus money runs through very tight circuits, without entering into investment or credit (compare Guyer 1995:9). When one person comes into some money, others are likely to make their claims on it; this is why some civil servants try to get themselves posted to parts of the island far from their kin. For those few people who have bank accounts, the main reason is to hide their money from others. As a result, money in Sumba does not always fully possess the properties of fluidity, impersonality, or abstraction, and, like exchange valuables, it often retains some indexical links to its sources and owners.[10]

THE VALUE OF RENUNCIATION

Recall the use of money as a token in marriage exchange, in lieu of a gold ornament. This context suggests that gold and money have more in common than simply their properties. Both take their value in part from constraints on their materiality—the concrete particularity that for Marx defined the use-value of objects is played down in favor of semiotic abstraction. This is one reason money is so often compared to the quintessential arbitrary sign: "Like money, language manifests itself in material form, but in the former as in the latter the manifestation is external to the nature of the means and does not really matter" (Coulmas 1992:10). This negative property of money was described by Simmel as the result of a process of elimination or suppression: "It appears that even the most useful object must *renounce* its usefulness in order to function as money" (1990 [1907]:152). Only in this way can objects serve to symbolize simple quantities of value (yet the very uniformity that sustains money's abstractness has historically depended on the uniform, divisible, and durable properties of the materials out of which it is manufactured [Crump 1981:4]).

But this renunciation is incapable of fully abolishing its alternatives: even money, for example, to the extent that it retains a material form, may take on new functions. Coins may become jewelry or bullion—as Marx put it, "For a coin, the road from the mint is also the path to the melting pot" (1976 [1867]:222). Not only that, the very absence of one possibility is a critical component of the meaning of what remains: in Simmel's words, "the value that money has, and that allows it to perform its function, may be determined by those other possible uses which have to be foregone.... The perceived value of the developed function is constituted by...the exclusion of all other functions" (1990 [1907]:155).

So both gold and money, when placed in the dish, take their value from a similar basic structure of deferred value: everyone knows that the object in the dish is convertible to other forms. The Rp 100 could, of course, become money again. Gold and cloth, too, can be diverted from exchange. Indeed, their persistence as valuables can be seen as a continual refusal to allow them to return to their original state. As I argued earlier, it takes the work of ritualization to maintain the boundary between the semiotics of exchange valuables and the alternative meanings and uses that things might possess in coexisting regimes of value.

Anakalangese descriptions of their world before "modernity" stress the absence of abstraction and a fetishistic clinging to the materiality of things. Anakalangese accounts of the naiveté of their forebears, however, contain an important subtext. People in the past ignored differences of quality because of their nobility. They eschewed such calculations because they refused to give in to their desires. Whereas for

Marx the concrete particularities of things were important as the source of their use-values (1976 [1867]:230), the apparent empiricism that Sumbanese ascribe to exchange is a mark of people's relative *independence* from use-value. To follow ancestral rules is a demonstrative refusal to calculate utility, which can be understood only as a function of need or desire. Desire is something that separates one simultaneously from one's own best self (a loss of self-control) and from others (by attacking the moral bonds of community), and thus it threatens one's claims to high rank. By stressing the conventionalized semiotics of objects, formal exchange displays the players' imperviousness to the appeal of utility or their own wants.

The abstractness and fluidity that are supposed to characterize money, by contrast, appear to place desire in the foreground. Unlike inalienable valuables, money realizes its value neither in transaction as a social performance nor simply in being held, but only in that which it obtains in a future expenditure. To the extent that money is abstract and its uses unspecified—that is, as it is free both of particular qualities in itself and of the constraints of ancestral rules—any particular expenditure represents a choice among possible options. Therefore it seems to express, above all, the wishes of the person who spends it. And to legitimate those wishes is to challenge the principles by which people are valued and particular relations of domination sustained.

ALIENATION

The multiple uses, mobility, and durability of exchange goods allow them to extend the agency of their producers and original transactors. But the same properties entail the possibility that they will become detached from their transactors altogether. This brings me to the second property of money, its relation to alienation. In most accounts of modernity, money is preeminently the instrument of alienation. It circulates promiscuously, without respecting persons or things. Ethnographic literature often describes it as dissolving the moral obligations that bind individuals into communities. Against this view of the multiply alienated conditions of modern life, Mauss saw the model of the gift as an attractive alternative.

Yet even Sumbanese exchange is never too far from the possibility of loss and alienation, both in practice and in fantasy. In practice, the capacity of objects to circulate threatens to become total detachment, a possibility that formal procedures and elaborate ritual speech work constantly to prevent. On the other hand, divergence from exchange can be an appealing fantasy, for even those who hold the greatest stakes in the play of exchange may chafe against the constraints it imposes on them, complaining, for instance, of the relatives who show up asking for help the moment one comes into a windfall. The alternative, a source of wealth free from social obligation, remains attractive. This, along with the risk that wealth will become detached from its possessor, is elaborated in a rich discourse about *yora*, the spirits of the wild who can become demonic patronesses of selected individuals. *Yora* have several features in common with those presented by market, money, and government development projects. The *yora* is a source of antisocial wealth that cannot reproduce itself, lead to social ties, or be transmitted to a person's children. It is also associated with illicit unions between men and women, thus exemplifying unrestrained desire. *Yora* represent the conjunction of wealth from beyond society with the threat of loss. It makes sense that such wealth is ephemeral, since it often manifests individual willfulness. The *yora*, like the government development project, is distinguished by the inexplicable entry of money from no comprehensible or stable source. The fact that this wealth is ultimately sterile parallels its lack of grounding in social interaction. Those who are considered most likely to deal with *yora* are either young, unmarried, adventurous men or, more rarely, men so rich and powerful that they can hope to enter into such dealings with impunity.

The links between the idea of *yora* and the problems of modernity are especially evident in the following story, well known throughout Anakalang. The version I pass on here was told to me by Umbu Dewa Damaràka, a ritual specialist.

> Ubu Nyali Malar was given a chicken by a yora. That chicken laid an egg which crowed from the inside. Once hatched from the egg, that rooster crowed continuously. As it grew, it kept on crowing. This crowing carried all the way to Java. Java over there heard that rooster crow. Now a man came from Java to Sumba wanting to buy that rooster. He wanted to buy it with money, but

> Ubu Nyali didn't want to sell it. He said, "Better than that, give me that gold ring on your finger." The man from Java really wanted that rooster, so in the end he gave up the ring. Now he had the rooster, which he brought home to Java. So that's why now the president is in Java. That ring is in Sumba. It had child after child, until they put it in the granary. The granary filled up with gold. Then Ubu Nyali's slave, Mùda, ran off with the ring. The ring kept having children. He put it in a granary, it filled up the granary; put it in another, filled that too. Finally put it in a cave, but that too filled. It's all gold in that cave. So now that's why in Java, it becomes the president, and in Sumba, we're rich in gold. So it's like that rooster: we hear that president wherever we are in Indonesia, otherwise, why is the president always from Java?

The fate of Ubu Nyali's gold displays both the promise and the hazards of antisocial sources of wealth. Reproducing on its own, it contains the possibility of autonomy and riches beyond the demands and politics of social interaction. Nonetheless it remains detachable from persons and thus vulnerable to loss. Once lost, it becomes the property of foreigners. This certainly accords with Sumbanese experience both historically and in everyday life in the 1990s. Sumbanese are reluctant to introduce money into dealings with clan fellows and affines, which are structured by formal exchange and informal debts, dependencies, and mutual assistance. In practice, most money is directly received from and paid back to non-Sumbanese, either the state or ethnically "foreign" traders (Vel 1994:68–69).

Even after Ubu Nyali's gold becomes a stolen good, it is wealth that reproduces itself independent of human agency. This foreign gold is unlike normal gold valuables, which, either as inalienable ancestral possessions held by clans or as tokens that circulate in ceremonial exchanges, are intimately linked to the social identity of their transactors. In contrast, this gold carries on regardless of proper ownership. As value uprooted from ancestry, it is alienable. As value that requires no reciprocity, it is self-contained.

Finally, the loss of the rooster forms an image of the colonial relations between Sumba and both Dutch and Indonesian rule. The rooster is a conventional Sumbanese image of masculine bravado, aggressiveness, and fame. With the rooster, Sumba surrenders power and self-esteem for wealth. Moreover, by Sumbanese standards, the very act of barter by which it is given away entails a suggestion of loss. Although barter in some form or other has long existed in Sumba, it is usually considered to be unworthy of proud people, since, unlike formal exchange, which is supposed to be dictated by ancestral mandates, it is visibly driven by personal, even bodily, needs or desires. It establishes no further relations, in contrast to the multigenerational ties of debt and ritualized obligations that are fostered by exchange. The result of Ubu Nyali's barter makes clear that local claims to wealth and authority now operate against a background of something that has been lost: the political control represented by the president will always be elsewhere, though his voice can be heard everywhere. Gold, self-reproducing and circulating without limit, enters as political autonomy departs.

PRODUCTION

Yora represent not only antisocial wealth but also its uncanny sources. This brings me to the final feature of money, its peculiar relation to its own materiality as a product. Money seems to many Sumbanese to have sources not only distant in space but also at a remove from the labor and agency of humans. In 1912, a Dutch official recounted the following conversation:

> A puzzle which our host would gladly have solved was why the "taoe djawa" (= foreign men, Europeans) came to have much money. He was asked what he thought himself. He said that in the foreign land three trees must grow, one which bears as fruit gold pieces (English pounds of which men on Sumba see much), another of silver (rijksdollars), and the third copper coins (2 $^1/_2$ cent pieces). At a certain time, as soon as there is a need, the king or kings order a harvesting. Guilders and smaller silver money are nothing other than unripe rijksdollars, cents still undeveloped "gobangs" (2 $^1/_2$ cent pieces). (Witkamp 1912:486; parentheses in the original)

Juxtaposed to the widespread interest in *yora*, this familiar story suggests that when people think about money, they think of uncanny origins that require no more labor than the plucking of fruit from a tree, a form of production requiring the minimal intervention of human agency. (This recalls Marx's satirical remark that those who fetishize capital assume it is "a property of money to generate value and yield interest, much as it is an attribute of pear trees to bear pears" [1967 (1894):392].)

But Sumbanese gold valuables also have uncanny and distant origins. People insist that "it wasn't *we* who made them" but rather the ancestors. Part of the value of gold, as I have suggested, derives from the fact that it is not produced locally, that it ultimately comes from nowhere in Sumbanese experience. Put another way, its value lies not in local control over the means of production but perhaps in the promise of an escape from the demands of production altogether, and in its capacity to supplement physical labor. In this respect money is like ancestral valuables to the extent that it represents the state as an absent origin. In a place like Sumba, money is one of the most pervasive everyday forms the state takes in most people's everyday experience. Money is legal tender because it is stamped with an inscription bearing the state's political authorization. The authority represented by money portrays itself on money's material substance: every coin or banknote carries some emblem of the state. It wears, in Marx's image, a "national uniform" (1976 [1867]:222; see Foster 1998; Hart 1986; Shell 1982). As a medium of alienation and an uncanny source of value beyond bodily labor, money is not always radically different from exchange valuables. Moreover, money is not necessarily even antisocial: like exchange, the use of money still requires trust (something made explicit, if sociopolitically obscure, by the slogan "In God We Trust" on American currency). It is just that the object of that trust has shifted from exchange partners and the ancestors to the state. To that extent, money does not so much abolish society as it institutes a different kind of society. So wherein is the distinctive difference that makes for modernity?

THE STATE OF DESIRE

In contrasting the casualness of market transactions with the formality of exchange, Sumbanese express historical imagination in terminology that reflects contemporary national culture, but they also manifest more specific concerns about the potential detachment of objects from persons, concerns that are implicated in exchange itself. If the risk of loss has *always* haunted the ceremonies of exchange, then this risk has become inseparable from the dominant regime of value. In the modern world, the authority of ancestral mandates meets an alternative authority in the pervasive presence of money.

Money, of course, is issued and backed up by the state, but, as I have noted, Sumbanese often associate its appearance in their lives with the state in other ways as well. As in many subsistence economies, the need for money was initially produced by the state's demands for taxes. Today most money in Sumba ultimately derives from the state, either in salaries or from businesses whose income is due largely to government projects. More generally, the state has established itself as the chief promoter of capitalism and endeavored to do away with what it sees as the more irrational forms of local expenditure. Economic rationality has been the constant topic of government exhortations and directives. Finally, most states that issue money try to extirpate any competition with or restraints on the free movement of its currency—something that tends to meet resistance even in highly developed capitalist economies (Zelizer 1994).

What the state hopes money will come to mean may not fully determine how people understand it locally. Sumbanese understand money's threats and promises in terms of the virtues and frustrations of exchange. The ways Sumbanese handle and speak about money seem to be responses to a dilemma posed by the state project of development. This dilemma is that, to the extent that money's origin lies in the state, it seems to be the state that guarantees the play of individual desires. Sumbanese describe the present era with the Indonesian expression "free era" (I. *masa merdeka*). In national discourse, the "free era" usually refers to liberation from colonial rule. But Sumbanese often use the expression in speaking of the abolition of slavery and the resulting challenge to rank distinctions and the exchange system that helps support them. Depending on the speaker's social position, or the extent to which he or she is at home in the world of rank and exchange, this is not an unambiguous good. The "free era" means that Sumbanese live in a time dominated by "economic thinking," a time of rampant individualism. The ostentatious suppression of use-value and economic profit that is displayed in the forms of ceremonial exchange is supposed to manifest the participants' nobility and public display of honor. Like other familiar critics of money, many Sumbanese describe the present day as a time of antisocial stinginess, a ruthless calculating of costs and benefits unconcerned with honor or rank. The two aspects are combined in the assertion that now people get ahead by virtue of "brains"—by which people ambiguously refer to both the economic rationality that development should produce and the cleverness associated with devious former slaves, people who, it would seem, have no honor to lose or ancestry to sully.

Of course not everyone has the same stakes in the regimes of value and the social hierarchies that money seems to threaten. Former slaves and unmarried women, for instance, may benefit from the promise of freedom both from rank and from material dependence as reproduced in exchange. But even those who celebrate modernity and economic rationality must have some account of the respective values of exchange and money. This is where Christian discourses of interiority and materialism often come into play, discourses that help give expression to shifting distinctions between subject and object (Keane 1996, 1998). Talk about "materialism" seems to incite people to a certain dematerialization in their understandings of the world. This is evident, for instance, in the effort to treat material goods as merely symbolic. For example, Sumbanese Christians must often face the question, what is the value that is transacted in marriage exchange? Few are willing to reject exchange out of hand, yet they also cannot accept the world of ancestor spirits and rituals at its foundations. Nor are they entirely comfortable with the apparent identification of persons with things that marriage transactions seem to produce. One solution, which I often heard, is to explain marriage exchange in functionalist terms, as fostering social solidarity. Another explanation is provided in this newspaper essay by a Catholic high-school student (Witin 1997).[11]

> Bridewealth in the form of traditional valuables like ivory, gold, buffalo, is at base only a symbol *(simbol)* in order to raise a woman's value and dignity. Demands for bridewealth show that a woman must be honored, valued....Bridewealth is only a symbol of the woman's self-respect....It is proper that bridewealth

> be retained, on the basis of its essence as a symbol of woman's own value and dignity—and not tend toward business *(bisnis)* or "trade" in daughters. On the part of women themselves, the most important problem is as far as possible that she be able to guard her self-respect so that the demand for bridewealth which is to be discussed by her family doesn't put her to shame. One should value oneself by way of one's patterns of thinking, attitude, and praiseworthy behavior, before one is valued by others, especially the groom, by way of the bridewealth that will be discussed.

The author makes explicit something that is implicit in the social functionalist explanation as well—and that underlies many Western views, such as Polanyi's (1944:46), that assume a clear opposition between material and social values. Both accounts dematerialize exchange and treat material objects as merely signs of some immaterial value, whether that be social solidarity or self-worth. (The self-conscious modernity of this is evident in Witin's unusual appropriation of the English words "symbol" and "business.") This dematerialization underwrites the world of money, in which the subject is supposed to be clearly separated from its objects and in which value can be fully abstracted from concrete practices and material forms. Yet in seeking to account for the value those objects hold for the subject, one is left with little but the willful and desiring subject itself.

Put in other words, the writer is describing how the modern subject must be the source of its own value. And there the subject encounters the promise and the threat of money, in the freedom that money seems to accord this subject. Money clearly proclaims a difficulty that other valuables also encounter, albeit more unobtrusively. It is hard to confine material objects to conventionalized symbolism and to constrain their motion to prescribed pathways. As the emblem of this social and semiotic fluidity, money bears a further implication. To the extent that it is abstract, it permits a potentially unconstrained range of choices among purchasable items. In coming to stand for those choices, for Sumbanese, it seems to point toward the desires that any given choice expresses.

But who stands behind money and its promises? Here the subject encounters the state, which, by authorizing money, seems to sponsor that willfulness. Yet certainly neither the state nor (for different reasons) most Sumbanese are willing to accept the consequences. The state's efforts to control willfulness and desire (as stimulated, for example, by elections or advertising) lie beyond the scope of this chapter. Sumbanese efforts are visible in the continued power of exchange in the 1990s. Recall again the use of money as an exchange valuable in the offering dish. To use money as a material token, emphasizing the underdetermined character of its materiality, is to deny the authorizing stamp on its face. To treat money as if it were gold is to deny the ultimate power of the issuing authority in favor of the semiotic value asserted by ancestral mandate. The use of the coin does not replace material use-values with symbolic values but rather asserts the primacy of one authorizing origin for signs over another. It asserts the superior power of exchange to suspend use-values in favor of claims to higher value. In the process, it seeks to deny the abstractness of money. Yet it does not necessarily do so by reasserting the materiality of meaningful objects. Rather, those objects are turned into signs of invisible values such as "social solidarity," "tradition," or "self-worth."

The tension between the two uses of money represents a tension between two sites of agency. In exchange, persons manipulate tokens of value in deference to the displaced agents of ancestral mandate. In commodity circulation, the state seems, unwittingly, to authorize the cleverness of desiring selves and the endless possibilities that money affords them. The individual who can buy and sell with impunity bears the warrant of the state, which itself remains invisible except in its effects, in the form of "use"-less, circulating signs of itself. This rather implausible vision is, in turn, an effect of that aspect of the ideology of money that celebrates abstraction, denies social mediation, and imagines that signification offers the subject an escape from materiality.

Notes

I am grateful to Fred Myers and Annette Weiner for their invitation to join the seminar at the School of American Research. My thanks to all the other seminar participants, especially Ivan Karp, Daniel Miller, and Fred Myers, for their comments. This chapter draws on fieldwork and archival research supported by Fulbright-Hays, the Social Science Research Council, the Wenner-Gren

Foundation, and the Association for Asian Studies and sponsored by the Lembaga Ilmu Pengetahuan Indonesia and Universitas Nusa Cendana. It was substantially revised during a year spent at the Institute for Advanced Study in Princeton, New Jersey.

1. At the boundaries of the properly salable in the United States we find things such as prostitution, fees charged for adopted children, the sale of body parts, and bribery. These are notable precisely for the discomfort, anxiety, or outrage they provoke. See Pietz 1997 for an insightful discussion of this problem as it was faced by the writers of liability laws for human deaths caused by machines in the early industrial age.

2. Albert O. Hirschman (1977) argued that the emergence of capitalism in the West was legitimated in part by the development of a conceptual distinction between the passions and the interests. The former were seen as destructive and irrational, the latter as subject to rational calculation. But like people in many other places in which other values are being challenged by the market, most Sumbanese find calculation and rationality themselves to be antithetical to social virtue.

3. Terms in the national language, Indonesian, are identified with an "I"; all other terms are in Anakalangese or cognate languages of Sumba.

4. Sumba, an island about the size of Jamaica, is dry, is sparsely populated, lies off the main trade routes across the archipelago, and itself offered little but sandalwood and slaves to attract traders. The Dutch took fairly light-handed control of the island in the first decades of the twentieth century. The postwar Indonesian state was too impoverished and distracted to attend to Sumba until the oil boom of the 1970s. What export and local trade now exists (in buffalo, horses, and local cloth) is controlled by ethnic Chinese, Arabs, and other off-islanders. Commerce in land is very recent and still highly constricted by the persistence of collective ownership and the general view that certain kinds of land should not be alienated. In the 1990s, most Sumbanese still depended on subsistence farming. Although there is considerable variation in systems of exchange and rank across the island, for purposes of this chapter, these can be overlooked, and I will speak of "Sumba" rather than "Anakalang" (Keane 1997), Kodi (Hoskins 1993), Weyewa (Kuipers 1990), and so forth.

5. I do not discuss the iconographic and other metaphoric features of exchange valuables here. Having done so in detail elsewhere (Keane 1997), I argue that these are insufficient in most cases to make sense of either the practices surrounding objects or the values imputed to them.

6. The association of modernity with desire and desire with money is made quite explicit in many parts of Indonesia. By the 1920s, the Minangkabau of Sumatra already contrasted the cooperative character they ascribed to traditional villages with the "desirousness" (I. *hawa nafsu*) that money induces in those who "eat wages" (I. *makan gaji*) (Kahn 1993:126). In Java, where conventionally it is women who handle money, people see both money and marketplace as stimulants to both sexual and material desire (Brenner 1995; Siegel 1986; for a Western analogy, see Hirschman 1977:9).

7. Even in parts of Indonesia where money and market production appeared much earlier than in Sumba, coins were often treated as valuables. In nineteenth-century highland Sumatra, for instance, pepper growers demanded payment only in Spanish "Carolus" dollars, whose high silver content was preferred for melting down into jewelry. Only coins with the full bust portrait of the king were acceptable for marriage payments, apparently for iconographic reasons (Steedly 1993:90–91).

8. In the 1990s, the most important sources of money for Sumbanese were government salaries paid to minor officials and schoolteachers. Some young unmarried men and women earned wages by working for non-Sumbanese merchants, but these were not sufficient to support a family. Other people engaged in petty trade in weekly markets, and a very small number sold everyday goods from tiny kiosks. Reports from across Sumba gave the percentage of the population with access to cash at between 2 and 10 percent (Hoskins 1993:188; Vel 1994:47). Given Sumbanese resistance to outmigration (Iskandar and Djoeroemana 1994:57), remittance income was apparently negligiable.

9. The anxieties raised by selling animals for money can be seen in the ritual precautions they provoke. If one sells a buffalo or pig that one has raised oneself, one should first pluck the eyebrows and place them under the household water pot so one retains a "cool corral." Otherwise the money will disappear or the remaining animals will not thrive.

10. When Sumbanese, at least in some districts, obtain a sum of money, it is not likely to enter into an existing stock of capital. Therefore, the sum obtained in a particular transaction tends to retain its identity. It is also likely to be earmarked for a specific expenditure. This has allowed Vel (1994:70–71) to rank spheres of money expenditure in parallel with spheres of exchange: one would sell a buffalo, for instance, only in order to raise money for something as important as university fees, but not for children's clothing. As Zelizer (1994) showed, earmarking is an extremely widespread means of constraining the

abstraction and fluidity of money even in full-fledged market economies.

11. The author happens to be from the neighboring island of Flores, but the ideas she expresses are being propagated in churches and Christian schools across Sumba as well.

3

Alienable Gifts and Inalienable Commodities

Daniel Miller

My central contention in this chapter is that in generalizing from an ethnography of shopping in North London, one can discern a basic dichotomy between two spheres of exchange involving gifts and commodities, respectively. The first of these spheres is based on an explicit classification and representation of social relationships in terms of money.[1] It allows people to develop highly rationalist and instrumental perspectives based on explicit calculation, perspectives that are employed in the process of selection. This sphere is gift exchange. It exists in opposition to the second form of exchange, which is based on the use of commodities that are not translated into gifts. In this sphere, which I call "provisioning," the primary agenda appears to call for either the creation or the acknowledgment of a transcendent goal in life that might well be termed the spirit of the inalienable. There are many elements within commodity exchange that seem to negate the elements of calculation, individualism, monetarization, and explicit rationalism that are most characteristic of the gift.

This conclusion is intended at one level to amuse, in that it systematically reverses what have come to be conventional ways of talking about the gift-commodity dualism. But beyond the initial moment of fun is a more serious aim, that of going beyond what has sometimes been a stultifying classification. My second concern in this chapter, then, is to address one paradoxical (and therefore perhaps also amusing) implication of this initial argument, which is that in North London, the equivalent of what Weiner (1992) has termed inalienable possessions is the commodity.

I imagine it would be generally agreed that one of the highlights of anthropological discussion in the last two decades has been what might be called Maussian revisionism—that is, work inspired by Mauss's book *The Gift* (1990 [1925]), but almost always developed as a creative critique of Mauss. Not all of this has come from within anthropology; there is an equally important component within French philosophy. One of the most influential uses of Mauss's work came in Bataille's attempt (1988b) to create a political economy of consumption, and more recently, Derrida (1992) offered an influential reading of *The Gift.* Within social anthropology, contributions have ranged from the more formal exposition of gift-commodity dualism by Gregory (1982; in 1997 he described the relationship between gift and commodity as "coeval") to continued exhortations toward the creative application of Mauss (e.g., Carrier 1995) and a sustained debate within Melanesian anthropology by Strathern (1988), Thomas (1991), Weiner (1992), Godelier (1999), and many others. Schrift (1997) provided a valuable guide to the extension of this debate beyond anthropology.

The most conspicuous trajectory through Maussian revisionism has been the critique of the basic duality of gift and commodity, in which highlights have included criticisms by Lévi-Strauss (1987), Sahlins (1972: ch. 4), and, perhaps most significantly, Bourdieu (1984:3–8). These were followed by a highly influential critique from Appadurai (1986), since which the dualistic element has certainly been in retreat. The direct inspiration for this chapter, however, came from my reading of Gell's (1992) argument that the gift was a secondary development of commodity-like barter in traditional Melanesia. Given the weight of academic investment in the opposite conceptualization of gifts and commodities, this seemed both an elegant closure to the debate and extremely funny. On reflection, however, there seemed to be room for at least one more contribution that could follow Gell's paper. It would undertake the same inversion of the conventional terms, but with respect to a context more akin to the France with which Mauss was ultimately concerned than to the Pacific. This is the ambition behind the present essay.

In starting to switch the terms "gift" and "commodity," I am clearly aided by the emphasis that followed Bourdieu (1977) on the roles of strategy and sometimes calculation in Pacific exchange. My clearest precedent is the contribution of Appadurai (1986), which has often been bracketed with that of Kopytoff (1986) in that their work attempted to create, for the Western commodity, a more flexible sense of the relationship between alienability and the inalienable. Since my intentions are directed toward this debate rather than toward the explication of ethnography per se, I do not try to describe in this chapter the considerable variation and complexity of exchange and consumption practices that I observed during fieldwork. The evidence about to be presented is structured by a highly normative dichotomy that demonstrates the consequences of applying the terms of this long-standing anthropological discourse to this particular ethnographic circumstance. I do not, therefore, follow Thomas (1992), who demonstrated the constraints of dualistic paradigms when applied to exchange in the Pacific and revealed a much wider range of exchange forms there.

The tradition I want to criticize is that which has tended to assume that when making comparisons between the Occident and the Pacific, the duality of gift and commodity can be retained as a basic opposition in which the term "gift" evokes a sense of the inalienable while "commodity" is taken as the essence of the alienable. The Pacific literature reinforces this opposition by continually returning to the idea of the "spirit of the gift" as something that in some sense prevents the development of commoditization. The result is evident in most of the work on gift giving in the United States by anthropologists and sociologists such as Caplow (1984) and Cheal (1988). For them, the gift is primarily an element within the domestic arena, where it assists the domestic in becoming a reservoir of affective relations within a market economy. The gift is understood as a small still remnant of socially embedded exchange within the swirling tide of alienable commodities that surround us. I, too, have worked within this tradition, as in my discussion of Christmas as the festival of the gift that in some ways tames the relentless shift to commoditization (Miller 1993).

WEINER: IT'S LOVE THAT STOPS THE WORLD GOING ROUND

Weiner's (1992) account of inalienable objects is an important stepping stone within my argument, because she clearly opposed what had become an extension of Mauss's work into a more general emphasis on reciprocity.[2] This had come about through the writings of Lévi-Strauss and others who threatened to turn reciprocity into some kind of general principle constitutive of society. In effect, her work was pitched against attempts to reduce all exchange to basic principles of equivalence.

Instead, Weiner emphasized the significance of a range of objects that are not usually entered into the practice of reciprocal exchange. Such objects are often the most powerful symbols of the group concerned and of its constancy and stability. It is the potential of these objects for negating exchange that turns them into sites for the objectification of transcendence. Weiner did not abstract the emotional context as an affective dimension, but there are many instances in the accounts she gives from various ethnographies where affectivity in the form of passion is at least implied, whether in Maori fighting over *taonga* or Pintupi devotion to original *tjurunga* (Weiner 1992:61, 108). What emerges clearly is that it is exchange, not love, that "makes the world go round." Love (or, to keep the terms in their appropriate context, obligatory devotion), by contrast, tends to act as the very negation of this sense of movement by confirming a stable and constant center to society's affective identity.

Weiner's other focus was on the role of women in many societies as the key devotees who maintain the power of the inalienable by standing for what cannot be reduced to exchange. Her emphasis was on images of the female that refuse sexuality as an object of exchange or reciprocity. A core example is woman as sibling rather than woman as wife, which raises the problematic status of love as passionate devotion when applied within the sibling relation (Weiner 1992:76–77). The implication is that the love for which women are responsible—both as devotees and as objects of devotion—is at the core of the devotional concern that constitutes the inalienable possession. My argument depends on the idea that in North London there is an equivalent ideal of women as associated with the practice of devotion and especially with love. Women, therefore, seek to retain objects of devotion that become symbols of all that transcends mere equivalence or reciprocity. To a degree, then, disregard for women's love or for the female as the objectification of the potentiality of love is disregard for her core relationship to the production and reproduction of that which is regarded as inalienable. I follow Strathern (1988) in understanding this ideology, which associates women with love, as the larger discourse that creates gender as difference, rather than understanding it merely as the elucidation of what a pregiven category we term "women" happens to do.

For my argument to work, however, there is a clear paradox. The central point of Weiner's book is that all this is achieved through the mediation of a genre of material culture termed "inalienable possessions." In my argument, another genre of material culture, the commodity—that most alienable of objects—plays the equivalent role. By implication, this poses a problem in terms of what women come to represent in the transition to a capitalist society (for which see Johnson 1998). Weiner helps me along by problematizing the more common assumption that we should be looking to the gift as our key emblem of the inalienable, because she treats the gift as the instrument of equivalence as much as the spirit of the inalienable. But this is still a long way from substituting the commodity within the same slot.

In North London it would be hard to evoke a deep mystical sense of the gift equivalent to the *hau* analyzed by Mauss, or even to privilege some ontological site for the inalienable in the philosophical tradition of Locke and Marx. From the ethnographic perspective, the inalienable can be said to exist only inasmuch as a given cultural tradition constructs relationships of material culture in that way. As I have argued elsewhere (Miller 1987), inalienability comes mainly through the consumption of commodities and the power of consumption to extract items from the market and make them social or personal. This is because it is the person who lies at the core of any local conceptualization of the inalienable. The vanguard of discussion has become a concern with topics such as the new reproductive technologies or organ transplants, where the core principles of the inalienable as a property of personhood come under threat (e.g., Edwards et al. 1993; Strathern 1996). In North London, then, inalienability is a rather fragile property of objects that comes to them from their attachment to groups or persons.

THE ETHNOGRAPHY OF GIFT GIVING

The ethnography from which the following material is taken was conducted during one year (1994–95) and consisted of a study of shopping on and around a street in North London. In part I was accompanied by Alison Clarke, who studied non-shopping elements of provisioning and is presently writing up further fieldwork on the same street.[3] The study comprised greater or lesser exposure to 76 households, of which 52 are in what I call Jay Road. Jay Road consists of council (state) housing on one side and a variety of housing types, ranging from small purpose-built maisonettes to large family houses, on the other.[4] In order to include a larger selection of middle-class households in our fieldwork, we expanded to households on streets that were almost all adjacent to Jay Road. For the sake of simplicity, I have amalgamated these in this account and refer solely to "the street."[5]

Rose is a working-class retired woman living in the council estate on Jay Road. She has been invited to the wedding of a friend who comes from a wealthier, middle-class milieu. Rose has a strong sense of what is appropriate in gift buying, an activity to which she devotes a considerable amount of her time. In this case she is more than usually anxious about what would be appropriate. She has therefore consulted some friends about what they feel is currently the "going rate" for gifts at the wedding of a friend, and they come to a firm conclusion that the answer is £20.

Following a common practice, the couple have established a wedding list. Rose does not much approve of this restraint on her selection, but real consternation follows when she inspects the prices of items on the list. Clearly, unlike the younger, middle-class couple, she is embarrassed at the idea of giving a single bedsheet as a present and astonished at the cost of the listed set of bone china, which would reduce her to giving a single cup and saucer. In the event, she selects a beach towel—one of only two individual items she can afford. It costs £15. She therefore decides to add an additional voucher from this same shop for £5 to make up the £20 total she believes appropriate for this gift. The resulting dual gift may perplex the recipients, but it conforms to Rose's own firm belief that she must end up with a gift of the precise monetary value appropriate to the occasion.

In this case, the purchase is complicated by the crossing over of class cultures, which is perhaps the most common cause of confusion in British exchange relations. But otherwise it echoes a characteristic element in gift purchasing. The buyer of the gift expects first to establish the precise monetary value appropriate to the relationship being expressed in the gift and its occasion. Where there is doubt, phone calls to friends and relatives allow some discussion about the current going rate. This enables a clear categorization of relationships. The going rate may be for a sibling at Christmas or a child's best friend's birthday. Even for the closest relationships, few people showed any difficulty with the idea of a going rate that was expressed as a sum of money.

One of the most prevalent forms of gift shopping on the street arose from the requirement that children take gifts to birthday parties. For several years during primary school, it is common to invite all or most of a child's class to a party. This results in a child's attending 20 or more parties a year. There was considerable discussion about the going rate for an appropriate gift. Largely this rate was seen as relative to a particular school; for example, one school was criticized as a place where parents spent too much on such gifts. Within this idea of a going rate, there was room for marking stronger relationships of friendship, either between the children or between the parents concerned, by buying gifts of a higher value or buying an especially appropriate gift. I also saw parents buy gifts of a lower value in order actively to discourage a relationship between their child and another. The idea of a going rate also enabled parents to make explicit certain strategies such as competitive giving. A device for spending less money than the going rate was to buy gifts abroad, so that people would not know how much the items cost, or at sales.

The alienability of money became itself an important element in gift giving. For example, one mother with somewhat older secondary school children had been arguing with them about the presents to be given to their friends for their birthdays. She had already discussed the issue with the mother of one child, who had indicated her desire for some sports equipment. Her son, however, intervened and insisted that she should give money as a present. It appeared that the two children had agreed to pressure their respective parents to give money rather than a gift, thus allowing the children to control the purchasing of their respective presents. The parents had wanted to avoid this partly because there was a disparity in income between the two households, and present buying could give the appearance of equivalence where it was not the case. Giving money meant that there had to be exact symmetry between the two.

Money had come to play an increasing role as the substance of gift giving for people on the street. In part this was a measure of the desire for autonomy by the recipients of gifts, as was clear in the case just described. Equally important was the feeling that since a "going rate" was becoming ever more explicit as the criterion by which presents were decided, one might just as well make this clear in the present itself. This logic could be true not only of relatively distant relationships, such as those manifested at weddings, bar mitzvahs, and similar life-cycle events, but also of gift giving between parents and children. There were still areas, however, where giving money was considered inappropriate; it was rare, for example, between partners. Furthermore, the ambiguity between money and gift was exploited by the ever-expanding range of gift vouchers and gift tokens that were available for providing money with the gloss of more traditional gift giving.

In several cases where the buying of Christmas presents for children was discussed, it was clear that a compromise was being established both in the problematic issue of allowing some autonomy to the children and in agreeing on the appropriate sum to be spent. This compromise was made through the use of a shop catalog called *Argos* (for details, see Clarke 1998). Most families possessed a copy of this catalog, which offered a wide range of standard toys and other items of interest to children. The *Argos* catalog emerged as the key means by which selection of items could be discussed at home, thus enabling people to avoid the experience of actually shopping with children, something disliked by most parents and most children as well. In the case of Christmas and birthday gifts, it also allowed a negotiation to develop in which parents indicated the appropriate price parameters and children indicated their preferences for a range of goods from which the parents could then select the actual "surprise" gifts for their children.

It appears, then, from observation of a wide range of gift giving, that it has emerged as one of the few arenas in which a relatively precise assessment of a social relationship, between either kin or non-kin, is made and translated into a price. As at least one stage in gift buying, the notion of the "appropriate" is assessed as an abstract idea of equivalence, which helps classify the relationship in strict monetary terms. What happens once this decision is reached depends upon the nature of the relationship. When the recipient is either little known or relatively distant, it is the abstract amount to be spent that remains dominant—that is, many items will serve as long as they cost the correct amount. When a close relationship or one with much affection is involved, a secondary stage takes over in which the concern becomes choosing an item that reflects the degree of fondness the giver has for the recipient.

In this secondary stage, the giver assesses how a whole range of aspects of the relationship might be expressed in this particular present. Many strategies are made possible by deviating from the going rate or by translating the sum of money into a certain gift, as well as by the way it is wrapped up and presented. The desire to fix the appropriate sum in no way lessens the giver's subsequent anxiety about how the gift itself will be read as an explicit statement about the relationship between giver and receiver.

Let me give an example of this sort of tension. Fiona went on a shopping expedition to Brent Cross Shopping Mall on 15 December. A middle-class woman with an academic background and a comfortable income, she normally would have been relatively relaxed about the selection of goods. This shopping trip, however, stood in marked contrast to other occasions when I accompanied her, in that this was the only time she came armed with a written list not only of what she wanted to buy each person but of where she should buy it and how much it should cost. She had decided on an overall cost for the typical Christmas gift (£15) and was concerned that individual unplanned decisions would lead her to more expensive alternatives.

The reason she had spent so much time and consideration on each purchase, even before she started shopping, was not, however, just to keep gifts to a desired cost. It was also because of her feeling that each gift was a clear indicator of a number of elements in her relationship with its recipient. The amount spent was one of several factors that made a gift more or less appropriate. A revealing conversation concerned the gift she would buy for her child minder. (A child minder is a woman, usually working class, with her own family, who looks after the child of another, often middle-class family for part of the week—for example, after school hours or when the latter parent works part-time.) Fiona noted that the previous Christmas she had deliberately bought the child of her child minder a rather more physical and playful toy than she would have bought for her own children, for whom she tended to buy gifts of clear educational value. Her assumption, following the lines of Bourdieu's (1984) argument in *Distinction* (which she might well have read), was that the appropriate gift for a working-class woman was a toy that had a high quotient of fun as against education. This had been a failure, since the child minder had clearly been disappointed in the present, and Fiona interpreted this as meaning that although the child minder did indeed tend to buy fun toys for her children, she had expected that Fiona would help balance this with an educational toy reflecting the background of the giver rather than the receiver. This Christmas, therefore, Fiona intended to buy a toy more akin to those she would buy her own children. This reasoning about the relationship was clear, explicit, and easily communicable to me.

Similarly, in a discussion I had with Fiona about books she was purchasing for some of her relatives, it again became clear how the gift was an assessment of neither the giver nor the receiver but of the relationship between them. This assessment might include an affective element when the relationship was based on love or deep friendship, which should be made evident in "the thought that has gone into" the selection—though even here this element came second to a decision about the appropriate amount to spend. On the same trip Fiona was also buying a gift for the next meeting of her National Childbirth Trust group of mothers and children. In that case her emphasis in discussion with me was on how important it was not to buy anything too expensive, since the gift needed to be on a par with the kinds of presents bought by the other mothers, some of whom were less well off than she.

In many ways the logics of gift giving are among the most overt and explicit of all those involved in purchasing. It is far easier to discuss gift purchasing than ordinary provisioning. It is a common topic of discussion, in which people feel relatively free and clear about the rationalization and processes of consideration that lead to a particular purchase. None of this is in any way incompatible with the points made by Mauss with respect to either reciprocity or the position of reciprocity in constituting the relationship. Nor is it incompatible with descriptions of gift giving in the Pacific in which the elements of calculation and strategy are stressed, as by Bourdieu. But in the North London case it is clear that calculation, strategy, and abstraction do not represent some secondary "weakening" of the socially constituted element of this building of relationships but together are the primary mode by which it is achieved. It is also clear that gift giving in the West is not a form of totalization as in the Maussian sense of prestation. On the contrary, it is a limited and "framed" dyadic exchange that classifies the relationship in that most alienable of media—money—in some cases prior to expressing the individuality of the relationship in the precise form of the object given.[6] Ironically, considering the tensions evident in the spread of money and the perceived threat to pregiven formal exchange systems (see Keane, this volume), in North London gift giving has become the main refuge of formal exchange.

PROVISIONING AND LOVE

The significance of the explicit abstraction represented by monetary evaluation that forms the first stage of gift giving becomes evident when it is contrasted with the bulk of mundane shopping for commodities, which I call provisioning. Provisioning is most often carried out by a female who is responsible for grocery shopping and for buying clothes for herself, any children in the household, and often also for a male partner. She also tends to dominate the purchase of general household materials and furnishings, although she is usually accompanied by a partner during the purchase of the latter.

Details of provisioning on Jay Street can be found in Miller 1998 and are not repeated here. In general they accord closely with those observed in a wide range of studies conducted by feminist researchers whose primary concern has been to foreground the work of the housewife as unvalorized labor (many examples are found in Jackson and Moores 1995). A finding common to all these studies is that the housewife sees herself as serving a more general set of needs and concerns to which she subordinates her own sense of desire. Typically, the one time a meal either is not prepared or is prepared with minimal effort is when she has only herself to feed. The main concern of these researchers has been to analyze the degree of effort involved in housewifery and to uncover the ideology that sustains the inequalities. DeVault (1991) has been particularly helpful in this regard because she includes all the intellectual work of planning, considering, and becoming anxious about provisioning as well as the labor required. By contrast, in almost all such studies informants are shown to refuse this perspective on their work. They maintain that as housewives, they represent a special, largely female contribution in which work should not be reduced to mere questions of equivalence and effort but rather should be respected as a manifestation of love, care, and devotion, which are in some sense "higher" ideals. There is, then, a direct conflict between the housewife's ideological premise and that of the researcher. Both my work and DeVault's suggest that feminism has had much less impact than might have been expected on who actually does what in the home.

In Miller 1998 I detailed four elements of shopping to demonstrate how, in practice, it is used to create and sustain the higher ideals to which many housewives consider themselves devoted. These four elements are thrift, the "treat," love, and the discourse of shopping. Provisioning is an activity in which concerns over money are generally at the fore, but in a manner quite distinct from the way they operate in gift purchasing. The central concern of provisioning is thrift. The primary ritual of shopping is a performance that begins with a discourse of spending money and often a vision of excessive expenditure but then transforms this into an experience of saving money and an emphasis on money as a substance primarily stored and retained rather than expended. In my 1998 book I rejected suggestions that this ritual was distinctly different from traditions of either peasant thrift (Gudeman and Rivera 1990) or bourgeois thrift (Vickery 1993).[7] I also described the vast number of ways in which modern supermarket technologies facilitate shopping in enacting this transformation. New retail technologies allow almost any individual purchase to be conceptualized as an act of saving money without the shopper's having to be involved in a detailed consideration of price. Indeed, housewives engaged in provisioning, unlike in gift purchasing, proved to be largely ignorant about actual prices and to have little knowledge of how much they were spending. What seemed to matter was that they could experience the individual purchase and the shopping expedition overall as an activity in which they had striven for and succeeded in saving money.

When I considered the beneficiaries of this thrift, I found it to be a core means by which the shopper objectifies an ideal higher or larger than herself, even though thrift does not involve the more concrete categorization of the house found in some studies (Gudeman and Rivera 1990). In effect, provisioning negates a vision of hedonistic materialism that dominates the discourse of shopping and transforms shopping into a practice that creates and sustains core values. This conclusion is strengthened by a study of the concept of the "treat." The treat is a common element in many shopping expeditions and consists of an extra item, often embodying some sense of extravagance or hedonism, that is purchased for a specific person. The shopper often gives it to herself as a reward for the labor involved in shopping, but she might also give treats to children or other members of the household. This genre of individualized purchase in effect helps render the bulk of provisioning a generalized purchase of goods that are neither individualized nor hedonistic. In short, the limited and framed treat helps define the rest of shopping as something other than merely treating.

In my 1998 book, I subjected provisioning to a larger argument based on studies of traditional sacrifice and especially a modified version of the structure of sacrifice as outlined by Hubert and Mauss (1964).[8] I suggested that an initial act of transgressive violence that dominates the discourse of sacrifice/shopping is transformed in sacrifice/shopping into a central means for creating and sustaining objects of devotion, be these deities or transcendent images of society. In effect, the act of consumption—which is also an act of using up or relinquishing resources—is, in Western society (and in most other societies), initially viewed as a destructive if not evil activity. Through the rituals of provisioning, shopping is redirected such that its essence is first used as obeisance to higher ideals. The remainder of the sacrifice/shopping is then passed back to the population in the form of an act of consumption—for example, a sacrificial/family meal—which is used to reconstitute the dominant social relationships, such as hierarchy or equivalence, among the consuming group.

In effect, then, the ideology of "care" or "love" (like the sacrificial offering [Valeri 1985:71–72]) becomes split into two elements, one of which is directed toward a transcendent ideal and the other toward a specific object of love. In Miller 1998, I also examined the changing forms by which this love or devotion has been objectified. I started with a consideration of devotion to deities in sacrifice and then considered the kinds of inalienable representations of society analyzed by Weiner (1992). From there I turned to the coincidence of the Enlightenment and the Romantic movement, which between them may be regarded as having shifted the object of devotion from religious ideals to an objectification in romantic partners. More recently, feminism has in turn removed the partner from such a pedestal, but ethnography shows a simultaneous rise of a cult of the infant in which, for example, feminist mothers negate their own projects of autonomy in obsessive self-elimination on behalf of infants. This has also been the subject of a separate study (see Miller 1997b).

This conclusion pitches two of the works of Mauss against each other. Although in *The Gift* Mauss established the idea of an inalienable spirit that was the very essence of the gift, this gave rise to a model of exchange as reciprocity and thereby, in turn, to a long-standing anthropological concern with commensurability and equivalence. It is the striving for equivalence that tends to end with the increasing alienability of things as commodities. By contrast, in many ways it is the work of Hubert and Mauss on sacrifice that has been more successful in sustaining a sense of the inalienable, because in that work they demonstrated that the primary concern of sacrifice is to establish a relationship based on difference or nonequivalence between the human and the divine.

This contrast suits exchange in North London. Whereas I have suggested that the gift cannot be regarded as an act of totalization, provisioning is central to any project of totalization in that it creates, through the domestic arena, the fundamental microcosm of all that most people in the study area understand as value. This distinction lies between the first stage of gift giving and the first stage of provisioning, and it takes the form of a search for thrift in the latter. In their secondary stages, however, gift giving and provisioning come together. Once the abstract notion of the "appropriate" sum is achieved for gift giving, and once provisioning has performed its primary ritual of transforming expenditure into saving, then there may emerge a secondary element that in both cases is about demonstrating one's concern for an individual relationship through the careful choice of a specific commodity. It is to this secondary element of creating the particularity of households, individuals, and, especially, relationships that I now turn. This involves a consideration of the second paradox of this chapter, which is the contention that it is the very alienability and diversity of the commodity that allows it to play a role equivalent to that of the inalienable possession as portrayed by Weiner.

THE MATERIAL CULTURE OF LOVE

Sasha was born in South America, as was her husband, but she has lived in London for 13 years, and although the two talk of returning, there seems no immediate likelihood of their doing so. They have children aged nine and three and live on the council estate. The longest debate held during Sasha's shopping trips was about the color of a new set of toilet and bathroom mats. She was unsure whether to buy two different sets to match the colors of each bathroom or to buy two identical sets that matched each other and might work better if they moved house. Although I certainly found shoppers who both enjoyed and cultivated decisions of taste as matters of personal and individual skill, Sasha neither particularly enjoyed nor identified with this activity. Rather, she saw it as an onerous but natural part of her role in creating a home for her family, a home that was pleasant for them and of which they need not feel ashamed when visitors come to the flat. Much of her purchasing was of items such as toilet rolls, milk, and washing powder that form part of the same sense of mundane provisioning of the home.

Other aspects of her shopping were directed toward individuals, but her decision making was still premised on the individual's being socially contextualized in complex ways. In the case of the younger daughter, who needed a dress for her birthday, Sasha noted that out of the available selection, her husband would have preferred the plain black dress and she would have liked the blue dress with flowers, but her daughter was allowed to insist on a shiny maroon dress with ribbons and lace. The children were also allowed to choose in grocery shopping—for example, the flavors of items. But these choices all lay within clear boundaries demarcating what would be acceptable to the wider world and just about bearable to the parents. Sasha was clearly disappointed that her daughter chose a brand-name fancy ice-cake for her birthday and refused the offer of a homemade cake on which her mother would have liked to have spent much time and attention, but the daughter's preference was respected. On many other occasions, such as when Sasha felt the family should have healthier food than they would have chosen for themselves or that they should have some South American foods to remind them of their origins, the daughters' and husband's choices were overturned, and Sasha followed her own feelings about what was appropriate. On the other hand, Sasha insisted the girls buy Easter eggs, even though this tradition did not exist in her homeland, because she felt that they should know about customs in the land where they lived. On occasion she and the daughters united to defy conventions. For example, the nine-year-old had reached an age for which the high-street shops no longer stocked a range of dresses suitable for younger girls but instead a kind of clothing that emulated more street-wise teenage fashions. But Sasha's daughter, who was generally quiet and studious, did not like such clothing, and her mother assisted her by going to a large number of shops in order to find an appropriate dress.

There are no rules to this decision making. The choices reflect a series of relationships between individuals and among members of the household as a whole, and they are made on the basis of varying interpretations of what is appropriate or socially conventional, as well as what is morally preferable. One cannot say that Sasha prefers South American foods in general, because what happens is that she decides she wants such items mainly when she feels she has ignored this factor for too long. Equally, a child's preference might be allowed simply because the parent has had to refuse so many more important matters, and it seems right to give the child a "turn."

Already in what is quite a simple case, it is clear that the shopper uses goods to express many contradictions in the nature of her relationships. One such contradiction is between the desire to educate her family to better or healthier choices as against the desire to respect their autonomy. But family relationships are far more complex than this. In most cases they are built from years in which a variety of emotions have undergone sedimentation—in memory, expectation, guilt, and aspiration. Any good work of fiction can spend a hundred pages examining the nuances and contradictions in a simple family relationship (the Anne Tyler style of novel comes to mind). It is the relationship that is constantly searching for modes of expression. So the idea that a shopper expresses love or devotion in making choices must evoke the whole sphere of literature directed toward an exploration of the complexity of love in relationships. In contemporary shopping, the prime example of this material expression of the complexity of love has increasingly become that of parents shopping for their children.

This consideration of literature and shopping requires a change in our perception of material culture. Earlier novelists such as Balzac tended to spend considerable effort in describing characters through an analysis of their possessions—for example, the furnishings of their homes. This device was effective, but it was based on the individual as a relatively static, established personality, with an emphasis upon status or position in life, background origins, and sometimes suggestions of future aspiration. Material culture in such literature was being considered within a form of portraiture as a background "still life."[9] The genre known as the modern "shopping" novel, although supposedly trendy and new, is in a sense quite conservative. Such novels emphasize designer goods and name dropping, with the same sort of emphasis upon the individual and status. But the material culture of most shopping is based on far more complex structures of change, stability, and daily shifting nuances of relationships. It is closer to that of hunter-gatherer societies in which people are reported to have moved each day, in part so that they could shift the position of their hut to reflect the current state of their relationship to particular kin.

Douglas and Isherwood (1979:ix–xii) noted the relationship of consumption to both social relations and the work of the novelist (in their case Henry James) in depicting those relations, but their concern was with the classification of social relations, which I see as more the role of the gift. Such classification is very different from the daily dynamics through which such relations are objectified. A similar point applies to Bourdieu's (1984) use of "taste" to study class as a system of categories (see also Sahlins 1976). Provisioning is not a process of representation or semiotics. Although I have used the term love, it is only in certain cases that this is the explicit legitimation of a relationship that is thereby being expressed. Provisioning is a continual practice that objectifies relationships both real and imagined, in the sense that they are in some measure the creations of that practice. The same practice subjectifies, in the sense that it creates persons as sources of desire. This is why the process may continue regardless of the evidence that it is commonly unvalorized by the people it is supposed to serve and fails in any instrumental criterion of actually improving these relationships. Provisioning may construct an ideal subject of its own, a subject created by the shopper notwithstanding the failure of any actual person to live up to the ideal. This is also why I found shopping for the household to be just as important in single-person households and in social units that bore little relation to any normative ideal of the household. North London is an area where gender and other roles have changed dramatically in certain respects (compare Beck and Gernsheim-Beck 1995 for Germany).

We can now start to resolve the paradox established through the consideration of Weiner's work. In it, devotion is directed toward and thus objectified in inalienable objects, through which people gain their social or cosmological identity and for which they might fight and die. In North London, it is persons who tend to be the objectification of the inalienable. As Kopytoff's work (1986) and my own (Miller 1987) have suggested, the degree of inalienability of an object results from the object's becoming part of personification or socialization through the act of consumption. Provisioning is directed by love through attempts to recognize as many nuances and subtleties of the relationship as possible. It is the attention to detail that is held to demonstrate the shopper's degree of concern. The key skill of the shopper as parent or partner is sensitivity and a seeming knowledge of what is wanted before the subject realizes he or she even had such a desire. Shopping as an act of subjectification that constructs others as the sources of desire therefore becomes the effort expended in all those complex considerations by which individuals and relationships are constantly reconsidered and reevaluated. This is by no means passive, since as both parents and partners, shoppers are likely to wish to mold, educate, and morally improve the persons for whom they shop, or at least make them more amenable to the image the shopper has of them. This interpretation is entirely compatible with the conventional critique of capitalism, in which the emphasis is on the exploitation and inequalities generated by relations of production and distribution. It does, however, imply a defense of consumption as a process of value creation and not merely one of passive acquiescence to capitalist motivation or mindless hedonism.

The sheer range of commodities that are available to form part of this exercise is enormous. I believe it is possible to account for a considerable part of the current forms and trends in modern consumption in terms of the complexity of the relationships among persons in a household.[10] For example, from the point of view of commerce, a key (and highly bankable) asset is the long-term brand—a specific make of commodity that has existed for generations, such as Heinz tomato soup. Such brands can become appropriated into a family's desire to constitute itself as a descent group. The notion of a descent group is often infused with a cyclical element in kin relations, a cycle in which parents, bringing up their children as future parents, return to the models and guidance they themselves received during their socialization by their own parents. A number of key brands such as Heinz and Kellogs are available for objectifying the concept of descent group simply because of their longevity and their memorialization of the love that was borne between members of earlier generations. Soup is perhaps an obvious such case, but it is possible for a brand of toilet roll or kitchen cleaner also to evoke such generational links (usually implicitly), precisely because it becomes an invariant feature of the grocery purchasing, something that the household should never run out of. No one such commodity can bear this weight of descent constitution alone, but in many households there is a group of long-standing branded goods that stand for a continuity transcending any one generation. After all, some of these brands remained little changed during a century that saw immense shifts in social structures and cultural ideology. Some commodities have been around long enough to represent tradition, stability, and history.

These branded products are the nearest equivalents to Weiner's inalienable objects because, though the individual exemplification might change, the brand retains constancy. A study such as Pendergrast's *For God, Country and Coca-Cola* (1993) illustrates how a brand can become a kind of Durkheimian representation of society. As Quinn has argued (1994:108–9, 134–35), the corporate logo becomes a metasymbol to be filled with a wide range of potential symbolic elements. But to generalize the material culture of consumption from such brands would be to extract a single element from a much more varied and complex range of forms.

In direct opposition to long-standing brands are fads and fashions, the designer labels whose whole purpose lies in their very transience. These are favored by youths whose primary concern is with fashion per se. They can also enter into relations of care, as in the case of a mother who is concerned that her child always have the latest thing so that he or she will not be looked down upon on the playground. The latest demand might be for goods linked to movies such as *The Hunchback of Notre Dame* or *The Grinch,* where it is crucial precisely in which week the items are bought, but the goods might also refer back nostalgically to *Bambi* or *Snow White* as the Walt Disney events of the mother's childhood. For the fashion conscious, timing comes to dominate over form, and this is especially important where consumption expresses relations of power (Bourdieu 1984; Douglas and Isherwood 1978).

There are many other polarities in commerce similar to that between the stable and the transient in brands. Writers who concentrate on the logic of commerce tend to assume that the existence of constant contradiction is itself evidence of the ability of commerce to fool the consumer. Thus Fine (1995:151–52) attacked the marketing of dairy goods, which literally creams off the fat in order to provide a wide range of low-fat goods such as milk and yogurt but then uses the same fat to make cheeses and creamed goods. From the viewpoint of shoppers, however, there is probably nothing better suited to the tasks of shopping than shelves that exhibit contradiction. There are few shoppers today who do not use low-fat, diet-conscious goods, and it is equally rare that those same shoppers do not also want to buy rich cream desserts that gain their specialness from their direct contrast with the low-fat norm. It is this wide register of fat content that allows the housewife to compose her unique melody of provisioning, a melody whose base notes of healthy diet harmonize with the high notes of treats and rewards. It is the same register that allows her to subtly fatten up the thin child who never seems hungry while keeping such goods away from the overweight child who is always raiding the refrigerator. Indeed, much subtler notes can be sounded, such as what "mood" the shopper is in or her displeasure when a family member has conspicuously failed to follow her advice or is behaving badly.

Behind these lie a wide range of other contradictions—whether, for example, to buy more expensive "moral" items such as organic vegetables or to emphasize the morality involved in saving money for the household by buying cheap, mass-produced goods (see Miller 2001: ch. 4). Is it worth the effort of making one's husband get involved in shopping in order for him to acknowledge its skills and importance if the result is going to be a whole set of inappropriate goods? Shopping that is often regarded as the most hedonistic, such as clothes shopping, is often just as hedged in by considerations of wider obligations, such as whether the shopper should buy goods that suggest a desire to "age gracefully" or insist on retaining clothing styles that now embarrass her teenage daughter. We might feel that the sheer variety of goods is outrageously developed, beyond any sense of need, but the primary "need" that is expressed in shopping, far from being any novel desire emergent from the presence of the goods themselves, is the preexisting and restless need created by the complexity of a social relationship. As any good novelist will demonstrate, the nuances of a human relationship manage to make even the vast range of commodities available for its expression look sparse and oversimplified. To conclude, the goods purchased by shoppers in North London did not, in the main, appear to be "about" merely social classification, nor about social status, power, exchange, or even identity. Rather, they were used to objectify social relations, a process in which the social life of things is formed through the object life of relationships, and within which all of these other factors may or may not have a presence.

One does not have to suggest that family and other relations have become more complex or nuanced as a result of the range of goods available. Insightful plays and books have been written about human relationships in plenty of periods and regions other than those of high capitalism. It is merely that objectification of those relationships is the core, pregiven need that literally feeds off the grocery store shelf as the range of commodities allows ever more precise and varied ways to meet that need. Because in Western society it is persons and relationships between persons that have come to be the primary media through which a concept of the transcendent or the inalienable has come to be objectified, it becomes appropriate to use these highly alienable and flexible forms of material culture in much the same way that, as Weiner argued, inalienable possessions are used in other societies—that is, as the means to create and sustain objects of devotion. This may be why it is often women who are most closely associated with projects of the inalienable in the Pacific and equally with commodity consumption in the West.

Reversing the usual implications of gift and commodity exchange might have a bearing on the other main topic of this volume. It may be suggested that the same search for an objectification of inalienablity can produce both art and provisioning. Within modernity, the inalienable is sought first through processes of subjectification—that is, the reification of personhood as the only true source of the inalienable. So the concept and practice of art as a defined genre in its contemporary sense arose first through the conceptualization of persons as artists, whose pure, creative labor was then objectified in their works. As is evident in Myers's chapter in this volume, there is still pressure to construct Aboriginal people as artists in order to designate their products as art. Provisioning, by contrast, starts with alienated commodities and proceeds with its own project of subjectification in that it creates subjects out of projected desire for goods.[11] This returns goods to their role in the establishment of social relations. Art, on the other hand, objectifies through a process of abstraction from social relations in order to construct another regime of value in which the inalienable is founded upon an aura of transcendence. In short, art and provisioning represent two ideal types in modernity's search for the inalienable. Art is a process that leads from subjectification to objectification, whereas provisioning is a process that leads from objectification to subjectification. But such dualisms cannot be presented without some caveat, which I give here in the form of a conclusion.

CONCLUSION

The original contention of this chapter is that the gift in Western society is not necessarily the correct form in which to seek equivalence to the kind of gift discussed by Mauss. Far from being the instrument of totalization and the creation of the inalienable, Western gift giving may be a highly restricted and dyadic medium by which money can enter into the classification of kinship and other relationships. Instead, there is evidence to suggest that it is the vast range of highly alienable commodities as used in basic provisioning that is germane to the primary process by which we seek to create a sense of the inalienable through the domestic microcosm, where our sense of values is objectified. Thus, if we wish to embark upon a project of comparative anthropology, we might advance farther if we reverse the gift-commodity dualism as we move from the Pacific to a Western capitalist context. Obviously, this can be reduced to a kind of semantic game. If we change the time during which the object is defined from after purchase to before purchase, the equations with terms such as alienability also change. By demonstrating how one could proceed with this discussion while reversing the standard comparison, my purpose is not to prolong the gift-commodity dualism but to end it.

The anthropological debate has not remained static. Gregory (1997) provided a robust assertion that the kind of coeval presence of the two systems that I have described in this chapter is common to most societies, and that our focus should turn to the relations of power between them, which has become a common theme. At first this seems both attractive and straightforward. We can see a kind of "hypercommodity" logic in the attempt by neoclassical economists to account for every aspect of social life, following mainly upon the example of Becker (see Fine 1998), whereas in some of the eco-warrior "alternative" lifestyle critiques of capitalism, one sees the imagination of a world where the logic of the gift overturns all other relations. Such a polarization is of course far too simplistic, and Mauss himself was trying to achieve a more considered balance in his interventions in French politics at the time. After all, as Godelier recently pointed out (1999:179–98), there are elements of the sacrificial logic of the gift that could be argued to be fundamental to the development of class and caste. And money had a fundamental if not essential role in developing modern concepts of equality (Simmel 1990). This chapter was also intended to demolish any simple relation between forms of exchange and forms of power. The task of determining how forms of exchange, or models of exchange systems idealized as gift and commodity, are employed in conflicting relations today (see Carrier 1997; Carrier and Miller 1998) can best proceed if we transcend any prior assumption that a particular form of exchange must perforce enable or constrain a particular form of power.

This point brings out the caveat that is required by any such playing around with the dualism of gift and commodity, or indeed art and commodity. Fortunately, that caveat is well presented in the introduction to this volume. This chapter may be taken as merely one example of the more general argument made by Myers that what is required in material culture studies is a wider understanding of the construction and use of systems of value. In achieving this understanding, we must be sensitive to the dynamics by which value is transformed and revalued, and we will discover that there are many routes and institutions through which we can observe the objectification of both exchange and the inalienable.

Notes

This chapter was originally composed before the publication of Miller 1998. There is some repetition between that book and the penultimate section of this chapter.

1. By the term "gifts," I refer to that category of objects given to individuals on special occasions that would be termed gifts by my informants.

2. For an alternative contextualizaton of this section on Weiner that considers these points in terms of a history of love, see Miller 1998:128–32.

3. Alison Clarke is a tutor at the Royal College of Art, London, and professor at the Design Institute of Vienna, but she is conducting this research as a graduate student in the Department of Anthropology at University College, London (see Clarke 1998).

4. Council housing in Britain does not have the same connotation as housing projects within the United States. Until recently, it represented around a third of all housing. Maisonettes are houses in which the top and bottom floors were built to be (or to be made into) separate accommodations.

5. We were unable to include all households in the study, the main reasons being the absence of many householders during the day and my inability, owing to family commitments, to conduct much research at other times. Following our leafleting and approaching of households on Jay Road itself, only 14 of those who were able to take part during the daytime completely refused to do so. This

means that although the study represents some 30 percent of households in the street, it represents some 80 percent of households where people were available to take part. The bias this produced is clearly in favor of the kind of family-based household in which the factors I dwell on in this essay would be more pronounced. The dominant group was housewives in part-time employment. The sample is less representative of single-person or dual-person households in full-time work.

6. Just to throw in a bone of contention for the volume as a whole, I would suggest that art is similar to the gift in that it purports to be a form of totalization but in practice is merely a highly "framed" variety of money.

7. I fully recognize that thrift has many other social and cosmological roles. For example, in my analysis of shopping in Trinidad, I emphasized a quite different competitive element to thrift.

8. My 1998 study of sacrifice was based on specific parallels between stages in shopping and stages in sacrificial ritual as analyzed by Hubert and Mauss (1964) and later writers. It was not intended to refer to the colloquial idea of the self-sacrifice.

9. See Sennett 1976 for a discussion of Balzac's representation of material culture during "the fall of public man," but also Schama 1993 for an assessment of the moral discussions involved in still life.

10. I refer here to an understanding of their consumption context, which in a wider study would have to be articulated with their production context (see Miller 1997a).

11. This point arose from discussion during the seminar; I am especially grateful to Claudio Lomnitz and Webb Keane.

Part Two

Nationalism

4

Elusive Property

The Personification of Mexican National Sovereignty

Claudio Lomnitz

From our point of view, the great novelty that independence brought with it was to expose colonial man to the inclemency of modernity.

—Edmundo O'Gorman, *México: El trauma de su historia*

In this chapter I discuss the secular process whereby the ideal of national sovereignty became embodied in the material apparatus of a postcolonial state.[1] I do so through a study of the historical development of the public persona of the national president in Mexico. Presidential power, symbolized in the president's body—in his demeanor and his position with regard to other national symbols—became a model of how sovereignty is achieved. Such models were used to tie the state to "the people," and successful presidential images were turned into state patrimony. They became part of the material inventory that could be deployed to uphold one of the principal claims of the modern state: that it is itself the inalienable possession of the nation, and not the instrument of special interests.

I analyze three different images of the president that were developed in succession during Mexico's first century of independence. These three forms of embodiment of national sovereignty were later recycled and recombined during the Mexican Revolution (1910–20), and they were carefully appropriated and harnessed by the revolutionary state, material relics and all.

In Mexico, the earliest successful images of the president as an embodiment of national sovereignty appropriated Christian models of sacrifice and spiritual guidance to lead the nation to freedom. Like the bodies of saints, presidential bodies that were possessed by the spirit of Christian sacrifice became powerful relics in the nationalist struggle. In another set of images taken up successfully by presidents somewhat later, the popular demand for equality before the law guided the nation, and presidential bodies again served as vehicles for enacting the ideal. Finally, in a third set of images, the judicious implementation of scientific advancement was to lead the nation to its independence. In each of these images, the nation's material and spiritual patrimony provided the symbolic repertoire for the historical development of the presidential persona and thus for the symbolic formulation of the relations of command that are implicit in the notion of national sovereignty.

THE MEXICAN STATE'S DIFFICULT RELATIONSHIP WITH NATIONAL SOVEREIGNTY

In Mexico, theories about national destiny have eclipsed broader concerns with human history. Development in Mexico has been national development, history has been national history, and theories of history have been theories of national history. This phenomenon is not caused by isolation. It is instead the result of a pervasive peripheral cosmopolitanism, an acute desire to catch up, to reach "the level" of the great world powers. The need to explain the dynamics of national history stems from the national project's failure to deliver its promise to free Mexico from subservience and to attain the ideal of national sovereignty.

Perceptions of the disjunction between the central tenets of national ideology and actual political practice are visible in Mexico as early as the independence movement itself. One clear formulation of the problem was framed by José María Luis Mora, a man who worked tirelessly and to a large extent unsuccessfully at creating the persona of the liberal citizen. Mora complained that his contemporaries believed "the constitution and the laws are here to place limits on a power that already existed and was invested with omni-modal power, and not that they are here to create and form that power" (1837, 2:52, my translation). In other words, the state's power was thought to *precede* the social contract. Mora relied on the temporal trope of "precedence" to stand in for a series of practices in which the state was not accountable to the people through formal or legal channels.

Lack of identification between the national community and state power has produced a chronic problem of legitimacy for Mexican governments and even, at times, for the state itself. Because the state and its power are independent from or, as Mora would have it, "prior to" communitarian consensus, the symbolism and material embodiment of national sovereignty always lie slightly outside of the state itself. Sovereignty lies with the people and so can be attained only by transcending the state as an existing structure—that is, by occupying the state and turning it against itself. Leaders who wished to stir nationalist fervor have tried to embody sovereignty by "rising above" the petty interests of the existing state or by "forcing it down" to the popular level.

Not surprisingly, perhaps, sovereignty in this context became an elusive property. I mean this in two ways. First, sovereignty could not be identified with the material apparatus of the state unless it was personified by a president himself. However, the embodiment of sovereignty in the president was often unconvincing because presidents were constantly in danger of being overwhelmed (or of being accused of being overwhelmed) by private interests. Second, because the idea of sovereignty is transcendent, its material embodiment in the form of inalienable possessions of the national community cannot always be successfully appropriated or harnessed by the state, and those possessions might be taken up in popular movements against the state.

The legitimation of the national state in Mexico therefore has had a long and cumbersome history. Early perceptions of a disjunction between the state and the people were matched by weak and highly unstable central administrations. This weakness of the Mexican state shifted great symbolic weight onto the national presidency, since it was the pivot of the entire national project. As a result, images of sovereignty, images of the realization of the nation's possibilities, were embodied in the national president. Mexican presidents and their entourages of flatterers and propagandists offered concrete formulations of the ideal of national sovereignty in the construction of their own personae.

A CATHOLIC NATIONALISM

Once the priest Miguel Hidalgo's movement for independence, launched in 1810, had ravaged several towns of the Mexican Bajío, the bishop of Michoacán, Hidalgo's erstwhile friend Manuel Abad y Queipo, decreed the excommunication of the priest and his followers. This act, and some of the insurgent clergy's reactions, set the tone for later metaphors of national unity and apostasy.

The bishop began his edict with a quotation from Luke—"Every kingdom that is divided into factions shall be destroyed and ruined"—and then reviewed the ravages of the wars in French Saint Domingue (Haiti), which were caused, he reminded his flock, by the revolution in the metropole. The result of that revolt was not only the assassination of all Europeans and Creoles but also the destruction of four-fifths of the island's black and mulatto population and a legacy of perpetual hatred between blacks and mulattos. No good could come from a false division between Europeans and Americans.

Abad then expressed particular chagrin that the call of disloyalty and to arms came from a priest who not only killed and injured Europeans and used his robes to "seduce a portion of innocent laborers" but also "insulted the faith and our sovereign, Ferdinand VII, painted on his banner the image of our august patroness, our Lady of Guadalupe, and wrote the following inscription: 'Long Live the Faith. Long Live our Holiest Mother of Guadalupe. Long Live Ferdinand VII. Long Live America, and Death to Bad Government'" (Abad y Queipo 1964 [1810]:37). After excommunicating Hidalgo, Abad y Queipo threatened to do the same to anyone who persisted in fighting on Hidalgo's side or aiding him in any way.

This edict, which was soon endorsed by the archbishop of Mexico, caused Hidalgo, the priest José María Morelos, and other members of the insurgent clergy great indignation and rage. Hidalgo made a formal reply in which he swore his loyalty to the Catholic faith: "I have never doubted any of its truths, I have always been intimately convinced of the infallibility of its dogmas." He then deplored his excommunication as a partisan and un-Christian act: "Open your eyes, Americans. Do not allow yourselves to be seduced by our enemies: they are not Catholics except to politic; their god is money, and their acts have our oppression as their only object" (Hidalgo 1964 [1810]:42). Hidalgo called for the establishment of a representative parliament that,

> having as its principal object to maintain our holy religion, will promote benign laws [*leyes suaves*], useful and well suited to the circumstances of each pueblo. They shall then govern with the tenderness of parents, they shall treat us as brothers, banish poverty, moderate the devastation of the kingdom and the extraction of its moneys, foment the arts, liven up industry, ...and after a few years, our inhabitants shall enjoy all of the delicacies that the Sovereign Author of nature has spilt on this vast continent. (1964 [1810]:43)

In sum, Hidalgo warned against the use of the true faith for the enrichment of foreign oppressors. He identified national sovereignty with the rule of the Catholic faith, a rule that was to be paternalistic in that it should recognize the specific needs and circumstances of each pueblo. He imagined a nation guided by a single true faith that would quickly become a kind of Christian paradise in which poverty was eradicated by the brotherly and benign intentions that existed between true co-religionists. Thus Hidalgo performed a kind of counterexcommunication of European imperialists who used Catholicism to "seduce" those whom they sought to oppress and exploit.

Hidalgo's position found concrete juridical expression in the edicts of his follower Morelos. In 1810, in his first edict abolishing slavery and Indian tribute, Morelos proclaimed, "Any American who owes money to a European is not obliged to pay it. If, on the contrary, it is the European who owes, he shall rigorously pay his debt to the American." Moreover: "Every prisoner shall be set free with the knowledge that if he commits the same crime or any other that contradicts a man's honesty, he shall be punished" (Morelos 1964 [1810]:55).

These laws portrayed "Europeans" as having exploited "Americans" to the extent that no possible debt to the Europeans had not already been paid handsomely. They also implied that the judgment of crimes under the Spanish regime was systematically unfair. In sum, the counterexcommunication of the Spanish clergy by Hidalgo and Morelos fused the national ideal with a Christian utopia. Paternalistic beneficence and brotherhood would be achieved in an independent Mexico ruled by true Catholics, instead of by oppressors who used Catholicism to pursue their un-Christian aims: the extraction of money and the oppression of a nation.

Morelos's political spirit perdured in Mexico because the defense of nationals against foreign extortion and the dispensation of Christian justice proved impossible to achieve after independence. Thus Hidalgo's image of sovereignty as the Christian administration of plenty remained a utopia, and Mexican governments after independence were just as subject to the politics of religious appropriation or excommunication as their Spanish predecessors had been.

So, for instance, a similar formulation of national ideals can be found, 100 years after Hidalgo's cry in Dolores, issuing from the pen of that foremost ideologue of the Mexican Revolution, Luis Cabrera. Under the title "Two Patriotisms," he blasted the official celebration of the centenary of independence just two months before the first revolutionary outburst of 20 November 1910:

> The celebration of our glories and the commemoration of our heroes is a cult, but those who suffer and work cannot arrive together at the altar of the fatherland with those who dominate and benefit, because they do not share the same religion. Just as the Christian's plea to pardon all debts cannot fit in the same prayer as the Jew's plea for daily bread exacted from profits, neither can there be a unified homage to our fathers by those with an insatiable thirst for power and by the noble desire for justice that moves the hearts of the pueblo that suffers and works. (1972 [1910]:55–56)

This significant foundational strain of Mexican nationalism saw the national state as the ideal medium for achieving a Christian community. In fact, the standards for sovereignty that were set by Hidalgo, wherein poverty would be banished "in just a few years," or by Morelos in his declaration of a clean slate for all, would be impossible to uphold. They were ill suited to serve as the basis for consolidating a huge territory peopled by a weakly integrated nation that had gained its independence in a moment of intense imperial competition.

DEAD PRESIDENTS

The consolidation of a central authority has been a complex problem in Mexican history. Although such an authority existed during the colonial era in the figure of the king and his surrogate, the viceroy, establishing a central state and authority after independence proved to be extremely difficult.

Monarchical solutions to this quandary were consonant with the ideology of Mexican independence, which leaned heavily on traditional Spanish legal thought to legitimate itself.[2] The dream of a smooth transition between the colonial and the independent order was simply not to come true. On one side, radical insurgents were not keen to see the precolonial status quo upheld so thoroughly. On another, Spain did not immediately relinquish its claims over the new Mexican Empire and attempted to reestablish a foothold on the continent for 10 more years, sufficient time for an anti-Spanish sentiment, which had been growing along with the construction of Mexican nationalism, to become virulent. Moreover, the United States was clearly and loudly opposed to the establishment of a monarchy in Mexico.[3] As a result, monarchists were forced to set their hearts on acquiring a European monarch with the simultaneous backing of all or most European powers, a solution that was tried with French backing in the 1860s and failed. Thus, the fractures in the nascent national elite were connected from the beginning to the contest between the United States, France, Spain, and Britain.

It was not until 1867, after the French departed and Maximilian was shot, that Mexico finally earned its "right" to exist as a nation in the eyes of all foreign powers. Until that time, no strong central state had existed, and the country's sovereignty was severely limited. In the words of an astute Porfirian intellectual, before the wars of intervention, "being a foreigner came to mean being the natural born master of all Mexicans. It was enough, as a few of the exceptionally rare honest diplomats acknowledged, for a foreigner to be imprisoned for three days on poor behavior or intrigue for that person to become a creditor for fifty or one hundred thousand pesos to the Mexican national budget as a result of a diplomatic agreement" (Bulnes 1904:819).

The state had become the guarantor of foreign interests against its own people. The bullet that killed Maximilian effectively ended the possibility of ever establishing a European-backed monarchy, and it made a powerful international statement about the sovereignty of

Mexico and its laws. Until that time, Mexico had been insistently "Africanized" in foreign eyes.

In the years between 1821 and 1867, Mexican leaders had tried a series of strategies for constructing central power, combining various forms of messianism with aspects of monarchical power, republicanism, and liberalism in a large number of short-lived presidencies. Given the nonexistence of a successful hegemonic block among early post-independence elites, and considering that those elites did not fully comprehend the foreign pressures that were being exerted until half the country's territory had been lost, constructing an image of national sovereignty and authority in the office of the president became a major cultural challenge. For whereas political ritual and the stability of office in the colonial period reveal a clear-cut ideology of dependency—that is, a combination of subordination, complementarity, and mutual reliance—the sense of interdependence between Mexico's regions and its capital was decidedly shaken and sometimes completely shattered after independence.

The difficulty of shaping presidential power was increased, too, by the weakness or nonexistence of modern political parties. Political organization around the time of independence flowed to a large extent through Masonic lodges. In the early independence period there was only one Masonic rite, the Scottish rite, which had been imported by Mexico's representatives to the Cortes of Cádiz in 1812. A second lodge, that of York, was established in Mexico by the first US ambassador, Joel Poinsett, with the explicit aim of introducing a federalist, republican, and more Jacobin organization into Mexico's political field. In neither case was the lodge open to public scrutiny, as political parties are meant to be, and political power was taken in the name of an ideology such as federalism, centralism, liberalism, or conservativism, with no party structure to back it.

As a result, the construction of the president as the personification of sovereignty was both important and highly problematical. It involved creating an image that could rise above and reconcile a regionally fragmented society but that could also be manipulated in order to seduce or frighten off imperial powers. These contradictory uses are surely part of the much-commented-upon gulf between the *país real* and the *país legal*—that is, between actual state practice and the normative order.

AN ARM AND A LEG

The salience of martyrdom in Mexican politics has often been noted in popular commentary. Mexico has a large pantheon of national leaders who were shot or martyred, including—to name only the most prominent ones—Hidalgo, Morelos, Allende, Aldama, Iturbide, Guerrero, Mina, Mariano Matamoros, Maximilian, Madero, Villa, Carranza, Obregón, and Zapata. The first martyrs of independence were Hidalgo, Allende, Aldama, and Santa María, whose heads were cut off by Spanish authorities and displayed in the four corners of the Alhóndiga de Granaditas, where Hidalgo's army had massacred a number of Spaniards and Creoles. Many other independence leaders were executed in later periods.

When it came to insurgent priests, Spanish authorities tried to degrade the leaders before and after execution. The subjects were defrocked in ecclesiastical courts and then turned over to civil authorities, who dictated their sentences. In cases where military officers had to take justice into their own hands, some officers "reconciled their duties as Christians with their obligations as soldiers" by undressing the rebel priest, shooting him, and then re-dressing him in his robes for burial.[4] Despite these and other degradations, the dead became the martyred "fathers" of the nation.

The use of the imagery of Christian martyrdom or sacrifice was a way of identifying the presidential body with the land. The relationship to kingly ideology is clear. Since Mexico was unable to enshrine its own king, in whom a positive relationship between personal welfare and national welfare could be state dogma ("the king and the land are one"), its national leaders had to create this relationship negatively, through sacrifice. Thus it was through personal sacrifice that the president could attempt to convince people of his capacity to represent the entire nation.

The president who most successfully relied on this strategy for fashioning his persona was Antonio López de Santa Anna, who dominated Mexican politics during the first half of the nineteenth century. Santa Anna was called to the presidency 11 times, alternatively as a liberal, a conservative, and a moderate. Ideological purity was clearly not the way to establish oneself as a durable choice for the presidency in early-nineteenth-century Mexico. Instead, as the historian John Lynch observed, Santa Anna saw himself as a preserver of order, not as an ideologically inconsistent opportunist: "The fault [according to Santa Anna] lay with the political parties, which divided Mexico and created a need for reconciliation" (Lynch 1992:336).

In the rhetoric of the period, nothing remained above the fray among political parties but the fatherland *(patria)* itself, and so Santa Anna cultivated his reputation as a war hero. He led the defense against Spain in 1829; his leg was amputated after he was wounded during the "Pastry War" against the French in 1839 (offsetting, somewhat, his humiliating defeat in Texas); and he organized the defense against the US invasion at a time of political disarray. In 1842 Santa Anna was once again called to power, and at that point he attempted to build the rudiments of a political geography that would have him at its center. He had a luxurious municipal theater built (the Teatro Santa Anna), with a statue of himself in front of it. A solemn and much-attended ceremony was enacted to inaugurate a third monument, a mausoleum in which his left leg was reinterred.

The significance of Santa Anna's leg—a limb that linked him to Hidalgo, Morelos, and all the dead heroes whose love for the *patria* was at that point the only ideology capable of unifying the country—can be appreciated in the lore of the era, which is well captured in Santa Anna's autobiography:

> The infamous words the messenger read me are repeated here:
>
> The majority of Congress openly favor the Paredes revolution....The rioters imprisoned President Canalizo and extended their aversion to the President, Santa Anna. They tore down a bronze bust erected in his honor in the Plaza del Mercado. They stripped his name from the Santa Anna Theatre, substituting for it the National Theatre. Furthermore, they have taken his amputated foot from the cemetery of Santa Paula and proceeded to drag it through the streets to the sounds of savage laughter and regaling....
>
> I interrupted the narrator, exclaiming savagely, "Stop! I don't wish to hear anymore! Almighty God! A member of my body, lost in the service of my country, dragged from the funeral urn, broken into bits to be made sport of in such a barbaric man-

> ner!" In that moment of grief and frenzy, I decided to leave my native country, object of my dreams and of my disillusions, for all time. (Santa Anna 1988:68–69)

Given Mexico's ideological rifts and the difficulty of creating a national center in the face of internal divisions and international pressure, the only good president was a selfless one. Dead insurgents became exemplars of this ideal, and the earliest viable presidential personas were built around the figure of the martyr—these were presidents who received no salaries, who sacrificed their families, abandoned their family fortunes, gave up their health for their country.

Santa Anna lost his leg, and it became the focus of contention. Alvaro Obregón, caudillo of the Mexican Revolution, president from 1920 to 1924, reelected for office in 1928 and murdered on the day of his election, lost an arm in the battle of Celaya against Pancho Villa. The arm was preserved in alcohol and became the centerpiece of a monument built in Obregón's name by the man who created what today endures as the Institutional Revolutionary Party (PRI). Obregón's martyrdom was thus used to funnel charisma into a bureaucracy that has insistently called itself revolutionary.

Two less well known and curious stories are the ends met by the bodies of Guadalupe Victoria and General Francisco (Pancho) Villa. Victoria, Mexico's first president, died in 1842. During the US invasion of Mexico (1848), American soldiers violated the tomb where his embalmed body and preserved organs were kept. According to one hagiographer, two US soldiers drank the alcohol in which Victoria's innards were preserved and died—the remains of Guadalupe Victoria were still powerful in the struggle for sovereignty. In 1862, just before the French invasion, Victoria's remains were transferred to Puebla by General Alejandro García (Villaseñor y Villaseñor 1962, 2:267–68), and they were placed at the foot of the Angel of Independence in Mexico City by President Calles in the 1920s.[5]

US patriots apparently also had a bone to pick (so to speak) with Pancho Villa, whose tomb was desecrated and whose head allegedly ended up in the Skull and Bones Society at Yale University, a secret society of which George Bush was once a member (Katz 1998:789). It appears that Villa, whom the US media initially portrayed as a popular hero and then demonized as a bandit who had the gall to invade Columbus, New Mexico, became the object of "scientific interest" by patriots in the United States—whereas Villa's invasion of Columbus is still a source of pride and pleasure for Mexican *revanchistes.*

The politics surrounding these remains reveal the degree to which the Mexican nation's inalienable possessions have been vulnerable to foreign appropriation and internal desecration. They suggest that martyrdom has been fundamentally linked to an often unworkable ideal of sovereignty in modern Mexico. Sovereignty has been a place that only the dead can inhabit, which is why Mexicans sometimes fight over their remains.

UNCONVENTIONAL CONVENTIONALISTS, OR THE FETISHISM OF THE LAW

It fell to Benito Juárez to create the first strong image of the presidency as an *institution* of power that was truly above the fray. His strategy was to present himself as a complex embodiment of the meeting between the nation and the law. As an Indian, Juárez could stand for the nation; as an inscrutable magistrate and keeper of the law, he attempted to create an image of the presidency as being above ambitious self-aggrandizement.[6] Francisco Bulnes provided a biting Creole perspective on Juárez's distinct public persona:

> Juárez had a distinctively Indian temperament; he had the calm of an obelisk—that reserved nature that slavery promotes to the state of comatoseness in the coldly resigned races. He was characterized by the secular silence of the vanquished who know that every word that is not the miasma of degradation is punished, by that indifference which apparently allows no seduction but that exasperates.... Juárez did not make speeches, he did not write books, use the press, nor write letters, he did not have intimate conversation, nor did he have esprit, an element that makes thought penetrating, like perfume. Nor was he subtle or expressive in his gestures, his movement, or his gaze. His only language was official, severe, sober, irreproachable, fastidious, unbearable. His only posture that of a judge hearing a case. His only expression the absence of all expression. The physical

> and moral appearance of Juárez was not that of the apostle, or the martyr, or the statesman; it was instead that of a god in a *teocalli,* inexpressive on the humid and reddish rock of sacrifices. (Bulnes 1904:856–57, my translation)

Juárez created a lasting image of what the relationship of the president to the nation should be. He had no need for the kind of martyrdom that Santa Anna utilized, because his identification with the Indian race already proved his link to the land. Neither, as Bulnes said, was he an apostle, in that his role was to *remind* Mexicans and foreigners of the rule of the law, a posture that was immortalized in his refusal to bend the law to the will of foreign leaders and pardon Maximilian's life. The result appears at first as an impossible combination: the legalistic bureaucrat as national fetish.

Juárez's construction of the presidential persona as the embodiment of the law depended on a racial element for its success. Mexican presidents who belonged to the local aristocracy could achieve full identification with the land only through the theater of messianism and martyrdom. Juárez, on the other hand, relied on the mythology of the Aztec past as a way of establishing a credible relationship to the land without relying on messianism. When he relied on biblical imagery, Juárez usually turned to Moses, the law giver and liberator, and not to Jesus and the martyrs. This was because Juárez's challenge was not to demonstrate loyalty to the land but rather to show that he could "rise above his race." The law resolved this problem to some extent. The Indian, who indisputably was connected to the land, could identify so fully with the law that he would become faceless: a national fetish of the law, an idol in a *teocalli,* or temple, as Bulnes said. This contrasts with the role of the law in the persona of the messianic president, whose attitudes in this regard were usually inspired by Napoleon.[7]

Juárez was aided in this project by the fact that he presided over the definitive defeat of European powers, the execution of a prestigious European monarch, the defeat of the clergy, and an alliance with the United States. He succeeded in identifying himself with the nation not through the greatness of his individual acts (as Bulnes would have liked) but through his sober image as the embodiment of the law.

With Juárez, two alternative images of that national fetish that is the Mexican president had been rudimentarily established: the president as messianic leader—overflowing with personality, ideologically inconsistent, and abandoning his fortune for the sake of the nation—and the expressionless leader who could claim the rule of law in the name of the nation by virtue of his Indian body. That the two could not easily be combined is evident in a satirical verse directed to León de la Barra, interim president of Mexico after Porfirio Díaz's fall in 1910 (quoted in Sánchez González 1995:64, my translation):

El gobernar con el frac	To govern with a tuxedo
y ser presidente blanco	And be a white president
es tan solo un pasaporte	Is only a passport
de destierro limpio y franco.	To certain banishment.

That is, you could use a tuxedo, like Juárez, if it underlined a fusion between the Indian and the law, but if you were white and sought to be president you could not take on the persona of the bourgeois or the bureaucrat—you needed instead the force of arms and a messianic language.

After Juárez, the image of saving the law in the name of the nation became a powerful way of claiming the presidency and shaping the presidential persona. During the Mexican Revolution, Madero revolted against Díaz in the name of the 1857 Constitution and was punctilious in setting himself up as a law-abiding citizen. Indeed, Madero combined the messianic image with that of the law provider in his "apostle of democracy" persona. Carranza's army called itself the Constitutionalist Army when it organized against the usurper Huerta; Villa and Zapata called themselves "Conventionalists" and claimed to be fighting Carranza out of respect for the resolutions of the Aguascalientes Convention. Finally, and perhaps most importantly, Mexico's dominant political party, established in 1929, saw itself as the institutionalized heir of the revolution, which was interpreted as the fount of national communitas, whose spirit was embodied in the Constitution of 1917. In each of these cases, including Juárez's, the nationalization of the law was a way to construct a viable presidential authority, even though the president's actual policies often had no more than a casual or after-the-fact relationship to the law.

MODERNIZATION AND PRESIDENTIAL FETISHISM

I have outlined two ways in which the president's persona was shaped: the messianic strategy and the indigenized-legalist strategy. These alternatives were developed in different moments, though both are components of contemporary Mexican "presidentialism." The messianic strategy was the first successful option because presidents had no way of feigning ideological consistency in the first half of the nineteenth century. The fetishization of the law occurred in conjunction with the consolidation of Mexico's position in the international system and as a result of the polarization of the country to a degree that only one party could conceivably emerge as victor.

The third and final strategy that I discuss concerns the nationalization of modernization. According to the historian Edmundo O'Gorman, referring to the early and mid-nineteenth century:

> We have two theses corresponding to two tendencies [the liberal and the conservative] which struggle against each other because of their respective aims and because they are founded in two different visions of the direction of history. However, these two theses end up postulating the same thing, to wit, they both wish to acquire the prosperity of the United States without abandoning traditional ways of being, because these are judged to be the very essence of the nation. Both currents want the benefits of modernity, but neither wants modernity itself. (O'Gorman 1977:33)

In other words, the contest for material and technological modernization was a high aim of the national struggle that was claimed by all factions, whereas cultural modernity was, in different ways, rejected. This tendency was clearly expressed at the turn of the twentieth century—when the contest between liberals and conservatives had been transcended—in *arielismo,* an ideology that took its name from an influential essay published in 1900 by the Uruguayan philosopher José Enrique Rodó. *Arielismo* posited the spiritual superiority of Latin America over the United States and envisioned modernizing the Latin American countries without absorbing the spiritual debasement created by the all-pervasive materialism of the United States.

Although Rodó's *Ariel* tied Latin spirituality to a Hellenic inheritance, the fundamental tenet of *arielismo* (greater spirituality that is nonetheless compatible with selective modernization) had multiple manifestations, some of which are present even today as *indigenismo* and nationalistic socialism. Taken at this level of generality, *arielismo* presupposed a certain cosmopolitanism and a high degree of education (at least at the level of the elites) combined with the maintenance of hierarchical and paternalistic relationships within the society. The cosmopolitanism and spiritual education of the elite was required, in fact, in order to guarantee a well-reasoned selection of modern implements and practices to import. In other words, *arielismo* was an ideology well adapted to the circumstances of Mexican political and intellectual elites from the end of the nineteenth century to the end of the era of import substitution (1982), because it cast Mexicans as consumers of modern products that retained an unaltered "spiritual" essence. This essence was embodied in specific, *unmodern* relations at the level of family organization, clientelism, corporate organization, and so forth.

Moreover, *arielismo, indigenismo,* and other avatars of this posture implicitly fostered a defensive cultural role for the state and its statesmen: to guard Latin societies against the base materialism of US society. Given this mediating position, the state was meant to be savvy about the consumption of modern products. Its knowledge was derived from the humanistic education of its leaders and the spirituality of communal relations in Latin America. This mediating position allowed the appropriation of modernization as part of the presidential manna. In short, the "white man's inventions" *(los inventos del hombre blanco)* became a third critical prop for creating a stable view of sovereignty and of presidential power.

For the early nineteenth century there are relatively few examples of this political usage of modernization by the presidential figure. One partial exception is the use of statistics, specifically those pertaining to deviations from the norm, to show that Mexico City was morally the equal of Paris, with lower percentages of prostitutes, higher educational levels, and other illusions.[8] Early imports were usually cultural rather than technological—Santa Anna's choice to build a theater as his most public work is an example. These cultural acquisitions, however, never had the nationalist power of the later technological imports.

The image of the state presiding over or introducing some major technological innovation or material benefit has been critical to the construction of the persona of the president since Porfirio Díaz's regime (1876–1910), when his introduction of the railroad did much to lend verisimilitude to his impersonation of Kaiser Wilhelm. More recent examples of the nationalization of modernization include the construction of the Mexico City subway under Díaz Ordaz (1964–70), the construction of the National University's modernist campus and of Acapulco under Miguel Alemán (1946–52), the development of Cuernavaca under Calles's hegemony (1929–34), the construction of the Panamerican Highway and the nationalization of the oil industry under Cárdenas (1934–40), and the electrification of the Mexican countryside under Echeverría (1970–76).

The identification of the president with modernization has at times been used against the more racialist images of the presidency as the embodiment of national law and of the nation's martyrs. This has especially been the case in times of great economic growth, when presidents usually show ideological eclecticism. The father of this eclectic style was Porfirio Díaz, who nonetheless concentrated in his persona much of the two earlier components of Mexican presidentialism (identity as racially Mexican and as war hero). Díaz's unparalleled personal success in combining all three strands of the presidential persona seems to have received divine sanction: the day of his namesake, San Porfirio, coincides with Mexican Independence Day, and so the births of the hero and the nation were celebrated on the same day.

This almost ideal overlap between a modernizing image (gained only by presiding over the country in a moment of economic growth) and an image of personal sacrifice and racial legitimacy has coincided only rarely since Díaz's time. To a degree, Alvaro Obregón (1920–24) had it: his pickled arm, which was blown off at the battle of Celaya, linked him to the earth, while his modernizing policies eventually gave him popularity with the United States and Mexico's industrial classes. Arguably, Lázaro Cárdenas (1934–40) also had a credible mix of these ingredients. After the Second World War, however, with peace in the land and sustained economic growth for several decades, the image of the modernizing president became increasingly significant.

Moreover, with the end of the policy of import substitution, variants of *arielismo* as an official ideology became increasingly untenable. Correspondingly, modernizing presidents since the 1982 debt crisis have gambled everything on a successful bid to be like the United States—materialism and all. As a result, the Mexican presidential image has suffered greatly, especially to the extent that presidents have failed in achieving the promised goal.

CONCLUSION

Although the idea of sovereignty was firmly entrenched in New Spain before independence, it became an elusive ideal afterward. The weakness of Mexico's position in the contest between imperial powers, along with its internal economic and cultural fragmentation, made the construction of a central power difficult. Straightforward identification between the state and society was impossible. Although the uncertainty of the state's claim to be the true instrument of popular sovereignty was felt most keenly in the periods 1821–67 and 1910–39, the cultural dynamics that were unleashed in these uncertainties have been relevant for the whole of Mexico's independent history.

The three strategies for constructing the presidential figure that I have discussed originated and culminated in different moments, though all three were routinized into the presidential office in the postrevolutionary era. Nonetheless, representing the nation internally while maintaining an adequate external façade has been a chronic difficulty. The importance of the nation's presentation to the external world, and the conflict between the state's needs in this regard and its connections to internal social groups, led to the invention of a state theatricality that was often divorced from the daily practice of state rule.

As a result of this structural problem, moments of governmental self-presentation before foreign powers have been vulnerable targets of public protest, such as those that occurred during Díaz's independence centennial celebrations in 1910, before the Olympic games in 1968, and on the day of the inauguration of the North American Free Trade Agreement (NAFTA) in 1994. Clashes between communitarian revivals of the ideal of sovereignty and stiff and self-serving international presentations of the state have often been understood by analysts as manifestations of what Turner (1974), in his classic essay on Hidalgo's revolt, called "primary process." These clashes were moments in which the original idea of sovereignty as a condition in which the Mexican nation would be free to construct its own destiny and to live in fraternal bliss has been revived. Nevertheless, these moments of communitarianism have always been betrayed because the popular and Catholic ideal of sovereignty has been a structural impossibility for Mexico. As a result, its history generates a characteristic combination of banality and passion, with long periods of modernizing innovation that are perceived, despite their novelty, as façade or farce, and short bursts of unrealizable communitarian nationalism that are perceived as manifestations of the true feelings of the nation. The martyrdom generated in these moments of primary process is subsequently harnessed and routinized by aspiring presidents and used as the blueprint with which to build a more stable political geography.

At the same time, the very strategy of constructing a national center by brokering modernity through the presidential office, and the strategies of nationalizing it through the cult of martyrs and the racialization of the law, is what has helped generate a national self-obsession. This obsession has been fostered to a large degree by the aspirations of liberals and conservatives, of *arielistas* and *indigenistas*, to modernize selectively and to attain the promised modernity within a national framework. *Arielista* cosmopolitanism, the cosmopolitanism of the statesman as the nation's official international taster, is at the heart of the preponderance of the nation as an intellectual object in Mexico. This cosmopolitanism, which sometimes conceives of itself as provincial, has forged sagas of national history that reach to the Aztecs or to the Spanish conquest for an understanding of the qualities and properties of the Mexican nation, but it is the state's constant need to assert its identity with the nation that generates this form of knowledge. The spent passions of national leaders and the mementos they leave behind form part of the inventory of this strained relationship.

Notes

1. Portions of this chapter are included in my forthcoming book, *Deep Mexico, Silent Mexico* (University of Minnesota Press, 2001).

2. The two principal documents written for the consumation of independence, the *Tratado de Córdoba* and the *Plán de Iguala,* both imagined Mexico as a republican monarchy.

3. See Delgado 1953, 2:192, for the views of the Spanish ambassador Angel Calderón de la Barca on these matters. Ambassador Poinsett, the first US ambassador to Mexico, arrived in the country saluting its independence and hailing the republic, which was "founded on the sovereignty of the people and on the inalienable rights of man" (cited in Delgado 1953, 1:303). He emphasized the identity between the two republics and conveniently omitted any reference to monarchical currents in Mexico.

4. This occurred to father Mariano Balleza, a kinsman of Hidalgo's (Villaseñor y Villaseñor 1962, 1:58).

5. For interesting comparative material on postcommunist use of dead heroes, see Verdery 1999.

6. Although Juárez seems to have mentioned his Indian origins only once in his writings, and that in writing to his children in his old age, he had an Indian body, and this made any profession of identity superfluous with regard to his ability to represent. For critical appraisals of Juárez's relationship to the law, see Escalante Gonzalbo 1992; Perry 1978; Weeks 1987.

7. It is worth noting that Juárez seems to have bent or broken the law often enough, and that others before him also often invoked and applied the law. What interests me here is Juárez's successful appropriation of the image of the president as a magistrate who used the law to save his people.

8. See Mayer Celis 1995. For an overview of the history of Mexican censuses, see Lomnitz 1999: ch. 10.

5

Appropriation/Appreciation

Settler Modernism in Australia and New Zealand

Nicholas Thomas

The effectiveness of material culture in political life derives in part from the sheer ambiguity of objects, which bear meanings but do not denote specific values. It is obvious that an artifact or work of art can possess different significances at the same time or over time. This essay is not intended to elaborate or demonstrate this general point but to explore the cultural politics of competing identifications in two related cases. In the antipodean settler colonies, anxieties around national identities have often been negotiated through art, and conversely, the value of art has often been adjudicated on the basis of its local authenticity and its adequacy as a vehicle for national distinctiveness. One of the most obvious routes to such national distinctiveness has been reference to, or appropriation of, elements of the indigenous art traditions of these colonial societies.

This chapter traces the debates around two antipodean modernists' uses of indigenous references. I argue that these appropriations were two-sided, because the artworks ambiguously validated the indigenous traditions from which they drew inspiration. Yet until recently, settler artists often saw their works as succeeding those of indigenous peoples: an evolutionary narrative was imagined that saw one authentically local tradition supplant another. Such an evolution was offered to viewers of the Carnegie Corporation's *Art of Australia* exhibition, which toured the United States in 1941. The show began with Aboriginal bark paintings and concluded with the Aboriginal-inspired work of the important mid-twentieth-century modernist Margaret Preston. The summary history of Australian art in the catalog made the message explicit:

> Finally, it has been left for Margaret Preston to strike the one original note in the development of a new outlook for Australian art. Already having made a name for her decorative painting of wild flowers, she has studied the work of the aboriginal artists all over Australia. She has combined her research and knowledge of their outlook and design with her sophisticated study of European art, and applied it very successfully to the rendering of Australian landscape. In carrying out this idea she has set herself the limitation of using only those colours which are to be found in the particular district which she paints. In this way she enters fully into the outlook of the aboriginal artists, who were limited in their portrayal of colours by the clays and pigments which were found in the various areas.
>
> The inclusion of her painting "Aboriginal Landscape" completes the cycle of this exhibition, which starts with the work of the aborigines, and ends with the influence of their work as the basis of a new outlook for a national art for Australia. (Anonymous 1941:28)

Some American critics must have been impressed, insofar as this line of argument was reproduced in reviews; but the most important feature of the story is that it was not at all persuasive to Preston's Australian audience. Although Preston's arguments for a national art were publicized widely through women's magazines and newspapers as well as through journals such as *Art in Australia,* her views were generally disregarded or disputed. Her work was celebrated despite rather than because of the engagement with Aboriginal forms that she advocated, and this for the most part remained the case after her death in 1963. Since the 1970s, a few commentators have credited her with being ahead of her time in taking an interest in indigenous art, but her paintings and prints that feature Aboriginal references are now marginal in comparison with her enormously popular flower works and views of Sydney Harbor. Margaret Preston is certainly appreciated today for the distinctively Australian qualities of her art, but the national appeal that her work now possesses is not at all the same as the appeal she herself made for it.

MONUMENTAL FLOWERS

Preston's work developed rapidly and entailed many shifts in direction, but it is not my purpose to chart them here (see Butel 1985; Butler 1987; North 1980). Suffice it to say that back in Australia during the early 1920s, after seven years in Europe, she became committed to the notion that the way forward lay in a national art—one that was formed by its environment and that drew something from indigenous traditions. She published a number of essays arguing for the "application" of Aboriginal art in craft and decorative art, but she apparently did not draw from indigenous forms in her own paintings and prints until 1940. Her work from the twenties and thirties is in fact diverse and includes many urban and suburban Sydney views, but it is dominated by images of Australian flowers and birds.

The best of her woodblock prints, such as *West Australian Banksia* (c. 1929) and *Australian Rock Lily* (c. 1933) (fig. 5.1), possess a kind of self-sufficiency and distance from discourse that is shared by decorative art and still life, among other cultural forms. It is certainly possible to talk about her works in art-historical terms, citing the influence on them of Japanese printmaking, or their Cezanne-ish shallowness, but such commentary seems at once to say too little and too much. Like any other artist, Preston responded to a host of stimuli, but to trace these is to neglect the solid presences that she so consummately evoked.

A newspaper critic suggested in 1927 that Preston's still lifes were "almost monumental in form" (*Daily Telegraph*, 9 September 1927). The comment draws attention to an apparent paradox. For the idea of national art is not easily reconciled with diminutive and decorative works, which have more obvious affiliations with craft and design than with the landscapes and history paintings that are the more conventional vehicles for the expression of national spirit and historical

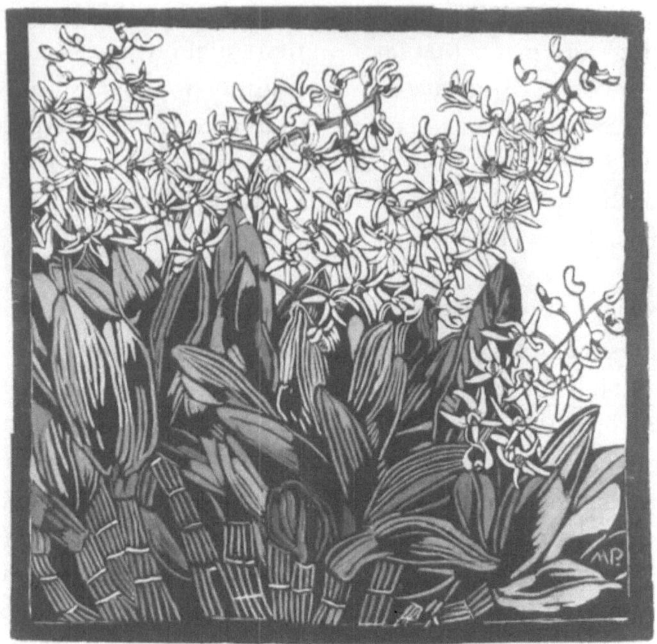

FIGURE 5.1

Margaret Preston, Australian Rock Lily, *ca. 1933, hand-colored woodcut, 45 by 45 cm, Art Gallery of New South Wales, Sydney.*

purpose. Whereas the latter are saturated with overt meaning and are almost measurable in yards rather than inches, Preston's banksias and desert peas seem attractive and domestic rather than moralizing and national.

To respond in this way, however, would miss the relation that Preston imagined between the home and the nation. Her claim that "the beginning should come from the home and domestic arts" and her hope that "the craftsman will succeed where, until now, the artist has certainly failed" warrant our attention (Preston 1925:n.p.). It is not anachronistic to understand Preston as a feminist, but my interest in her affirmation of domestic cultural expression arises more specifically from the way both her polemic and her practice broadly anticipated the recent arguments that inform this book. These arguments acknowledge that while social theory has generally been preoccupied with ideology and language, material objects are no less significant for the formation of personal and collective identities (Appadurai 1986; Miller 1987; Thomas 1991; Weiner 1992).

Acquiring ordinary things, dressing in a certain mode, and decorating one's home in a particular style are expressive activities that variously convey attachments to local and cosmopolitan values, religious and political affiliations, and class, ethnic, and subcultural solidarities. Further, as Preston asserted, the domestic practice and application of craft and design may anticipate rather than merely express developments in high art, among other cultural domains. If we eschew her preoccupation with progress toward the realization of national cultural distinctness, we can nevertheless gain something from exploring the implications of the obvious point that "domestic arts," understood broadly, are arts of self-fashioning.

The woodcut *West Australian Banksia* depicts the native flower in a fairly severe modernist vase. The accomplishment of the print rests in part on the fact that the solid black cylinder at once echoes the bulk and form of the banksia while contrasting with its provoking and highly textured irregularities. Yet the vase is not there just for these compositional reasons, nor because Preston happened to own at least a couple of this kind. The container does make it explicit that these flowers are displayed, presumably at home, and thus sets the work apart from a project of botanical illustration. But the domestic aesthetic that is presented is not just any domestic aesthetic. As I mentioned earlier, Preston campaigned against what she called "South Kensington dullness" and insisted on the need for forms that were shaped by the land and by the environment, which she understood in a national rather than a peculiarly local sense. Her insistence upon the importance of decoration contradicted the enduring idea that it meant mere adornment and feminine prettiness. For this artist, decoration was like architecture; it was culturally expressive, and it needed to be appropriate to epoch and place. Her friend and sometime pupil Gladys Reynell's vase was suitable to an Australian living room both for its creative expression of the spirit of its own time and for its particular (though presumably fortuitous) formal correspondence with the weight and substance of the banksia cone (cf. Butler 1987:8–12, 149).

From this perspective, Preston's flower works are not decorative in any belittling sense. They can be seen, rather, to possess an argumentative dynamism in insisting on the significance of the subjects depicted instead of merely recording them, deliberately elevating certain subjects through representation in art. What the works described and insisted upon was the presence of an Australian flora. Preston gave these flowers new meaning simply by drawing attention to their presence. The masculine project of national myth making via the evocation of awesome and remote topography always suffered the paradox of cultivating human attachment to dehumanized landforms. If the enduring appeal of the domesticating, periurban landscape painting, such as that associated with Australian impressionism, arises in part from the suppression of distance, from the painters' aestheticization of familiar bush and beach, then Preston literally brought the bush right into the living room and into the domestic routine of unheroic self-fashioning. This was not the validation of a pioneer myth but an affirmation of domestic practices that were true to their antipodean environment.

There appear to be inconsistencies, if not contradictions, between Preston's statements about floral imagery and her extensive use of it. For example, she made disparaging observations about the pervasiveness of gum leaves, wattle blossoms, and kookaburras in design (quoted in Thomas 1999:116). These, she suggested, needed to be repudiated in favor of Aboriginal forms. Yet her own art in the years immediately following her most polemical statement along these lines was dominated by Australian wildflowers and birds, including kookaburras. It might be added that earlier designers such as Eirene Mort, whose imitators Preston would primarily have been reacting against, had dignified their twiddling with gum leaves and wattle through recourse to the importance of a national approach to decorative art. They broadly anticipated, in other words, the terms of Preston's arguments as well as the subject matter she actually used, as opposed to the Aboriginal references she advocated but seldom employed in the period between 1924 and 1940.

In part, Preston was conflating issues of national authenticity with those of artistic style and modernity. It was presumably not the gum leaves and kookaburras themselves that she objected to, but certain ways of handling them that seemed traditional and deadeningly realistic. Her work speaks the modernist preoccupation with form more loudly than that of most of her Australian contemporaries. But she did more than replace one approach to representation and decoration with another. Her engagement with the flowers, which she depicted as forms rather than as sprays of color or ornamental motifs, effectively presented them, as the 1927 critic noted, in a "monumental" fashion. A monument is a public edifice that marks historical fact and encourages quasi-religious contemplation. The connection could easily be strained: of course Preston's woodblocks do not make deliberate or specific historical references, they are not allegorical, and they are not excessively grave—though they are mostly serious rather than pretty or cheerful. But the prints do present the flowers as aesthetically compelling objects. As a set of works, they also display an array of *Australian* flowers: nationality seems to be not only an artifact of human histories and political relations but also a property of the environment, which in turn is understood to shape human types in particular countries.

So these works do more than simply connect Australian natural forms with the business of home- and self-making, with mundane aesthetics. A personal response to certain flowers, or the practice of displaying them, has little weight unless the sentiment or the activity is somehow validated and given public meaning—as other activities, such as football or cricket, may be dignified through their connection with patriotic competition. It is not always true that art affirms the subjects and relations that it depicts, but Preston's art can certainly be seen to validate and bestow meaning upon the use of nationally distinctive flowers in the arts of the home.

FUSION OR COMBINATION?

In the 1930s and 1940s, Preston's arguments at once complemented and differed from those of a number of literary nationalists. They felt generally that Australian culture had been stifled by its British inheritance and that an engagement with the Australian environment was essential if anything distinctive and vital was to emerge. There were, however, significant variations in emphasis. P. R. Stephenson, for instance, in his *Foundations of Culture in Australia*, referred to indigenous people only in passing, noting their irrelevance to the emergence of a "new nation" and "a new human type" in Australia (1936:11–12). In contrast, the Jindyworobak group of poets declared an interest in

Aboriginal spirituality—though, as Humphrey McQueen pointed out (1979:126–29), the movement's label exaggerated the extent to which indigenous culture, rather than the desert wilderness and related images, was actually exploited in their work.

In 1940, Preston's interest in Aboriginal art became dramatically more evident in her own work. During the 1940s, in any event, she was to participate in the field trips of the Anthropological Society of New South Wales to examine the rock engravings around Sydney; she also later traveled through central and northern Australia visiting Aboriginal communities and especially galleries of rock art. She drew upon Aboriginal art in a number of quite distinct ways: by working with ochre-like colors, by quoting the patterns of shields and carved trees, by emulating what she took to be indigenous compositional principles, by illustrating Aboriginal legends, by presenting biblical subjects in Aboriginal settings, and by reproducing rock art fairly directly.

Her most successful "Aboriginal" works surely include the landscapes deriving from the earliest phase of this experiment, such as her 1941 *Aboriginal Landscape.* It is worth raising the question of what the adjective "Aboriginal" here actually refers to. It hardly suggests that the generic tract of country depicted was inhabited or owned by Aboriginal people. Although just one late work must be seen as a harsh comment on the Australian government's neglect of the indigenous population, it cannot be said that Preston generally displayed much interest in the history of settler-indigenous relations. Her national concerns were forward looking rather than retrospective, and though by 1941 she certainly celebrated Aboriginal art for itself as well as for its uses in a new Australian culture, she was not concerned to expose the history of dispossession or remind viewers of the fact that the country had once been owned by Aborigines. An anachronistic reading of *Aboriginal Landscape* could take it to affirm the Aboriginality of the country, but Preston's admittedly cursory remarks on color and related matters point to a more circuitous association. The pigments employed in Aboriginal art reflected those of the land because they were derived directly from it. More generally, theirs was an "aesthetic form that is of our land," which accordingly pointed the way for a "modern" artist who wanted to grasp the truth of the environment (Preston 1949:11): the grey and ochre palette furthered that aim. It may perforce have

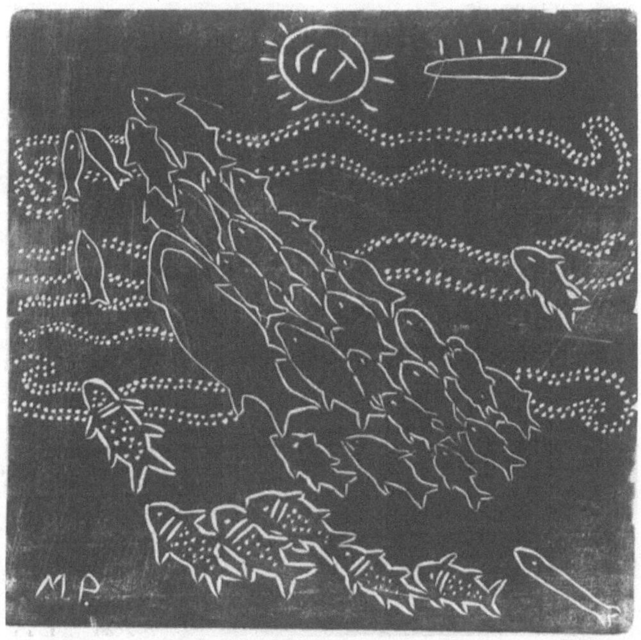

FIGURE 5.2

Margaret Preston, Fish, Aboriginal Design, *1940, woodblock print, 34.6 by 34.8 cm, National Gallery of Australia, Canberra.*

acknowledged an Aboriginal presence, but it was not part of an artistic statement that emphasized or foregrounded one.

If this is apt as an interpretation of these particular works, Preston was at other times more concerned to display elements of Aboriginal culture. Some works, such as the 1940 woodblock print *Fish* (fig. 5.2) and the 1946 monotype of the same title, can be seen essentially as illustrations of Aboriginal art forms, and a later series depicted incidents derived from legends. Where she provided captions or comments on works, she often made it explicit that she took the Aboriginal element to provide a direct route to national distinctness. In *Aboriginal Still Life* (1946), she aimed "to create a still life that would owe its existence to this country, and not to Holland or any other nationality" (Preston 1949: caption to pl. 5). This overriding purpose required little engagement with Aboriginal people or culture, though Preston's appreciation of Aboriginal art deepened during the 1940s, and she became

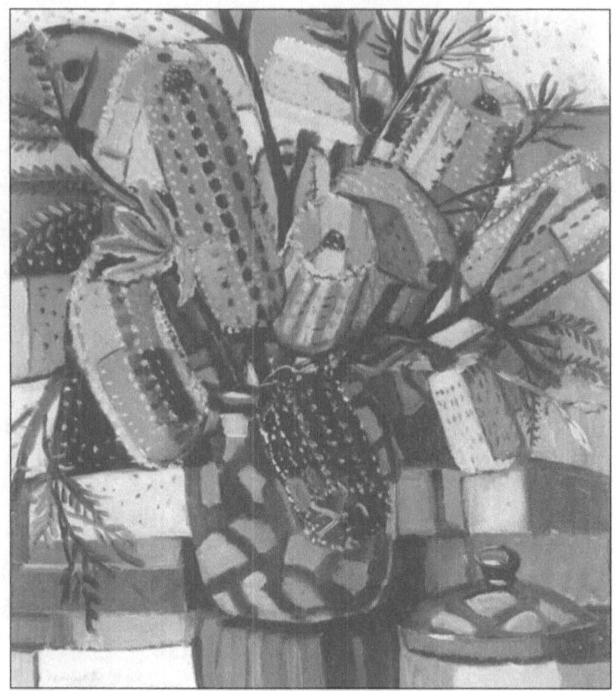

FIGURE 5.3
Margaret Preston, The Brown Pot, *1940, oil on canvas, 51 by 45.8 cm, Art Gallery of New South Wales, Sydney.*

concerned to challenge widespread misapprehensions such as the idea that there were essential affinities between "primitive art" and children's art. Not being really a painter of people or a social realist, she never depicted the living conditions that she must have witnessed during her travels in central and north Australia. It was left to communist painters such as Yosl Bergner and Noel Counihan to image the marginalization and impoverishment of the Aboriginal people.

Preston's "Aboriginal" corpus is too diverse to be dismissed for merely seizing upon indigenous reference as a shortcut to national distinctness, despite the simplistic character of some of her own statements to that effect. The Aboriginal landscapes of 1941–42 are predated by *The Brown Pot* (fig. 5.3), a somewhat more radical painting that places the familiar banksias on an essentially abstract background clearly divided into bars and fields of white and ochre browns. The pattern recalls north Queensland shields of the kind Preston would have seen in the Australian Museum, and one in particular that she had discussed in her 1930 article, "The Application of Aboriginal Designs." A similar combination—a bowl of flowers against an indigenous pattern—appeared in the 1943 masonite print *Aboriginal Design, with Sturt's Pea,* which reordered the elements of an Arnhem Land bark. The same general principle, with varying emphasis, featured in a number of other works.

The interest of these works lies in the fact that cultural combination appears as a formal problem. In this respect, they differ from most of the classic modernist appropriations of tribal forms, and this difference is closely linked to a significant contrast between the logic of primitivism in general and the special mission of settler primitivism. In the best-known works of Picasso and others, and in the great majority of the works reproduced in the Museum of Modern Art's compendious catalog *"Primitivism" in Twentieth-Century Art* (Rubin, ed., 1984), tribal forms are assimilated into new compositions, not introduced as separate motifs that are marked off from the rest of the work. Whereas the European modernists used whichever "primitive" elements interested them, without regard to their particular ethnic origins, Preston was concerned specifically to draw on Aboriginal art, and in these works she juxtaposed the indigenous elements with other, avowedly modern ones. As she noted with respect to a 1946 monotype based on the masonite cut I just referred to, "the flowers are the creation of a twentieth-century artist, while the bowl and background belong to a primitive aboriginal art" (Preston 1949:15, caption to pl. 16).

The larger trend of Preston's writing suggests that she may have intended a simple synthesis of the "modern" and the "primitive" elements in these compositions, and this synthesis would have exemplified the indigenized white Australian culture that she so frequently advocated. The effect of her works, however, is rather to make the fact of difference explicit. They lay bare the contrivance of synthesis and give the viewer the option of regarding it as awkward or impossible. In juxtaposing genres of Aboriginal art with practices that may have been Asian influenced but that still belonged firmly to Western art traditions, Preston presented combination rather than fusion, a possibility rather than an accomplishment, a problem rather than a solution.

STUBBORN ABORIGINAL TERRITORY

Over the last 20 years, Margaret Preston has been praised by a number of writers for her forward-looking appreciation of Aboriginal art. At the same time, her Aboriginal-influenced works have received far less exposure than her wildflowers and birds. Certainly there is some embarrassment among those otherwise inclined to celebrate the artist's accomplishment. In 1985, Elizabeth Butel acknowledged that "many of her statements about 'applying' Aboriginal art come down to us today with an unpleasant clang" (1985:53). Surprisingly, though, Preston's use of indigenous material has been subjected to only one powerful critique, in a brief but important essay by Ann Stephen (1980). Reacting particularly against McQueen's effort to equate Preston's work with Australian modernism, Stephen emphasized the marginality of modernism in the period and the compatibility of Preston's landscapes with conservative affirmations of national strength and nobility. In a section entitled "Modernism goes hand-in-hand with racism," she drew attention to the crudity of the artist's early writing on the "application" of indigenous art but found Preston's later position problematic in a different though perhaps more fundamental way. Preston "assumed that she was able to transcend cultural differences; and that her values were not in direct opposition to and complicitly involved in the destruction of aboriginal culture" (Stephen 1980:14–15).

If we had to choose between these positive and negative adjudications of Preston's work, we could attempt to theorize the practice of appropriation and measure the extent to which cross-cultural borrowings are to be construed as legitimate exchange, productive mutual acknowledgment, or the robbing of colonized peoples by exploitative European and settler cultures. But the political meanings of appropriations are not susceptible to such generalized measuring. Although I agree with Stephen that McQueen's presentation of Preston as an oppositional artist is unconvincing, the general statement that she was complicit in ongoing colonization is inadequate, too. If appropriations do have a general character, it is surely that of unstable duality. In some proportion, they always combine taking and acknowledgment, appropriation and homage, a critique of colonial exclusions and collusion in imbalanced exchange. What the problem therefore demands is not an endorsement or rejection of primitivism in principle but an exploration of how particular works were motivated and assessed. Hence I am concerned with the way Preston's efforts were received in the 1940s.

It is notable that with a few exceptions, her Aboriginal works had a bad press. In 1942, the influential news magazine and review, the *Bulletin,* set the tone, crediting Preston with an "infallible color sense" and finding some her works "strikingly beautiful." But: "Her latter-day experiments with the Australian abo.'s idiom, however, are more interesting than aesthetically fruitful" (*Bulletin,* 1 April 1942). Seven years later, the same magazine featured a more extensive critique of the fairly lavish Ure Smith publication *Margaret Preston's Monotypes:*

> In the aboriginal paintings Margaret Preston is exploring stubborn and dangerous territory. Where...the Aboriginal motives are used purely to make a decorative pattern, the effect is pleasing. But where, as in the crudely symbolic trees of "Bimbowrie Landscape," which might have been drawn by a child with its thumb, or in "Drought, Mirage Country," with its kangaroos that look like a cross between a fox-terrier and a rocking horse, the pictures are meant to be something more than decoration, they fail.
>
> It is impossible to respond to them with that instantaneous delight which a work of art evokes, for the interest is focussed on the crudity of the technique; and they are at best curiosities....
>
> She is allowing the aboriginals—a people, as she admits herself, too limited in sensibility and technical capacity to have attempted to paint the wildflowers—to debilitate her talent; but what is really required is the opposite process—the enrichment of primitive art by the infinitely greater technical and spiritual resources of the civilized artist. (*Bulletin,* 17 August 1949)

The writer here ignored Preston's attempt, in the text reviewed, to dismiss the notion that "primitive" art was either childlike or crude. His response is predictable, but it is significant for its direct contradiction of Preston's claim that something might be gained from the study of Aboriginal art. Given that Preston's body of Aboriginal-influenced work aspired to exemplify a national culture but was for the most part greeted with indifference or hostility, it was surely more at odds with the culture of the period than "complicit" in the wider destructive colonization of Aboriginal societies.

This political situation, of being at odds with a dominant racism, is less easy to assess than overt affirmation or resistance to that ideology. As I have already noted, Preston did not explicitly criticize the wider marginalization of the Aboriginal population, though she did positively promote Aboriginal art through her writing and through involvement in a major UNESCO exhibition. What may have been most important, though, was not the political statement she made or failed to make, but the effect of her work. In a book on Australian art published in the same year as the *Bulletin* review I just quoted, the critic and painter Herbert Badham applauded Preston's "colourful and delightfully fresh flower pieces" but found that her adaptations of Aboriginal motifs amounted to "derivation *in extremis*": "There is undeniable refreshment in judicious use of this aspect of primitive culture, but it can, in all reasonable truth, hold but fragments of its pristine intention—fragments which may, through repetition and function moulded by an alien setting, bore to insufferable tears" (Badham 1949:79–80).

Like the *Bulletin,* Badham found that the work failed. In his judgment, though, this was not because of the crudity of the source material but because the adaptation that Preston attempted was inherently problematical. Badham implied that Western and indigenous art systems were incommensurable. Borrowings on the part of Western artists must reduce the "primitive" culture quoted to fragments that were profoundly distorted in the "alien setting" that was unavoidably imposed. Yet Badham proceeded to suggest that the art might have unintended value: "It is in this connection that Margaret Preston's work is important. Although she has chosen the part of one convention, her pictures themselves draw us irresistibly to an element in art formerly ignored as unworthy of the white man's attentions, an element which embraces the dawning spirit of humankind, and holds it aloof from the soiling touches of modernity" (1949:80).

This is prescient. The effects of Preston's work at once fell short of and went beyond her intentions. If Badham's response is anything to go by, the very awkwardness of some of her Aboriginal compositions drew attention to the indigenous art forms that seemed unsatisfactorily translated. Just as the 1941 exhibition at the Australian Museum inadvertently revealed the strength of the indigenous aesthetic forms that were introduced only in order to display their potential "applications," so Preston's work deflected the attention of her viewers. They might be drawn not toward her grand notion of a national culture but "irresistibly" toward the neglected indigenous art traditions themselves. Those traditions pointed in turn toward the indigenous presence, spotlighting a stubborn and enduring obstacle to the idea of settler nationhood.

RECONTEXTUALIZATIONS

Preston's prints and paintings were never quite comfortable with the rhetoric in which she captioned them. In the case of the New Zealand artist Gordon Walters (1919–1995), there is a still more complex succession of tensions between the works and the ways they have been contextualized, more by a series of advocates than by the artist himself. Indeed, the history of commentary around Walters provides an intriguing case of art-world myth making. Though his hard-edge optical abstract work is wholly unlike Preston's work stylistically, it raises many parallel issues concerning not only the specific character of artistic primitivism in settler societies but also the relations between high art, design, and national culture.

The hallmark of Walters's work has been a formalized version of the *koru* stem-bulb form abstracted from curvilinear Maori designs that featured on engraved gourds, in facial tattoos, and in painting on canoes, paddles, and houses, particularly on the rafters of the famous Maori meetinghouses. In the 1980s and 1990s, it was a sign of the times that the artist's use of an indigenous motif should have become highly contentious. Oddly enough, the problem of appropriation was initially acknowledged by one of Walters's supporters in 1983 (Bell 1983). It was not until 1986 that a Maori critic, Ngahuia Te Awekotuku, condemned the artist's "repeated and consistent and irrefutable exploitation and *colonizing* of that symbol" (Te Awekotuku 1986).

These remarks provoked less reaction than those of a younger curator and commentator, Rangihiroa Panoho. In a 1992 essay in the catalog of the *Headlands* exhibition, a major survey of New Zealand art at Sydney's Museum of Contemporary Art, he argued that Walters's work formalized the *koru*, leaving behind its spiritual associations. Though his harshest observation, that the *koru* works entailed a "residual colonialism," seems more moderate than Te Awekotuku's charges, Panoho's criticism provoked an extraordinary backlash that highlighted the extent to which an international touring exhibition was understood as an exercise in cultural diplomacy. The show was seen as a context in which New Zealand art ought to have been affirmed, not questioned, least of all in the exhibition catalog itself. Walters reportedly said that he felt as if he had gone out to fight for his country, only to be shot in the back. Though there was much angry correspondence and comment in reviews, the debate gave Walters's work new prominence and boosted the prices it realized at auction. Subsequently, the Auckland City Art Gallery staged a major retrospective by way of vindication, and one critic, Francis Pound, devoted a book, *The Space Between* (1994), to refuting Panoho's few pages.

Pound had earlier argued that art criticism in New Zealand had been dominated by nationalist thinking that had celebrated landscape painting to the exclusion of modernist abstraction. The most advanced artists—abstractionists such as Walters and Milan Mrkusich—were consequently marginalized. An "embattled minority of...fully abstract painters [was] condemned during the Nationalist time to relative silence and invisibility, or subjected to pejorative critical remarks" (Pound 1992:187). Walters, in particular, had rigorously pursued his own vision in isolation, unrewarded by public recognition. Yet during the 1970s and 1980s the attitudes of an enlightened minority gained wider acceptance. A "postnationalist" countercanon emerged in which Walters and others were finally given their due. The appropriation debate, however, raised new and quite different concerns about Walters's work. What had previously been celebrated for its apparent counternationalism now seemed caught up in a peculiarly national primitivism. Here, my claim is that Walters's use of indigenous reference was not antagonistic to wider trends in antipodean settler culture. Rather, it resonated with them, though without ever being quite the same in its intentions or effects.

WHAT TO PAINT IN NEW ZEALAND

Gordon Walters became interested in European modernism—in Tanguy, Klee, and Miro, among others—in the 1940s. During the same period he was encouraged in his interest in Maori art by Theo Schoon, a Dutch-born Indonesian artist then engaged in documenting South Island rock carvings, who was later to study and revive the traditional Maori incised gourd. Yet according to Walters's own later accounts of his development, it was only when he visited Europe in the early 1950s that he gained a sense of what direction his art should take. "I saw the use that some French abstractionists circa 1950 were making of Pacific Art. The penny dropped. This was one way out of the dilemma of what to paint in NZ. I was elated with this discovery, but between the insight/inspiration and the realization of the idea was a huge gap" (Walters n.d.).

In the mid- to late fifties, Walters produced a number of studies based on Marquesan forms; though he would go back to these from time to time over the years, it was Maori art rather than "Pacific art" in general that became his most conspicuous point of reference. He began experimenting with the *koru* in 1956, but it was not until the mid-1960s that he was satisfied with the results. The early works retained curvilinear forms, whereas he later worked toward a harder geometric adaptation of the motif, influenced by the op art of Vasarely and Bridget Riley. The first fully realized *koru* paintings, such as *Te Whiti* (1964) and *Painting No. 1* (1965) (fig. 5.4), led to several series over 20 years in which the scale, organization, and density of the bulb forms were varied. Though Walters also worked with a number of other geometric elements, it was the *koru* that he explored most extensively and that became his signature. Some of his paintings, including the very fine *Aranui*, used colors other than black and white, but these seem in retrospect almost departures from the core of Walters's project. That effort centered upon the manipulation of binary relations, relations that were most effectively foregrounded by the formal opposition of black and white.

That Walters did not exhibit the *koru* works until 1966 is frequently adduced in discussions of his supposed marginalization, but it is plain that his own rigor, indeed perfectionism, held him back. It is not clear that there was as much hostility to abstract painting in New Zealand as has been maintained, but in any event his work received almost immediate critical acclaim and institutional recognition. He was included in survey exhibitions at the Auckland City Art Gallery in 1966 and 1967, and some of his work was sent to a group show at a dealer gallery in

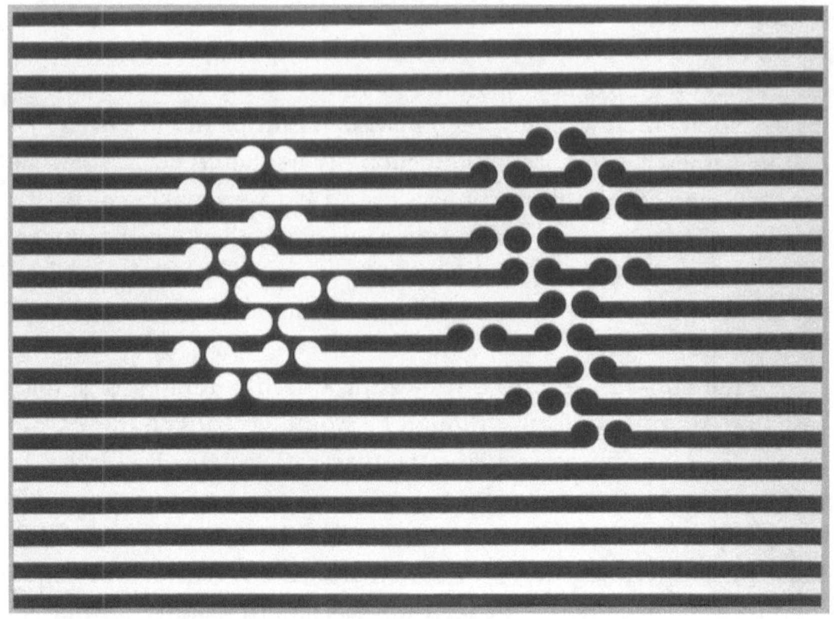

FIGURE 5.4

Gordon Walters, Painting No. 1, *1965, PVA on hardboard, 114 by 154 cm, Auckland Art Gallery Toi o Tamaki. © Gordon Walters Estate.*

Sydney in 1968. The paintings attracted generally favorable local reviews and brief but positive comments in international periodicals. One of the leading critics, Hamish Keith, suggested as early as 1970 that it was time for a retrospective; the artist, apparently concerned about potential damage to the work in the course of a tour, turned down a proposal in the mid-seventies, but the Auckland City Art Gallery eventually mounted such a show in 1983. Walters received an Arts Council Fellowship in 1971, and subsequently other government grants, and he was appointed visiting senior lecturer in painting at Auckland's Elam art school in 1972. To be sure, he was by this time in his early fifties, but he had nevertheless moved fairly quickly and smoothly from the situation of a nonexhibiting artist to that of an established figure. The cultural history of his art needs to work from the fact that these paintings were successful, not from the claim that they were ignored.

Yet the terms in which they were successful are contradictory. One of Walters's early advocates, the critic and dealer Petar Vuletic, was

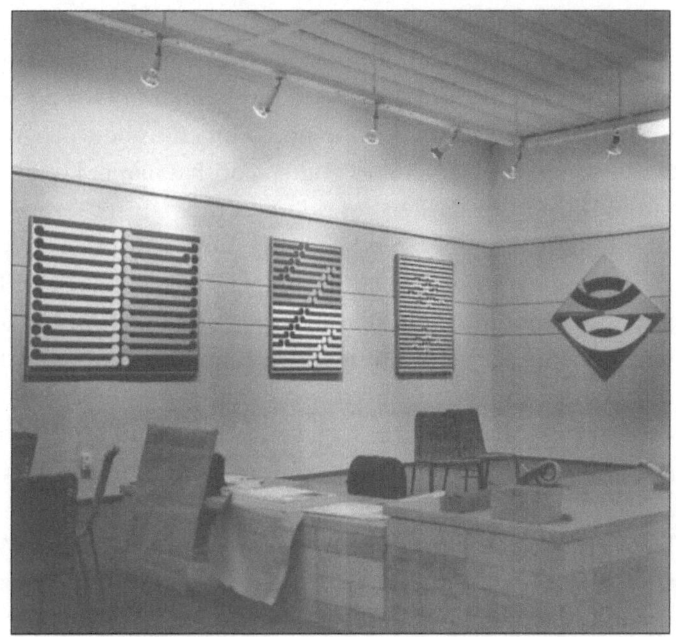

FIGURE 5.5
New Vision Gallery, 1968, displaying works by Gordon Walters. Courtesy Auckland Art Gallery Toi o Tamaki.

vehemently antinationalistic. He championed Walters's work for its affinities with hard-edge American abstraction, and Walters's own statements in commentary seem to sustain this reading. The dealer's brochure for his 1966 and 1968 shows (fig. 5.5) quoted him: "My work is an investigation of positive/negative relationships within a deliberately limited range of forms. The forms I use have no descriptive value in themselves and are used solely to demonstrate relations.

Some critics initially read the work in these purely formal terms, and a Maori woman was prompted to write to the *New Zealand Herald* (10 June 1968) in response to one such review, pointing out that the stripe ending in a circle was "the traditional Maori koru motif." Yet if attention needed to be drawn to the indigenous reference in one context, Walters had used Maori titles such as *Te Whiti* since 1964. Though many works were untitled or simply numbered, by the early 1970s his paintings carried Maori words more often than not. In some cases, the works were actually titled by Walters's Wellington dealer,

Peter McLeavey; in 1971, he opted for well-known Maori terms such as *Karakia* (prayer) and *Waiata* (lament). These and similar titles have been extensively debated. Whereas Te Awekotuku (1986) pointed out scornfully that there seemed to be no connection between Walters's cool *Mahuika* and the fiery Maori goddess of that name, Pound (1994) drew attention to the similarities between the painter's approach to titles and that of the American hard-edge abstractionist Frank Stella. Stella's titles referred to jazz clubs, places in Colorado, and Islamic cities; they were not intended to evoke specific references but to point "in the general direction of the Islamic, in homage to a powerful predecessor." In the same way, Walters's titles did not imply that particular gods or historical Maori figures such as Te Whiti were represented but instead alluded to the Maori in a more generalized way (Pound 1994:110).

The further point that has frequently been made in Walters's defense is that many of the Maori names he employed were actually Wellington street names, from the neighborhood in which he grew up. "These names had a strong emotional significance for me," he said. "By using them to title my works I was able both to pay tribute to the Maori tradition, which has meant a great deal to me, and to re-interpret it in terms of my own art and my immediate environment" (quoted in Dunn 1983:125).

Pound therefore proposed that Maoris concerned about appropriation, such as Te Awekotuku, might take their complaints to the Wellington City Council rather than to Walters. What this glib suggestion points to, however, is the extent to which Walters's work is tied up with the cultural geography of New Zealand cities. These are settler places that draw commemorations of empire (Queen Street, Khyber Pass) and indigenous names uneasily together. The significance of these place names in Walters's biography marks the distinctness of his art from the northern hemisphere artwork that it formally resembles. Unlike Stella, Walters did not use series of titles referring variously to bars, streets, towns, and exotic places. He opted either for untitled neutrality or consistently for Maori allusions.

It is the consistency of this reference that is crucial. Along with many European and American modernists, Walters was informed about a variety of indigenous art traditions, as was Margaret Preston in

Australia. Like Preston, however, he foregrounded the indigenous art of his own country and declared its local specificity. Unlike her, of course, he never vaunted such reference as the basis for a national culture, and his personal style was entirely different—he promoted his own work far more discreetly and did not seek the stature of a cultural commentator, as she did. But his lack of engagement with nationalist rhetoric ought not to disguise the fact that his work constituted an answer to the problem of "what to paint in New Zealand." Although the trend toward interpreting his work in national terms developed during the seventies, he had put it in these terms himself in a 1968 interview:

> It was during this period [while living overseas] that I was able to see myself for the first time as a New Zealander and began to come to terms with the implications of this. I never much liked the idea of being a New Zealand painter, I just wanted to be a good painter and the more I saw of European and American painting the more the provincial nature of most New Zealand painting became clear to me. At the same time it was only by coming to terms with my being a New Zealander that I could go on to paint. (Walters 1969)

Here the artist defers reluctantly to nationality. Not nationalism: one may be unenthusiastic about patriotism or preoccupations with building a national culture, but it seems that one must nevertheless acknowledge the formative significance of place, or particular background, upon one's cultural expression. And it is strangely axiomatic that this means nationality. Walters might conceivably have aimed to ground his art in forms derived from his local environment or from the antipodean Pacific in a wider sense. Indeed, in some ways he did both of these things, by referring often to Wellington street names and by drawing upon non-Maori "Pacific art" forms. Yet what was foregrounded is consistent with "being a New Zealander," a generalized and encompassing native and/or national reference.

Walters's account of his work in these terms would be less important had it not been taken up by his audience. Though journalists initially stressed the work's op-art interest, its national distinctiveness was increasingly cited—most significantly, perhaps, by those outside the art world, who were less concerned to commend Walters's internationalism.

There is some irony in the comparison with Preston. Whereas Australians were generally unconvinced that her indigenous works laid the foundation for a national culture, Walters was said to have succeeded in doing exactly that, though he had "never much liked the idea of being a New Zealand painter." "I believe that you have essentially solved the problem of representing New Zealand's identity," a corporate designer wrote to the painter in 1983 (Walters n.d.). By this time the observation that Walters had successfully fused the country's Polynesian and European cultures was becoming commonplace.

"HIGH" ART AND COMMERCIAL APPROPRIATION

New Zealand art historians have generally dissociated Walters's art from the widespread use of indigenous motifs in settler design, often by simply ignoring the latter phenomenon altogether or by asserting that the *koru* became widespread only during the 1980s. It is true that its use in logos proliferated in that period, but indigenous motifs and patterns were extensively drawn upon earlier and were ubiquitous on the banknotes that New Zealanders carried around until the introduction of decimal currency in 1967. Leonard Bell raised the question of whether this kind of quotation amounted to "pernicious neo-colonisation," but he proceeded to say only that "no doubt sometimes it is, other times not" (Bell 1989:16). Even if we are to find in the end that indigenous references are diverse and typically contradictory in their effects, surely we are stopping at the point where we need to start.

It has been fairly pointed out that Walters drew attention to Maori art and treated it as art, as Preston had done for Aboriginal work, during a time when attitudes toward indigenous culture were generally disparaging. As in Preston's case, the accomplishment can equally be read negatively, as entailing the assimilation of indigenous culture to settler nationalism. If Walters was claiming a right to define antipodean nationality on the basis of an indigenized modernism, he was doing so only implicitly, and it seems unfair to find him culpable on the grounds of his own technical brilliance. But the fact that his art is visually authoritative enables the wider conclusion that his works (and not those of any Maori) "solve the problem" of New Zealand's identity.

This reading of Walters's work—a result of its canonization, not of the painter's own practice—is not too remote from the assumptions of those advocating the "application" of Aboriginal designs in Australia in the 1940s: they, too, imagined that national culture, though drawing on Aboriginal art, would be produced by and for whites. Their rhetoric failed because the work itself was weak and deflected attention onto the indigenous source materials themselves. The case of Walters's art is, like that of Preston's, more complicated. This is so in part because there were multiple connections between his art and the business of signifying the nation. The paintings were bought by the Foreign Affairs department for display in New Zealand embassies, and they were used in New Zealand corporate collections in a similar way. They have been reproduced on book covers and were rendered central in an education department teaching kit, *Emblems of Identity* (1987). More importantly, Walters himself worked in commercial design, producing at one time a logo for the National Library with what he called "a discreetly New Zealand emphasis," and at another, devices for the New Zealand Film Commission that were based more directly on the *koru* paintings (fig. 5.6). The widespread commercial use of *koru*-based designs from the 1980s onward owes a good deal to Walters. One of the most visible logos, that of Air New Zealand, features a straightened, simplified version of the motif, and it is hard to believe that this was not stimulated directly by Walters's work. Ironically, given the appropriation debate, the most widely used travel guide to New Zealand has, in every reprint since it was first published in 1973, used a cover clearly indebted to Walters, without acknowledgment of any kind.

In this context, the assumption that abstract art was "ultramodernist" and hence estranged from popular culture is misleading. Over the decades, landscape has probably always been the most widely appreciated style of painting in New Zealand. Walters's abstraction, like Bridget Riley's, differed from most avant-garde art in that its optical play appealed to a wider audience while its flatness and hard edges were easily adapted to commercial applications. Just as Riley's art was almost immediately plagiarized by fabric designers, Walters's was reproduced in print and in other media.

Francis Pound was surely right, however, to insist that Walters's *koru* works related to the larger history of Pakeha (European New Zealander) uses of Maori motifs "as at once a continuation and a difference" (1994:74). They were a continuation in the sense that they

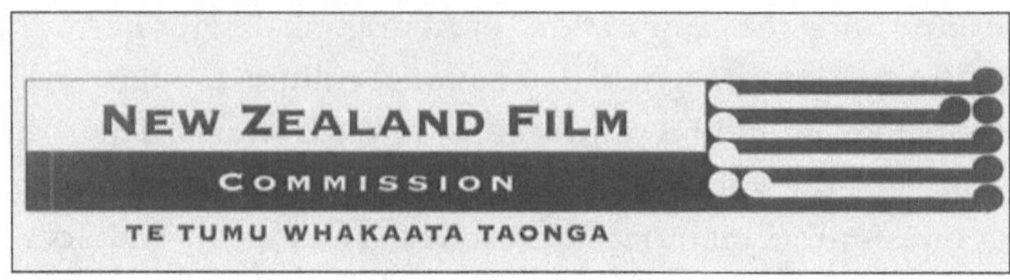

FIGURE 5.6

Gordon Walters's banner design for the New Zealand Film Commission. © Gordon Walters Estate.

were inescapably part of the wider cultural effort of a nation of settlers to symbolize local identity through indigenous reference. Yet they were also not the same, because the domain in which the effort took place was different. The adaptation of indigenous art in design might give Maori or Aboriginal signs public visibility, but it could not give them dignity because commercial design, like craft activity, was not in itself a dignified or prestigious practice. These hierarchies of cultural creativity and genre have, of course, been endlessly contested, but even now they are discredited only in theory, because there are too many art-world and public investments in their maintenance. Whereas the incorporation of indigenous references in "low" genres could not elevate the forms quoted, the high-art status of painting might ideally work conversely to celebrate them. In European modernism, this cannot be seen to have proceeded in any consistent way, because work from different regions was drawn upon eclectically and generically, and often almost surreptitiously. Tribal art in general may have been affirmed, but not in a way that made much difference to the indigenous people in any particular place.

Where, on the other hand, modernist artists in settler societies drew upon the native traditions of the place, the proximity and specificity of their interest was potentially more consequential. This may have been true of Preston's work in the longer term, though its initial reception reminds us that wider racist attitudes can hardly be changed overnight; for the *Bulletin* critic quoted earlier, her art was "debilitated" by the Aboriginal element. Walters was working later, with different material, in a different style, and in a more sympathetic environment; his incorporation of a Maori form did not attract criticism of this kind.

In the 1960s, the emerging group of modernist Maori artists seems generally to have welcomed Walters's work: they took it as an affirmation of the *koru* rather than as a cheapening of it. By the 1980s, however, and certainly by the 1990s, a deeper sense of cultural heritage and cultural property would make indigenous references of this kind visible as instances of appropriation, and hence as essentially illegitimate. Although assessments of the works in question remain various, and questions of appropriation remain contentious, the narrative projected in mid-century, which saw a creole settler art succeeding indigenous art as an authentic expression of antipodean nationality, had become implausible, and irreversibly so.

Note

This chapter draws on material discussed at greater length in my book *Possessions* (Thomas 1999), which includes a much fuller range of the visual sources. In this version, citation has been limited generally to works quoted, and I have refrained from reviewing the wide comparative literature on appropriation (but see Ziff and Rao 1997). For suggestions that helped refine my arguments, I am grateful to all the participants in the SAR seminar, and especially to Annie Coombes, Barbara Kirshenblatt-Gimblett, and Fred Myers.

6

The Wizards of Oz

Nation, State, and the Production of Aboriginal Fine Art

Fred R. Myers

In the years between 1973, when I began fieldwork in Australia with Pintupi-speaking people, and 2000, there emerged an enormous interest in and market for a range of objects (and performances) made by Aboriginal people. Estimates are that Aboriginal "arts and crafts"—a catch-all phrase that includes everything from fine-art-quality bark and acrylic-on-canvas paintings to handcrafted boomerangs, carved animals, tea towels, and T-shirts—generate anywhere from $18 million to $50 million Australian in sales per year (fig. 6.1). Aboriginal painters in the small communities of the Western Desert in which I lived are represented by the cooperative known as Papunya Tula Artists. The "company" has regularly had sales of between A$700,000 and A$1 million per year. Literally hundreds of exhibitions of these acrylic paintings have been mounted in Australia, the United States, Canada, and Europe (see Altman, McGuigan, and Yu 1989:78; Perkins and Finke 2000). About them many journalistic articles have been written, catalogs published, government studies made, and policies articulated. Aboriginal art is a sociocultural phenomenon of considerable weight, sustained by a complex set of practices and institutions, and for that

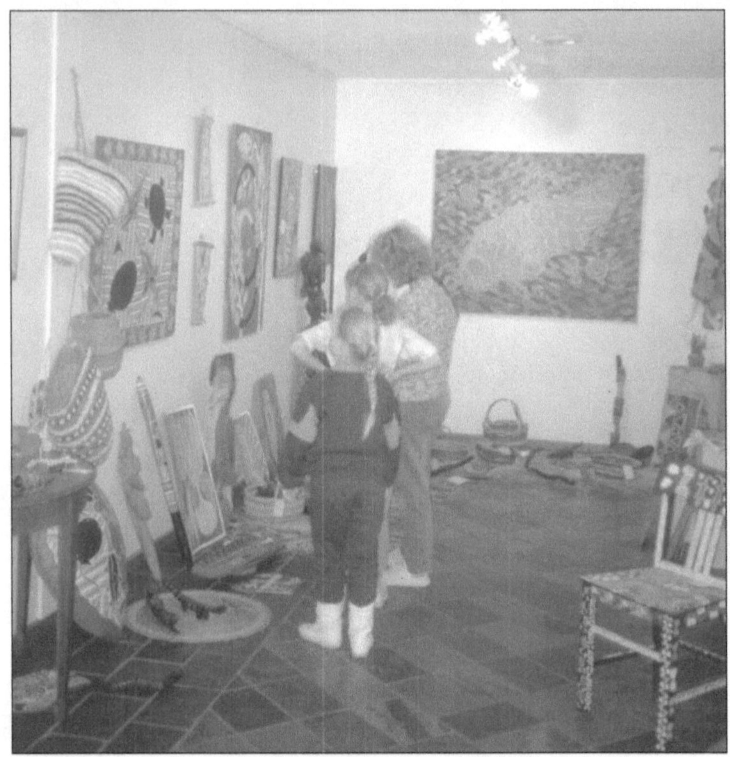

FIGURE 6.1

Aboriginal art for sale in a gallery in Alice Springs. Photo by Fred Myers.

reason it is a particularly interesting location for the study of intercultural formations.

One account of the development of Papunya Tula Artists (Johnson 1994) predicated its success on its having been included in the category "contemporary Australian art." While this may be true, my interest is in what this means and how it was accomplished. In the story I discern, a particular commodity formation—Aboriginal fine art—emerges in relation to a specifiable form of "modernization" in Australia: transformation of the managed Australian economy, a postcolonial shifting of cultural identifications, and the ascendancy of a new technocratic-managerial class at the heart of the "enterprise."

Discussions about Aboriginal art's "success"—and there have been many—have tended either toward the "triumphal" or toward critiques of it as "appropriative" and "exploitative." Both sorts of discussion derive from distinct *critical* perspectives on "Western cultural practices," perspectives that are elaborated within the arts and that imagine the possibility of an authentic cultural realm (see Lattas 1990, 1991, 1992). A third strand of discussion and practice has focused on the policies of developing an Aboriginal arts and crafts "industry."

Whatever the first two approaches might tell us—and they have been very productive—they ignore what, from the point of view of the practitioners, was actually accomplished, and how. Thus, I want to look at the very placement of acrylic paintings in the category of fine art. I want to consider the material "practices" through which these objects have moved and explore some unexpected linkages between the market for fine art and Australian national redefinition. My focus is on delineating the effects of distinct discursive formations and specific institutions that have as part of their function the "re-presentation" of Aboriginal culture.

The shifting discursive formulations of Aboriginal art (in the form of acrylic paintings), from "art as enterprise" to "art as cultural and spiritual renewal" or "art as Aboriginal identity" (see Myers 1989, 1991, 1994), have significant implications. First, far from being simple artifacts of an enduring Western or Australian culture, these discourses are mobilized not only within some general national culture but also within the bureaucratic institutions of the Australian nation-state, by community arts cooperatives and art galleries, and by specific segments of the populace. Second, these arts and their aesthetic values are articulated within frameworks of broader cultural policies—policies toward the culture of some of the government's subjects—and are therefore an aspect of "governmentality." Policies for Aboriginal people aimed at "protection," "assimilation," and "self-determination" (as they were successively described in the twentieth century) are themselves culturally formulated or produced. In other words, such policies are increasingly brought under the direction and administration of bureaucracies and producers of specialist knowledge (anthropologists, sociologists, patrol officers, welfare workers) in distinct institutions. What is particularly interesting and challenging about these institutions and practices as sites of cultural production is the centrality of the discourse of "economics" in assessing production and consumption, which I believe must itself be subjected to interpretation as a kind of sociocultural transformation.

Finally, orientations to these objects and their circulation seem simultaneously to be formulations of the personhood—indeed, of the nature of people as subjects—of those among whom they circulate. Although the narrative of the arts and crafts industry's development and the policies addressed to it imagine and implement impersonal processes of bureaucratic rationalization and commoditization, the story I discern is one in which these processes are countered, if not "resisted." They are countered not only by the strong presence of personal relations, claims, and identifications among the participants but also by the value such personal traces have for the peculiar commodity of Aboriginal "fine art." At the point where the personal and the impersonal processes run into each other most directly, one finds the institutional role of the "art adviser," or "arts coordinator," whose situation is central to my understanding. We should view the "aesthetic" appreciation or recognition gained by the paintings not as a universal attribute that might be taken for granted but as something *produced* in specific historical actions and contexts (see Miller 1994).

These are shifting and contested formulations. The paintings are circulated, defined, and transformed in meaning and value through a network of persons and a range of institutions. One could impose on this a neo-Marxian analysis emphasizing the articulation of different modes of production. One *does* want to track the way acrylic painting has been commodified through the market processes of consumer capitalism, through the practices of the Australian state, and through the demands of Aboriginal activists for greater recognition. To leave the analysis there, however, risks losing the rich, often ironic, sense that ethnography provides of the way these new formations put people into different relations to each other. In each of these formations there are complex sets of social relations in which the everyday vagaries of social life are played out.

Thus, I hesitate to circumscribe this nexus as the "art market" or the "arts and crafts industry." To a significant extent, these terms are signs, cultural constructions that define a reality as much as they represent an already existent one. The "market" is not simply the mechanism through which value is assigned to Aboriginal paintings; it is also understood as involving a specific attitude toward kinds of cultural value as enmeshed in debates about value. It emerged at least partly in relation to self-conscious planning and policy concerns on the part of the state, which attempted to integrate a range of political, social, and economic goals.

In analyzing the growth and development of the category "Aboriginal fine art," I discuss three periods or "moments": the beginnings (1972–81), a time of little demand and serious cash flow problems; the boom years (1981–89), which saw a dramatic growth in sales and exhibitions; and the privatization period (1989–2000), with its "settling out" or establishment of a distinct and calibrated market for Aboriginal "fine art."

ORIGIN STORY

If, in numbers of sales, Western Desert acrylic paintings (fig. 6.2) are but a small proportion of all Aboriginal arts and crafts, they nonetheless represent a significant component of it and one particularly identified with the "success" and rise to prominence of Aboriginal art. These paintings, produced mainly for sale, are a transposition onto canvas of stories and designs derived from central Australian Aboriginal religious and iconographic traditions in which the images are usually made as ground or body paintings. It was as recently as 1971 that Aboriginal men began to paint these designs on canvas at Papunya, Northern Territory, which was then an Aboriginal settlement maintained by the government for about 1,000 persons (Pintupi, Warlpiri, Luritja, Arrernte, and Anmatyerre) (see Bardon 1979, 1991).

There is, of course, an origin story for this practice, and although it is contested by some (see Johnson 1990, 1994), it is adequate for our purposes. Such painting, a culturally hybrid form, grew out of the collaboration between several Aboriginal men living at Papunya and Geoff Bardon, a schoolteacher-artist originally from Sydney, who saw in the designs they showed him something of great aesthetic value (Bardon 1979, 1991). His evaluation was soon supported by events outside the settlement. In August 1971, Bardon recorded, Kaapa Tjampitjinpa's painting *Gulgardi* shared first prize in the Caltex art competition in Alice Springs, bringing to the painters a sense of what Bardon identified as cultural esteem, but coded in cash: "That weekend, over $1300

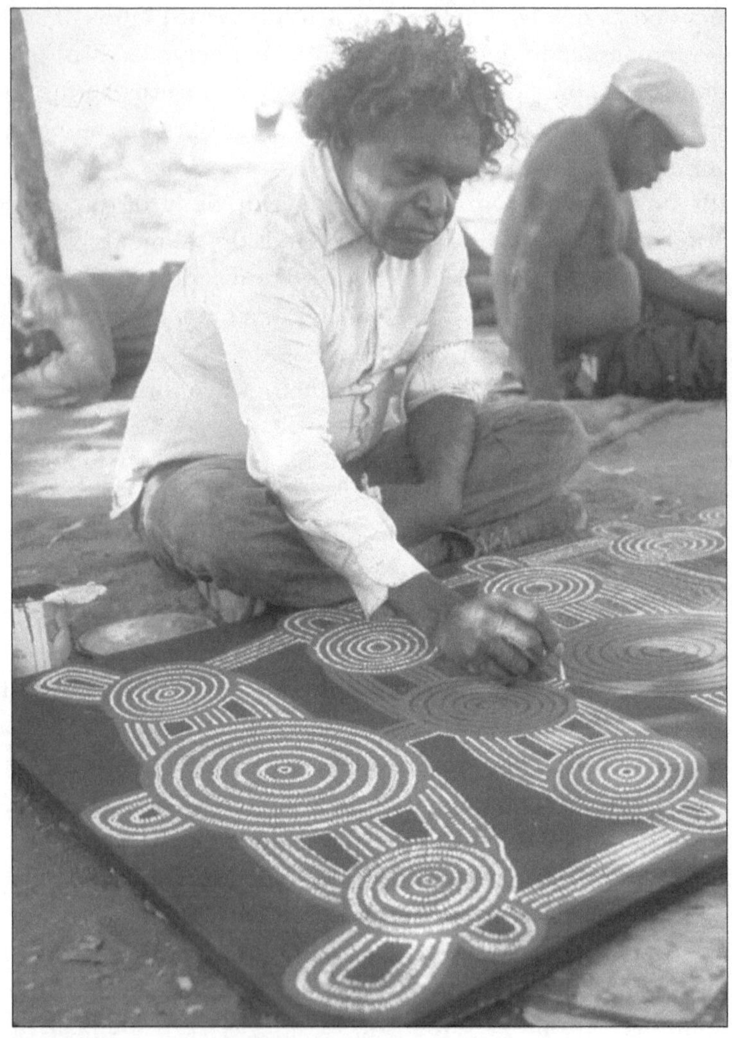

FIGURE 6.2

Freddy West Tjakamarra making an acrylic painting, Papunya, Northern Territory, 1981. Photo by Fred Myers.

cash was raised from the sale of paintings. It was a sensation at Papunya. The Aboriginal men were jubilant. At least five large cash sales were made during the following months, involving some six hundred paintings by twenty-five men" (Bardon 1991:34).

There is some political stake, obviously, in whether the painting originated in "authentic" Aboriginal aspirations and creativity or in Bardon's leadership, but roughly speaking, the events conform to Bardon's account. His emphasis on Aboriginal artistic creativity and its value is evident in his letter of application for a grant from the Australian Council for the Arts to support continuation of his work at the time. Reporting that the painting movement had already earned more than A$3,000 from the sale of 170 works in just four months, he argued that "the story paintings [as he called them] and designs show great vitality and intelligence and as Gallery Art [the work] clearly is a valuable contribution to the reputation of aboriginal culture" (Papunya Tula File at Australia Council/Aboriginal Arts Board 76/840/022 II, 26 January 1972).

Named after the local Dreaming site, Papunya Tula Artists was incorporated as a company of limited liability in 1972, with 11 original Aboriginal shareholders; by 1974 the artists' cooperative had 40 producers. Throughout this early period, the producers were almost entirely senior Aboriginal men, and certainly all were post-initiatory, fully indoctrinated in their own ritual heritage.[1] The number of participating artists has at times risen toward 80 and has come to include some women, but the number of shareholders has remained steady at 40. The cooperative is a community-based enterprise, owned by the Aboriginal shareholders, with emphasis on group decisions and choice of arts coordinator. These sorts of enterprises are commonly known as "art centers."

Although the wholesaling and retailing of artwork is one of the principal objectives of such centers, at Papunya a particular set of practices emerged that emphasized group identity and Aboriginal values—quite in line with the emerging national policies of Aboriginal "self-determination." Purchases of paintings are managed by the arts coordinator, with payment usually made at the point of sale. Moreover, arts coordinators have felt obliged to purchase all the paintings produced, although they have sometimes been able to reduce the payment for those found unsatisfactory in quality. Similarly, outside retailers seeking material for exhibitions have usually not been allowed to specify the works of individual artists but have been expected to take a consignment of paintings that included the work of many members of the cooperative. This was consistent with the local Aboriginal position that *all* the work was valuable ("dear"), because it all represented the Dreaming (see Michaels 1988; Myers 1989). A growing complaint by dealers in the 1990s concerned precisely this practice, which they saw as preventing the true quality work from emerging and maintaining its value, supporting instead "inconsistency" in quality (Altman, McGuigan, and Yu 1989; Kronenberg 1995). The fine art world's logic or mechanism for establishing hierarchies of aesthetic quality means keeping the "cheap stuff," the "dots for dollars," out of the same circulation as the good work.

THE STATE AND THE PROBLEM OF "ENTERPRISE" ACCOUNTING: 1972–1981

One cannot understand how acrylic paintings circulated beyond Papunya (and its outstations) beginning in the early 1970s without recognizing the role of the Australian state, its policies and institutions, and its changing relationship to Aboriginal people. The social and cultural value of acrylic paintings has generally been articulated within two main components of this complex: Australia's administration of the so-called Aboriginal problem and its development of a consensus, managed economy. The components are related, of course, in that both represent areas of social practice submitted to rational, directed planning. I hope to show that in the 1970s and 1980s, these arenas of practice were coordinated by and identified with the ascendancy of a distinctive class fraction, the public managerial class or, as Barrett (1996:128) described it, "the bureaucratic bourgeoisie: the public servants, teachers, academics, community workers and art and culture workers, the expanding administrative class which had grown over the previous decade [before Whitlam] as Australia had developed the character of a resource-based industrial democracy."

The "Aboriginal Problem"

For much of Australia's history since colonization, from 1788 until the 1930s, Aboriginal people were seen as primitive, inferior, lacking civilization, and having no rights to land; their culture was considered valueless. As they were being killed off ("dying out") along the moving frontier, evolutionists of the nineteenth century endorsed the policy of displacing or missionizing them for their own "protection." Later views led to arguably more enlightened policies of education and assimilation in order for Aborigines "to take their place in a civilised community" (Tatz 1964). These policies at best saved lives, but they destroyed or erased traditional cultures, which were seen as impediments to progress: these cultures were too collective, too kinship oriented, too attached to place. First articulated in 1939, such policies had by 1954 come to be accepted by the Australian government as a commitment to planned, directed change that would produce "useful black citizens...who would perhaps gradually migrate to 'better places'" (Davis, Hunter, and Penny 1977:11).[2]

It was only in 1967 that Aborigines gained the rights of citizens in Australia and official policy began to move away from the modernizing fantasy of assimilation toward a goal of "self-determination," the program endorsed by the Australian Labor Party on its election in 1972. Especially important was that after 1967, Aborigines became a federal responsibility, a subject of *national* concern and political technologies. The Gove land rights dispute in 1969 further figured an Aboriginal culture and identity acceptable for national recognition: the "traditionally oriented" Aboriginal with religious and spiritual links to the land—and far from white settlement. This was the Aboriginal identity circulated in acrylic paintings. It was one that did not overtly confront white Australians with its physical presence or with political conflict.

An important part of the administrative response to the Aborigines' continuing poverty and high mortality was to find them a place in the economy. The assimilationist programs of training had largely failed to get Aborigines to take up the "worker" role imagined for them. Indeed, reports frequently mentioned the difficulty of getting Aboriginal people to adopt a Western concept of work. With the perception of this failure came a sense among administrators and critics that cultural difference needed to be recognized in a different way, that ripping people away from their cultural roots was not good, leading rather to demoralization and despair. These realizations, at least in part, underlay an interest in providing "culturally meaningful" work, which could itself be one discursive link (though not the only one) to a concern with preserving or maintaining Aboriginal culture(s). Perhaps, it was thought, Aboriginal people would be motivated to participate in their changed situation if theywere able to do things that interested them, activities linked to their own cultural values and ways of conduct.

This was clearly a theme resonating at Papunya. Built in the late 1950s to house a growing population of varied, displaced language groups, Papunya was part of the Commonwealth government's assimilation policy, which sought to prepare Aborigines for entry into the dominant society by educating and training them (see Rowley 1972). By 1972, however, Papunya was known as a troubled and demoralized place with a high rate of morbidity, riots, violence, and visible disrepair.

Geoff Bardon and Peter Fannin, who had both come to Papunya as schoolteachers (Bardon 1971–72, Fannin 1972–74), were the first two people to act in the role that became known as "art adviser," and their time with Papunya Tula overlapped the end of this assimilationist administrative regime. In Bardon's writings (1979, 1991) and Fannin's letters to the Aboriginal Arts Board, the two framed the significance of the art in that context. Bardon's fuller, later account (1991), with some bitterness characterized the government's policies and agents as committed to breaking down Aboriginal people, to demoralizing them—the government was unable, he wrote, to recognize these men as human, much less as talented. The counterpoint offered by Papunya Tula's success and the promise he believed it held for its residents' self-esteem and independence was significant (Bardon 1991:36). In this sense, the recognition of their art's value stands as a stinging indictment. Bardon articulated the value of the paintings through a humanistic discourse, writing that "the painting movement had brought forth an enormous passion in the desert people to develop their own style and their own sense of self. In a way they were being freed, and redeeming themselves and their culture, by their creativeness" (Bardon 1991:41–42). Through this art, Papunya people could find confidence, rather than demoralization and despair, in activity linked to their own values.

In Bardon's account, the economic valuation and the cultural valuation of the paintings compete for relative, if not absolute, significance. These two kinds of value represent distinguishable visions of Aboriginal personhood as articulated within the context of "Aboriginal policies" and an educated Sydney-sider's understanding of the conditions of modern Australian cultural life. If art could glorify and restore, then money was the corruption that undermined the communion

Bardon had with the men and turned them into a "travesty of what they had once been." He furnishes a recognizable narrative about the destructive effects of capitalism on cultures not built on a monetized economy:

> I seemed to find it much harder to communicate with the painters after that first demand for money and, though I was still liked, I knew somehow everything had changed. While the men were painting, I had witnessed the sense of the glory that the Aboriginal people bring forth in their ceremonies and dances and songs. Now there seemed to me only the stale, sick stench of the camps, the awful physical nearness of the used-up sand, the filth, and the destitution of the alcoholic faces about the tracks and streets....
>
> It was in the painting shed itself that the final blow came. The painters were waiting for me, surrounded by paintings half-completed or just begun. There must have been as many as forty men there that day in June 1972 and when I came in they threw their paints and brushes on the sand. They would not paint, they said. Nor could I prevail upon them to paint without money. The monstrousness of it was not lost on me as they began to chant in their own languages amongst themselves, then at me: "Money, money, money." (Bardon 1991:44)

In 1972, Bardon left Papunya, and Peter Fannin, a fellow Papunya schoolteacher who had earned a B.A. and a B.Sc. from Sydney University in the mid-1950s, took over from him as art adviser. Two years after Bardon began, Fannin found Papunya to be more open to the aims of the artists' cooperative, because the settlement had come largely under Aboriginal control. And though he still experienced the somewhat changed political realities as harsh, Fannin expressed a kind of primitivist nostalgia for what he saw as "non-materialist culture" that offered an alternative vision for what he, like many other Australians, perceived to be Australia's crass materialism. Fannin saw the art as providing emotional insight into a way of life that was totally different from his own, in a way "no verbal description can hope to match" (Fannin to Department of Education, 12 October 1974, Papunya Tula Art file, Australia Council 76/890/00).

I hasten to add that it was not only Bardon and other art advisers who recognized value in these objects (see Myers 1989). The Aboriginal producers continued to think of their commercial paintings as related to and derived from ceremonial designs and rock paintings associated with important myths, and therefore as possessing value other than that established merely in the marketplace. Nevertheless, by at least 1973 they expected (with continual disappointment) this value to be reciprocated in appropriate sums of money. For both artists and their white intermediaries, the promise of combining culturally meaningful work with money was an intriguing policy possibility for a situation some saw as desperate.

Success in supporting the enterprise probably owed much to the way in which proponents tacked back and forth between the two poles of value. It was in this context that forms of "Aboriginal crafts" could hope to receive governmental support and interest, and in its earliest stage, the "sudden flowering of art in the [Papunya] area" received critical support from H. C. (Nugget) Coombs at the Aboriginal Arts Committee of the Australia Council for the Arts and the Office of Aboriginal Affairs (Papunya Tula file, Australia Council/Aboriginal Arts Board 76/840/022 II). Much of Papunya Tula's early support came from the Aboriginal Arts Board, which was formed in 1973 out of this earlier body, especially through the special interest of its director, Robert Edwards, in Sydney and the presence of local Aboriginal representatives on this national body. Edwards was particularly interested in the Papunya paintings, and through the Aboriginal Arts Board he worked creatively to satisfy the producers' need for financial support to continue their painting.

Edwards occupied a distinct social location for an aesthetic framing of Aboriginal art. As curator of ethnology at the South Australian Museum, he took an interest in recording Aboriginal sites and protecting cultural heritage. In the 1960s he was excited to recognize that many of the Aboriginal craft traditions that had produced material culture still survived (Edwards interview, 5 May 1994). His concern to allow such traditions to be preserved and even to thrive grew into an interest in what he called "the living arts." From this orientation, it made sense that Aboriginal art ought not to be included with other Aboriginal needs and activities, such as health, under the rubric of an institution like the Australian Institute of Aboriginal Studies, where funding for art might have to compete with funding for research. Putting it in the Australia Council for the Arts, he said, "included Aboriginals with other artists."

The framework articulated by Edwards represented acrylic painting as having significant value, but it was somewhat different from Fannin's "spiritualization" or Bardon's emphasis on artistic creativity. Edwards's support through the Aboriginal Arts Board tended to emphasize the paintings' basis in local knowledge and practice—their preservation as a living art. This formulation, partly a response to painters' desires to renew their inspiration by visiting their sacred sites and partly reflecting an interest among some art advisers to participate in that knowledge, was shared by Dick Kimber, an art adviser in the mid-1970s. Kimber defined his role as combining development of the sale of Papunya painting, through education and improved documentation, with preservation of what he sometimes called "the living culture" in the form of frequent trips with Aboriginal men to visit the sacred sites represented in their paintings. He worked to preserve, as Bob Edwards wrote to him in a letter of acknowledgment, "an ongoing interest in an Aboriginal way of life." Like many others hopeful of a modern cure for modernity's own problems, Edwards and Kimber imagined a governmental intervention of mimesis to reproduce—in artificial form—Aboriginal culture.

Despite this sympathetic policy and recognition of the art, money was always short. Incommensurate systems of value and circulation intersected in defining these objects, and the contradictions and conflicts came to rest most heavily on the art advisers. A crisis atmosphere was developing that long endured.

Government and Art Enterprise

Although the arts and crafts industry was never simply an economic enterprise, maintaining the cash flow to support its objectives was nevertheless a critical problem. Throughout the 1970s, two institutions provided the bulk of support for Papunya painting and Aboriginal arts and crafts generally—the Aboriginal Arts Board and the Aboriginal Arts and Crafts Propriety, Ltd. (AACP). These governmental enterprises originated, to some extent, in distinct discursive formulations of the Aboriginal situation, and they increasingly came to represent the objectives of supporting the production, respectively, of cultural value and economic value. Moreover, in policy terms, the delineation of Aboriginal painting as an economic enterprise tended to increase in importance over time.

The two government enterprises differed in the way in which they integrated the values of culture and enterprise. At its inception, the AACP had little to do with what the government funded formally as "the arts." It emanated from the Office of Aboriginal Affairs and was delineated primarily as an economic enterprise, a means of economic development for Aborigines.

The Aboriginal Arts Board

In 1973, following the first election of the Labor Party in several decades, Aboriginal policy was officially transformed toward the encouragement of "self-determination" and then "self-management." Both goals emphasized greater respect for Aboriginal culture. At the same time, a broader program of cultural policy endorsed increased support for the arts generally; indeed, Prime Minister Gough Whitlam was also minister for the arts. In the expanded and renamed Australian Council for the Arts, a separate Aboriginal Arts Board was established to provide grant support for a range of arts activities—visual arts, literature, theater, and film. This transformation of the government's role in relation to "culture" was perhaps the salient mark of a new direction in Australian national life.

This new organization, funded significantly by the federal government, was unusual in the extent of Aboriginal control, both substantive and procedural, over its decision making. According to the minutes of the first meeting of the Aboriginal Arts Board, in May 1973, members were told that "the Prime Minister [Whitlam] was seeking their advice on arts." This was a new age for Aboriginal self-determination, and the minutes register that direction: "On procedural control, it was noted particularly in the meeting that, 'Board members agreed that Aboriginals should be in charge of promoting the Arts in Aboriginal society and protecting existing cultural values and practices.'"

Robert Edwards regarded this development in procedure as central, and he took pride in his support for such a transformation. But the transformation was not simply a policy paternalistically handed down. Aboriginal activists, operating under the banner of "black power," had already shown their political muscle in a variety of outspoken ways. At the founding Seminar on the Aboriginal Arts, meeting in Canberra just prior to the establishment of the Aboriginal Arts Board itself, Edwards's diplomacy held potentially explosive events to a productive course, resulting in a number of serious resolutions that guided Aboriginal Arts Board policies. The degree of Aboriginal involvement appears to have been an innovative step in more than one way. Edwards was clear about the way in which he organized an effective Aboriginal autonomy, namely, by allowing Aboriginal members to make the decisions and having an able (largely white Australian) staff who could figure out how to implement the plans in a way acceptable to government accounting.

The structure of the Aboriginal Arts Board was perhaps overdetermined. At a time when Aboriginal activism was putting pressure on the Australian state for more resources and a greater role in the national narrative, the state responded by giving money for cultural activities that Aboriginal people could allocate themselves. The approach was also consonant with the ethos of Whitlam's government and its new breed of public servants. Participants in this new bureaucracy experienced the times as heady ones. One person I interviewed likened the ethos of Whitlam's government to that of "America's New Dealers" (Anthony Wallis interview, 1 January 1996). As Edwards said, they were "not concerned to make money, but to do a job."

Of course, it took money to do this job, and Edwards was adept at finding accountable ways to allow money to be spent in sustaining Aboriginal objectives. Part of what kept the Papunya Tula company afloat during the 1970s was the support of the Aboriginal Arts Board, whose funds seem to have paid for the largest number of paintings. The board purchased paintings for exhibitions such as one organized by the Peter Stuyvesant Trust for Canada in 1974 and others in Nigeria and Indonesia. Dick Kimber, at least, from his position in Alice Springs as supporter and sometime adviser of Papunya Tula, regarded Edwards's interventions as critical: "Bob Edwards is the key reason why it kept going....There were no other people with an interest" (Kimber interview, July 1991). And for Edwards, with his lifelong interest in Aboriginal material culture and heritage sites, purchases made through the Aboriginal Arts Board not only contributed to an emerging "industry" but also supported an activity valued by Aboriginal men that helped to preserve, maintain, and record traditional Western Desert skills.

With expertise gained in his early career in business, Edwards knew how to make the bureaucracies and rules work and how to build a market. At the Aboriginal Arts Board, he did so in order to make possible the Aboriginal cultural activities that had been his real passion. "Most paintings are of superb quality," he advised in an internal memo, "and should be stock-piled for museums and exhibitions in order to enable the artists to continue painting." Donating collections of paintings to foreign governments—Korea and Canada, for example—was an explicit policy, supported by the Aboriginal members of the board. Work sent overseas for exhibition should be given—left there—rather than returning to clog the Australian market. Thus, through a subtle comprehension of the market, demand of a sort was maintained and activity sustained in the Aboriginal communities.

The Aboriginal Arts and Crafts Propriety, Ltd.

The AACP's beginnings can be traced to a combination of factors, including a tourism plan for central Australia that recommended Aboriginal arts and crafts as a basis for economic development in Aboriginal communities and a proposal put forward by the Foundation for Aboriginal Affairs (Peterson 1983). In 1971, this proposal materialized when "the then Office of Aboriginal Affairs established Aboriginal Arts and Crafts Pty Ltd.... to both wholesale and retail Aboriginal artefacts" (Altman 1988:52).

The first appointment to the AACP, or "the Company," was the market research officer, Machmud Mackay, who was chosen "to undertake a survey of production, distribution and marketing of Aboriginal art and craft to place the industry on a sound footing" (Peterson 1983:60). The goal was to increase economic returns to artists and craftsmen and to stabilize the flow of income. In his second report, Mackay argued for a tightly controlled market for Aboriginal arts and crafts, rather than a free enterprise arrangement, "because it was the key to the control of the supply, making it possible to influence the quality of the art and craft and the selection of outlets" (Peterson 1983:60). Aboriginal communities would sell to the Company, which would wholesale to retail outlets in all the major cities. The Company's special mission was to market Aboriginal art and craft work in order to "encourage high standards of artistry and craftsmanship with a view to creating greater appreciation of and respect for traditional skills and the preservation of the culture; foster the production of arts and crafts as a means of creating employment opportunities; [and] ensure maximum possible economic returns to the artists and craftsmen" (Peterson 1983:61).

This mission was soon subjected to rationalization. After rapid growth in its subsidies from the Department of Aboriginal Affairs (A$220,086 in 1973–74), management consultants appointed to study the Company in 1975 suggested that its objectives be redefined with an emphasis on becoming economically self-sufficient (Peterson 1983:62). This redefinition was articulated not only as a consequence of some extravagant failures in Aboriginal expenditures but more significantly as deriving from the economic downturn facing the entire Australian economy soon after Whitlam's election. The AACP's sister organization, the Aboriginal Arts Board, was to take on the broader, complementary responsibility for encouraging and reviving pride in and knowledge of Aboriginal culture by "assisting the best professional work to emerge in the arts among the Aboriginal people."

Despite the attempt to split the economic from the cultural, a central problem was to manage marketing and promotion in a way consonant with "the integrity of Aboriginal cultural traditions," avoiding what one marketing study called "the ill effects of commercialisation" (Pascoe 1981). From an economic point of view, however, the marketing was not particularly successful. During this early period, and following shortly on the 1975 report, the Company's wholesaling function expanded, yet it did so not as a result of increased sales but rather in order to boost production (Peterson 1983:62). The development was not market driven; in some communities, 70 percent of production was being bought by the Aboriginal Arts Board itself.

As Aboriginal arts and crafts production grew in volume, it came to be evaluated in terms deemed appropriate for "economic enterprises," and concern was expressed about the continuing need for government support. On the other hand, given the mixed and sometimes contradictory goals imagined for Aboriginal arts and crafts, participants to the policy debates recognized that assessing the value of government subsidies was not a straightforward matter. There were other grounds on which artifact production might be valued as important to Aboriginal communities—for example, "in maintaining cultural life, in capitalizing on unique skills, in allowing wide community participation, in giving individuals an opportunity to earn money, and in providing communities with their only export" (Pascoe 1981).

By the late 1970s, as the Australian economy began to sink, the development of Aboriginal art did not look an easy task. In meetings of the board of directors of the AACP, where discussions had once included questions of whether the Company should emphasize fine art or crafts, increasingly they were about how to survive the next cut of funding. The Company was meant to be self-sufficient rather than simply to support Aboriginal employment. As soon as it began to generate money, the bureaucrats thought they could move it over to what they regarded as "enterprise," reducing subsidies.

The emergence (or development) of Aboriginal "fine art" should be understood in relation to the actual practices through which objects were moving. The central dynamic of the AACP was "cash flow," which also defined the relationship between Aboriginal producers and a "market" that those producers understood to be the government body rather than any abstract economy. The cash flow problem was this: the Company did not buy on consignment, as most dealers would, but instead paid up front for the objects it acquired. Aboriginal producers received their payment as soon as they transferred their objects. Increasingly, as the Company failed to sell as much as was sent to it, a huge stock accumulated, and all of its capital was gone, tied up in stock and out to the producers. No new paintings could be purchased—something the producers took as a sign of disrespect or of failure on the part of the art adviser, which led to acrimony and recrimination.

The difficulties with cash flow led to a change of operation. After finding that it could not continue to acquire more stock, the Company shifted to a system of waiting until it had an item for 60 days before sending the money. This form of operation, it was hoped, might allow the Company to sell some of the work before having to transfer the money to the producers.

The "60-day system," however, merely transferred the problem to the art advisers, who collected the work and sent it to the Company. Now it was the advisers who had the "workers" angrily asking where their money was. The producers began to sell the best of their work to outsiders, not to the Company, in order to get cash. Consequently, the Company was getting the lower-quality work, unsuitable for sale, which meant it piled up in their storerooms and ate up their capital. Such a conflict between two sets of values—between the market for art and community-based enterprise—was experienced as a flaw in the policy and practice of the AACP.

It also put tremendous pressure on the art advisers, whose role was central to brokering Aboriginal cultural products to the marketplace and the wider public. In the early years, the art advisers mediated primarily between the Aboriginal communities around Papunya and either the AACP or the Aboriginal Arts Board, whose grants were the life-blood of the cooperative. The position, as Bardon found early on, was an impossible, even tragic one; when he left Papunya in 1972, it was after having undergone what many presumed to have been a nervous breakdown. Fannin, too, ended up leaving the position for medical reasons—nervous exhaustion—after rolling his vehicle over during a trip between Alice Springs and Papunya. Fannin's letters to the Aboriginal Arts Board read eloquently of cash-flow and work-load problems, the difficulty of providing documentation, and vehicle failure, repair, and destruction. The stress came preeminently because of the pressure from Aboriginal painters for payment and purchase of substantial numbers of paintings even when, as in Papunya's first several years, the cooperative's unsold stock was reaching levels of 500 paintings or more. Intercultural communication across these domains of value and expectation, where there had already been a long history of cheating and suspicion, was vexed.

The art coordinator's job was not (usually) just an economic or business mediation, which made it both desirable and destructive. From early on, the relationship of the art enterprise to cultural knowledge was a significant consideration of government support, especially for the Aboriginal Arts Board, but the link was also representative of Aboriginal views in which the paintings were considered an intrinsic part of the painters' relationship to country and ceremony. To accept this link was to acknowledge that painting, as an economically viable activity, and looking after their country composed a single cultural domain of activity and to reject—somehow—the claims of a modernizing impulse that would separate "painting" from "religion."

In the daily life of the art adviser, balancing two cultural worlds, these conflicting values were dramatically played out between completing the annotations and the account books and taking the painters out to their country. The quality of knowledge desired of an art adviser gave "travel with the painters" value, too. Because the amount of money charged to the government budget for vehicles and travel was sizable, Aboriginal priorities were very real and challenging to government values and the rationalizing impulses of cost accounting.

THE "INDUSTRY": EXHIBITION SUCCESS AND ECONOMIC RATIONALIZATION, 1981–1989

In the 1980s, Aboriginal art became a new "social fact" through a combination of state support for a cultural formation that was "good" for the state and economic processes that further transformed the new commodity. The move was toward arts and crafts as an "industry," however, more than an activity of cultural preservation. The issue of Aboriginal art was increasingly constructed along lines of economic enterprise—in terms of profitability rather than subsidy. The years from 1981 to 1989 were also a period in which acrylic painting began to receive legitimation and purchases by Australian cultural institutions. Public, journalistic attention to the artwork and its producers emerged, institutional recognition and acquisition grew, and retail galleries, collecting, and curatorship all expanded.

The Australian government under the Labor Party leadership of Hawke and then Keating—corporatist in orientation (Alomes 1988) and given to managed consensus for the economy—was, overall, trying to *remove* government from enterprises. The 1980s were characterized by the growth of marketing surveys and government policies that emphasized Aboriginal employment and the arts and crafts industry as keys to Aboriginal development, as well as accountability for the tax dollar. Many commentators have recognized this complex shift in Australian national political discourse toward economic rationalization and "enterprise accounting." The balancing act between economic and cultural valuation had always been unsteady, and the increasing scrutiny now given to budgets for Aboriginal affairs intensified this contradiction between ways of evaluating the worth of Aboriginal acrylics.

A marketing study conducted by Timothy Pascoe for the Australia Council and the AACP in 1981 really ushered in the new era. It was particularly concerned with the relationship between commercial activity and cultural integrity, but it took a strongly economic orientation and produced a special kind of knowledge of the circulation of Aboriginal products as an "industry." The study identified and evaluated different effects for different kinds of products. For example, it found that a few kinds of products sold by the AACP made up a disproportionate share of total production and sales. "Paperbark landscapes," small bark paintings, small carvings, and boomerangs were 80 percent of the items sold and 40 percent of the sales value. Thus, items of low economic and cultural value for the Aborigines were the dominant product groups. Other components of the study suggested that Aboriginal economic need was the strongest spur to production: more production came from communities with fewer alternative sources of income. Such an orientation to the market, the study claimed, might suggest that selling artifacts would lead to a tendency to produce small souvenirs and to deterioration in quality. Other studies, however, suggested that "quality items" earned a better hourly rate (Morphy 1977, 1980, 1983, 1992). They implied, moreover, that the effect of this pattern of remuneration was actually positive on valuing skills and did not destroy the "artistic system." Thus, commercial activity was *not* deleterious to maintaining the standards of Aboriginal cultural integrity.[3]

If, in Pascoe's study, economics were allowed to support the cultural arguments, the study itself seems to have paved the way for a different approach in cultural policy. In the broadest perspective, the shifting formulation of "Aboriginal arts" among such bureaucratically relevant categories as "enterprise," "cultural renewal," or "social welfare activity" (generating community esteem) should be seen as resulting from the intersection of different technologies of intervention into Aboriginal life. Yet there is no doubt that the discourse of economic rationalization was ascendant, subsuming other forms of value within its own.

Indeed, as forms of Aboriginal material culture become commodities, their properties enter into a process of symbolic transformation that needs to be understood as much as it is criticized. The circulation of Aboriginal material culture is a varied phenomenon, with distinct streams—"product classifications"—through which objects move. Recognizing that different classes of objects have different sorts of value and properties for consumption, marketing surveys are forms of cultural practice that both represent and transform the social phenomenon of intercultural circulation. Such surveys rely on existing implicit notions of value in delineating their versions of what Appadurai (1986) called "the social life of things," because classes of objects have different sorts of value. The original four classes recognized by the AACP, for example, were arranged in terms of a theory of acculturation: "traditional," "transitional," "adapted," and "market." Borrowing from Graburn (1976), the 1981 marketing survey adjusted these frameworks to clarify how the streams of objects might be differentiated according to the intersection of two other axes of value—Aboriginal cultural value and Western aesthetic value (Pascoe 1981:20). The result was a four-cell matrix (fig. 6.3) that defined types of artifacts and delineated for each group of objects the "likely customers and therefore the type of marketing needed to reach them."

Thus, the category of "bicultural" artifacts—which would have included the acrylics—was seen as "of high cultural value for Aboriginals and aesthetically appealing to non-Aboriginals." Along with acrylics, quality but non-sacred bark paintings and carvings fit into this class as objects "suitable for art collectors as well as museums and collectors of ethnographica." According to the study, bicultural artifacts needed presentation in "specialist commercial gallery surroundings" (Pascoe 1981:21).

The so-called bicultural artifact was indeed a category in which expansion took place. Papunya paintings began to enter into the category of "contemporary Australian art" through exhibition and marketing that focused on "quality." Throughout the late 1970s, demand had been slight, and rather than encourage painters, the art advisers felt they had to slow down production. In 1980, the Australian National Gallery in Canberra purchased its first acrylic painting, Old Mick Tjakamarra's *Honey Ant Dreaming* (1973), and this began the process of legitimation. Later that year, the South Australian Art Gallery made its first major purchase of a Papunya work, *Men's Love Story* by Clifford

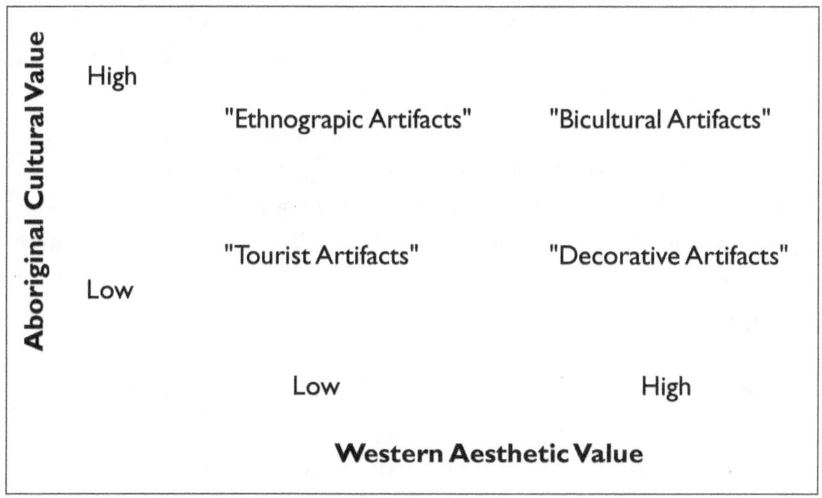

FIGURE 6.3

Classes of aboriginal artifacts as they relate to different categories of value (after Pascoe 1981:20).

Possum Tjapaltjarri, and hung it in its display of contemporary Australian art, an act of curating that Johnson (1994) regarded as particularly significant. In 1981, curator Bernice Murphy included three major Western Desert works in the inaugural "Australian Perspecta" exhibition at the Art Gallery of New South Wales.

Overall, however, Johnson attributed the breakthrough to Andrew Crocker, the art adviser from late 1979 to the end of 1981. "The new manager," she wrote, "had a different attitude toward the paintings from all previous incumbents of the Papunya job.... His insistence that the paintings be seen as contemporary art rather than ethnographic artifacts had undoubted effectiveness as a promotional strategy in attracting the art world's attention to works it had previously thought of only in the context of an ethnographic museum" (Johnson 1994:55). A Cambridge graduate, Crocker was neither ethnologically oriented nor Australia identified, and he sought to turn the enterprise into one with a sounder business footing. In terms of sales, however, not much changed until Crocker sold a substantial collection—26 paintings—to the wealthy Australian businessman Robert Holmes à Court.

Although the purchase gave a push of legitimacy to the movement,

Holmes à Court did not pay a large price. It was only after Daphne Williams took over as art adviser in 1982 that Papunya Tula's earnings began to grow. Its sales in Australian dollars went from $382,595 in 1985–86 to $595,168 in 1986–87 and $1,050,395 in 1987–88 (the year leading up to the Australian Bicentennial). This was an unprecedented rate of growth and volume of sales. Not only was Papunya Tula's work suddenly the subject of enormous publicity, but its sales were the highest of any art center in Australia. A number of factors facilitated this upsurge—the Bicentennial and the accompanying growth of tourism, for example—and the whole Aboriginal arts and crafts market grew during this period. The placement of acrylic paintings in the category of fine art was critical to that economic success.

The growth in sales, however, owed little to private galleries of the sort thought likely to handle "bicultural artifacts" during the early part of this period. Sales to the ordinary tourist market, even with support from AACP, were unable to satisfy the producers' aspirations. The 1981 marketing survey showed that less than 5 percent of all tourist sales were of acrylic paintings. The producers were kept going only through sales of these paintings to museums and governmental collections.

Even when sales began to pick up, a substantial number of paintings apparently still went to the public sector rather than to private consumers. In other words, the "Aboriginal art phenomenon" was not a simple case of consumer interest, in that there were never many collectors or investors. According to Anthony Wallis, who in 1986 took over the former AACP, by now renamed Aboriginal Arts Australia, there was never much of an external market for arts and crafts; this is corroborated by other materials I have seen. At Aboriginal Arts Australia, Wallis in one year raised sales from $1.5 million to $3 million, mostly from sales to government offices. The paintings sold, for example, to Artbank, which rented out art to government office buildings.

Sales to the public sector created an impression of massive success, which the "industry" aimed to do. There is some evidence for a deliberate sort of staging in which the art market had no real foundation in consumption. It reminds me of the film *The Wizard of Oz*, in which an effect is created for the public by an operator behind the scenes—in this case by the Australian government, which primed a belief in the art's value. Anthony Wallis claimed that he once spoke to the director of a general art gallery located in a major department store. The director was impressed when he heard that Wallis did $3 million in sales, and said that in 10 years the gallery had never actually made any profit (Wallis interview, 21 December 1995). Its exhibitions of art were sustained, it seems, in order to give some class to the overall retail operation. This anecdote indicates that the art market is full of wizardry, smoke and mirrors, by which objects acquire stature and value—a process amusingly figured in the famous scene in *The Wizard of Oz* when the dog pulls back the curtain to show the wizard as a little man turning cranks on a machine to create the illusion of power and authority. This is a normal part of art market practice, but in Australia it is shaped in a particular way because of the inescapable connection of "Aboriginality" to changing formulations of Australian national culture and the reframing of the national image.

Thus, one of the puzzles about the so-called "market" is that few Australians were really interested in or knew much about Aboriginal art, even at the time of a 1993 review of the industry (MacMillan and Godfrey 1993). The government purchases were clearly inspired by a changing national construction that embraced Aboriginal culture as part of Australia, a construction that must have been supported, if not among the majority of Australians, then at least among those involved in politics and cultural production.

At the same time that pressures toward economic rationalization were being realized in the organization of an "arts and crafts industry," another, apparently contradictory cultural shift was equally noticeable. "Aboriginal culture" increasingly came to be formulated as central to a distinctive Australian national imaginary linked to the land and oriented away from the country's European ancestry or its American "big brother" (Hamilton 1990). Not only did the Australian government need to respond to growing, visible Aboriginal protest about inclusion, but also in the 1980s the image of the nation—its self-representation—moved away from Europe and America and toward the commodification of its tourist market, for which traditional Aboriginal art and culture took on new value. Aboriginal art, and acrylic painting in particular, came to be associated with a formation of Australian national identity. This was marked most explicitly and dramatically in the selection of Michael Nelson Tjakamarra's Western Desert painting design in

1985 for the mosaic forecourt at the new billion-dollar Parliament House in Canberra, dedicated on 9 May 1988. The embrace of Aboriginal culture (in a limited sense) in the national imaginary is also indexed by the widespread acquisition of Aboriginal art for government offices.

The contexts for this shift are both specific and general. The Australian Bicentennial in 1988 provided the occasion and the resources for renewed cultural production around questions and problems of national identity, for Australians were faced with the necessity of staging themselves in public, not only for themselves but also for a large tourist audience. Predictably, these stagings became occasions of social drama in which enduring hierarchies of value were contested and became unstable. It was not only Aboriginal political activists who placed themselves at center stage in the ensuing "debates," by contesting the celebration of "discovery." Bicentennial funding also supported the exhibition of Aboriginal culture and art on a new scale, allowing it to play a significant role in celebrations of "Australia." Representations of "the Aboriginal" were constructed, additionally, in the form of an artistic "primitivism" that received considerable attention from critics in the arts during the 1980s, especially for the complex role of the "primitive" in constituting the "modern" (see Clifford 1988a; Foster 1985b; Said 1978). Critiques of modernist primitivism drew attention to the themes of nostalgia for an organic relation to place, a tie with a premodern Australia, and a specifically Australian modernist interest in the "other," inspired by the Vietnam War's impact in pushing Australians toward the international counterculture (see Hamilton 1990; Lattas 1990, 1991; Myers 1991).

As in the case of Native American culture at important times in the United States, Aboriginal forms provided Australia with a native, local identity, a means to distinguish itself from its European colonial past. This transformation was already well under way by the late 1970s, as ties with England were severed after World War II and new relations were forged in alliance as America's "junior partner." The new positioning was signaled, according to Barrett's (1996) study of "Whitlamism," by cultural allegiance on the part of Australia's new elite to a kind of "modernist internationalism," which itself began to falter with the economic downturn of the mid-1970s and Australia's detachment from the

"American century." Barrett maintained that the National Gallery of Australia's controversial, costly acquisition of Jackson Pollock's abstract expressionist *Blue Poles* in September 1973 marked the modernist internationalist aspiration of Whitlam's government, which was endorsed by the rise of a particular class fraction in Australia, the bureaucratic bourgeoisie. In turn, the ascension of Aboriginal art to its status as a representation of Australian distinctiveness filled the gap left by the collapse of the modernist fantasy. *Blue Poles,* to speak metonymically, opened up a new space that came to be filled with Aboriginal art, in ways reminiscent of the development of the Southwest Indian art market in the United States after World War I.

I find Barrett's delineation of this rising Whitlamist class very suggestive. National imaginaries, as they have been called, are tied to changing political economies and are produced by specific social sectors. Indeed, although Aboriginal art and Aboriginal identity gained a place in the Australian national imaginary, that place appears to have been sustained by the taste and hegemony not of the working class, the immigrant ethnic groups, or the elites of the old "squattocracy" but of the historically distinct class fraction of university-educated public servants and bureaucrats who took over the Australian Labor Party. These technocrats were presumably the people into whose offices one-third of Papunya Tula's paintings, purchased by Artbank, went and whose "cultural" (national) identity was expressed through such appropriation. There is, therefore, a revealing link between economic rationalization and the cultural reevaluation of Aboriginal art, a link whose compromise formations made the artistic success of acrylic paintings a significant national symbol. The linkage was fashioned by a new class of Australian elites in a specifically "postcolonial" situation that was both economic and political.

These sensibilities did not fall from heaven. They were produced. Unquestionably, art criticism—the institutional domain in which aesthetic value is appraised—is important in providing a basis for discrimination. Exhibitions are the raw material of art critical writing and curatorship because they provide occasions for the practice of these activities by bringing objects into the arena of evaluation. Art criticism and curatorship are both necessary for the structure of art selling because they provide a means for establishing connoisseurship or "quality control"—a knowledge of the objects and their relative worth. The problem for dealers (sellers of art) is to synchronize the market with the criticism. It is clear that during the 1980s, a time when interest in "ethnic arts" was burgeoning throughout the West, positive critical reception from outside Australia secured a sense of value for Aboriginal art and acrylic painting in Australia. This sense of value had not existed earlier. For example, James Mollison, curator of the Australian National Gallery, was completely uninterested in Aboriginal work until 1980. This new reception was important for the cultural value assigned to the "Aboriginal" as well as to the monetary worth of the paintings.

Moreover, these sensibilities and imaginings were produced in particular, located social actors—namely, members of the professional managerial class. My evidence for this is more anecdotal and inferential than I would like, although it is implied by Lattas's (1990, 1991) discussions of Australian intellectuals as well as by Barrett (1996). The results of a 1993 marketing survey (MacMillan and Godfrey 1993), conducted in several cities, suggest that the new interest in Aboriginal art as part of Australian national culture was not the sentiment of a majority of Australians. The largest part of the market for Aboriginal arts and crafts was still overseas customers (travelers and tourists), and not Australians themselves. Only 38 percent of adult Australians had "ever bought" Aboriginal arts and crafts, including T-shirts. The Australians who did buy were likely to be high-income earners and those with at least some tertiary education. These were said to be the people most likely to visit displays. And the most popular items were not fine art objects but weapons, clothing, carvings, and accessories with Aboriginal designs. Despite the enormous publicity of the 1980s, studies of focus groups found that most Australians had "only a limited experience of Aboriginal people and their arts" (MacMillan and Godfrey 1993:15).

Such information suggests that the cultural themes dominant in the formulations of Australian intellectuals should be located within a context of ideological "struggle"—in a specific, globalizing political economy and in the tastes (or identities) of a specific class fraction (Bourdieu 1993b)—a fraction that is to be understood as the professional managerial class. These people were, it seems to me, those who participated most definitively in the Whitlam "revolution." I think we have seen their brothers and sisters elsewhere—in *Songlines* (Chatwin 1988), for example, as the quirky whites of the Aboriginal industry, trying to find an Australian identity in absolutely non-European practices. These were people who, for their own identity, needed to constitute Australia as an authentic cultural space, and they put intellectual energy into creating an authentically Australian culture as "culturally productive." The "managed economy" was not, as one might expect, at odds with these new national imaginings; the two were, instead, deeply connected. Cultural export has played an important role in Australia's self-conception.

My emphasis in considering the "middle period" of acrylic painting and the development of the Aboriginal arts and crafts "industry" has been on the material practices of cultural production, the infrastructures through which an Aboriginal practice and product moved on the way to becoming something like a commodity. The issue has been how the broad category of "Aboriginal fine art" was manufactured and sustained. First, I have tried to show that the paintings were subsidized by the state, originally as a solution to the "Aboriginal problem" and then as an aspect of the production of national identity—which has always struggled to place Aboriginal people in relation to the state through policies and practices ranging from destruction and assimilation to self-determination. Second, I believe the machinery of the state was mobilized to this end by a particular set of agents and the Whitlamist concern with culture. Those agents were the class fraction I call "the wizards of Oz," prefigured by Robert Edwards. Aboriginal culture had been something otherwise unassimilable with which they had to deal—and through art, it could be assimilated, either economically or culturally. Like the wizard in the film, the agents of this class were involved in the production and circulation of imagery, mobilizing, often to good ends, the tricks of the bureaucratic machinery of Oz to create the structures of Australia against an unknown and magical landscape.

Because of the substantial absorption of acrylic production first by the government and later by galleries in the context of Australia's changing self-definition and the wizardry of its new managers, acrylic painting came to broader attention as a success. It became its own "thing," a social fact, acquiring an aura that combined its economic success, aesthetic recognition, and Aboriginal authenticity. It lay somewhere between the pure commodity—value defined in market discriminations—and the Aboriginal artifact—value defined by use as signs within a community. This Aboriginal "presence" in the paintings was critical to the value of the commodities: consumers preferred to "buy direct from makers rather than retailers" and "to buy only genuine, original hand-crafted Aboriginal arts and crafts" (MacMillan and Godfrey 1993:17).

Now that the category of Aboriginal fine art was a social fact, now that the paintings had status as "commodities," dealers wanted to exploit them to their own ends just as the government wanted to divest itself of its subsidizing role and to subsume Aboriginal art to economics. After 1989, "Aboriginal fine art" as a signifier came to be further separated from its cultural base as the selling of Aboriginal art was increasingly dominated by the structures of the Western art market, in which the need for "discrimination" and "quality control" defined the practice of its mediation.

BEYOND ABORIGINALITY: 1989–2000

In this last section, I can sketch out only briefly the most recent period in the acrylic painting market. It has been characterized by an emphasis on connoisseurship, a delineation of a hierarchy among painters, and a movement away from the emphasis on "Aboriginality" and national identity. This transformation followed on the dismantling of the centralized system for marketing the paintings in the 1980s, which happened not only because of conflicts over centralization, which were spearheaded by arts coordinators, but also because of attention to the economic rationality of government subsidies, which was articulated by private retailers. Both were set in motion by overall emphases on "rationalization."

In 1987, Aboriginal Arts Australia (AAA, successor to the AACP), then under the control of the Aboriginal Development Commission, came under attack from the arts centers and coordinators when the minister for Aboriginal affairs, Clyde Holding, announced a policy of intensifying the centralization of marketing. With all funding for art centers to be passed through AAA, the proposal was threatening to the arts coordinators, who resisted it with a strike that eventually led to the dismantling of AAA. With the demise of centralized marketing, a substantial number of private dealers and galleries moved in. Whether buoyed by reality or by illusions of success, the retailing of Aboriginal arts and crafts no longer lacked for players.

The practices of retailing and the identification of distinct streams of art products led to differentiation in outlets. Altman and colleagues (1989:74) found three broad types of specialist outlets: "Aboriginal fine art outlets," "Aboriginal tourist art outlets," and "mixed outlets." These differentiations depended upon the recognition of a class of "fine art." As Anthony Wallis and others had recognized, people would not pay large sums of money to buy paintings in a shop cluttered with tourist souvenirs. Not uncommonly, specialists established different outlets to straddle different market segments. The Dreamtime Aboriginal Art Centre, for example, had tourist venues in the Argyle Centre in Sydney and a fine art gallery in Paddington (Hogarth). Coo-ee had an "emporium" for tourists and a nearby gallery for collectors (Altman, McGuigan, and Yu 1989:75).

The differentiation of outlets—and especially the sustaining of a higher-end category of fine art—required retailers to present themselves as knowledgeable. Interest in buying "direct from makers" and in buying "only genuine, original hand-crafted Aboriginal arts and crafts" reflected the value of the items as mementos or souvenirs of travel that needed to be indexed to a location and people. Correspondingly, the meaning or "story" associated with the items was considered to be an important dimension. For visitors who purchased such items, they represented a mnemonic of tourism. For this category of consumer, such "art" was a turn to an aesthetics in which objects were memorable not because of their intrinsic value but because of the effect they had on their viewer at specific times and places.

On the other hand, the interviewees in MacMillan and Godfrey's (1993) marketing survey—suspicious consumers, apparently—believed that retailers in cities would carry only low-quality stock, and best-quality artwork would be available only at the source of production. This information suggests a combination of interest in "authenticity," personal significance (associated with the connection between producer and consumer), and a concern to get the best value. There was a corollary defining the terms of a dealer's self-presentation as knowledgeable and connected with producers: "In the event of buying Aboriginal art from a local source, consumers often felt that they would need to obtain reassurance and guidance in purchase from an art expert or dealer. Understanding the meaning and stories associated with Aboriginal art was also thought to be a means of assuring authenticity" (MacMillan and Godrey 1993:17).

"Knowledge" is critical in mediating sales of objects, in making them fine art (Plattner 1996; Savage 1969). This is not particular to Aboriginal art. Where information is lacking on value, as is the case with Aboriginal forms, the seller's mediation becomes even more important. For good Western art, the question is the track record of the artist, which is somewhat harder to show for Aboriginal artists, although dealers are evolving in that direction. In Alice Springs, as the market changed, dealers attempted to enter it on terms related to their closeness to "supply," upgrading their own reputations as connoisseurs and "sources." One such practice on the part of retailers involved taking the stories that came with the paintings from an arts cooperative (that is, documented by the art adviser) and copying them so that the gallery appeared to be the authenticator, the source with close ties to the producer.

Even if the largest part of the market has been tourist mementos, the separation and reaggregation of tourist art and fine art is an ongoing issue. "Fine art" seems to require a less cluttered context, a presentation or "framing" of the product separately from other products. The number of tourists who will buy $400 to $500 items is apparently small, but galleries have evolved to engage these persons. The reason Aboriginal Arts Australia's Kent Street gallery in Sydney was good, Anthony Wallis told me, "was that it looked classy. It had books in it.... People could feel they were getting educated and that they were getting something worthwhile." Younger tourists, whom he classified as "backpackers," typically bought this art. They were, he said, even willing to pay $2,000 to $3,000 for a painting: "They thought it something authentic."

This account presents "fine art" as being secured and legitimated by the (modernist) context of the gallery, a context strongly in contrast with that of shops in Sydney's "the Rocks" tourist district, with their more jumbled interior displays. People do not want to pay large sums of money for something that looks like part of a tourist enterprise. Galleries, dealers, and a modernist style of exhibition began to emerge in the 1990s along with curators and dealers from the government enterprise known as Aboriginal Arts Australia, such as Djon Mundine, Ace Bourke, Gabrielle Pizzi, and Gabriella Roy, all past employees, and gallerists such as Christopher Hodges.

The opening up of the market introduced another set of meanings through the effects of competition. At least 161 different venues for selling Aboriginal art and crafts were identified in the database in Altman, McGuigan, and Yu 1989, and there was a good deal of competition among them and among the art centers. The arts and crafts industry had become less a "cultural" question and more an "enterprise." Increasingly, participants discussed the movement of the paintings in terms that delineated the structure of the fine arts world, where value was sustained by distinctiveness, trajectory, and quality control. The common phrase I heard was "settling out," referring to the drying up of demand for any old kind of acrylic painting and a discrimination of quality. This meant that there would be a different market for work regarded by retailers as of lesser quality, which might have to move to outlets of a different order.

The remarks of a well-known curator with a long career in Aboriginal art to some extent celebrate the turn to "quality," "taste," and "discrimination." In an extended interview at the Hogarth Gallery in Sydney in 1991, Ace Bourke told me,

> I think what's going to happen with Aboriginal art is that a few people have had a good run under the Aboriginal umbrella but now it's just coming down to the Gordon Bennetts, the Tracey Moffatts, the Trevor Nichols, I mean, the real artists. The ones who just compete on an international art front. It's just going to be as simple as that. The novelty of Aboriginal things has worn off, particularly from the media's point of view. I mean, they're just not interested. They think it's yesterday's news. In fact, the art is extraordinarily gorgeous. You know, the dot paintings are an extraordinary phenomenon in the world...history of world art, well, this century especially. So it's just especially good and it's got something to say, there's real weight behind most of it.

> So it's very simple why people are interested in it. And the interest has only just begun. And there are real problems like overproduction. Too many paintings indiscriminately evolved....It's shaking out. Getting better rather than worse.

The curatorial realities that Bourke referred to are illuminated in his remarks about a then-current show at Aboriginal Artists Australia, where he had once worked and toward which he was somewhat ambivalent: "These days you don't get a package deal. You have the good artists, and the bad ones can just go fuck themselves. You know, *why carry them?* It's just unprofessional and it's just not how it's done.... [It] just shows amateurism as far as I'm concerned. Why carry a bad artist? You don't sell anything. You don't do the artists any good, and it just makes you look bad. It takes away from a good show."

Although his comments in this case referred chiefly to urban-based artists, his curatorial position is quite at odds with the expectations of painters in places like Papunya, who have expected, as Gabrielle Pizzi said, "that all work there would be purchased on completion" (quoted in Kronenberg 1995:7). To some extent, such practices had helped guide curatorial practice for a while, in the form of an emphasis on group shows, even if they unintentionally colluded with the practices of shadier "entrepreneurs" who sold and displayed paintings without regard to their effect on the painter's career.

In the accounts of dealers and curators, if "standard" practices prevailed, then the good would survive and the so-called "weaker" painting would dry up. These accounts outline the common understanding of how a fine art market is structured. "I was finding it increasingly hard," Gabrielle Pizzi said in an interview, "to promote Aboriginal artists, both in Australia and internationally, when their work was simultaneously being sold in tourist shops and vanity galleries.... That means mediocre work is finding its way onto the market and, more damagingly, is being sold in commercial outlets, and this can lead to a destabilisation of the market" (quoted in Kronenberg 1995:7–8). Such a "lack of control in the market" might compromise a dealer's "professional integrity and reputation" (Pizzi in Kronenberg 1995:8).

This is not, I should say, simply a hostile position that greedy dealers take against Aboriginal interests. There is great concern about a "flood" of poorer work being marketed by those who want to make a quick dollar, and this is distinguished from responsible participation.

The remarks of Christopher Hodges, who represents Papunya Tula in Sydney's Utopia Gallery, extend this analysis of the "new market" and the changing place of Aboriginal fine art. Hodges's central concern is the development of connoisseurship, or knowledge, as a basis for appreciating artistic value—as a way to discriminate "quality." This requires education of the viewer and the capacity to know individual styles through "research," something in which a good dealer must engage. At this point, Aboriginal fine art—articulated for the high-priced world of collecting and connoisseurship—is becoming detached from its base in Aboriginal cultural practices. Hodges told me:

> There's no doubt in my mind that every one of the artists that is producing work at the moment is producing it for a marketplace and knows it gets exhibited. They're not producing it for sacred ceremonies. It's a viable income-producing form of labor....
>
> Their paintings are influenced by what's happening to them. They're important statements about the big issues, and the fact that it's abstract fitted in with the Western tradition of abstract painting. And so abstract painting had lost its punch by the seventies, by the late seventies, abstract art had run full cycle until it was pretty much looking up its own navel, and so when this stuff came along it was full of content, it was powerful, it had all the energy in it, and it was volatile. And most of the art at that time had lost its real vitality. And so it went into the art world as a fresh, new thing, which continued a tradition that had begun in completely different cultures. We use the phrase, "beyond Aboriginality." And the idea was that once the work had transcended the specific culture, it still has an effect on people who know nothing about the specifics of the work. The best pictures, they hit you. That ability to hit, even though there are no cultural records. It really makes a difference. (Hodges interview, 21 June 1991)

Entering into this fine arts world does not, in Hodges's view, necessitate indulging in "primitivist nostalgia" for the "noble savage."

Hodges was very clear that what he expected to sell was "painting," rather than "Aboriginality," and the expensive paintings were sold on the basis of knowledge—moving buyers ever further toward "stronger" art. Hodges explained his idea of appropriate relationships as involving what he called "proper representation." But this is exactly what most of the so-called reputable dealers believe is not occurring:

> There's a lot of potential to do things internationally with this art. There are lots of chances to go and show this work to a larger audience. But it's got to go out in the proper way. It's got to go out supported well. Go out with the same care the work of the top white artists [goes out] with. If that's going to happen, it means cooperation from everybody on a long-term call. Ninety-nine percent of the people involved with Aboriginal art, I reckon they just rank out of it. The places that show art in Sydney, most of them started out as tourist shops that have become galleries. Like Hogarth—down at The Rocks—who runs a tourist shop, and then they've got a museum and gallery, and then they've got the Dreamtime Centre Gallery in Paddington. So they come from a background of splitting their options three ways. (Hodges interview, 21 June 1991)

This sort of comment, not uncommon among dealers, reflects the relationships of competition among them, too. At the time of my interviewing, Emily Kngwerreye's work was receiving the greatest critical attention, and galleries were vying for her paintings. Indeed, "representation" could be said to have become meaningful entirely within this entrepreneurial environment.

> I believe in representing artists. To do the right thing for your artists, you have to support them. You have to work together. But your aim is to develop their reputation so that they have a long-term future in the arts. Now because of the exploitation by opportunists who don't understand the art market, who don't understand anything about art, wouldn't know a good painting if they fell over it...many of the major artists...are basically hugely undervalued, because the opportunists stop proper representation occurring.... The entrepreneurs have just under-

> mined the pricing. Every time somebody is nominated, you know—like Emily Kngwerreye—they took advantage of all the efforts that had been made by everybody before that. Coventry Gallery actually mounted an Emily Kngwerreye show. Gabrielle Pizzi mounted one and Hogarth Gallery has mounted an Emily show. (Hodges interview, 21 June 1991)

These shows were obviously the point of the competition, but they clearly reflect the difficulty of the "unsettled" art market. The dealers all struggle with "opportunists" and entrepreneurs who have no long-term involvement, which seems to be understood as the stabilizing force. Ace Bourke had complaints about competition, too, and seemed to dream of a curatorial autonomy that was denied him in the mercurial world of Aboriginal art:

> We've got Balgo [the Balgo art cooperative], and Balgo showed at Coo-ee earlier in the year and wanted to show in Kent Street later in the year. And I'm the monster because I said no way [to a Balgo show at his own gallery, the Hogarth]. I'm just sick of it.... They can be as amateurish as they like. [If] they're going to show with someone, they're going to show with me and they're going to show once a year or I'm not interested. They can just drop out or drop dead. It's not like a big chocolate cake you share around; you know, have a go at the Hogarth and then move on to Kent Street. (Bourke interview, July 1991)

The future of the Aboriginal fine art market seems to be the system familiar to Western art, but in the new guise of Hodges's version of "proper representation." And this future will follow the "settling out" of the finer artists from the others, not the continuing endorsement of Aboriginal identity per se.

> When all this stops, and people really look at it, and the entrepreneurs have dropped out, and we have people capable of making judgments about Aboriginal art the same way they are capable of making judgment about white art, with the same degree of scholarship and commitment. And you'll have somebody say, "Turkey Tolson's stripe paintings from the late eighties, early nineties, those are the best paintings he ever did." I think that's what will happen. (Hodges interview, 21 June 1991)

There are aspects to what is afoot, however, that may be depressing to some of those involved in the fine art market. Sales have declined overall, and "unscrupulous" dealers have been able to get into the market. This is perhaps the expectable result of the shift toward Aboriginal arts and crafts as an industry. According to at least two recent accounts I heard, Papunya Tula is having trouble that is indicative: a problem keeping its artists. The cooperative is undermined by people who want access to the Aboriginal communities but gain it by sowing discontent among painters who are not selling well at the time. This is something that has long been visible: People are angry because their paintings are not being sold, and so someone in Alice Springs tells them they are being robbed. The artists have begun to sell to anybody in town, and dealers are coming to Alice Springs to take advantage of this. Indeed, one rumor was that a gallery down south had managed to have an assistant from Papunya Tula act as its agent, bypassing the cooperative and sending work directly to the gallery. One "mixed outlet" from Melbourne was also reputed to have an agent in Alice Springs and to pay artists on the spot—with cars. In another case, a shop owner in Alice Springs reportedly told an artist, in order to get him to paint for him, that Papunya Tula did not look after him properly and the dealer would do so. The artists never had a great deal of loyalty to Papunya Tula, always feeling themselves impelled by need to sell where they could, but their association with the cooperative has been further eroded.

Dealers who operate in this fashion cannot provide accurate provenience information, which is critical for selling paintings at the high end. Before, they could guarantee authenticity for buyers with a number on a painting that linked it to a document on file at the cooperative. As a result of the changes, I understand, the market has now turned back to the earlier period of the art, when paintings were inherently limited in number, controllable, and linked to more culturally "isolated" times. Apparently, paintings from that early period are going for large sums.

These changes may challenge the "authenticity" of the work, both commercially and culturally. One view holds that after the generation passes for whom this art is really linked to ceremony and traditional concerns, the movement will die. What people buy it for, in this view, is that connection with Aboriginal culture. But it may also be that the demands of the art market always move on, and that different explorations will take place from a basic cultural repertoire. The tropes of modernism and modernization take us just to here, for now.

Notes

I want to thank the many people involved in Aboriginal art who have given me generously of their time and thoughts. Most of them are mentioned by name in this chapter, but there would have been nothing to write about had I not had the experience of being taught about this business by Pintupi painters themselves. Work on this chapter has been supported by grants from a number of agencies over the years, including the John Simon Guggenheim Memorial Foundation, the National Endowment for the Humanities, ACLS, and the Institute for Advanced Study in Princeton, New Jersey, and by a sabbatical from New York University. Earlier versions of the chapter have been presented at the Departments of Anthropology of Cornell University and Princeton University and at the Institute for Advanced Study. I have benefited greatly from critical comments by T. O. Beidelman, George Marcus, Toby Miller, Gwen Wright, Annette Weiner, and Vincanne Adams, but I am especially indebted to Faye Ginsburg for her many contributions. I thank Jane Kepp for her wondrous editing. The essay is dedicated to my friend Annette Weiner, who died before its publication.

1. That the painters were almost entirely male is probably a consequence of the relationships that Bardon had—principally with men—when he initially formed a group of painters. Aboriginal women of ritual standing, likely participants in painting, would not have been on such close terms with a white man. It was certainly the case that at that time, male painters took great pains to ensure that women in their community would not see the paintings, lending credence to the view that painting was necessarily "men's only."

2. The legal framework for the implementation of these policies was provided in the Welfare Ordinance of the Northern Territory Legislative Council (1953), which replaced the Aboriginals Ordinance (1911–47).

3. The study showed that there had been little growth in sales since the Company's founding in 1973. In 1981 the system was still substantially subsidized by grants from the Aboriginal Arts Board and by Aboriginal communities—to the tune of $1 million. In terms of total revenue, artifacts were seen to contribute less than 1 percent of Aboriginal revenue, and in terms of disposable

cash income, they accounted for 4 or 5 percent on average. These crass economic findings were arrayed against "cultural values," however, allowing the authors of the report to maintain that "artefact production is still very important to Aboriginal communities" (Pascoe 1981:16). It was said to be important in "maintaining cultural life," for example, because "most artefacts produced for sale also have a physical and spiritual role in the traditional life of Aborigines. Production for sale as well as for use helps to keep the culture alive." In retrospect, many commentators regard arts and crafts as almost the only successful Aboriginal enterprise.

Part Three

Border Zones

7

Rights of Passage

On the Liminal Identity of Art in the Border Zone

Christopher B. Steiner

> The question of what is and what is not art has agitated mankind since the first Cro-Magnon scratched on the walls of his cave in the South of France. Government has repeatedly attempted to settle the question, with almost uniform lack of success. In fact, governmental approval of an artist or work of art is a pretty accurate indication of mediocrity.
>
> —*Hartford Courant*, 24 February 1936

Without attribution, this passage from the *Hartford Courant* might well appear to have been published in the late 1980s or early 1990s in response to the controversial debates in the United States Senate regarding the artistic "merits" of certain photographs by Robert Mapplethorpe and Andres Serrano. In an effort to reduce what Senator Alfonse D'Amato called "the abuse of taxpayers' money," legislators took up the role of art critics and judged several sexually explicit images by Mapplethorpe to be pornographic and *Piss Christ*, an image by Serrano of a plastic crucifix submerged in urine, to be blasphemous and antireligious (Bolton 1992). Written in 1936, however, the quoted statement was actually in response to the detention by United States Customs Service examiners of a shipment of photographs from Italy of Michelangelo's frescoes in the Sistine Chapel, on grounds that the images were obscene.

When the state is called into service to discriminate between art and non-art, or, in this case, between divine passion and indecent exposure, objects are removed (both physically and conceptually) from their original cultural contexts and examined in the harsh light of legal discourse. Things that were once valued, in Weber's sense, as "charismatic" are now "subjected to classification and a rational approach that, in effect, bureaucratizes them," in the same manner as the rationalization of political power in the modern nation-state (Fisher 1991:12).

Much has been written in recent years on the social construction of the category "art" and on the institutional frameworks or so-called art worlds that function to create or establish artistic meanings and values (for an excellent overview, see Marcus and Myers 1995). The primary art worlds that have been considered in recent literature are those of the museum and the marketplace, both being sites where diverse bodies of art are brought together for cultural consumption and exchange and where they are, in the process, reinterpreted according to the logic or structure of their new institutional location. One juncture of the art world, however, that has received far less attention than the cultural or the commercial is the legal sphere, in which art objects have increasingly become enmeshed. Whether the litigation is over title, authenticity, import duty, repatriation claims, or reproduction rights, the discussion of art in the legal arena never fails to raise controversial issues that bring into question the social, economic, and political identity of material culture.

This essay is about the legal definition of material culture, in particular "fine" art, within the transnational space of the art world and the global networks of collection and exhibition through which objects circulate.[1] Specifically, it is an exploration of what happens to objects of art when their transnational flow is momentarily interrupted at the international boundary, where duties are negotiated and where sometimes the "undesirable" is denied entry. In this sense, the essay is an exploration of the relationship between two precise institutional locations, or, better, semi-autonomous social fields (Moore 1978:57–59), that are temporarily brought together at the border zone: on one hand, the academic art world, in which definitions of art condition the canonical status of objects, and on the other, the courts, which must disentangle, in Thomas's (1991) phrase, "entangled objects" and, at least for the purposes of imposing tariffs, make temporarily commensurate a seemingly incommensurate body of material things.

I use the term "border zone" in the sense intended by McMaster (1995) to indicate a space of negotiation, arbitrariness, and liminality. "My own tactic," McMaster wrote, "is to combine two terms as one metaphor: 'zone,' for it recognizes an area (in the abstract sense), and 'border,' which demarcates a space, like the slash in centre/periphery or inner/outer. For my purposes, the border zone spatializes cultural possibilities" (1995:80). Clearly the term "border zone" is not unrelated, either, to Pratt's (1992) and Clifford's (1997:188–219) notion of the "contact zone." However, while contact zone implies a sense of "copresence, interaction, interlocking understandings and practices, often within radically asymmetrical relations of power" (Pratt 1992:7), the border zone is far more "indeterminate, as in the liminal zone where everyone is status-less" (McMaster 1995:82). The border zone is a deterritorialized space, pregnant with possibilities, situated between two different cultural systems, where values and meanings are negotiated, transformed, and rearranged. In the rapid transnational flow of material culture, a flow that animates the world of material objects, the border zone offers a period of suspended animation—a liminal space between two worlds where category alternations and conceptual shifts are poised to occur.

In part, this essay is also intended as a revisitation of some of the arguments put forth in Appadurai's edited volume, *The Social Life of Things*, (1986). Since it first appeared, a good deal of fruitful research has been conducted in the spirit of Appadurai's volume, including my own work *African Art in Transit* (1994), which in particular is indebted to Kopytoff's (1986) useful model of the "cultural biography of things." One of the reasons Kopytoff's processual model of commoditization has had such a large impact both in anthropology and in other fields in the social sciences and humanities is that it coincided with a broader disciplinary change in practice and theory—one that redirected the unit of analysis from the "local" to the "supralocal" or "global" and from single-site field research to multisited ethnography that aims at tracking persons and things through their various movements in space and time (see Clifford 1997; Marcus 1995; Steiner 1995).[2]

One of the aims of this essay is to expand and rethink the "cultural biography of things" model in at least two ways. First, I believe that a lot of the research spawned by Kopytoff's original essay attributes far too much "power" to objects themselves. Kopytoff, in his original essay, was quite clear that he was dealing with the way in which the meanings of things were "constructed *by people*" (1986:83, emphasis added). Yet in their zeal to explore the social identity of material culture, many authors have attributed too much power to the "things" themselves, and in doing so have diminished the significance of human agency and the role of individuals and systems that construct and imbue material goods with value, significance, and meaning. Thus, commodity fetishism has been inscribed as the *object* of the model rather than its *subject*. Whereas Kopytoff's aim was to redress the distinction between people and things, some of those who have spun theories of material culture on the basis of his model have actually fallen back on a fetishized construction of the commodity or material object. Hoskins (1988), for example, invoked Kopytoff's model in her discussion of the anthropomorphizing of ritual objects in Kodi.[3] Although there may indeed be a transformation of objects into persons in the context of Kodi healing rituals, Kopytoff's model was intended primarily to explain the etic transformation of objects rather than alterations in their purely emic identity. Another example is the way in which Rovine (1997) summarized Kopytoff's argument as the foundation of her analysis of the "biography" of a Malian textile. She noted that the cultural biography model "treats the material world as an active, continually shifting subject rather than as the passive, stable object of academic study" (1997:42). To be sure, it is useful to shift the focus of inquiry from persons to things, but in the final analysis it must be made clear that the meaning of things is limited and bound by the "systems of cultural signification" (Bhabha 1990:1) through which objects are interpreted and transported. The point is not that "things" are any more animated than we used to believe, but rather that they are infinitely malleable to the shifting and contested meanings constructed *for them* through human agency.

Second, the emphasis on commodities and commoditization that characterizes the essays in *The Social Life of Things* has, to some degree, detracted from the other qualities that objects accrue in their circulation through space and time. Although much of the world's art travels the globe in the name of "international commodity flows," some art circulates for other purposes and gets caught up in different processes of classification and collective (mis)representation. In seeking to expand the model of the "cultural biography of things" beyond the pure commodity realm, I focus particularly on the legal identity of things and on the relationship between material culture and various aspects of the law. Furthermore, I draw upon some of the recent literature in refugee and migrant studies to refocus attention on the relative power*lessness* of objects and on the concomitant authority of those who construct the meaning of things within the sphere of legal discourse. What is interesting about objects in judicial contexts is not their putative "voice" but rather their silence—as people on either side of the court "put words in the mouth" of things and, in what often appears to be an entirely arbitrary fashion, assign value and meaning to subjects that cannot "speak for themselves."

OBJECTS IN EXILE

In a recent article titled "What Do Pictures *Really* Want?" Mitchell (1996) argued that it might be high time to scale down the rhetoric of the "power of images." "Images are certainly not powerless," he wrote, "but they may be a lot weaker than we think" (1996:74). Mitchell was arguing for a shift in the interpretation of visual culture from power to desire and "from the model of the dominant power[, which is] to be opposed, to the model of [the] subaltern[, which is] to be interrogated or (better) to be invited to speak" (1996:74).

Although his argument was focused on a problem quite different from the one I consider in this essay, I take his point regarding the relative powerlessness of objects to inform my argument on the characteristics of material culture in legal arenas. In many ways, as I have already suggested, a hasty reading of Kopytoff's model of the "cultural biography of things"—which has become the dominant model for interpreting the movement of material objects through channels of trade and exchange—gives too much authority to objects and not enough to those who imbue objects with meaning. By shifting our focus from the "disembodiment" of objects in motion to their embodiment in the sociocultural space of legal and judicial process, we can begin to see material culture once again as "objects," without claims of subjectivity or personhood, whose meanings are opportunistically readjusted within the legislative framework of classificatory bureaucracies.

Anthropological theory is heavily indebted to studies of classification and taxonomy. The work done on classification by Van Gennep (1960), Douglas (1966), Turner (1967), and Tambiah (1985), for example, lies at the heart of much anthropological theory of ritual order and process. But on the whole, until recently, the study of classification has largely avoided the political implications of taxonomy and the social construction of the "national order of things" (Malkki 1995b). Drawing on Malkki's (1995a, 1995b) recent writings on the "ethnography of displacement" and the political implications of classifying people in migration, flight, and exile,[4] I suggest that the classification of objects at the interstitial nodes of national borders provides a unique opportunity to witness a highly politicized form of categorization and the emergence of definitions of value out of the very liminality engendered by transit and passage across formal boundaries. Just as racial categories of identity are constructed, defined, and perceived in the transnational space of migrant dislocation (Charles 1992; Goldberg-Ambrose 1994), so too the very definition of "art" is contested as a result of the deterritorialization of objects. Obviously, the human consequences and tragedies of art migration are not even remotely comparable to those of human exile, but the processes that are revealed in tracking art across international boundaries demonstrate, often with profound clarity, the political and economic consequences of (re)classification in the indeterminant space of the border zone.

THE DENIAL OF ART AS COMMODITY

In his writings on the complex relationship between art, class, and taste, Bourdieu has argued extensively on the logic of art "devaluation," or the cultural denial of the economic foundations of art collection and appreciation. In a typically dense statement on the subject, Bourdieu noted that "the challenge which economies based on disavowal [*dénégation*] of the 'economic' present to all forms of economism lies precisely in the fact that they function, and can function, in practice...only by virtue of a constant, collective repression of narrowly 'economic' interest and of the real nature of the practices revealed by 'economic' analysis" (1980:261). Writing specifically about the international trade in European art, Bourdieu went on to say that the "art business, a trade in things that have no price, belongs to the class of practices in which the logic of the pre-capitalist economy lives on" (1980:261; cf. Bourdieu and Derbel 1990 [1969]:165 and Bourdieu 1968:610–11).

Most of the research that has spun off of Bourdieu's ideas on the construction of "cultural capital" in the realm of art worlds has focused on practices of collecting and on the self-fashioning of the art connoisseur's identity (e.g., Cramer 1994; Marcus and Myers 1995; Phillips and Steiner, eds., 1999; Price 1989; Steiner 1994). In a characteristic assertion that points to the profound ambivalence between art and money in the mind of the connoisseur, Lord Kenneth Clark, for instance, declared in the early 1970s: "I hate the whole idea of art being turned into a kind of stock exchange or gambling parlor. I hate the whole thing; I won't go to an auction—one might as well go to a roulette or gambling house. I hate the whole idea of art becoming a form of stock exchange investment. It's a ruinous, wicked, degrading thing" (*Art News* 1973:16).

In different periods of American and European history, art has been perceived by financiers as a more stable form of investment than other commodities. In 1974, a year after Lord Clark made his disparaging comments about the speculative nature of the new art scene, the *New York Times* reported in a headline that "Investors Trust in Art When Other Assets Slide" (14 January 1974). The article quoted New York gallery owner Klaus Perls as saying, "People don't have confidence in money and stocks. They place trust, however, in art. Rather than let their money sit around and evaporate, they buy gold, precious stones and art. They buy anything they feel has a permanent value." In the same year, the British Rail Pension Fund invested $64 million in art as a controversial hedge against inflation and an otherwise weak economy (Rubin 1997). Although studies of art and money have pointed out the contradictions between the speculative nature of art collecting and the cultural overdetermination of art appreciation, little has been said about the "official" channels through which art (as both cultural capital and commodity capital) flows. The disavowal of art's economic value not only is part of the collector's presentation of self but also serves as a financial stratagem to lower or eliminate import duties and taxation on works of art. In other words, the disavowal of the economic is often profoundly *economical.*

In this section of the essay I hope to demonstrate the role of government, and especially the role of tariff and tax law in the United States, in mediating claims of art and value. The history of United States tariff law as it applies to works of art is complex and characterized by shifts through time. The Tariff Act of 1832, which was conceived as a highly protectionist measure, placed all works of art on the free list (Anonymous 1822). Art remained untaxed in the United States through a succession of legislation until the Wilson Tariff Bill passed in 1894. At that time it was declared that only art that was "over a hundred years old" was to be admitted free of duty; all other works were to be assessed at 15 percent ad valorem. In 1909, following heavy lobbying on the part of museums, art leagues, art associations, art dealers, and artists to abolish duties on the importation of all art, regardless of age, Congress compromised and passed the Payne-Aldrich Bill, which removed duties from art that was more than 20 years old. Contemporary art, however, was to remain taxable at anywhere from 15 to 20 percent ad valorem.

In 1912, Woodrow Wilson ran for president on a platform of lowering international tariffs and encouraging world commerce. Shortly after his election, in early 1913, the Association of American Painters and Sculptors, under the direction of Arthur B. Davies, organized what would become the most revolutionary exhibition of modern art in America, the *International Exhibition of Modern Art*, or what later came to be known simply as the 1913 "Armory Show." Under the existing stipulations of the 1909 Tariff Act, all 1,600 "modern" paintings and sculptures that were being brought in for the exhibition from collections in Europe would have either been taxed or placed under exorbitant bond until they were shipped back overseas. The exhibition organizers, however, never intended the works to go back to Europe. In order to defray the high costs of the show, the objects were intended to be sold in the United States at the end of the month-long exhibition. The New York attorney and art patron John Quinn, who had been engaged by the Association of American Painters and Sculptors to assist in legal arrangements for the exhibit, was asked by Davies to lobby Congress in favor of amending the current law so as to allow free entrance into the United States for all the art objects included in the Armory Show. Quinn, who had established a reputation as an expert in financial law, was a tireless art collector and passionately devoted to the cause of promoting art.

In 1913, Quinn testified at the tariff hearings before the House Ways and Means Committee. He offered a fervent plea for the removal of importation duties on all classes of art. He spoke not only for the sake of the objects that were to be imported for the Armory Show but also to relieve a financial burden that hindered his own collecting of contemporary European art. As Quinn's biographer, B. L. Reid, noted in his book *The Man from New York,* Quinn "was finding the customs duty a heavy expense and a grievous nuisance in his own dealings for paintings and sculpture" (1968:157).

Quinn's argument employed two brilliant strategies that were intended to cut to the core of the Democratic plank of the new Wilson administration. First, he argued that art duties and taxation encouraged class distinctions in America and favored the wealthy over the middle class and the poor. He said: "This Committee should bring it within the means and within the power of the man of moderate means—yea, even the poor man—to acquire works of contemporary art before they become twenty years of age and appreciate in value and then fall into the hands of dealers and then become merely the hobby or exclusive possession of the rich" (Tariff Hearings, Schedule N—Sundries, p. 5696). He went on to note that the "popular misconception as to art being a luxury is largely due to the fact that the 'old masters'—some of them spurious—are bought for large sums by a class that would least feel the proposed taxation" (Quinn 1913:19).

His second argument was that tariffs on works of art posed a cultural liability that would negatively affect the overall economic progress and success of the nation. He said:

> Art is a necessity not a luxury.... The French people, as a people, sell millions of dollars' worth of things to the rest of the world, mainly because the artistic instinct and spirit has been fostered in them generation after generation. Where people have an artistic instinct and sense their products are certain to be finer and better and to be bought by other nations.... If we want to compete with the rest of the world in the finer grades of products, and if we want to raise the standard of our export

> products so that we can compete with the works of Germany and France, where art is *fostered and not taxed*, it will be only good business for us to encourage, at least to the extent of removing the duty on contemporary art, the practice, study, and knowledge of contemporary art. (House Hearings, Schedule N, pp. 5694–95)

After testifying before the committee, Quinn wrote a legal brief entitled "A Plea for Untaxed Contemporary Art: Memorandum in Regard to the Art Provisions of the Pending Tariff Bill," which was submitted to the House and circulated to whomever else he though might be able to assist him in his crusade. In his brief, Quinn expanded on the two arguments he had already made and in particular stressed the noncommodity status of art objects. He wrote:

> It is an absurdity to argue that art is merely a luxury. It is a degradation to treat it as though it were something like opium or a drug or an adulterated food or like a contagious disease, and it is uncivilized and reactionary to consider it merely a means of raising a little revenue, as if it were leather or wool or machinery or tobacco or bananas or cotton goods or like any other article of utility that need[s] "protection" or afford[s] a chance to raise a little revenue from. (Quinn 1913:16)

His argument was shrewdly interwoven with enough allusions to nationalist sentiment to tweak Congress's paranoia. "To tax art would be something like taxing religion.... Art should be untaxed because art has a civilizing influence and it tends to drive out things that are pernicious with hatred and fanaticism" (Quinn 1913:18). Finally, in a statement that smacked of current rhetoric in "refugee" discourse, he portrayed art objects as "citizens of humanity" with extended kinship ties that stretched across the greater "family of art." As such, art should be allowed free and safe passage across international frontiers (cf. Malkki 1994). "Art knows no country," Quinn argued in his legal brief, "and its cultivation should be as free as can possibly be made" (1913:3). Ironically, while arguing that the cultivation of art was "good" for the nation, Quinn simultaneously claimed that art was located in a universal sphere and that it was neither territorialized nor rooted within a single political system. In this sense, the passage of art from Europe to the United States was not an uncanny act of "uprootedness" but rather part of the normal flow of objects within their natural sphere of universal circulation. Quinn's argument against a delimited location of art appears, in a way, to anticipate Clifford's (1988b) point that "common notions of culture are biased toward rooting rather than travel" (quoted in Malkki 1995a:15). It also coincides with one of the foundational myths of modernism, that "art is something universal and timeless" (Staniszewski 1998:70).

Quinn had remarkable success in his lobbying efforts, and Congress swiftly ratified the new Underwood Bill, which allowed free entry into the United States of all art objects regardless of their age.[5] The law was passed just in time for the newly arrived shipment of art objects from Europe to clear customs duty free, and the Armory Show was able to open as scheduled. The press and much of the public ridiculed the Armory Show and lampooned those who claimed that the material on view was "art." Among the more illustrious visitors to the exhibition was Theodore Roosevelt, who conspicuously visited the Armory Show instead of attending Woodrow Wilson's inauguration. Roosevelt described his visit in an essay titled "A Layman's View of an Art Exhibition," which was published in *The Outlook* in March 1913 (reprinted in Munson-Williams-Proctor Institute 1963:160–62). In it he extolled the strength of American artists and denigrated the European "lunatic fringe," unfavorably comparing "Duchamp's nude to the Navaho rug in his bathroom" (Altshuler 1994:69). Marcel Duchamp's *Nude Descending a Staircase* was, in fact, the subject of most of the critics' derision. J. F. Griswold of the *Evening Sun* published a cartoon showing rush-hour mobs going down to the subway, which he titled *The Rude Descending a Staircase.* In the same paper, the political cartoonist John T. McCutcheon took up the Cubist theme in a cartoon depicting "Woodrow Wilson proudly painting a falling faceted figure entitled *Tariff Descending Downward*" (Altshuler 1994:73). The critics had thus come full circle, and in the end the government and the Underwood Bill were portrayed as accomplices in the free passage of "non-art" into the United States.

Given all of his arguments to Congress regarding the noncommodity status of art, it is ironic that John Quinn purchased the most sizable share of the Armory Show collection, spending $5,808 for 20 works by Derain, Duchamp, Manolo, Redon, Signac, Duchamp-Villon, Eugene Zak, and Walt Kuhn. In fact, there is no doubt that Quinn was attracted to art collecting as a form of commodity investment or speculation. As Zayas noted of Quinn's art-collecting activities: "There were only two [major] buyers in New York, Arthur B. Davies, who knew all there was to be known about buying pictures, and John Quinn, who just bought and bought. Neither of the two needed to be lured into buying.... Davies and Quinn were old timers and knew the marked (French) value of modern works of art, and also knew that they were getting 'bargains'" (1996:94).

Following the Armory Show sale, Quinn's passion for collecting escalated. He became consumed particularly with the work of the Romanian sculptor Constantin Brancusi, whose work was introduced to him in 1914 by Alfred Stieglitz at his Photo-Secession Gallery, where Quinn purchased *Mlle. Pogany* (Zilczer 1985). His commitment to Brancusi grew "to the point of actually commissioning a sculpture, a version of the Kiss in stone...and of requesting the right of first refusal on Brancusi's next important work" (Andreotti 1993:147). Brancusi in fact became financially indebted to Quinn to the point where he could scarcely keep up with the demands on his production. In a letter written in 1917, Brancusi apologized to his chief patron and noted, "I am sorry that I cannot go quicker and that I am making you wait." Quinn also took advantage of Brancusi's financial indentureship, as well as his desire to concentrate his works in one collection, "by offering at times half, or less than half, of what Brancusi had asked for them" (Andreotti 1993:147).

Upon Quinn's death in 1925, his collection was dispersed, and large portions of it were sold to European collectors—nationally uprooted objects shipped back to where they had originally come from (Zilczer 1990). Brancusi sent Marcel Duchamp and Henri-Pierre Roché to New York to buy back his works. "He was afraid that if they were put up for public sale," Duchamp recalled, "they would make only two or three hundred dollars a piece, when he had already sold them for a lot more." Duchamp arranged with Mrs. Charles C. Rumsey, a friend of Brancusi's, to buy back from the Brummer Gallery 22 Brancusis (from the Quinn collection) for $8,000. "We split three ways," Duchamp continued. "We reimbursed Mrs. Rumsey for what she had put up, and then we—Roché and I—had about fifteen Brancusis, which we divided. This commercial aspect of my life made me a living. When I needed money, I'd go to Roché and say, 'I have a small Brancusi for sale; how much will you give me?' Because at that moment the price was very low. That lasted for fifteen or twenty years" (Cabanne 1971:73–74). In the end, then, not only did most of the objects Quinn fought so hard to bring into the United States end up back in Europe, but the objects for which he claimed pure aesthetic value with no commodity interest ended up functioning as mere currencies in a small commercial network of subsistence exchange.

ON THE LEGAL IDENTITY OF THINGS

Every first-year student in contract law is taught the 1960 case of *Frigaliment Importing Co v. B.N.S. International Sales Corp.*[6] In this case, which was heard before the United States District Court of New York, the Swiss plaintiff argued that the chickens his company had received from an American poultry supplier were not the quality he had expected or been promised. "When shipment arrived in Switzerland, plaintiff found on May 28, that the 2 1/2–3 lbs. birds were not young chickens suitable for broiling and frying but stewing chicken or 'fowl.'" The defendant, on the other hand, claimed "chicken" to mean any bird of that genus that met contract specifications on weight and quality, including what it called "stewing chicken" and what the plaintiff "pejoratively terms 'fowl.'" The defendant's principal witness, a Mr. Weinberger, who operated a chicken eviscerating plant in New jersey, testified that "chicken is everything except a goose, a duck, and a turkey." In the end, Circuit Judge Friendly concluded "that plaintiff has not sustained its burden of persuasion that the contract used 'chicken' in the narrower sense." But the ambiguity surrounding the definition of "chicken" was never fully clarified in the case. If the law has trouble defining what is or is not a chicken, how can it ever hope to define an even more nebulous category such as "art"?

In 1928, the photographer and art collector Edward Steichen attempted to import into the United States Brancusi's abstract statue *Bird in Space* (fig. 7.1).[7] The statue, which stands just over four feet tall, is crafted of highly polished bronze with a brilliant reflective surface

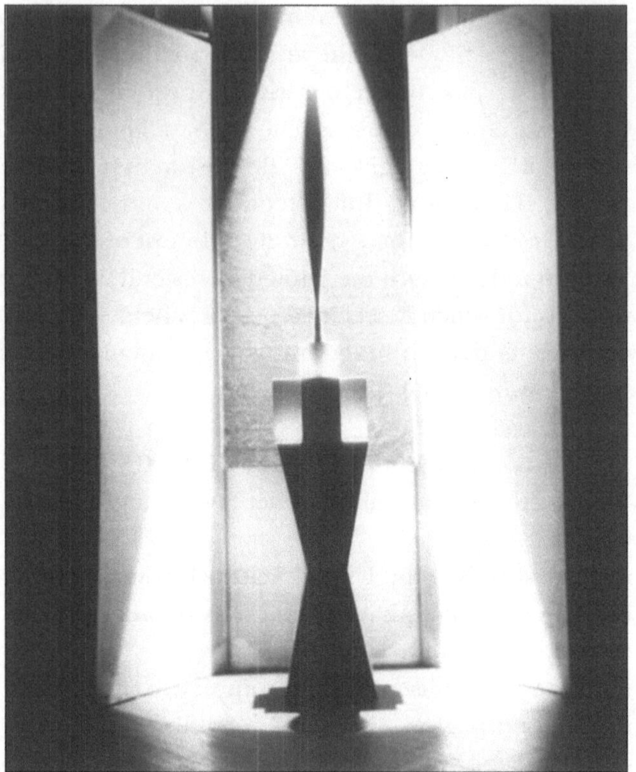

FIGURE 7.1

The object in the border zone: Brancusi's Bird in Space *as photographed by Edward Steichen. "Exhibit 2" in the case of* Brancusi v. United States. *Reproduced by permission of the International Museum of Photography at George Eastman House.*

and is mounted on a base of stone and wood. In shape, "it is basically a gently curving cylinder, wider in the middle than at the base but tapering again to a point at the top" (Hartshorne 1986:94).

Steichen sought to import the statue duty free, entering it as a "work of art" under Paragraph 1704 of the Tariff Act of 1922 (Steichen 1962:57). The sculpture, however, was detained in New York by the United States Customs Service, and the examiner F. J. H. Kracke, "acting on the advice of several men high in the art world," decided that it was not properly a work of art and thus was not entitled to a duty-free passage into the United States. Citing the limitations of the Tariff Act of 1922, which allowed to enter the country duty free only "original" works of art whose subject was principally "imitations of natural objects, chiefly the human form," Officer Kracke declared that nonrepresentational and abstract forms, such as *Bird in Space,* fell outside these guidelines.

The word "original" was initially inserted into the law as a result of John Quinn's efforts to block the importation of fakes and replicas into the United States. In a letter written shortly after the passage of the Underwood Bill in 1913, Quinn wrote, "I read into the law for the first time the word 'original.'...I did that deliberately to put the importers, largely Jews, I am told, of fake Corots and Raeburns and so on, out of business" (quoted in Reid 1968:159). One of the unintended consequences of his action was that ultimately the term "original" would come back to haunt the very art and artists that Quinn admired most.

Bird in Space was classified according to the criteria of Paragraph 399, as interpreted by the United States Customs Service, as fitting into the category of manufactured items and was therefore to be assessed a 40 percent ad valorem duty, which was prescribed for household and hospital utensils "composed wholly or in chief value of iron, steel, lead, copper, brass, pewter, nickel, zinc, aluminum or other metal" (United States Treasury 1929:428). In his report on the importation of *Bird in Space,* Officer Kracke noted that one of the art historians he had called in for advice on the artistic merits of the statue told him, "If that is art, then I'm a bricklayer" (Hartshorne 1986:94). Another commented, "Dots and Dashes are quite as artistic as Brancusi's work" (Adams 1976:38). The idea of assessing an artist's work "by the yard" or "by the pound" is, of course, the ultimate insult to the valuation of artistic worth. The indignity was not lost on Steichen, who paid under protest the amount assessed, $229.35,[8] and then sued the United States Customs Service to recover payment. Under advice from Gertrude Vanderbilt Whitney (founder of the Whitney Studio Club, which later became the Whitney Museum of American Art), Steichen named Brancusi as the principal plaintiff in the lawsuit. Whitney, who also covered the financial aspects of the suit, "suggested that since this was such an important and far-reaching case, it should be officially instigated by the sculptor himself, so as to make it 'Brancusi, Plaintiff, vs. United States, Defendant'" (Steichen 1962:57).

Testifying on behalf of the plaintiff were the sculptor Jacob Epstein, Forbes Watson (publisher of *The Arts*), Frank Crowninshield (editor of *Vanity Fair*), William Henry Fox (director of the Brooklyn Museum), and the art critic Henry McBride. Drawing upon the same appeal to democratic principles and patriotic discourse as John Quinn in his 1913 "Plea for Untaxed Contemporary Art," the attorneys for the plaintiff stated in their trial brief that works of art ought to be compared to ideas; both "were entitled to free currency among the nations of the earth, and to fall into the error of bounding 'art' is almost sufficient to destroy the principle of its right to free entrance" (quoted in Adams 1976:57).

On the part of the government, two witnesses were produced "who have had experience in art and sculpture." Robert Ingersoll Aitken and Thomas Jones, both New York sculptors, "pronounced the importation to be neither a work of art nor a sculpture" (United States Treasury 1929:429). Jones, also an instructor of art at Columbia University, added that although Brancusi was "a wonderful polisher of bronze," the sculpture in question "was not art" (Adams 1976:40). In his deposition, made in Paris, Brancusi had to argue for the status of *Bird in Space* as art under the criteria established by United States tariff law. Principally, he had to demonstrate that he was a professional artist, that he had worked on the materials by hand and not by machine, and that the work was an "original" and not a reproduction or copy (fig. 7.2).

> This work was made by me. I personally took the bronze cast out of the mold. The theme in bronze is my very own special invention and execution. The second reproduction is not yet finished. I certify that no second bronze version of it exists, nor does the work exist in marble, stone or wood. The bronze that I sold was the original. I finished this sole model in 1926. After the piece was cast, all the work was done with my own hands, and the polishing was also done by hand. No polishing machine or any other mechanical instrument was used for this. (Quoted in Steichen 1962:57)

Following a long courtroom battle, and after keeping the case under advisement for two years, Justice Waite, speaking also on behalf of Associate Justices Young and Cline, ultimately ruled in favor of the appeal and determined that Brancusi's sculpture was indeed a work of art and not an industrial metal commodity (fig. 7.3). For the record, he

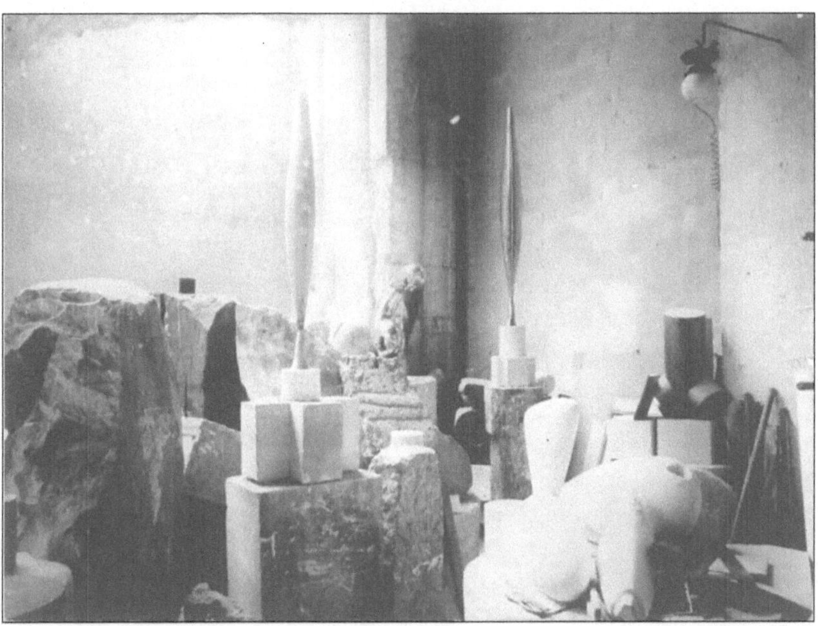

FIGURE 7.2
The object in the studio: Bird in Space *as photographed by Brancusi in Paris, about 1924. Musée Nationale d'Art Moderne, Centre George Pompidou, Paris.*

noted the following finding:

> The decision [that works of art as defined in paragraph 1807 refer to imitations of natural objects] was handed down in 1916. In the meanwhile there has been developing a so-called new school of art, whose exponents attempt to portray abstract ideas rather than imitate natural objects. Whether or not we are in sympathy with these newer ideas and the schools which represent them, we think the fact of their existence and their influence upon the art world as recognized by the courts must be considered. (United States Treasury 1929:430–31)

It is fitting that the struggle over "art" versus "commodity" in the early decades of the twentieth century should have taken place at a port of immigration—a point of respite and cultural evaluation wedged momentarily into the otherwise rapid transnational circulation of

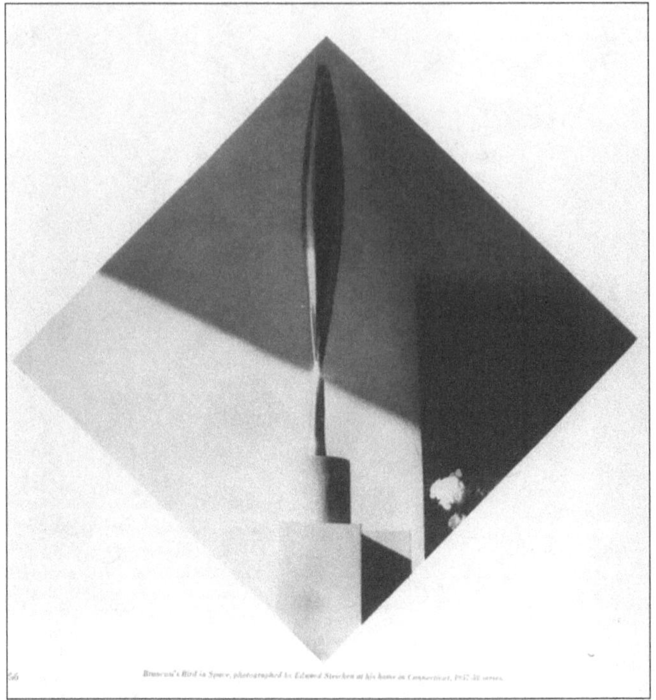

FIGURE 7.3

The object in the collection: Brancusi's Bird in Space *as photographed by Edward Steichen at his home in Connecticut, about 1957. Reproduced in* Art in America *50, no. 1 (1962): 56.*

goods in the world market. Definitions of art, artifact, and commodity typically occur at such interstitial nodes, which act as sites of negotiation and transaction where things must continually be reassessed according to national or regional criteria and local definitions. At each point in its movement through space and time, an object has the potential to shift from one category to another and, in doing so, to slide along the slippery line that divides art from artifact from commodity.

In the landmark case of *Bird in Space,* it is the object attempting to cross an international border that stands as the unknown and potentially subversive "other"—an anomalous icon threatening in a way the very essence of American cultural identity. As Chicago's *Journal of Commerce* reported years after the Brancusi case: "The discussion began on the dock. A crowd gathered—symbolic, we suppose, of the patriotic impulse to withstand the enemy at the very shore" (Punchon 1936).

Why was so much fuss made about the importation of *Bird in Space?* Was it, as Tom Wolfe asked with characteristic wit, "a case of dismal workadaddy civil servants instinctively hating abstract art—this lump of metal some greaser had the audacity to polish up and ask fifteen hundred for?" Or "do they really think that unscrupulous rack-jobbers are going to import job-lots of corkscrews from Japan and exhibit them as art objects on the docks of San Pedro, California, thereby evading millions in duty before unloading them on housewives in the Sanitary Stores?" (Wolfe 1976:ix–x).

Although the case of *Brancusi v. United States* was judged in favor of the plaintiff, this was by no means the end of the legal confrontation between art importers and the United States Customs Service. Until the 1958 amendments to the tariff law, which more accurately reflected the definitions of "art" reached in court cases beginning with *Bird in Space,* customs officers consistently continued to impose duties on objects they deemed unworthy of being called art, and "the courts continued to struggle with many subtle and somewhat arbitrary distinctions between art and non-art" (Duboff 1975:3). In some instances, importers simply paid the tax instead of fighting a costly court battle. As *Art Digest* reported in 1936: "Rather than get into a long, legal argument with the Customs authorities, the Valentine Galleries, New York, paid, under protest, a duty of 33 1/3 per cent on two works in wood by Arp, which recently arrived in this country." But others chose to fight—not only for the money but more importantly for the principle.

In 1936, nearly a decade after Brancusi's successful day in court, the Museum of Modern Art became embroiled with customs officials over the importation of objects brought from Europe for Alfred Barr's exhibition *Cubism and Abstract Art* (fig. 7.4). Philip Goodwin, a member of the museum's board of trustees, "wrangled with United States Customs officials over what he estimated to be $100,000 worth of abstract sculpture from Europe" (Lynes 1973:138). This time, citing Paragraph 1807 of the Tariff Act of 1930, customs ruled that certain objects fell outside the government's definition of art, which *still* stipulated that art consisted of "imitations of natural objects, chiefly of the human form...in their true proportion of length, breadth and thickness." Reflecting on the incident in his anecdotal history of the

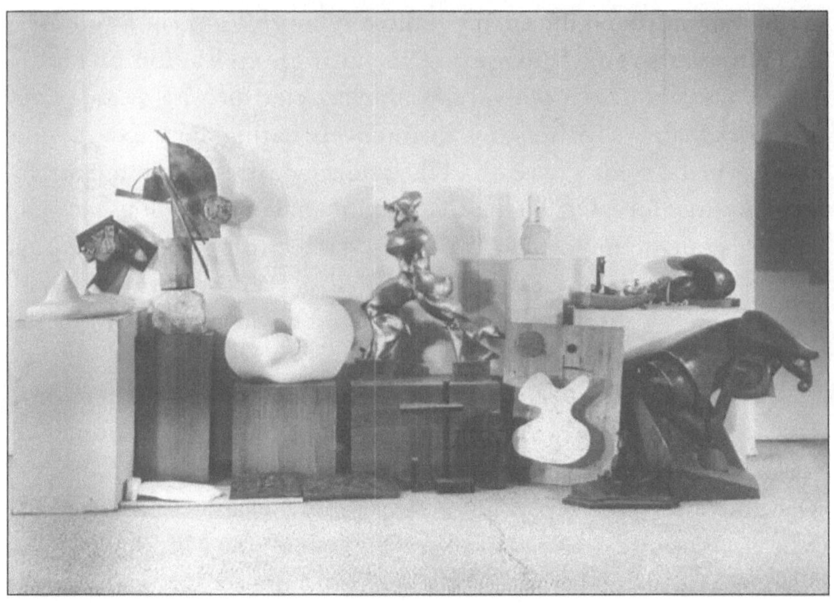

FIGURE 7.4
Foreign loans to the exhibition Cubism and Abstract Art *at the Museum of Modern Art, 1936. "These nineteen sculptures were refused entrance by customs examiners as works of art." Photograph by Beaumont Newhall, courtesy of the Museum of Modern Art, New York.*

Museum of Modern Art, Russell Lynes recalled, "There were nineteen pieces which Barr had borrowed that the men in the customs house could not measure properly or put heads or tails to—three each by Giacometti, Laurens, Vantongerloo, and Duchamp-Villon, two by Boccioni, and one each by Arp, Moore, Gonzales, Nicholson, and Miró" (1973:138).

The problem of importation was not limited to modern European art but also extended to definitions of non-European art, particularly objects of African origin. In 1935, just a year before the Museum of Modern Art wrangled with customs over the works for the *Cubism and Abstract Art* exhibit, the museum faced similar problems in bringing into the United States from Europe objects of African art (fig. 7.5). As was reported in the *Bulletin of the Museum of Modern Art:*

> Many objects in its exhibition of African Negro Art had been refused free entrance [into the United States] because it was

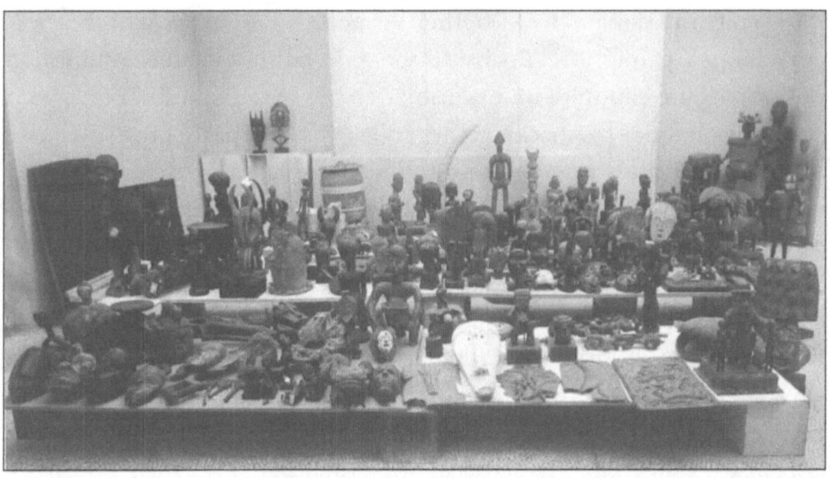

FIGURE 7.5
Objects laid out for customs inspection before installation of the exhibition African Negro Art *at the Museum of Modern Art, 1935. Illustration in* Bulletin of the Museum of Modern Art *(March–April 1935).*

> impossible to prove that certain sculptures were not more than second replicas, or because the artist's signature could not be produced, or because no date of manufacture could be found, or because ancient bells, drums, spoons, necklaces, fans, stools and head rests were considered by the examiners to be objects of utility and not works of art. As a result the Museum was forced to give bond, the premium on which amounted to $700. (Museum of Modern Art 1936:2)

The problem faced by African art entering the United States was not its abstract qualities but rather its status as "utilitarian," which by definition denied it access to the legal category of art. According to the case cited by the government as precedent, *United States v. Olivotti & Co.,* in which the United States Customs Service disputed the importation of marble fonts and seats under the rubric of art, "utilitarian articles do not become sculpture by reason of being adorned by the carving of a sculptor, unless the sculptural decorations be so compelling that the utilitarian achievement of the artisan is lost in the realized sentiment of the artist" (United States Treasury 1916:587).

While the debate over whether Brancusi's *Bird in Space* fit the category "high art" might seem absurd today, in light of its now established position in the canon of modernism, debates over the utilitarian versus aesthetic qualities of African art are still very much part of the discourse of art history, anthropology, and the philosophy of aesthetics. Writing on the history of modern displays of decontextualized African art—which began famously in 1914 at Stieglitz's Photo-Secession Gallery—Vogel noted that "the impulse to strip African art of its visible cultural context has roots in the desire to make it resemble art of the West and conform to our definition of what art is. An essential quality of Western art is that it exists for its own sake, that it has a higher ambition than to be useful in any pedestrian sense. That African art is functional...can appear to compromise its status as art" (1988:14).

In the 1935 Museum of Modern Art exhibit *African Negro Art,* the aim of the display was to separate function from form in order to highlight the aesthetic attributes shared by the "modern" and the "primitive." Curator James Johnson Sweeney "felt that if African art was displayed in the same manner as European and American sculpture, viewers would evaluate it using the same aesthetic criteria" (Webb 1995:32). No information was provided in the exhibit to instruct viewers about an object's function. Unobtrusive identification labels identified provenance but nothing else. As Webb put it, "the objects were to 'speak' for themselves" (1995:32–33). Ironically, what the exhibit was trying to hide from the public in order to gain acceptance of African art as "art" (i.e., the largely utilitarian nature of African material culture) was nonetheless "discovered" behind the scenes of the museum exhibition by United States Customs examiners, who were unwilling to grant these objects the status that the museum sought to accord. Were the objects "speaking" for themselves in the galleries? Were they "speaking" for themselves on the dock? Or did they remain *silent* throughout this process of transcultural exchange, in which the various individuals who interacted with the collection chose to "listen" to very different messages regarding the identity of the objects according to what they were predisposed to "hear"?

CONCLUSION

In a recent article on materiality in narrative fiction, Brown (1998) drew a valuable distinction between the history of things and the history *in* things. "If the history of things can be understood as their circulation, the commodity's 'social life' through diverse cultural fields," he wrote, then "the history in things might be understood as the crystallization of the anxieties and aspirations that linger there in the material object" (Brown 1998:935). A reading of the history of art through legal discourse is a reading of the history of objects at critical moments of "crystallization" or, perhaps better, semiotic sedimentation. Indeed, one of the unintended consequences not only of the trial of *Bird in Space* but also of more recent hearings on works such as Mapplethorpe's *X Portfolio* and Serrano's *Piss Christ* is that it is impossible now to think about these things without recollecting their status as objects of contestation and debate.

With the development of new arts, new audiences, and new potential markets for art in America in the twentieth century, the United States Customs Service has been flooded with unfamiliar material culture brought from around the world. While the academy struggles to classify and order this newly emerging system of objects, the government, in its own way, struggles to interpret the same body of material culture. In an attempt to calculate the value of objects across such a diverse spectrum of styles and categories, the government tends to reduce things to their "thingness": weight, size, metal content, function. The academy, on the other hand, tries to elevate objects above the burden of their material content: for example, Marcel Duchamp's urinal, *Fountain* (1917), doesn't flush, and Robert Gober's sink, *Untitled* (1985), doesn't run water. Although in the end the debates resolve little about the status of any particular "thing," they remind us forcefully of the fickleness of taxonomy and the subjectivity inherent in the construction of categories of art and the sign system(s) of an art world.

The contexts of travel and dislocation, which have become popular metaphors of postmodern identity in recent writings, bring into sharp focus the construction of material categories at "official" points of (e)valuation in the life history of an object. As Sally Falk Moore has made clear in her seminal writings on the anthropology of law and judicial process, it is in the very nature of legal discourse to exploit the indeterminacy of social situations and the ambiguity of liminal categories. Art, by definition, is a contested terrain, and when it is dragged through the halls of justice its indeterminacy is bound, as it were, to shine. Years after the Brancusi trial, Edward Steichen (1962:57) recalled in his description of the courtroom in lower Manhattan the vitality of the material object in the otherwise lackluster space of the border zone: "Behind the long bench sat the three dignified Justices ...in their judicial robes, against the background of a large, dusty-looking American flag. The Brancusi *Bird in Space,* triumphant in all its clean, serene beauty, was of course the chief witness."

Notes

I am grateful for the insightful comments and critiques offered by all members of the advanced seminar, and in particular to Webb Keane and Barbara Kirshenblatt-Gimblett for their extensive discussions of my paper. I am also indebted to the guidance and direction of Sally Falk Moore, without whom I would never even have thought to hazard into the clouded waters of art law. Finally, my thanks to Rebecca Steiner for sharing with me her bibliographic references, comments, and critical insights.

1. This essay is my first foray into a larger project that will deal with the relationship between art and American law. Whereas this essay focuses specifically on tariff law, in the larger project I hope to take into view other major issues that speak to this relationship. The closest works that currently exist on the subject are, in anthropology, Dierdre Evans-Pritchard's doctoral dissertation, "Tradition on Trial: How the American Legal System Handles the Concept of Tradition" (1990), and, in art history, a largely descriptive study by Laurie Adams entitled *Art on Trial: From Whistler to Rothko* (1976).

2. Outside anthropology, Kopytoff's essay has perhaps had the greatest impact on the field of art history, where his model of the "cultural biography of things" coincided with a disciplinary shift toward interest in the structure of markets, the circulation of works within the international art world, and the movement of objects across both geographic and conceptual borders. See, for example, Aronson 1992; Berman 1996; Cutler 1991; Goldthwaite 1989; McNaughton 1987; Pointon 1997; Rovine 1997.

3. "The paper explores the significance of the drum and spear in Kodi healing techniques, and describes their anthropomorphization into ritual actors, almost equivalent to persons. Through the recitation of a personal history or 'biography,' the drum acquires the power to heal, and becomes a symbolic double of the patient" (Hoskins 1988:820).

4. Malkki's work is itself heavily indebted to Anderson's (1991) on the importance of classificatory, taxonomic practices in the exercise of colonial state power.

5. Quinn's influence on the passage of the new law was helped by the fact that the chairman of the House Ways and Means Committee, Oscar W. Underwood, "had old debts" that he owed Quinn (Reid 1968:157).

6. I am grateful to Sally Falk Moore for bringing this case to my attention.

7. Steichen's relationship with Brancusi went back to the 1910s, when he was instrumental in getting the artist's work included in the Armory Show and when he initiated the artist's first one-man exhibition, in March 1914 at Stieglitz's Photo-Secession Gallery (Zilczer 1985).

8. The figure reported varies slightly. In 1962, Steichen recalled that the sum paid was $210 (1962:57).

8

The Object of Translation

Notes on "Art" and Autonomy in a Postcolonial Context

Annie E. Coombes

It would seem anachronistic, at the least, to talk of Western metropolitan identities being shaped in relation to representations of former colonies, no matter how unambiguous the economic power relations existing between such entities. And yet the relationship between culture, consumption, and power remains complicated in particular ways by this legacy. Crucially, it is spectacle—the public art exhibition, for example—that remains one of the primary means of asserting metropolitan identities still dependent on the assumption of a set of references from a shared colonial past.[1]

By way of explanation, let me give you a passage taken from a review of the blockbuster exhibition *Africa: The Art of a Continent*, which opened at the Royal Academy of Arts in London's West End at the end of 1995:

> On Monday night I put on my best suit and attacked the African art show, talk of the town at the Royal Academy.... Outside were a dozen prancing Zulu war drummers, skimpily clad in raffia briefs, beaming and whooping at the passing guests. The guests

> had no idea how to react. Were these renegade militants, satirising the white man's image of Africa? Or were they one of the exhibits, "performance art"?...Should we throw coloured beads or raise a fist in salute? Ambassadorial limousines cruised the forecourt menacingly, as if about to spew AK 47s and mow us all down. Or would the president of the Royal Academy stand up and read from *Jock of the Bushveld?* There is no knowing these days. (Simon Jenkins, *Times,* 7 October 1995)

Obviously, the meanings attached to the Royal Academy spectacle were not as reassuringly stable as the familiar tropes of regimented pomp and circumstance of the era of high imperialism. Indeed, we might infer from the review that the primary characteristic of the exhibition was the kind of flux and instability of meaning typically laid at the door of the postmodern condition by contemporary commentators. And yet, flippant as it is, the review could have been written only by someone well aware of developments in contemporary art practice that have challenged traditional notions of the art object, and by someone knowledgeable about the complexity of representation and agency and the political stakes that are raised as soon as race or gender is implicated. Although the glib tone signals the writer's reactionary reluctance to engage seriously with any of these developments, the review cannot but draw attention to precisely these issues. Paradoxically, this ultimately positions them at the very heart of the spectacle.

Africa: The Art of a Continent (fig. 8.1) was one of a number of exhibitions in Britain focusing on the culture of the African continent as part of the larger "Africa 95" festival.[2] A high-profile event, exhaustively covered in the national and international press, *Africa: The Art of a Continent* moved from London's Royal Academy to New York's Guggenheim Museum in the summer of 1996. Meanwhile, as part of the same celebration of African culture, the city of Birmingham in the British Midlands also hosted a large exhibition, *Siyawela: Love, Loss and Liberation in Art from South Africa* (fig. 8.2).[3] Unlike the Royal Academy show, *Siyawela* received minimal press attention.

Questions of regional versus national and of center versus margin arise, of course, but what interests me more is that despite the evident differences between the two exhibitions—the accusations of "decontextualization" leveled at the Royal Academy show as opposed to the

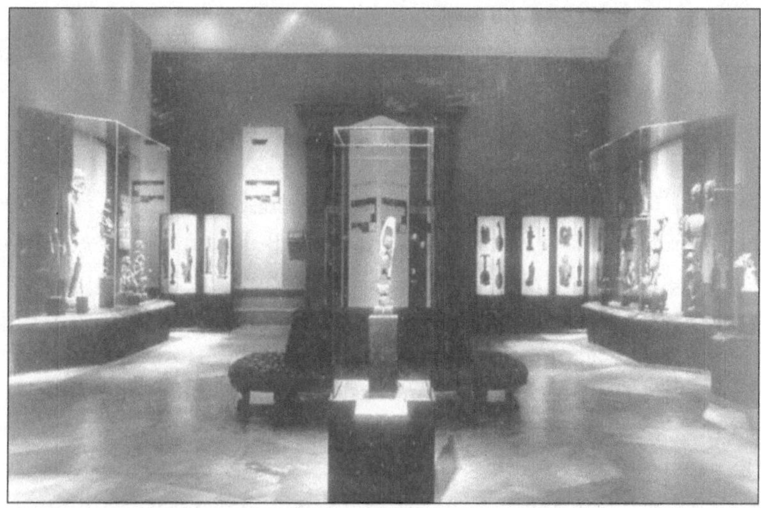

FIGURE 8.1

General view of the exhibition Africa: The Art of a Continent *at the Royal Academy of Arts, London, 1995. Courtesy of the Royal Academy of Arts.*

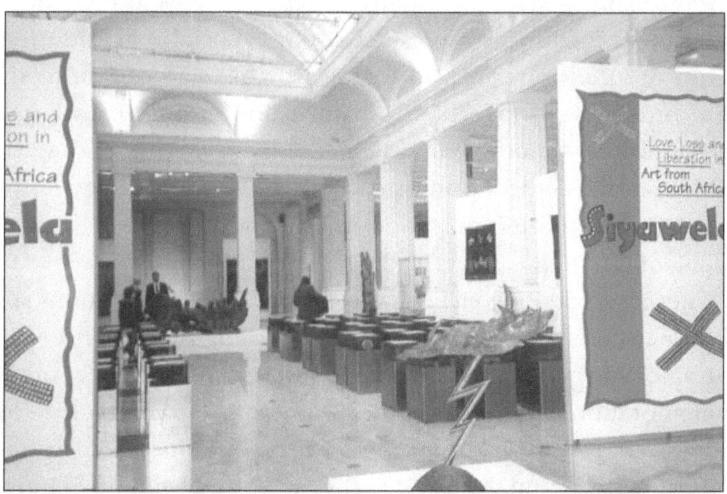

FIGURE 8.2

General view of the exhibition Siyawela: Love, Loss and Liberation in Art from South Africa, *Birmingham, 1995. Photo by the author.*

densely worked metanarratives of *Siyawela,* which derived from a proliferation of textualization, both literal and metaphorical; the hugely presumptuous containing of a continent in 10 rooms at the Royal Academy in contrast to the careful confinement of *Siyawela* to the specificities of the South African contexts—despite these differences, a common assumption lay at the heart of the two exhibitions. Both were fundamentally concerned with reinstating the notion of art's redemptive power.

There is nothing new about this designated role for the art object. It has a long legacy with many incarnations. But what these exhibitions, taken together, allow us to do is to explore how the "redemptive" project becomes inflected with other and specific meanings once it is underscored by a colonial or "postcolonial" dimension.[4] It also enables us to explore the possibility or impossibility of meaningfully representing a productively dialectical relationship between the colonial past and a postcolonial future via the medium of one of the most common spectacles of public culture in the 1990s—the temporary exhibition.

Given the exhibitions' shared utopian project, which prioritized the power of the object and the status of "making" and "art," what was the reason behind the radically different look of the two exhibitions, and why did *Siyawela* simply sink from sight? It seems strange that so little was made of the Birmingham show, especially considering the amount of attention given in Britain to coverage of South African affairs and Britain's investment historically (in both emotional and material terms) in South Africa, together with the impending visit of President Mandela to London early in 1996, both as patron of the Royal Academy exhibition (though he had to cancel his visit to the opening of the show) and as leading elder statesman.

There is something else, however, that the two exhibitions shared, and perhaps it is this that provides a key to the silences either in the curating or in the reviews. Both shows were centrally concerned with commemoration. In this sense they were both "monuments"—one to the power and creativity of ancient civilizations, once denied by colonial presumption, and the other to the power and triumph of humanity over the barbarism of apartheid. In another sense, they were both atonements for the colonial past. But therein lies the paradox. For the Royal Academy exhibition, which should have been the ultimate in grand commemorative and conciliatory gestures, turned out to be about forgetting. It was instead a grand displacement. Conversely, the curators of *Siyawela* could easily be forgiven for skirting the delicate task of commemorating the anti-apartheid struggle on what was then the eve of the Truth and Reconciliation Commission hearings in South Africa. In the wake of the euphoria of the new democratic government, it was certainly the case that, for all sorts of complex reasons, forgetting had become the order of the day—both out of guilt and out of pain and the desire to start anew. And yet *Siyawela* was an exhibition dedicated precisely not just to remembering but to the painful processes involved in the act of remembering and to the importance of historical memory. What I want to suggest is that if both exhibitions are understood as representations of history and as appeals to a postcolonial future, then the one performed this through displacement, dismemberment, and amnesia, and the other through embodiment and commemoration.

Because, in some senses, all exhibitions are dialogic, the linguistic metaphor of "translation" is particularly useful for this analysis. Reading Benjamin's essay "The Task of the Translator" (1968a), I am struck by the similarities between writing and reading historical narratives and his conceptualization of the act of translation. He describes translation as having "a vital connection" to the original that is driven not simply by the task of reproducing or, rather, mimicking the original but by that of actually bringing out something of the essence of the work, enhancing the work. He even goes so far as calling it a literary form: "Translation is so far removed from being the sterile equation of two dead languages that of all literary forms it is the one charged with the special mission of watching over the maturing process of the original language and the birth pangs of its own" (Benjamin 1968a:73).

The essay describes translation as an act of exchange that has the potential to transform both the object (the subject of translation) and the very tools that effect this transformation. Understood as a thesis about exchange and transformation, his suggestive essay has fundamental implications for the way we think about the relations between cultural value, historical narrative, and agency. Benjamin's thesis is also a creative way of rethinking the fine line between maintaining the integrity of the historical moment and recognizing the mediating process necessarily involved in the act of representation—the process of construction, the backing and forthing of logic, of different logics belonging to the past and the present, piecing together and laying out the contradictions rather than smoothing them over. History is always the sum of its parts, but it is also more than this. "In the same way a translation, instead of resembling the meaning of the original, must lovingly and in detail incorporate the original's mode of signification, thus making both the original and the translation recognizable as fragments of a greater language, just as fragments are part of a vessel" (Benjamin 1968a:78).

If we conceive of the "exhibition" model in this way, we become aware that in both the Royal Academy and Birmingham examples, the twin concepts of "history" and "memory" are the pivotal nodes around which the "object"—the displayed artifact—marks out a complicated trajectory. Both exhibitions presuppose a privileged space for the object as a vessel for "translating" history—as the bearer of memory. In other words, they presume a metonymic role for the object. Crucially, the central differences between the two are founded on the different ways in which they (explicitly or implicitly) articulated the relationship between cultural autonomy, on the one hand, and historical experience and social processes, on the other. These are distinctions that rest on the degree and nature of the attribution of particularity to certain kinds of cultural expression—on a willingness to suspend disbelief and credit a transcendental quality to the art object, for example. The exhibitions take us back to the thorny issue of the relationship of art's (relative) autonomy to the lived experience of the social. I want to suggest that what Bersani (1990:1) characterized as the negative aspects of the Kant-derived redemptive model of "willed isolation and alienation of art from the rest of life" may be differentiated from the redemptive features of Adorno's (1977:120–26) attempt to wrest the aesthetic from the jaws of the "culture industry." It is the way in which the two exhibitions articulated this relationship that is the subject of this chapter.

Some of the contradictions regarding this relationship in the Royal Academy exhibition are revealed through criticisms of the exhibition and the curators' defense of their project. The criticisms, which came from a number of different quarters, revolved around three issues: the ethics of exhibiting objects whose provenance was unknown or that were known to be stolen; the lack of "contextualization"; and the fact that the show was planned and curated by a white artist who was himself a Royal Academician and had no professional expertise concerning African culture(s) other than the fact that he owned a considerable collection of objects from that continent. Added to these was skepticism over some of the funding sponsors for the show, particularly De Beers, whose more recent history as a direct beneficiary of the apartheid system in South Africa lent a rather sinister cast to the show's advertising campaign. As one commentator put it,

> The rest of the £2.7 million raised so far has come from outsiders with links to Africa. These links may tell us more about their attitude to Africa than to African art. British Airways, for example, the "official airline to Africa 95," has cut its routes in Africa in the past seven years from 26 to 16. The *Times*, sponsoring the Royal Academy exhibition, portrays Africa, if at all, as a hopeless, helpless war zone. It has the poorest coverage of Africa among British broadsheets. Another sponsor, the Meridien Bank, a bank owned by a Zambian Greek Cypriot, collapsed in unexplained circumstances earlier this year. Its generosity to "Africa 95" won a prize from National Heritage—not much consolation for the ruined African depositors, mostly small businessmen and farmers. Anglo-American and De Beers, the South African companies owned by the Oppenheimer family, grew fat during the four decades of apartheid in South Africa. (*Spectator*, 30 September 1995)

Just as telling in terms of what it suggests about the cachet of cultural capital and its power to deaden the memory of the links between capitalist entrepreneurs and oppressive political regimes was the financial support from the Nigerian business elite. An example of the emollient properties of cultural sponsorship is that the period of the Royal Academy exhibition and "Africa 95," which accepted the munificence of Nigerian businesses, also witnessed the execution by the Nigerian government of Ken Saro-Wiwa and five others protesting the pollution and devastation caused to Egoni land by Shell Oil's extraction of petroleum in the area.

The discussion over sponsorship raises, on the one hand, obvious ethical and moral issues. Although these concerns should of course be taken seriously, the sponsorship issue also raises, on the other hand, concerns that are intimately bound up with the concept of cultural autonomy and the political implications of such an ideology. The acceptability of such sponsors tells us much about the status of the objects in the Royal Academy exhibition. Given the potentially politically volatile nature of the show, and considering that the organizers were evidently aware of this (although naively starting off on the wrong foot), the arguments for accepting this funding constitute a disavowal of sorts. I suggest that it is a disavowal made possible precisely through the belief in or promotion of the notion of an autonomous cultural sphere.

An attachment to cultural autonomy surfaces in many different contexts relating to the Royal Academy exhibition. One good example is the defensive response to charges of the academy's flouting the 1970 UNESCO "Convention on the Means of Prohibiting and Preventing the Illicit Import, Export and Transfer of the Ownership of Cultural Property."[5] Despite the fact that Britain is, significantly, not a signatory to the convention, museums there nevertheless generally follow the guidelines laid down by the International Council of Museums (ICOM). They state that museums should recognize an obligation never knowingly to accept a loan (or sale) of an item that has been exported illegally, either after the introduction of national legislation or after the acceptance of the UNESCO convention, whichever occurred earlier (Bailey 1995:14). During the Royal Academy exhibition, two cases of alleged theft were associated with objects that the curator, Tom Phillips, wished to include in the show.

One of these cases concerned a tenth-century terracotta vessel from Nigeria unearthed by Professor Thurston Shaw in an archaeological dig at Igbo-Ukwu in 1959 and stolen from the University Museum of Anthropology and Archaeology at Ibadan in October 1994. Phillips's version of the "pot" story was a complicated narrative from which he emerged as a heroic figure of *Boy's Own* proportions, tracking down the "lost" pot in the shop of a Brussels dealer, Pierre Loos. The vessel, apparently brought to the dealer by an African "runner," was handed over to Phillips for the Royal Academy show. Since no money had yet been exchanged, the dealer was apparently "happy" to get the now clearly stolen pot off his hands. Phillips's intention was to ceremoniously present the vessel back to Professor Adebisi Sowunmi, head of archaeology at the University of Ibadan, at the Ibadan museum *after* the exhibition, with Thurston Shaw in attendance.[6] Shaw's presence was to be an important symbolic feature of this spectacle, because he was a well-known campaigner on restitution issues and of course was historically associated with the trajectory of the pot. Shaw, however, in an angry lecture delivered at the School of Oriental and African Studies in London after the close of the exhibition, expressed scant regard for Phillips and dismay that he had at no point informed Interpol of the theft (and that Phillips was; in any case, none too fussy about the provenance of objects in his own collection). Fairly early on in the preparations for the Royal Academy exhibition, Shaw resigned from the organizing committee because of Phillips's intention to display the vessel.

London has lately acquired quite a reputation as a center of world trade in looted antiquities. According to Lord Renfrew of Kaimshorn, writing in the *Journal of Financial Crime:* "The traffic in looted antiquities is now said to be second only to that of drug smuggling and there is evidence that the traffic in antiquities and the traffic in drugs often go hand in hand" (quoted by Colin Renfrew, writing in the *Times,* 9 October 1995). Renfrew was one of a group of peers who criticized the government's dismissal of the Treasure Bill in a heated debate that finally extracted a promise that the bill would be reintroduced into the House of Lords in the next session. As one might imagine, the criticism leveled at the Royal Academy exhibition was that it tacitly condoned such illicit trade by displaying and publicizing privately owned artifacts of dubious provenance. As a corollary of display in such a prestigious venue, the value of these illicit collections must inevitably increase.

The second case, involving terracotta figures from Djenne in Mali, reinforced this view. The Malian government has traced more than 250 of these terracottas to museums and private collections in Europe and North America, where they were illegally acquired after having been smuggled out of the country regularly since the 1970s.[7] The terracottas are something of a cause célèbre for activists, who had already effectively forced the closure of a Paris exhibition displaying some of them and shut down a private authenticating business apparently run out of the Archaeology Department at Oxford University. In 1994, ICOM organized a conference in the Malian capital of Bamako. Discussing the illegal export of antiquities, the Malian representative informed the gathering that 85 percent of its archaeological sites had been looted in recent years and, equally tragically, any "evidence" provided by the sites had been destroyed by teams of thieves digging trenches up to 100 feet long. There were also fears that the trade was proving so lucrative that mechanical diggers might be brought in to speed up the process.

Small wonder, given this recent history, that the Malian government refused to give its blessing to the Royal Academy's desire to show the looted terracottas, despite the organizers' reassurances that they would publicize the problem of looting, its relation to the international antiquities trade, and its consequences for various African states, including Mali. Notwithstanding this rebuff, the academy went back to the Malian government and expressed an interest in borrowing items from the Bamako Museum, which itself owned some of the Djenne terracottas.

Ultimately, however, these were deemed by the Royal Academy organizers to be of "unsuitable quality" for display in the London exhibition. And indeed, it is the question of "quality," allied as it is to the concept of autonomy, that is the key issue here. It is the same criterion that was used to justify the questionable sponsorship deals for the show. The Royal Academy organizers attempted at various stages to extricate themselves from the controversies attaching to both the sponsorship deals and the display of stolen antiquities. They also needed to come up with some policy statements in order to short-circuit the demands for restitution that were inevitably raised by such an impressive collection of ancient artifacts from the African continent, especially once it was established that so many of the loans were from private European or North American collections or from museums outside of Africa.

One of the early decisions taken, therefore, involved establishing an arbitrary borderline between "acceptably" looted artifacts—those taken during the colonial period—and "unacceptable" thefts, which occurred post-independence. Piers Rodgers, the secretary of the Royal Academy, explained this convoluted justification by establishing an insoluble barrier between art and history. Writing in *Asian News* (10 July 1995), he said: "Part of the answer lies in the colonial period, so for us it is history. A private institution like the Royal Academy, *devoted to art* [my emphasis], is not really in a position to right the wrongs of history. If that can be done at all it is a matter for the governments."

This case for the autonomy of art, and therefore of institutions whose business is art, was the main claim deployed to extricate the Royal Academy from the restitution debate. It was also the argument that justified the Royal Academy's flouting of the ICOM agreement and the basis for its pursuing its request to display both the tenth-century Igbo vessel and the Djenne terracottas. "We never knowingly show stolen property but we cannot refuse to show *great works of art* [my emphasis]. They cannot be kept in the cellar forever," wrote Rodgers in the same article.

Both the Igbo vessel and the Djenne terracottas were described in terms that asserted their aesthetic importance. Their historical significance was conceived of primarily in relation to the development of art practices, not only on the African continent but, importantly, in all "art." Other reviewers of the show confirmed the suggestion of transcendence contained in Rodgers's statement:

> Whatever was true for the men and women who originally made and beheld these things, what is important is how *we* see them. This strategy works because the quality of what has been chosen is uniformly high. We can move with no difficulty from the familiar aesthetic of ancient Egypt to strange objects made in relatively recent years in Tanzania and Rwanda because artistic excellence transcends geography and time. (Richard Dorment, *Daily Telegraph,* 11 October 1995)

And finally, as irrefutable proof of the shared vision of all artists across huge expanses of time and space, Waldemar Januszcek, the long-established art critic of the liberal *Guardian* newspaper, offered up Phillips's selection of a plaque of green and white ceramic tiles borrowed from a Moroccan museum. He observed that there was little that was remarkable about these tiles except that the pattern had a meditative quality when seen as a whole. Instead, what was significant about such a choice was precisely that "in an exhibition filled with important masterpieces of world art, many being given their international due for the first time, an ancient Moroccan artist has spoken to a modern one [Phillips] who lives in Camberwell [S.E. London], and the two of them clearly understand each other perfectly" (Januszcak, *Sunday Times,* 8 October 1995).

In other words, a universal aesthetic was being invoked. The attachment of such a presumption to objects from the African continent inflect it with particular meanings, given the postcolonial context. The African context makes such presumptions particularly susceptible to originary accounts, which carry with them their own dangers: "Primitive is a word which cannot be discounted, for there remains a sense in which it describes perhaps the chief virtue and justification of so much of this work. For we should remember that in its origins, through its eternal power to touch the imagination, art was always at one with magic, ritual and religion, and the artist in his way a sort of priest" (William Packer, *Financial Times,* 7–8 October 1995).

The dangers of "corruption," historically tainted with the horrors of degeneracy, are consequently never far from the scene, in a rehearsal of what Clifford (1986:113) usefully coined as the "salvage" paradigm. "However much we study this African art for its essence, purity and its concise representation of cultures, we know that it will soon be corrupted by the contemporary global and technological world" (Tim Hilton, *Independent on Sunday,* 15 October 1995).

Benjamin, quoting Rudolf Pannwitz, insisted on the importance of what is now often referred to as "hybridity." Specifically, he insisted on its inevitability and on the necessity of "contamination" as part of the process of translation: "The basic error of the translator is that he preserves the state in which his own language happens to be instead of allowing his language to be powerfully affected by the foreign tongue.... He must expand and deepen his language by means of the foreign language. It is not generally realized to what extent *any* language can be transformed" (Benjamin 1968a:81).

Also interesting in this paradoxical invoking of the autonomy of objects is the extent to which this increases their exchange value. Though premised on a denial of the market and the economic incentives that could be said to have "influenced" those private collectors whose collections were enhanced by inclusion in the exhibition, the Royal Academy's assertion of aesthetic autonomy could only add to any market value.

This disavowal of economic interest and recourse to the old Kantian standby of "disinterestedness" was neatly and unwittingly unmasked in an article in the *Times* (4 November 1995) titled "The

Art of Investing in an Emerging Market." It reported on Africa as potentially "the emerging market story of the next few years" and then detailed certain new initiatives in Botswana, Kenya, South Africa, and Ghana. The text of the article framed a large photograph of an eighteenth-century Akan terracotta head, and the caption flagged the fact that it was on display at the Royal Academy. The conjunction of text and image is eloquent. Significantly, the same funerary head accompanied a short notice of the *Africa: The Art of a Continent* show in the *Wall Street Journal* on 17 November 1995. Now that the colonial past was neatly dispensed with and the postcolonial present negotiated into a settlement that included the "payoff" of a place in the great universal aesthetic, was this any more than the kind of recuperation that we have come to expect? Perhaps.

Important in the postcolonial context is that a place in the great Eurocentric canon is mediated by a particular relationship to history, through "forgetfulness" and disavowal. Despite what the issue of sponsorship and the mounting of arguments around "quality" as a selection criterion demonstrate about the exchange value of the objects on display (together with other reminders such as the financial report in the *Times* and the numerous issues of craft and interior design magazines dedicated to the adaptability of African textiles and carvings that year),[8] the question that responses to the show raised with extraordinary regularity was, "But is it art?" There is a remarkable déjà vu aspect to all this.

The responses ranged from the thoughtful to the banal. "Whether you call these Kongo sculptures fetishes or power objects or ritual tools, one thing they are not is art. Or not until Westerners get their hands on them. To treat them as such is a category mistake; it is to fetishize the fetish" (John Ryle, *Times Literary Supplement*, 20 October 1995:18–19). Or again, "African art is art in the first meaning of the word: skill. Its art grows out of practical things. In Europe we don't ask of a painting 'But what is it for?' In Africa don't ask of a spoon 'But is it art?'" (Dowden, *Spectator*, 30 September 1995). The latter writer continued, "There's no aesthetic art in Africa, just practical objects which we...happen to think are beautiful."

One of the most wonderfully willful examples of the Royal Academy's indiscriminate aestheticization was the display of a five-seated

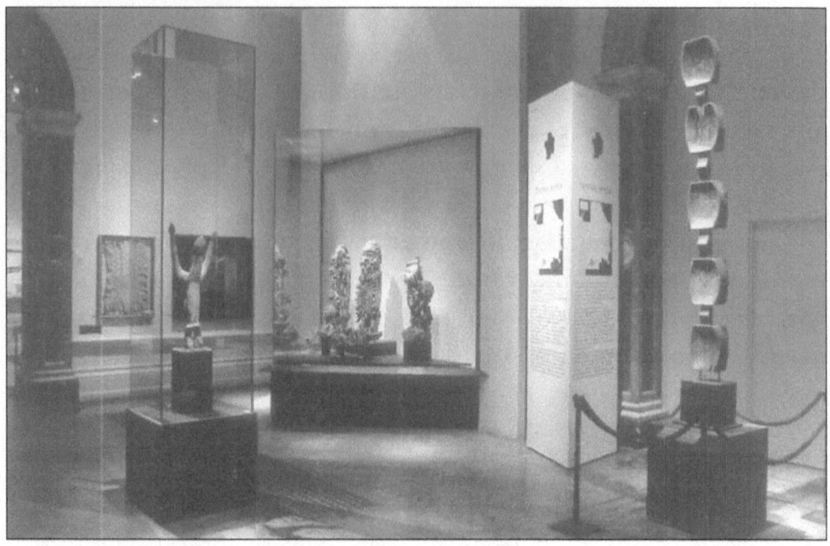

FIGURE 8.3

Ngombe stool, Zaire, on display in Africa: The Art of a Continent, *London, 1995. Courtesy of the Royal Academy of Arts.*

Ngombe stool from Zaire, up-ended on a plinth so that its original function became improbable if not impossible (fig. 8.3). Appiah (1995) usefully attempted to turn the tables on this anxiety over the "artness" or otherwise of the objects by indicating that the term "art" might have no equivalent in any African culture. He suggested, however, that this did not necessarily eliminate aesthetic and formal considerations, and that in any case one would have to recognize the heterogeneity of African production. Given that this is a well-worn rebuttal by now, what should concern us instead is why such old objections should continue to exercise the critics and what significance might be served by this reincarnation of an old debate at such a moment.[9]

Disavowal here takes the form of a restaging of the moment of modernist appropriation while at the same time denying that these things have ever been seen before in the West or, indeed, that such appropriations have ever been acknowledged. "Almost everywhere one looks there is something strangely familiar. A mask that is surely by Modigliani, a wooden totem pole which must have been carved by

Brancusi [a reference to the Ngombi multiple stool!], a fetish out of a Picasso painting" (John Russell Taylor, *Times,* 4 October 1995). Even reviews that acknowledged the distortions created by viewing the collection through this prism reinstated its primacy by cataloging the instances of this "meeting" of cultures: "No-one in the West can see African art without seeing it through the distorting mirror of Modernism" (James Hall, *Guardian Weekly,* 22 October 1995). Meanwhile, in the *Financial Times,* William Packer could repeat with apparent impunity, "Even now when we think of Africa, it is still that dark continent of the explorer, the empire-builder and ethnographer, that comes to mind" (*Financial Times,* 7–8 October 1995). And: "Africa is the invisible continent. What do we know of African culture beyond a few random offerings: the bare-breasted dancers of Ipi Tombi, the carvings and bangles of ubiquitous beach traders, the outrageous body-wiggle of the footballer Roger Milla?" (A. Lavender, *Times,* 4 August 1995).

Most poignant for me, perhaps, is that this "forgetfulness" was reproduced in the form of the old narrative of awe and wonder, now reinvented as if for the first time. In 1897, following Britain's punitive raid on and sacking of Benin City, European museums fought over ownership of the loot. When doing my research on the intersection of the aesthetic, scientific, and political discourses produced by anthropologists, art historians, and other constituencies of the colonial elites both in Britain and among West Africans, I expected a fairly homogeneous set of responses from the British contingents to the "bronzes" and ivories taken from Benin. I anticipated that the narrative I had read so frequently in contemporary historical accounts would be confirmed by my research. In other words, I expected the European colonials uniformly to proffer arguments about the origins of the "bronzes" that would deny their African origins and identify them firmly as the work of Portuguese craftsmen, or at least as having been generated by the colonial encounter in the fifteenth century. I discovered that this was far from the case, and that there were a number of competing accounts. Among these were some written by prominent figures from a number of arenas who claimed (in 1897) that the "bronzes" were indeed West African in origin and who likened them to the bronze work of the Italian Renaissance (particularly appropriately, since they were made at roughly the same time and used the same "lost wax" technique) (Coombes 1994). I also discovered that despite the prominence and circulation of such ideas in the first decade of the twentieth century, subsequent "histories" of the events of 1897 and of the responses to the "bronzes" were consistently written in a tone of surprise, awe, and disbelief, as if, at the time, there had been universal denial of their African origins.

In 1995, I came across the same expression of awe, disbelief, and "discovery" in reviews of the Royal Academy show. A familiar comparison, repeating almost word for word the narrative of awe from the nineteenth century, drew comparisons with Italian Renaissance bronzes:

> But the highlight of the exhibition has to be an astounding display of Benin bronzes, surely among the most beautiful works of art ever made by man. A naturalistic seated figure made by a Yoruba artist from Tada, Nigeria, between the 11th and 14th centuries shows an understanding of the bones and muscles of the human body that we do not see in European sculpture until Donatello a century later. The crispness and detail of plaques from the palace at Benin (15th century) can only be compared to Lorenzo Ghiberti's bronze doors for the Baptistry of Florence of roughly the same date. (*Daily Telegraph,* 1 October 1995)

More explicitly: "If the ugliest of these heads resembles the art dealers of Bond street, the most beautiful, made by the Yoruba of Nigeria, vaguely dated 12–15th century, is of such a quality that its attribution would not disgrace a master of the early Italian Renaissance" (Brian Sewell, *Evening Standard,* 12 October 1995).

Such commentaries culminated in the oft-repeated "We shall never look at African art in our old innocent, patronising naivety again" (*Financial Times,* 7–8 October 1995). Or as one commentator put it: "Such objects will certainly shake received opinion" (J. McEwan, *Sunday Telegraph,* 8 October 1995). Clearly, such overwhelming evidence is no insurance against "forgetfulness."

I have always been reluctant to seek answers in psychoanalytic theory, but there are, after all, some features of such an analytic system that might be productive in unpicking the seams of this narrative of forgetting.[10] For this was clearly not a conscious operation but a collective amnesia, all the more evident because the authors offered their responses as "positive" accounts of the exhibition. In this sense they were not "willful." And yet the constancy with which such arguments were advanced borders on neurotic repetition. Freud's thesis on memory (which is in fact a theory of forgetting) "assumes that all experiences, or at least all significant experiences, are recorded, but that some cease to be available to consciousness as a result of repression, this mechanism being activated by the need to diminish anxiety" (Rycroft 1972:90; see also Laplanche and Pontalis 1973:212–13, 390–94).

We could say that one of the "effects" of this process is a masking of economic relations and their actual exchange values, partly, as in this case, through recourse to the resurgence and insistence of the autonomy/universalism model of "art." But Freud's thesis might be useful as a way of thinking about the deeper-seated issues at the heart of this forgetfulness, and so perhaps we need to imagine what anxiety might be lurking there and why its repression should take this form of repetition as a mechanism of defense.[11]

The model of cultural autonomy in which the Royal Academy is still so invested is one much discredited in anything other than the most conservative art historical circles, and it is interestingly aligned to a concept of art that is grounded in the metaphor of organic entity and wholeness. It is a very different concept of artistic autonomy than that advocated by Benjamin's colleague Adorno, for example. For Adorno, "it was the different ways in which art's irreconcilability to reality is expressed in...modernist or 'non-organic' works that...demonstrat[ed] the decisive superiority of the modernist aesthetic" (Osborne 1991:5; see also Jay 1984: ch. 4). In his *Aesthetic Theory*, Adorno suggested that for art to be in any way effective (or affective), it must operate as "an articulated 'system of contradictions,' an 'antagonistic totality'" (Osborne 1991:34).[12] In other words, it must be dialectical. This is precisely what is missing in the claims of "autonomy" in the critical responses and official justifications relating to the Royal Academy exhibition.

I want to turn now to the Birmingham exhibition, *Siyawela: Love, Loss and Liberation in Art from South Africa.* One of the meanings of the Ndebele word *siyawela* is "we are crossing over." In 1995, the word immediately signaled the momentous changes occurring in South

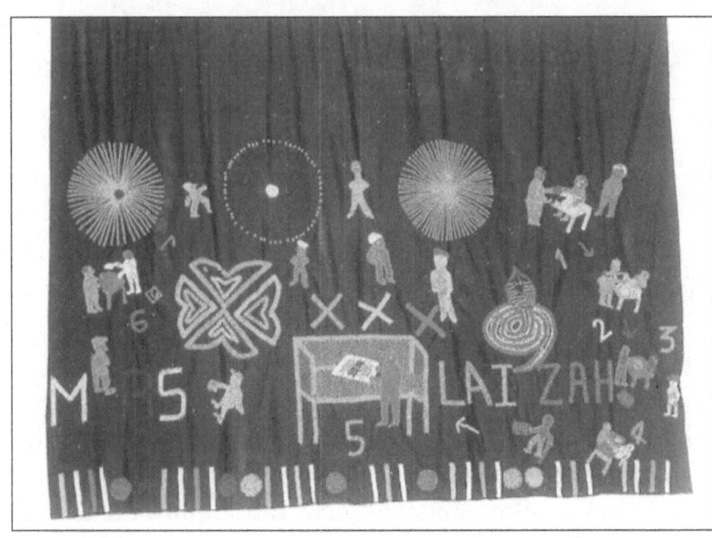

FIGURE 8.4

Mrs. Laizah, Voting, *1994. Beads on cloth. Collection of Kim Sacks, Johannesburg. Photo by Annie E. Coombes*

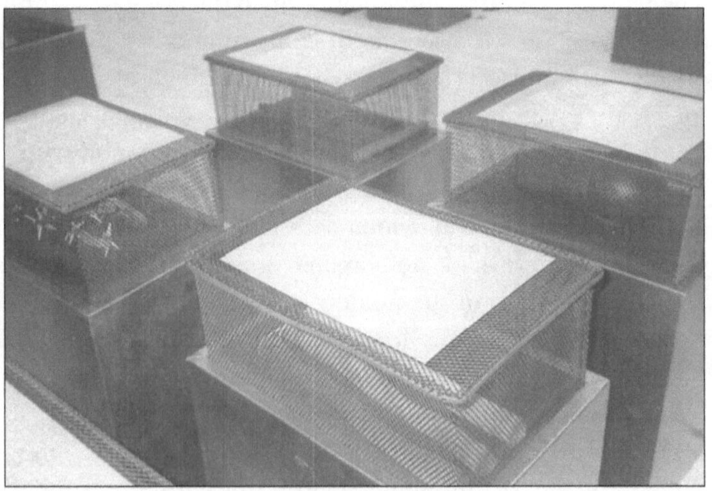

FIGURE 8.5

Willem Boshoff, Blind Alphabet B, *1987–94. Metal boxes containing wooden carvings, with plates in Braille as lids. Collection of the artist, Johannesburg. Photo by Annie E. Coombes.*

Africa. That is, the Birmingham exhibition represented art as a "bridge" between the horrors of the apartheid regime and Mandela's new government of national unity (the crossing over to the other side)—a means of survival and a beacon of hope. And in the hands of the exhibition's curators, Colin Richards and Pitika Ntuli, *Siyawela* took on other layers of significance. Again the metaphor of "translation" is useful. As with the Royal Academy show, there are narratives to uncover here, but they are never simple and rarely linear. The texts that guide us in our passage through the exhibition are suggestive markers that function in a complex relation to the objects they accompany.

We move from *minceka* (wraparound cloths worn by Tsonga-Shangan women in the northeast of South Africa) embroidered with beads showing scenes commemorating the election of 27 April 1994, inspired by voter education material produced for an electorate that had never before had the opportunity to vote (fig. 8.4). Farther on we encounter Willem Boshoff's conceptual sculpture *Blind Alphabet B* (metal boxes containing wooden carvings, with plates in Braille as lids) (fig. 8.5). The *minceka* are accompanied by a tender testimonial from Tatamkulu Afrika, "Against All Odds My Heart Sings":

> Later, sun low, tide running out in me. I bus to the township shack of my dear love, my need for her never so strong. She is sitting in a corner of one of the two rooms' perpetual gloom, her crippled leg hidden under the blanket over her knees, her hands quite still.... My spirits plummet. Has anything changed for her this Day? Will this Day heal her leg, restore her to what time and terror so remorselessly have taken away? She reads me, smiles, her eyes soft in the room's dusk, her hands beckoning me to come. "It is done," she whispers. "We have walked the last mile!" Later still, I helped her to the bed. We are careful with each other as though we hold a fine glass, and my heart sings. Yes, against all odds, my heart sings. (Afrika 1994:13)

The Boshoff piece is accompanied by a directive: "This exhibit has been designed to be fully accessible to blind people. We therefore respectfully request that sighted visitors refrain from touching it, unless with the help of a visually impaired guide."

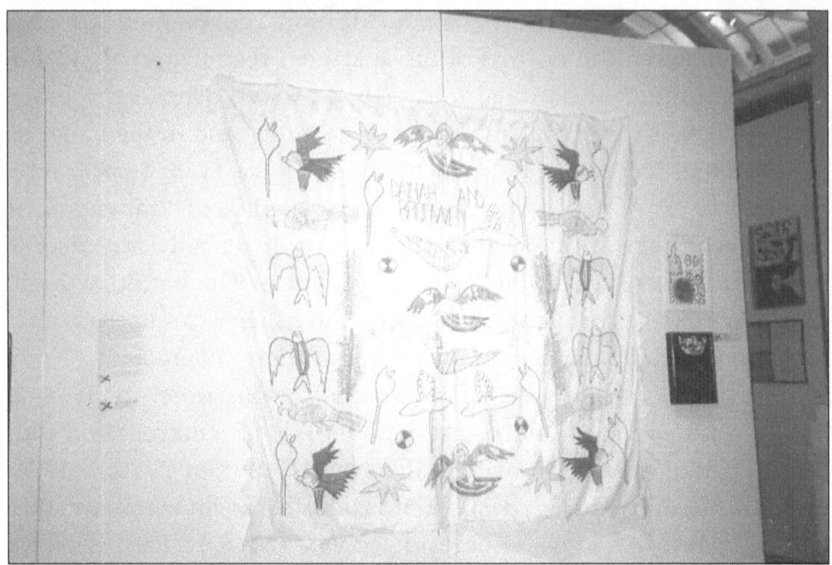

FIGURE 8.6

Bronwen Findlay and Daina Mabunda, Angels, Flowers and Birds, *1992. Cloth and embroidery threads. Collection of the artists, Durban. Photo by Annie E. Coombes.*

Later the viewer comes to an embroidered cloth made by Daina Mabunda in collaboration with a Durban artist, Bronwen Findlay (fig. 8.6). Angels inspired by Giotto's *Lamentation,* via Findlay's screenprint of angels and aloes, sidle with peacocks and *chabalala* birds. This is a crossing over of another kind. The accompanying text is a translation of Mabunda's commentary, by her son Moses Mabunda, and a statement by Findlay about her long-standing collaboration with Daina Mabunda.

Texts beside soccer "badges" from Robben Island and certificates from the "Robben Island Academy of Fine Arts" and "Robben Island Football Club" speak of the significance of football and fine art for the political prisoners interned on Robben Island. There is a testimonial by Bika Muntu Maseko about the role football played for those growing up in the townships under apartheid, and an extract from Neville Alexander's official statement, *Robben Island Dossier: Report to the International Community* (1994).

Accompanying Penny Siopis's photographs of the casts of Saartjie Baartman's body lying in the basement of the Musée de l'Homme in Paris and her work *Dora and the Other Woman* (1988) is a statement by the artist making reference to her sources: Helene Cixious's work on Freud and Freud's own writings about a patient of his known as "Dora," and his infamous observation that the "sexual life of the adult woman is the 'dark continent' of psychology." An extract from a report on Saartjie Baartman (who was also referred to historically as the "Hottentot Venus") from the *Times* of 1810 is included alongside the images, together with a historical analysis of the spectacle made of Baartman, written by a contemporary American academic, Bernth Lindfors (Lindfors 1983). Siopis's concern with this conjunction of text and image is to demonstrate the ways in which both "Dora" and Baartman have been objectified through spectacle and so-called scientific objectivity.

Another section of the *Siyawela* exhibition contains a selection of work done by British schoolchildren from Birmingham and children from the Mokhele art therapy and education project in Soweto, under the direction of Maggie Makhoana, painting their responses to living in South Africa today.

Siyawela, then, was an experiment in "translation" by curators who hoped viewers would grapple with the concept of "art" rather than take its meaning for granted as homogeneous and stable—the apparently "universal" aesthetic of the Royal Academy show. The art in this exhibition might have been transcendental in some ways, as well as redemptive and certainly utopian, but it was located in historical time and geographical place. Perhaps it was able to occupy a critical space precisely because the "autonomy" it invoked, which recognized the importance of making and envisaging, was a *relative* autonomy. It provided a space to comment on life, not to abscond from it, even though the exhibited work itself might have offered a fantastical escape from the grimmer aspects of it. The narratives of explication in *Siyawela* were multifaceted—like the work itself, they came from different sources that inform and construct and make sense of our world: poetry, autobiography, official documents, and historical interpretation. Perhaps we could argue that *Siyawela* was one instance of Adorno's "articulated system of contradictions" presented as an "antagonistic totality." It was also an exhibition that relied on a sense of time and historicity rather than denying it.

The definition of cultural autonomy recycled in connection with the Royal Academy has particular ramifications in the context of the African exhibition, precisely because of the objects' historical inscription as "ethnography" and the legacy of colonialism that this recalls. It is also a definition that negates the value of history just as it denies its inscription. Such a course fuels the rehearsal of awe and wonder and eases the passage of historical amnesia. Since this history is bound up with a colonial past, its denial has particular implications for the ways in which future relations between the West and postcolonial African states (for example) can be imagined and reinvented.

If we return to the passage by Jenkins that I quoted at the beginning of this essay, one of the things it demonstrates is that meaning is hard to pin down. It eludes commentators. They do not know how to respond. They do not know where they stand. This might be said to be one of the effects of the "postmodern condition," particularly for commentators who have no clear understanding of the economics of the art market and of what is at stake in the game of cultural value. For them there is something reassuring about the notion of an autonomous art object with its immanent internal logic. In the context of the Royal Academy show, this is doubly gratifying because of the assumption of paternalistic generosity through the act of inclusion, an act that might assuage any residual guilt for the colonial past. More than this, the quoted passage suggests that the "subject" of the exhibition has eluded definition and, by implication, containment. Not only do the critics not know where *they* stand, but also the object of their critical attention does not know *its* place. This is an "anxious" moment exacerbated by the concurrent exhibition of contemporary South African art, Birmingham's *Siyawela* show. The work displayed in it could fit into any and all categories: modernist, postmodernist, didactic, and suggestive.

If the historian's task is "to brush history against the grain," then Spivak's reader-as-translator (1993:197) further complicates the question of agency in a highly productive and constructive manner (both of these words also in their literal sense) by reading between the lines.[13]

Whereas for Benjamin, agency rests with the translator, for Spivak it is also produced through the act of reading itself, which can become an "other" layer of translation in the context (for Spivak) of a willful postcolonial critique. In a sense, *Siyawela*'s narratives, though rarely directive themselves, anticipated just such an "active" reader who would recognize, if not necessarily understand, the significance of those in-between spaces. Its various "voices" prompt us to unpick rather than take for granted the connections between objects and to engage with the objects' metonymic properties. For any thesis dealing with "exchange"—a term that already contains within it a notional equality—such a recognition of heterogeneous agency provides a necessary antidote to a version of "history" that would have us sleepwalking through the present in an attempt to defer the lessons of the past.

Notes

I wish to thank Neil Lazarus for critical comments on an earlier version of this chapter and Colin Richards for stimulating discussions on the work selected for *Siyawela* and for providing copies of the texts from the exhibition. Thanks also to Patrick Burton for generously sharing his cuttings collection on *Africa: The Art of a Continent* and consequently saving me a great deal of additional work.

1. Several examples of such exhibitionary spectacles have been subjected to considerable scrutiny. See, for example, Clifford 1988a; Coombes 1992; Foster 1985a.

2. *Africa: The Art of a Continent* was held at the Royal Academy of Arts in London from 4 October 1995 to 21 January 1996. See *African Arts*, Summer 1996, for critical reviews of the exhibition and its accompanying catalog and of other exhibitions put on as part of "Africa 95." Also see Nicodemus 1996.

3. *Siyawela: Love, Loss and Liberation in Art from South Africa* was held at the Birmingham Museum and Art Gallery from 21 October 1995 to 14 January 1996. It was co-curated by Colin Richards and Pitika Ntuli.

4. The cultural criticism of Walter Benjamin and Theodor Adorno contains some of the most fruitful discussion of both the contradictions arising from and the necessity of the redemptive potential of art, and the political implications of this. See, in particular, Adorno 1978; Benjamin 1968b. See also their correspondence with each other regarding autonomy and the redemptive potential of art, reproduced in Bloch et al. 1977. See also Bersani 1990.

5. This convention has been officially adopted by 80 nations, but in practice only the United States, Canada, and Australia apply it with any degree of regularity.

6. It was indeed presented to Sowunmi on 21 September 1996.

7. Nigel Evans's 1990 television documentary "The African King" traced the fate of the Malian terracottas.

8. See, for example, the October 1995 issues of *World of Interiors, Harpers and Queen,* and *Chic.*

9. The "anthropology of art" and questions of aesthetics, cultural value, and the relevance of terms such as "art" and "artist" were popular concerns in anthropology in the 1970s. With a few notable exceptions, such issues were explored much more critically in anthropology than in art history.

10. For an exposition of psychoanalytic theory in relation to historical analysis, see Roth 1987. See also the essays in Antze and Lambek 1996.

11. On the use of repetition in the psychoanalytic sense of the term and in relation to colonial discourse, see Bhabha 1994.

12. On the question of the autonomy of art in bourgeois Western society, see also Burger 1984; Williams 1981.

13. See also Spivak 1989, especially pp. 270–73, where she writes of "reading" Marx's *Capital* as a "diasporic postcolonial."

9

Reflections

Barbara Kirshenblatt-Gimblett

Our original goal during the seminar was to reevaluate the relationship between material culture and exchange theory and to do so in light of critical theories of value and consumption and avant-garde art practices. The chapters in this volume configure this theme in relation to three distinctions—gift/commodity, alienability/inalienability, and art/artifact—across a wide range of cultural contexts. Their immediate topics range from how customs officials evaluate Brancusi's sculpture as it crosses a national border to the indigenization of money in Sumbanese society and the circulation of Pintupi paintings in the international art market. Read in relation to one another, these essays confound the distinction between gift and commodity, unsettle assumptions about the inalienability of valued objects, and point to the implications of taking material culture as the point of departure for theorizing exchange.

GIFT/COMMODITY

The two sites for exploring the gift/commodity distinction are ones in which that distinction is vital for the actors themselves, different as the cases might be from each other: ceremonial exchange among the Sumbanese and shopping for gifts in North London. Money is central to both cases, but in ways that are refreshingly counterintuitive.

Webb Keane uses the Sumbanese case to look at how money appears from the perspective of gift exchange, whereas Daniel Miller looks at the gift from the perspective of a monetary transaction. Keane prepares the ground for his analysis by showing how money operates "in the absence of a full-fledged monetary economy." He demonstrates how the Sumbanese use the formality of exchange events to "keep gift and commodity distinct," whether the token being exchanged is a piece of cloth, paper currency, or a gold coin. The challenge in exchange is to make the material qualities of tokens into "signs of persons," no matter what the nature of the token. To realize this goal, it is not enough to identify tokens with persons. It is also necessary to detach those tokens from persons. Only then can tokens "exteriorize and represent their possessors in circulation." The materiality of tokens is what allows them to endure from one transaction to another. It is the task of ritual to control the category by prioritizing the sign value of the token and displaying "the players' imperviousness to the appeal of utility."

The indigenous theory of money that arises from the Sumbanese case posits the sterile wealth associated with *yora,* "spirits of the wild who can become demonic patronesses of selected individuals." This wealth is sterile because it is "antisocial wealth that cannot reproduce itself." It is antisocial because it "requires no reciprocity." For these reasons, "it is alienable." At the same time, the Sumbanese, when they "treat money as if it were gold," make wealth fertile—that is, they attend to its materiality, identify tokens with persons, circulate these tokens through a series of reciprocal transactions, and use the formality of ritual to give meaning priority over utility. In the process, they distinguish between ancestral authority, which gives to money its symbolic value, and state authority, which determines the use value of money within a market economy. As Fred Myers suggested during the seminar, this chapter raises the problem of unproductive value and the state's preoccupation with this issue in relation to indigenous populations. How is the state to deal with systems of value that lie outside considerations of utility and monetary calculations of value?

Siting the problem of gift/commodity in North London, Miller proposes that we think of the calculations entailed by the gift and the gift qualities of commodities in an emotional economy of love that is predicated on thrift and sacrifice. Contrary to the assumed contrast between gifts and commodities, Miller argues that gifts can be calculating and, conversely, commodities can have giftlike qualities. In the process, he shifts the discussion of inalienability away from its classic locus in the anthropological literature, namely, the gift itself in so-called gift economies. In doing so, he enlarges the range of sites under consideration and challenges the long-standing typology of societies and economies based on the gift/commodity dichotomy. We have tended to think of them separately from one another for the purposes of contrast. Miller and Keane establish a certain parity by staging, if you will, the same problem in two different economies. Neither one turns out to be as true to type as might be expected.

Miller focuses on the basic opposition between the gift as the essence of the inalienable and the commodity as the essence of the alienable. His goal is to show how that most alienable of alienable objects, the commodity, operates in gift transactions. The challenge for his subjects is to use "the power of consumption to extract items from the market and make them social or personal." Their task is to create and sustain a sense of the inalienable through consumption, not outside of it. To get at how this works, Miller identifies an opposition between gift giving and what he calls "provisioning," both of which are forms of exchange within domestic consumption, and he explores how commodities are used to create the "objectification" of love. He argues that whereas reciprocity has been central to theories of gift exchange and inalienability, sacrifice may be even "more successful in sustaining a sense of the inalienable." The two differ in the sense that reciprocity involves considerations of commensurability of tokens and participants, whereas sacrifice is predicated on the incommensurability of the human and the divine. It is through sacrifice, as expressed in the calculations and thrift of North London shoppers, that social relationships can become the medium for objectifying the inalienable.

ALIENABLE/INALIENABLE

If the gift is the privileged site for thinking about the inalienable in gift economies, then art is the privileged site for thinking about the inalienable within capitalist economies. Where we site the problem at hand will direct where we are likely to go with it. Thus, to make art the site for theorizing inalienability requires attention to the notion of art's autonomy. Siting the problem in unexpected places is a first step in charting new theoretical directions. Here again, two chapters, by the way they site the problem of art's inalienability, speak to each other and to the larger problem in counterintuitive ways.

Nicholas Thomas explores the use of aboriginal motifs in the paintings of Margaret Preston in Australia and Gordon Walters in New Zealand, and Fred Myers examines the circulation of acrylic paintings created by Aboriginal members of the Papunya Tula artists cooperative within an international art market. The emergence of Aboriginal painting, in Myers's view, is about the development not of autonomy but of the "category of fine art." And the fundamental condition for this development is the market, not the autonomy of art.

Moreover, the essays in this volume suggest that it is easier to discuss theories of the gift in capitalist societies than to discuss the inalienability of art in so-called gift economies. The reasons for this disparity go beyond any purported historical distinction between precapitalist and capitalist societies. They have rather to do with the nature of the typologies themselves and the historically formed cultural practice of distinguishing the alienability of the commodity from the autonomy of art, even though art itself is one of the most highly valued commodities.

Thomas and Myers complicate the discussion of art's autonomy by showing how considerations of indigeneity locate the question of inalienability outside of the autonomous art object. Discussions of appropriation transfer the problem of alienability from the autonomy of the work of art to the indigenous sources for its inspiration. However, it is the ideal of autonomy—freedom from utility and the market—and not inalienability that undergirds the distinction between art and artifact.

The essays in this volume thus frame the problem of alienability by way of two distinctions: art/artifact and art/commodity. These are not simply two formulations of the same problem, but they do entail each other. With respect to the art/artifact problem, a question is put to a particular object: Is that object now and was it ever art? If what is shown is not art, what is it? Under what conditions does this problem present itself? The issue is not ontological but contingent, as Annie Coombes suggests in her analysis of the blockbuster exhibition *Africa: Art of a Continent.*

By choosing modernist painting as the site for his analysis, Thomas established the normative baseline for our discussion of art's autonomy during the seminar. That baseline is defined by the history of modern art, with its privileging of painting, formal concerns, art's autonomy, artistic intention, faith in the universality of art, and circulation within a national and international art system. As Myers demonstrates, it is precisely within this system that Pintupi paintings circulate, with unpredictable and sometimes unintended consequences.

ART/ARTIFACT

The chapters in this volume locate the art/artifact problem in two places: inside the work itself or between the work and the spaces in which the work moves. Both Thomas and Myers locate the art/artifact problem inside the work itself, but they come at the problem from two different directions.

Thomas, who asks that we attend to the formal qualities and materiality of the paintings, focuses on modernist uses of the indigenous. In his analysis, these practices do not call into question the alienability of art. They call into question the alienability of the indigenous. Thomas's problem is not whether the paintings of Preston and Walters become commodities or whether they are alienable. For the purposes of his analysis, those issues are moot. Instead, if we are to deal with the issue of alienability, we must direct our attention to the use of indigenous motifs, iconography, citations, quotations, and appropriations, by whatever name.

While Thomas looks at modernist uses of indigenous material, Myers examines indigenous uses of modernist artistic practices. Both are concerned with the ramifications of these practices within a larger political economy and a national project that finds in Aborigines and their culture a wellspring for the national imaginary. In the Pintupi case, issues of intention and artistic autonomy are particularly important because the painters Myers studies do not consider themselves artists and do not value their work as art. Rather, the value of a painting derives from its relationship to the Dreaming. What are the implications of these understandings for the objects as art, quite apart from the fact that they are paintings? At what point in their circulation do they become art? Will the object be defined as art at its destination by virtue of its reception?

Myers's analysis of Pintupi painting resituates the alienability issue by asking whether the Pintupi are selling or selling out. Are they giving or giving away? Or does painting let them keep while selling, because they can sell the object without selling, or giving away, the Dreaming? This case dramatizes incommensurabilities between modern artistic practices and indigenous understandings and the consequences for the art/artifact distinction. If the producers do not understand themselves to be making something called art, and if these objects do not circulate in their own circles as art, what then have they produced? That the Pintupi may not consider the painting a work of art does not mean they consider it an artifact.

To better understand how this anomaly presents itself, I turn to those chapters that locate the art/artifact dichotomy between the work and the spaces in which it moves or comes to rest. Christopher Steiner and Annie Coombes come at this question from two different directions. Steiner explores what happens when art moves across national borders. The border is a prime site for analyzing legal definitions of art because it is at the border that those definitions are activated and contested. However, legal definitions of art are also at work within national borders. The problems that Edward Steichen encountered when he tried to import Brancusi's *Bird in Space* from France to the United States could arise as easily within the borders of France or the United States as on the border itself. I found it especially interesting that the gatekeeping practices of customs officials at a national border should be so at odds with the internationalism of modern art and its utopian faith in a universal language of form. Whereas the international art world is, ideally, a world without borders, *Bird in Space* had to negotiate national borders whose gatekeeping practices were at odds with its free passage. The Brancusi case dramatizes what happens when the law is out of step with the cases that it is intended to cover. If *Bird in Space* is not art, what is it?

If legal definitions of art demote *Bird in Space* to the status of the materials from which it is made, then the Royal Academy of Art exhibition that Coombes analyzes promotes objects to the status of art, whatever the intentions and understandings of their makers might have been. Whether the destination of an object is a private collection, a public exhibition, or an international border along the way, understandings at the source are out of alignment with meanings produced at the destination. Thomas and Myers also deal with this problem, but they launch the argument from within works that are intended or, better said, *engineered* to be more or less in sync with their venues and markets.

Nonetheless, there are situations in which even Brancusi's *Bird in Space* is not art, not even artifact, but something less—nothing more than the material from which it has been made. Even within the art system itself, art's materiality arises in such practices as pricing by size. Size is a material attribute. Size has nothing to do with quality. Similarly, when an artist gives a work of art to an American museum, the basis for calculating a tax deduction is the value of the materials (paint, canvas, stretcher), not the value of the art. Art's materiality is thus precipitated even in contexts where the definition of the work as art is uncontested and the value of the materials is irrelevant to the value of the work. In the case of a sculpture commission, where the cost of materials and fabrication can be very high, the work may be priced accordingly and the deal structured so that the dealer's commission is based on the price minus the cost of materials and fabrication.

The practice of considering materials and labor in calculating the price of a work of art has a long history, as Baxandall (1988) explores in his study of art patronage in fifteenth-century Italy. Such practices preserve a historical link between artisan and artist. It has taken considerable cultural work to sever that link, establish art as an independent kind of object, and create the conditions for producing incalculable value of a particular kind.

ART AND COMMODITY

Is art now and has art always been a commodity, claims to the contrary notwithstanding? Art circulates in a commodity form, even as it asserts its autonomy. Its autonomy is constitutive of its inalienability. Art is a very particular kind of commodity because there is something incalculable, even irrational, about the way in which it accrues value. Its value seems to elude calculation—it is priceless—without precluding the assigning of a price tag. The commodity status of art is another way of stating the alienability problem. It could be said that alienability and inalienability are stages in the social life of art.

The first stage is production. Taking the baseline of modernism as set out by Thomas in his discussion of Preston and Walters, the difference between an artist and an artisan is disinterestedness, as summed up in the aphorism "art for art's sake." Of course, both artists and artisans sell their work, but they are supposed to differ in their relationship to the market and in the marketing and pricing of their wares. Theoretically, although an artist wants his work to sell, he or she is not supposed to produce work for the market. Purity of motive, intrinsic value, and autonomy from the market are constitutive of the ideal of art. If it were possible to identify a stage in the social life of art where a work of art could be said to be "inalienable," then the first instance would be the production stage.

The second stage in the social life of art is the market. Some works may never make it there. Others may bypass the market altogether and head straight for the museum. It is when art moves into the market that it enters its commodity stage. Art, however, is no ordinary commodity. Value, particularly within the context of art auctions, can soar to astronomical heights, beyond rational calculation. Nor is there any denying that art is a commodity. Art has a price tag and changes hands for money, which is not to say that the value of art can be reduced (or elevated) to the price asked or paid.

The third stage in the social life of art, and in some cases the ultimate destination, is the museum. Ideally, the museum returns to art its inalienability by removing it from the market, though even the museum has difficulty insulating itself from financial calculations. Art must be assigned a value for insurance purposes. It has become increasingly difficult to lend or borrow works of art, because the cost of insuring them for travel is prohibitive. Museums that deaccession works and sell them to make up a shortfall in their operating budgets have come under severe criticism. Repatriation issues configure the problem in the reverse direction by insisting that museums have no right to particular holdings and are morally obliged to return them to their rightful owners.

Even as the museum removes art from the market, it is implicated in that market. Museum exhibitions increase the value of particular works simply by exhibiting them. Museums are taken to task when they fail to protect themselves from conflicts of interest in their relationship with private collectors, as the Brooklyn Museum discovered when its *Sensation* exhibit really did create a sensation, and an unwelcome one at that. Financial considerations aside, the circulation of art in and through museums increases the value of art as cultural capital. The museum does not remove art from circulation, though much work languishes in storage. Rather, the museum arrests the commodity stage of particular objects while stimulating the market for related work. Matters are never categorical or simple. Suffice it to say that the alienability/inalienability of an object is a processual issue.

MATERIALITY

Claudio Lomnitz comes at the issues of materiality and gift by way of the embodiment of sovereignty and the role of sacrifice in Mexico's political history. Given the misalignment of nation and state in Mexico's history, where could sovereignty be materialized? It could not be lodged in the material apparatus of the state itself, because the state was misaligned with the popular will. When sovereignty was sited in the president (his office, persona, and body), it was vulnerable to private interests. Finally, given the transcendence of sovereignty and the slippage between nation and state, there was always the question of who would control sovereignty—the state or popular movements against the state.

Materiality figures here not only in the literal sense of relics—the president's actual body, whether alive, dead, or in pieces—but also in the sense of image, iconography, and symbol. Of course, image and symbol have their concrete manifestations, whether in the form of statues, monuments, mausoleums, and ceremonies or in the form of capital improvements as subways and highways, but this not the focus of Lomnitz's analysis. Rather, he is concerned with the materialization—and more specifically the embodiment—of such intangibles as the nation, the popular will, the national community, the state, and sovereignty. At the heart of his analysis is how the president attempts to embody, literally in his actual body and figuratively through image and symbol, the ideal of sovereignty, given that sovereignty rests neither with the nation nor with the state. His contribution intersects with discussions of the gift in this volume in relation not to commodity but to sacrifice. It is martyrdom that is the supreme sacrifice and ultimate gift. Thus, the inalienable possessions at the heart of Lomnitz's analysis are the material embodiments of the idea of sovereignty, which he does not limit to objects but extends to performance—to the "state theater" for governmental self-presentation.

His essay prompts us to consider the implications of privileging materiality in discussions of alienability, the gift, the commodity, and art. Keane's paper stresses the formality of exchange, the performance of ritual language and actions, in imbuing material tokens with significance and value. Services and performances can be gifts in their own right, and the materiality of art is no longer a given within contemporary art practice. How does focusing on the materiality of objects constrain our efforts to theorize the gift, the commodity, and art?

Our theoretical concerns are part and parcel of the historical formation of the very phenomena we are studying. They are not separate from the paintings of Margaret Preston, Gordon Walters, and Papunya Tula Artists or from the exhibition of African art at the Royal Academy. So naturalized have the assumptions of modern art become that we need to remind ourselves of their historical specificity. We have predicated our deliberations on modernist formalism, which privileges painting as the premier genre of visual expression.

Even there, where art's materiality would seem to be assured, there are critical debates about "objecthood," the term Fried (1998) uses for work that calls attention to itself as an object. Such work, in his view, fails as art. Minimalist sculpture is the primary target of his attack, though painting is not excluded. As O'Doherty (1986) argues in his deconstruction of the white cube, the kind of art that Fried decries engages the space in which it is exhibited: the exhibition space is active and the work of art does not maintain its separation from the space in which it is shown. Moreover, Fried locates the problem of art's autonomy in the very nature of the object itself and its independence from what is around it, not in its relationship to the market.

Since the 1960s, when these debates were launched, and in light of a long history of avant-garde practice, artists have been defying the commodity status of art by dematerializing the object. They produce works that cannot be bought, sold, and collected in the way that paintings can. They intervene in art's materiality, which they understand as a precondition for its commodity status.

By siting our normative baseline within the history of modernist formalism, which fits our cases very nicely, we may be missing theoretical possibilities suggested by the historical avant-garde and contemporary art practice, including critiques that are internal to art practice. As already mentioned, the dematerialization of the art object complicates considerations of the materiality of art and its commodity status. Process and performance art shift the ground for discussing art's autonomy, theoretically and materially. At the very least, these kinds of practices suggest that there are material conditions for producing autonomous objects, to cite only the frame, which sets a work apart from its surroundings. Installation art challenges our working premise that the production of art is a process separate from its exhibition. Consistent with these developments, the emergence of the curator as auteur, artist as curator, and exhibition architect as artist are indicative of important shifts in the ways the kinds of objects that concern us here are being exhibited and engaged.

While much has been said about the decontextualization of objects and their recontextualization in exhibitions, the developments to which I refer are as material as the objects that we discussed during the seminar. They do something more and other than decontextualize or recontextualize, terms that lack the necessary materiality to capture what is happening.

In discussing material culture and exchange, we found ourselves returning to art. Art became a meeting ground between indigenous culture and modern formalism, African treasures and metropolitan exhibitions, inalienable possessions and the international art market, legal definitions of art and modern formalism. We would be the poorer, however, without the cases that did not focus specifically on art. They resolutely kept the gift/commodity question in play. They raised the question of objects and subjects, objectification and subjectification. They configured the problem of inalienability in radically different kinds of settings, from Mexican national history to the indigenization of money in Sumba. What might have remained concepts internal to our cases and to our own indigenous understandings, first among them art's autonomy, became problems requiring ethnographic research in their own right, as Lomnitz suggested in discussion. Myers noted that artistic autonomy entails a category of persons, a set of institutions, and social relations. He returned us to the theme of exchange and reminded us that inalienability is a theory of value that, in the work of Annette Weiner, is also a theory of persons.

10

Art and Material Culture

A Conversation with Annette Weiner

Fred R. Myers
and Barbara Kirshenblatt-Gimblett

During the SAR seminar, we decided to interview Annette Weiner when it became clear how much we missed her participation there. After some discussion, we decided to begin with the question of how Annette (AW) came to be interested in material culture. We would then move to what she thought were the defining moments in *her* thinking, and from there to where she saw the subject of material culture and exchange going. Since Fred Myers (FM) had known Annette for 25 years, the questions were not innocent of expected replies, such as the possible connection between Annette's earlier interest in painting and her concern for material culture. The participation of Barbara Kirshenblatt-Gimblett (BKG), however, allowed us to ask some of these very basic questions. We hoped Annette might illuminate the workings of an unusual life and career as a woman in anthropology and also respond to current issues in the field. She had read the original papers circulated before the seminar, and much of her discussion was connected to these examples.

The following interview with Annette Weiner took place on two separate occasions, the first in December 1996, shortly after the SAR seminar, and the second four months later. We have edited the interview to echo the opportunity for reflection between these times.

INTERVIEW, PART 1

New York City, 6 December 1996

Trajectories: A Woman's Career

AW: I think my interest in material culture started with painting. I painted from the time I was very young, and I used painting in a way as a bridge, because I had not gone to college when I graduated from high school. I felt very diminished by the fact that I hadn't. I got married when I was very young and I had two children. I found myself searching for something else to fill out my life, something to do intellectually—although I was by no means an intellectual. I hadn't even read any literature of note. I read pop best-sellers at the time.

I guess I was in my early or mid-twenties when this was going on. It was a very difficult time for me. Also I guess the most difficult of it was that I was pretty much in isolation for some reason, because all the people that I knew, the other women that I knew, were all basically like me: they had small children; they lived in the suburbs; they took care of their children. It was very much a Jewish princess sort of life. You had someone to come in to clean once a week, and you went out with the girls.

I started to paint. I found a painter—I can't even remember how I found him in Philadelphia; I lived outside of Philadelphia then—who had painted with Hans Hoffmann and he gave lessons one day a week. So I started to paint again, and I felt renewed but also not quite sure where I would go with this. I was lacking in self-confidence then, and I never really felt enormous talent or I would have been painting furiously all the time.

Finally I decided that all this talk about being sad because I hadn't gone to college—that there was really no point why I couldn't go. My children were five and seven at the time, and I enrolled as a freshman at the University of Pennsylvania. I still painted, not with this artist but at home, until I went to graduate school.

That was it. Graduate school stopped everything else. That was in 1968, which is amazing to me. In '68, so much was going on. I was right in the midst of it as an undergraduate, yet I was always hurrying to get home to my children and just get my work done. I didn't really have time to engage in all of the ferment that was going on, nor did I really know any undergraduates. I knew them in classes, but I wasn't around to make friends with them. So I still had not really hooked up with other women and was still struggling with this need to do something else, to be something in my own right. For a while when I started at Penn, I decided I would be an art major, and then I decided where would that really take me? Would I end up teaching art in some place? That idea didn't seem very interesting to me, having written off the fact that I could really be an artist. I mean, that seemed to be something that I couldn't be, because I got no support from anybody around me. My husband at the time was supportive in that he encouraged me to go to school, but in the environment in which I lived, people thought I was crazy. They thought my paintings were crazy; they thought everything I did was kind of off the wall. I was a real radical in this group, and yet I wasn't very radical.

So I found anthropology along the way as an undergraduate. Someone I knew gave me a copy of Hortense Powdermaker's *Stranger and Friend* [1966]—which presented the romantic notion of living in New Guinea. What could be more spectacular? It was all so wonderful! I had never really heard of anthropology before, and there I was. I was totally convinced that *that* was it. Love at first sight! And I thought that this person Malinowski must be really important because she was always referring to him. So I went and I ordered a hardback of *Argonauts of the Western Pacific* [1922]. I had only read this book and there I had *Argonauts*. About six years later, I'd be there! It was quite unbelievable that that was going to be my life. So I went to the University Museum and signed up as an anthropology major.

The other thread of this material culture interest began at the end of my first year of graduate school, at Bryn Mawr College. Ben Reina from the University of Pennsylvania—who had worked in Guatemala as a cultural anthropologist—decided that it would be interesting to do some exploration of archaeology—historical archaeology—in the capital, Antigua, and use ethnography with archaeology. This was rather new at the time. I said I would love to go; could I go with him? So he and I and another student went, just on an exploration. I think we went for about three or four weeks to see if it was feasible and possible.

Everything seemed to work out. We did a few little excavations; I had no idea what I was doing actually, I'd never done any archaeology, but Freddy de Laguna [Frederica de Laguna, a senior anthropologist at Bryn Mawr] was giving me advice.

Archaeology suddenly seemed the answer, because my big problem—from the minute I decided I wanted to be an anthropologist—was, how would I do fieldwork with my two children? How would I leave them, how would I manage all this? With archaeology research, you go to the field for six weeks, eight weeks, often in the summer. So you can take your children. It's a group. An archaeological expedition, even if I had to go quite a few times, didn't seem as onerous as trying to figure out what I would do going away for a year or two years. I didn't know how I would begin to manage that. So it seemed like a compromise. But in my heart of hearts, I knew it was a real compromise. I have to say I've always felt that the questions archaeologists ask are by far the most interesting. The big questions: "When did food production begin?" "How did villages come about?" But when you get down to the actual nitty-gritty, and you're faced with nothing but potsherds, it's hard to get those potsherds to talk.

[In Antigua] there were something like thirty monasteries and convents in the space of maybe twenty square blocks. It's phenomenal to think about. You think about all these bells ringing at various times during the day. Anyway, we excavated in about four of these convents and monasteries, but there wasn't much that we had except pottery. I think this is a problem with historical archaeology: it's fascinating, the questions are interesting, but if you have potsherds you already envision that you're going to have some dishes and plates from Spain and you're going to have some stuff that's made by the Mayans, and we didn't see much of an intermingling of these things. And then what do you really say? That the Spaniards came and set up this monastery? The Indians were here? You need the archives if you're going to really find something. At least in that situation it seemed very difficult to just rely on the potsherds and the archaeology.

More and more I was convinced that this maybe wasn't such a great compromise. I began to realize that my original idea was naïve: "Well, I have to get this dissertation done, and afterwards I can be anything I want because I'll be an anthropologist." The more I got into it, the more I realized that when you write a dissertation, it's the accumulation of a lot of work and you're really into a subject and into a field and you can't just move out into something else.

Becoming an Ethnographer: Defining Moments

We went there [to Guatemala] in the summer, the three of us, and then the next summer we did a much bigger expedition and I actually took my two children with me, and Ben Reina, his wife and two children came. We had quite a group together and that was when I really began to have my doubts. Was this really what I wanted to do? Fortunately, I was a student at Bryn Mawr and not at Penn, and I still had a choice, which was rather lucky for me. At the end of the summer, I told Ben that I thought I couldn't continue on this project, that I would analyze one major site I had been working at—which I did, I wrote a paper for him analyzing the pottery—[but] I really had to do ethnography. And he said his wife had already told him that. Because she saw me...I had gone up to the hills outside the city to visit some Indian villages to see how these women used the pottery, how they cooked, to try to expand what I knew about the use of these things. She went with me, his wife, and she told him that she saw me there, talking to these women and she knew that that's what I was, and that I wouldn't make an archaeologist, that I really should be an ethnographer. So I think my concentration during that period of two years on pottery and thinking about how people use these things and how they went to the market and the circulation of them—since a lot of this Mayan stuff was still in pretty much the same form—was triggered again.

Going to the Trobriands was the fatal attraction. I went originally to study art and economics. I was going to do tourist art because the Trobrianders had this very beautiful wood—striped ebony—and they were carving for tourists who came every weekend on day-and-a-half trips flown in small planes, private charters. My idea was actually to see how the carvings had changed over the years, because Trobrianders had been carving for tourists since the [nineteenth] century, when ships were passing through. There are some very early collections of stuff and you can already see in those collections how they [the Trobrianders] were accommodating, taking Western ideas and carving them, [carving] anything they thought somebody would be interested in buying. I wanted to see how that was changing with more cash coming in, how that might be changing any parts of the traditional economic system Malinowski had described. But I actually expected to see vast changes in that system.

So when I got there, all this was going on, but the very first day I went to live in the village where I was setting up, the women took me to another village where a distribution of something was going on, and this something was hard to describe. It was made of [dried] banana leaves and it didn't look like you did anything with them. Yet women had huge baskets, maybe six feet long, filled with these things that actually looked maybe like larger than whisk brooms but the same sort of things: tied at the top but instead of being stiff they were of flimsy leaves. They kept saying to me, "It's just like your money." They even gave me some and threw me into the center of the village to put them on these piles, very large piles, that other women would come and gather up and bring back to their piles of bundles.

I had no idea what was going on and I was sort of panicked because I thought, "Malinowski must have described this, but I missed it. What could this possibly be?" It was my very first day there and women were in the center of the village, women were doing something that they told me was like my money. Women? At that time women were supposed to be on the periphery, if you remember Levi-Strauss's [1949] diagram of a Trobriand village. Only men are in the center, and women are on the periphery of the village. Of course, women aren't supposed to be handling something that's considered money.

At any rate, it turned out to be true. The bundles of banana leaves—I named them that because I didn't know what else to call them and it was the most descriptive term so that people might have an image of what they might be like—they were a form of currency that really very much involved men. Not only were they [the bundles] essential in these distributions, which occurred six months after a person died, but also in order to get more of these bundles than any one woman could make, a woman took cash or a pig or some very large object of value from her husband. If she took cash, she went to the trade store and bought tobacco and tinned fish and rice and went around selling them to other villagers for payment in bundles. Or a pig would go to a man in another village who would then have to return *X* amount of bundles for this pig. So it definitely involved men's wealth. Men did this. At least, they usually did. Some didn't, and they were treated very badly by a woman's relatives if they didn't.

When I got home that night, after that first visit, I went through all the Malinowski books that I'd got, half in fear that I would find something about it and half that I wouldn't. And I didn't find anything about it. I know that he saw these things, because much later I found a little slip of paper in his notes. There's material at the Museum of Mankind because he did a collection of Trobriand artifacts for them, and he's got a little piece of paper that says "nununiga" (which is the Kiriwina word for bundles)—"Very important in mortuary rituals." And that's it. He said it was being done when he was there. I realized that *kula* shells looked bigger and they're more beautiful in their own way to Western eyes: they look substantive, they last—speaking of "perishable" [a topic we had discussed in the seminar].... And women were throwing this stuff.

After I had written *Women of Value* [1976], there was a trader from the Seychelles who lived in the Trobriands, [and] he said to me, "It's really amazing because all these years I saw these women with these baskets on their heads and saw they were going to this village or that village, I thought they were all just going to cry over somebody who had died." What's fascinating is that his business would increase, because people would buy cloth. They would more and more exchange cloth in addition to the bundles and skirts, if they didn't want to make traditional skirts. As one part of the exchange you need skirts. So nobody on the island while I was there had any idea about these bundles. Harry Powell, who did work there in the fifties, took photographs of these women, and after my book came out, he insisted that he saw that. But he didn't ever write very much. He wrote a few papers, and he didn't ever get into it. It was something that wasn't just invented. I think it certainly has become enormously inflated and today some women are actually trying to get women to stop making bundles because they tell them they're worthless. Because they [the men] are working in Port Moresby and they are using their cash for these women, for these bundles, and they see what's happening: that it's taking cash and turning it into nothing. So there's still controversy about it.

FM: We had always spoken about banana leaves as money. In our seminar, we talked about commodities and inalienable things and different kinds of exchange, about exchange and commodities and money, but I never realized how central the interest in money as another form of exchangeable was—from the very beginning. It was not just motivated from outside, but it's really from inside....

AW: Before they had a lot of cash to get things in the trade store, they would make things like mats and little carved betel spoons and things like that. It was harder to accumulate large amounts of bundles, so that's why there wasn't as much inflation in the system, but coconuts or pigs or whatever. And when the men went on *kula* and brought back more exotic things, they were great to take to other villagers and trade for payment of bundles. So there always was this kind of internal circulation that one could call, loosely, "commodity." You can see how trade store merchandise just fit right in. What happened, of course, is that when I first went to the Trobriands in 1971, one bundle was equivalent to one stick of tobacco. That was ten cents then, or ten kina. When I went back in 1989, one was about somewhere in the neighborhood of thirty cents. So even in the monetary value of these bundles as against how they were being measured and exchanged, they were definitely hooked to the market in that sense.

I guess these three strands really came together—painting originally and then the archaeology and then these bundles. Just following the trail of these bundles led me to begin to reevaluate what Malinowski had said about exchange. Because yams are connected to bundles. If a person gives you yams that are raw, you have a debt to him or her that's payable in bundles when he or she dies. And it has to be a certain kind of bundles, not old bundles but new bundles. If it's cooked food you can use dirty bundles or old bundles. So even within the narrow margins of these exchanges, when someone dies there are all these differentiations being made between clean bundles, new bundles, old bundles, and women will take apart some old bundles and fashion them into "clean" ones. "Clean" means that all the leaves are straight and that there's a kind of puffiness to the bundle—like crepe paper—which is achieved by running a knife, and stretching it a bit so that it's a little full. It's all about labor, the labor intensity of working at these bundles. The more labor you put in, the more value they have, as opposed to other bundles that—You need all kinds, but don't try to give these old bundles to somebody who gave you raw yams or you're nowhere!

So I began to see differentiations in the way objects were used.

FM: It's very different from the way most people got interested in exchange. They mostly started from Malinowski or Mauss or some imagined exchange theory. They mostly didn't start from objects.

AW: In Webb Keane's paper, I was really struck by his discussion of "perishable" versus "permanent" [objects]. This was one of the first big questions I had. In fact, the first paper I wrote after my dissertation was about yams. I wanted to explore, string out, and show the differences there could be in kinds of yams and what you got back for each kind, and the relationship between these yams and the bundles. Similarly, the yams that are already cooked are of lesser value that will last [only] for a while and you can trade them off to other people for other things. I came up with an idea that actually I got from a Nobel prizewinner at the turn of the century. He talked about things that have a permanence having energy, and they continue to have this energy. That's what allows them to circulate and to become other things. Something that is iron can be smelted down, it can have another life; these things continue. But when you have food and you cook it and you eat it, the energy is gone into your body and that's it. That seemed to me to be a good way to think about perishables....

FM: I don't remember if you were already in the field, but we had a seminar [at Bryn Mawr] on Melanesia, where we were doing a whole thing on the difference between taro and yams.

AW: I remember that.

FM: Taro has to be replanted, you can't eat it all.

AW: It's in my book [*Women of Value*]. I talk about that, where you cut off the leaves of the taro and then you replant it. When you give somebody an entire taro plant, you're giving them both food and also the possibility for another plant. So, again, it's a different kind of presentation to a person than if you just give the tubers, which is just food alone.

BKG: This issue of "perishable/durable" was very important to us in the seminar. One of the issues that came up had to do with materiality and material culture, with the idea that the properties of the material culture were consequential. One divide was between whether it was perishable or durable—we want to understand that better. For me, "perishability" is a way of talking about the temporality of the material.

There's a certain kind of drama in the perishable because it isn't that "now you have it, now you don't." It's that you have to renew it, and the process of renewal is of a different order than with the "durable." The durable circulates in other ways. But the idea that you have it, then you consume it and it's gone and that's the end of the story of the perishable? It's not the end of the story. It points to the event, the doing. That's why fruit is so interesting in that respect.... So the issue of materiality: what are the properties of this material thing that are consequential for the transactions we're looking at?

AW: Well, what fascinates me is the imagination of people to give longevity to something that has a much shorter life cycle, let's say, than another kind of object. The work at making something last before it is reduced to food—I find really amazing. The work in the Trobriands, for example, of building the yam houses, which are beautifully constructed to keep the air flowing through the yams so that they will last as long as possible? These yam houses are enormous undertakings. The ingenuity of their creation is amazing. That's what I mean—how you take that and you keep it. There are other examples. To make something—cloth, for example—that may be perishable and yet is kept in certain places and stored in special ways and taken out and aired so that it lasts longer. And that push toward keeping things going longer, as long as they possibly can, is fascinating. It shows an incredible creativity.

FM: Well, Barbara, I remember you and I had a question that we imagined coming at another point, but let's just jump right ahead to Mauss. Barbara has mentioned this, the way in which the attributes of the person adhere to the thing in exchange. This is central to Mauss but is disregarded in most of the subsequent exchange theory.

BKG: It's very clear that this is central to *kula* and to the shells. Annette, these banana bundles are so mysterious! I don't get it exactly.

Materiality: Why Banana Bundles?

AW: They were mysterious for me for a long time. How did they arise just in the Trobriands? I searched the literature on Melanesia, other islands around the Trobriands. There was nothing of which one could say this is an offshoot. I think the leaves actually come from the idea of giving skirts, and giving skirts as part of what you can give away in various cultures is an occurrence that does happen in various parts of Melanesia. But where it explodes is when you turn to Polynesia. I went to Samoa several years later—I think it was '77 or '78—because I saw in Mauss a reference to Samoan fine mats and that they were different from other things Samoans exchanged. They had the essence of the clan, kinship, the family, embedded in them.

I was incredibly curious about it. So I went and did some fieldwork in Samoa, where fine mats are like bundles only much more elaborated because they're worth so much more. They take so much longer to make, and each mat is graded, and people have all sorts of strategies when they give them to somebody else. They put the best ones on the bottom because they don't want to give the best ones away, but if somebody brings a really good one to them, they'll be forced to pull out from the bottom a best one. Hundreds and hundreds of strategies.

And then the bundles made sense in a larger context. I know we don't talk about these things anymore, but Trobrianders have a great affinity in terms of their culture with Polynesia.... You see it throughout Polynesia, because then it became not just Samoa but Tahiti, and these feather cloaks for the Maori. These things all had the same attributes. They had more value, they were supporting much greater hierarchy in terms of the political system, but they were basically all the same kind of thing.

BKG: But could you imagine—the discussion of Samoan fine mats as just like money? Could you imagine a conversation?

AW: They are just like money. Today, in American Samoa, they don't make any fine mats, and they send suitcases full of money to Western Samoa for fine mats, because now people give money in every exchange.

BKG: I understand that, but tell us what it *is* about the banana bundles. I'm thinking about the meaning of their materiality. I appreciate the way you indicated the issue of cleanness, newness, oldness, the labor that's involved in making them and all the rest of it, but there's something about the sheer massive accumulation of them, the idea that they could be counted and heaped and measured and calculated, and then they can be divided up. You don't start cutting them in pieces, do you?

AW: Well, when they get old they fray and a piece will often be really valuable. The mat has frayed...

BKG: Okay. I understand that, but the thing about the banana bundles is that like currency they represent a unit, although some of those units have more value than other units. But they're kind of a unit. And although they could potentially be made into something, very often they're remade as bundles and recirculated as bundles. Now do they gain value by attributes of the person adhering to them in the way that *kula* does or…No? So then, why?

AW: Well, it is a different system, in that *kula* is a fundamental platform for political organization. It upholds the notion of chiefs and chiefly people and the hierarchy of [some] men being higher than other men.

FM: Qualitatively, not quantitatively.

AW: These are not necessarily chiefs in their villages, but in *kula* they're like chiefs. I think it frames the whole Massim [area of Papua New Guinea of which the Trobriands are a part]. There aren't chiefs in other islands, but I think the Trobriands with their chiefs are projected out into the rest of these islands so [in *kula*] you could be *like a chief.* If you get a big shell, you return to your village and I think—I don't know this for a fact, but I think that—you could act like a chief. It is not that your position would be inherited necessarily, but you could organize people in some way. You wouldn't have to be so egalitarian, because people would be afraid of you. You have this big valuable, and that means you have big friends who have magic and who have poison magic. All of that is embedded in *kula.* It's like a fantasy of being "big," where being a chief is not really part of the constitution of this society. Yet it can occur through *kula.*

Whereas the banana leaves are resolidifying the whole social system. I didn't go into all the details of kinship that surround the banana leaves. They are the payment for everything that many people have done for this dead person during her or his life. The relatives of the dead person must repay.

FM: Well, that does make them currency. They are the measure of value that all these relations are…

AW: That's why I think that they're like units, that they don't have a personal connection. Once in a while, a woman will put her name on something that she makes, but by and large it's really about the preservation of the *dala,* of the lineage, through time….

The distributions of the bundles primarily go to the father of the dead person and all his relatives and the spouse of the dead person and all of her or his relatives. This can constitute a really large number of people and extended people from them—all of whom who have supported this matrilineage. So it's not just about the person who died—although it is to some degree—but it's also about the lineage. It's also about the ability of this lineage to sustain a death, because every death is perceived as an attack on the lineage, a weakening. People are really afraid of this. They talk about it all the time, of lineages dying out. You can see it. I see this incredible shift of configuration in the village in which I worked. A village is divided into hamlets which constitute these lineages—one hamlet that was pretty vibrant and now there's hardly anybody living in it, and another one that was okay, but now is burgeoning and they don't have enough room for everyone. The shifts that occur over time are quite interesting, but usually you're not there long enough to see that shift of generations. So the bundles are a social cement, I think. It's a grand accounting.

BKG: One of the things we were trying to get at is how form is consequential. Why *this* material and why in *this* form? That is to say, does it have to be shells? Could it have been stones? Could it have been wood? Did it have to be banana leaves? Could it have been some other material in some other form? Is it arbitrary? Will anything do? Of all the things they've done they've picked this, and that's it?

I ask it not really as a historical question. I don't really want to know the origin. I ask more, what are the analytic consequences of asking the question? What is it you have learned by looking more closely at the material itself?...Why banana bundles here, shells there? There may not be an answer, but that was something that we were curious about. I don't know if you have thought about it.

AW: Yes, I've thought about why banana leaves work for years and years and years. It is interesting, because it's really one kind of banana leaf, and there are many different species of bananas. I'm sure at some point they experimented and found that maybe this kind held up better, it was easier, you could make it stiffer. It had some properties that other banana leaves didn't seem to have.

You can say, "What kind of money is this?" (You should probably call it currency rather than money.) You can just go out and pick it. Do they run out of leaves? They often do, and they have to find a relative in the south of the island where there's a little more tropical jungle area, and they get these leaves. But why? I don't know. And the shells? I have these stories, but...

BKG: Well, you describe men taking the shells out and being totally entranced by them, completely absorbed in handling them and looking at them. One of the issues for us was not only how social interaction and systems of exchange help to create value, but also the degree to which the object has actual properties that make it compelling. So with some of the *kula* stuff you can see how that would work. But with the banana leaves it's harder.

AW: I know, and banana leaves now are changing into cloth.

There was always some cloth in the exchanges, with the skirts. Not all women have skirts, because skirts take longer to make. Women would buy cloth in the trade store and carry that. There's a big long distribution at the very end where skirts are given, and cloth. But now they do this distribution in Port Moresby, in the capital, when somebody really well known in the Trobriands dies. Their relatives put on one of these distributions in the capital for the people who are living there, the Trobrianders. They don't have bundles, so they use money and cloth. So I suspect that eventually in the Trobriands—of course unfortunately these women in the villages, they won't recognize until it's too late that this isn't really freeing them from making bundles, it's just going to be harder to get more money to have cloth.

It is strange, I've asked myself a million times, why bundles? As far as I could get with that was to see their elaboration elsewhere. Samoan fine mats are also currency. Traditionally if you wanted somebody to build you a house or build something else for you, you paid the person in fine mats. Today you would probably pay the person in cash. But you would always put fine mats on top of it. When the Germans came to Western Samoa, they actually made laws making it illegal for people to have fine mats and exchange them because they saw it as a waste of money. So they move the same object, which is a woven long piece with some feathers on the end. That same object will be currency, will be the incredible support of a political hierarchy, will be the statement about a particular kinship group. But this is so much more elaborated because the fine mats themselves are so much more valuable, each one.

Commensurability and Kinds of Objects: The World of Cloth

FM: The banana leaves are interesting, if you think about them as opposed in the form of value to the *kula,* as the title of your book—*Women of Value, Men of Renown* [1976]—marked. In the seminar, we were talking about Appadurai's concept of "regimes of value" [Appadurai 1986], which I think really fits the notion of this. Banana leaves are very hard to make into distinctive, memorable objects. They're not really differentiable, no matter how hard one tries. The banana leaves work quantitatively. You can communicate your dissatisfaction with people, but it's always qualitative. It can't be turned into an objective marker. If you give me an object that's a distinctive one, it's it forever: I know you gave me this one and it's this one. What is consequential, it seems to me, in terms of those social relations is that you can give people equivalent bundles. You can never give people fully equivalent objects, especially if they are noted. And for *dala* [lineage], if I understood correctly what you wrote in the Trobriander book [1988], you're actually recovering personal items back to the *dala,* they become *dala* property. So what's given out that really represents personhood, these decorations, is actually paid for by a currency that is no longer marked by who it came from. The gift of banana leaves clears it, because you're not giving anybody anything that reflects you.

BKG: Right—because one would assume that anything more elaborate has to be better than something less elaborated. This, of course, is a ridiculous assumption. You have to ask yourself why they have created something that resists a certain kind of elaboration. What does that enable? What does that make possible?

AW: That chieftaincy, ultimately.

BKG: The idea that the bundles are not authored, are not signed, are not differentiated in a certain way is strategic. That they should be in a sense dumber, that they should be without elaborate iconography, without the same kind of elaborated and transmittable histories as individual bundles—it makes it possible for them to operate in other ways.... It's precisely the issue of calibrating equivalence and their divisibility. Those kinds of things are very consequential. I think that actually, if we thought it through hard enough, we could begin to see why this and not stones, twigs...There has to be a way, because I think this is on the right track...

FM: Webb Keane had that very interesting case in his essay. They give them the money, but people are so focused on the qualitative differences: "This money is not the same as that money; it's dirty."

BKG: It's like giving a crisp hundred dollar bill for a bar mitzvah gift instead of a bunch of grubby ones.

AW: Exactly. From Polynesia, I thought there were bark cloth and feather cloaks and fine mats all functioning in certain ways. The basic ways are very similar, and yet much more elaborated. And then I put cloth to it and then I saw this world of cloth that seemed to me totally overlooked in all discussions of exchange and any evolutionary stories about food. But cloth didn't enter into these stories. Archaeologists now are looking at cloth, but this is very recent. True enough, it [cloth] doesn't always last. But other things do—spindles and things like that. And those were just added and counted up and put into the report, and nothing much was made of it.

That's why I got involved in the problem of cloth. It was after Polynesia. There, I was just so excited by the relationship between this bark cloth stuff and bundles.[1] And then when I saw cloth, it was like this whole world opened—of these exchanges, these places in the world, in every part of the world, where cloth is a vital part of certain exchanges. When you begin to look globally—Jane Schneider and I did in our book *Cloth and Human Experience* [Weiner and Schneider 1989]—there are places where men do the weaving. But often you find that it's women who do some part of that production process. They may do the spinning. Or, as in some places in Africa, like where Mary Douglas worked, she wrote all about men making this raffia cloth. But actually women were the ones who put on the material that makes a design on the cloth. And it doesn't mean very much unless it has this design on it.

I found examples like that which had largely been neglected. I've always thought that there was something about cloth as opposed to bone, shells, stone, that really hard stuff, and cloth as a wrapping. Human beings wrap themselves in cloth; they disguise themselves in cloth; they're buried wrapped in cloth, in bark cloth or some kind of cloth. There's an intimate connection between bones and cloth, and bones are sacred. Claudio's paper [Lomnitz, this volume] shows that—the way bones were used. In medieval times, you couldn't start a church unless you had [bones]. The legitimation of that church was the bone of some saint. Just go to Saint Patrick's [Cathedral, in New York City]. I don't know who's there, which saint, but there's an arm or a hand or something there. So that's where I think it leads you: this cloth that's so different from hard stuff.

BKG: For me, cloth is very mysterious. There's something that has to do with the idea that you start out with fiber that's a mass, then you make it into something that's a thread, and then...There's something about the internal structuring and repetitions and putting together a fiber that is very powerful. And then it creates this flexible material that can take the shape of what it surrounds and can hold things together...

AW: There are the metaphors from the ancient Greeks, too, and from all over. Every place you look there are metaphors about keeping the social fabric together, the threads that bind people to each other. There's a beautiful saying from a group in Indonesia about a particular kind of cloth. They always keep one end unfinished because it marks the end of life and the beginning of a new generation. It's very beautiful in the way they articulate it. You are basically talking about the nature of life and social life and keeping people together. And that's why women are primarily the agents of cloth. In Elisha Renne's material in Nigeria where she worked,[2] only men are weavers and there are sacred cloths that men use in their initiation rituals, but women have other sacred cloths that they make which are equally important and therefore different sets of ancestors.

Reciprocity: The Question Unasked

FM: I want to track the transition...It seems to me that in a lot of your work, when you start to look at these different circuits of exchange and different materials, the notion of exchange as the focus of reciprocity is gone.

It seems to me that there are two directions. One of them is toward objects mediating other relations more generally, following the cloth, and the other one is the gift. I know that your paper [for the seminar] was going to be about reciprocity.

AW: "The Questions Unasked," I was going to call it. This is a long answer. You said earlier that I came to exchange differently because it was through objects, through material culture, and exploring how things moved around, what they meant with all these different properties, while most people came to exchange more formally through Malinowski, through Mauss. I have to admit that I hadn't really read Mauss when I first went to the Trobriands. I was accepting Malinowski. I wasn't redoing exchange. I was accepting all of that. I was doing something different.

So at any rate, *The Gift* [Mauss 1990 (1925)] became a bible for me when I read it. I underlined it, I memorized it, I thought it was just so right, so magnificent, his insights, that part about the gift as part economic, part political, part social, all these things. He was so right. It was only Mauss that resonated with me. Other people who were then writing on exchange seemed to not quite get it, but actually I didn't get it either. I didn't know what the problem was, but I knew that Malinowski was wrong because of the way objects moved. He cut it off, he never followed the movement of something. An example? His great problem and the thing that people argued over and argued over was why men give yams to their sisters and not their wives. The eternal problem. He saw that every year men created gardens for their sisters, and so he had all these ideas: "They're feeding their sisters' sons because they're going to inherit from them," and "matrilineality"—all these things. Well, in point of fact, the yam exchanges are directly linked to the bundle exchanges because as I said earlier, if you give these yams to your sister... [then] when you or somebody else in your lineage dies, your sister has to come up with a lot of bundles if you've been making big gardens for her. Her husband is the one who's got to help her get those bundles. So it pulls this in-law into the very close relationship between a brother and sister.

Malinowski just didn't see any of it because he didn't follow women at all. This also made me see very early, against most of the other women writers at the time, the interrelationship between male and female. You couldn't just analyze men over here and women over here. That bipolarity just didn't work.

So it was this following something and seeing where it connected. It wasn't just this exchange that was given and that was it and then the next year was given again, and you got cooked food back or whatever. People give you cooked food when you bring these yams, but it's very short term. It's saying thanks for your work, minimally, thanks for bringing these into the village. But the real payoff is later. It was following things like that, between yams and women's wealth, that made me very uncomfortable with a lot of the notions about reciprocity. And then I saw the word "gift," which I began to realize was a kind of non sequitur because what does "gift" tell you? Nothing. It was the way people could talk about exchange without having to pursue all the things you've been asking me: what is the meaning of this? Are yams all the same? Are banana leaves all the same? You just call it "gift." They bring it in and put it down. You ask the person, "Why are you bringing this gift?" He tells you. "What are you going to give them back?" He tells you, and you write, "That's the exchange: A goes to B and B goes to C." I have to say I think it was an easy way to get information. Not that people were doing it because it was easy but because those informants were giving you an answer that they thought you wanted because that's what you asked for.

Now it's interesting that after my book *Inalienable Possessions* [1992] was published, I got quite a few letters from anthropologists who wrote and told me that when they went back to the field—and this is mostly in New Guinea—their informants told them about these shells that they had hidden away. And they worked just like I was talking about: they were trying to keep them. So it's again not asking the right questions, not pushing further, not seeing that reciprocity is the tip of the iceberg. I think that although Mauss was my great hero for so many years, I now have to say that I think he misled all of us down this very imaginary path. Although there is much richness in Mauss. Still there are other ideas to get from him. He did recognize that fine mats were inalienable, and there are a couple of sentences about this stuff which triggered my mind to think about going to Samoa.

I think that in the turn of the [nineteenth] century—and I think this is what really needs to be explored more fully—reciprocity was an incredibly powerful social theory that for quite a few reasons fit the "primitives" very dramatically. If you go back several centuries more, in the seventeenth and eighteenth centuries, philosophers were really arguing at that time about the nature of individuals, their greed. People were very worried: the market's coming or is here, people are greedy, there's no restraints on them any more, and how that sustained the market. A very well-known philosopher writes about how people who have land are looked at differently than people who don't have land, because land makes you attend to other people. You're much more careful because you want to keep this land for the next generation. And people trust you more because you have land and all that goes with the care of that land as opposed to people who have just commodities and are just trading the money in commodities, who are fly-by-nights. You can't trust them; you know nothing about them; they're not interested in generations; they're interested in now.

BKG: They have a long-term investment.

AW: Right. There's a whole track one could take about corruption and how people see corruption as really necessary for the running of capitalism. You just have to keep it in check and not let it go too far, but it's absolutely essential because it's part of how you're going to make money in the capitalist way. I'm not sure about the nineteenth century and what happens there. Off the top of my head, I think that grand theories really replaced this concern with "individual guilt" or "corruptibility." The rights of individuals had already been established. So you have with Spencer and then Marx, the big theories of society now, and now the system of capitalism is evil and bad. I think somewhere in there the "primitive" takes on this new form—like you [referring to FM] talked about in your paper [this volume], suddenly Aboriginal culture takes on this specialness that it never had before in all the years of Australian history. And I think that happens with "primitives." You have in Durkheim's book *The Division of Labor in Society* [1984 (1893)] a glorification of the primitive and reciprocity as the fundamental node of society, and the primitives do it much better. And Mauss then saying, "Oh, if we could only be like that. If there were only more reciprocity in our lives, then this capitalism would be better."

And the "primitive" really takes off, and reciprocity becomes a theory that is not even seen to be an arguable theory. It's an inherent part of what people are. So Malinowski goes to the Trobriands and he documents this reciprocity all over the place. Even in *kula,* he never followed *kula* out because all he looked at was people saying, "Yes, I give it to him and he gives it to me," which is not the way it works at all. So it all seems so obvious. Anthropology was supposed to be like science, and science should be reducible to its most elementary form and it should be replicable and simplifiable and there it was.

So I think, like being nurtured on mother's milk, that's what you did. That's what you thought was occurring in these societies. You didn't think too much past what A gave to B and what B gave back to A, or A, B, C or whatever. Even Lévi-Strauss's [1949] exchange of women was so limited. By focusing only on the exchange of women, [it] wiped completely off the map the critical relationships between women and their brothers. At any rate I think that's pretty fundamental and set us up for dealing with exchange. And if you look at the history of people writing on reciprocity you see that nobody gets out of it. There are times when people really try and push against it like in the seventies when Barth and Leach—they're seeing that it's not just so automatic, that people are using strategies and it doesn't always come out right. And they're kind of pushing at the limits.

It was called transactional analysis. It's so funny because in *Women of Value* I didn't know what to call myself. So I said that I was following the transactionalist ideas because it seemed to me at least that there you got processes going on and you got an attention to negotiation and strategy. I knew that I wasn't really like them, but at least that part of it seemed to make sense to me.

So I think just like other things that have happened in the last twenty years in anthropology, I think we have to really throw off the notion of reciprocity as a fundamental concept and to see it as the very opening between people. And know that that's only the beginning. If the relationship is going anyplace, there's going to be much more that's happening. I envision it in this linear way of looking at transactions, that it's really building up. And it's building up in certain ways—maybe it really does become a hierarchy. Maybe it can only build up a little bit, maybe with just one thing like the *churinga* or something.[3] You have to recognize that societies have different kinds of potential for a whole range of reasons. So how much [can] they build up and how much stuff [can] they get flowing, because in order to get that hierarchy, you've got to have a lot of stuff flowing in this system. Not all societies have the stuff to enable them to do that.

I also think, there's a word that I used in a paper [Weiner 1994] I wrote a couple of years ago to describe these—I was trying to find a way to describe the processes that would be descriptive in a more abstract way of these objects as they moved in this kind of scale or layers instead of only looking at them back and forth. I used the word "density." I thought of objects which, as they were able to move, became more dense and that was through value. It's really *value* that I was talking about, but I thought density would give people the visual notion of making something heavier by a name associated with it, by the aesthetic value of it, by the people who have owned it before, what its history is and its circulation. As you get higher and higher, that density gets very heavy so it protects the object.

I have to say that the whole thing is always a struggle. In listening to the tapes [of the discussion at the seminar], there was a discussion at some point about inalienability—that it was a category and it should be a process. Well, from the beginning that's what I've argued: It's totally a process and it's practically not achievable, and yet it may be achievable for a generation. In some societies, a generation is spectacular. Imagine in New Guinea that you could keep a shell out of circulation for twenty years! This is an unheard of accomplishment. And that's what we have to recognize. It's like an engine in the system that's always pushing to make something more than it is. But it's very hard to accomplish that. So if you achieve it for just two generations or one generation, whatever, it's a great accomplishment—but then it's going to be lost. It's going to go to somebody else. It's too valuable.

Value and Hierarchy

FM: If people are creating inalienability as part of the project of hierarchizing themselves, then the objects come to stand for that hierarchy as well.

AW: Exactly. If you got a feather cloak from a brother who was already king in Hawaii, you would really be your brother. It's what the objects finally stand for. And in the literature you find people talking about the object being the person.

BKG: This is very interesting because basically, in the reciprocity discussions if I'm not mistaken, the gift becomes a privileged form for talking about reciprocity. The assumption is that other forms of exchange are in a sense known territory—barter, money, etc. Because the gift becomes a privileged form, one talks about "gift societies" as if there were societies where they didn't have those notions—it's very strange, isn't it?

AW: People have a hard time viewing the dynamics of these movements, in large part because when they're in the field, they don't follow out the dynamics that are behind them. It's like when people discovered that women were doing things in society that nobody paid attention to. I think that's what this is. It [the traditional view] is a whole way of looking at exchange that's been so powerful. If you think about it, it's the only "theory" that anthropology has had in the last hundred years that hasn't been dismantled or actually fought about. It's just been accepted. There have been refinements to it, like [those of] Marshall Sahlins [1965]—but his work is a refinement on Malinowski's.

BKG: We found ourselves having difficulty [during the seminar]. We needed your help desperately. We recognized the degree of calculation in the gift which is not supposed to be so calculated.

FM: Danny [Miller] set it up that way.

BKG: Exactly. In fact he argued that gifting is more calculating than provisioning.

FM: Because the irony was supposed to be in that.

BKG: Right. But also it comes out from what you've said, that exchanges that may have a character of a gift can be very calculated, number one. Number two, that inalienability—also associated with that which can't be sold but could be exchanged in a more giftlike transaction—is a process, not a category. And this business about persons adhering to things, there's something about the relationship of those things. For me one of the most powerful moments in Mauss is this business about things retaining some of the qualities and attributes of the person associated with them. This is very powerful.

AW: I don't think it's one person. It's the former owners. I don't think something gets really, really valuable until it has a history, its own genealogy of famous lineages, famous kings, till it really represents not just me, but more than me.

BKG: Until it has density and depth. For that depth, it requires time and it requires movement of some kind, either through a family or through these transactions. But the inalienability thing was for us a real conundrum. It was a very difficult thing to work with. Is that fair?

FM: Well, we had to work through it. I argued in your [Annette's] name—the issue about the equality of objects. This came up with Webb's paper and the fundamental argument that you made—there are two kinds of arguments that you've been making. One is almost an evolutionary one and the other is about how exchanges are managed. And at the level of an actual exchange, what are the politics of what you give or don't give and how much you give or don't give. The achievement of equality is the exception. That is something that has to be carefully managed. This is, especially, the reason that banana leaves are so interesting. For *any* objects, it's really hard to make them the same. So it seemed to me that later, when you got more interested in hierarchy, the issue that was the flip side of the politics of exchange was actually in the fact that the objects involved in exchange—whatever they may be—have properties that make their equivalence problematic. Therefore, hierarchy is always a potential property of any exchange.

So you were arguing that people worked to keep it out. One of the major efforts is to create equivalence, so the reciprocity is the result, not the background of it. One is making people equal. It is not that there's an expectation of reciprocity. Rather, these are social acts to produce, at least for a moment, equality.

AW: They also work hard to make people unequal. In the Trobriands, you can make people by something you give or don't give, showing what you think about them. And in these other places I think too, a man [in Samoa] told me the real thing to do is to give a fine mat that's just a little bit better.

FM: This is why material culture matters—because it's a register for these differentia and similarities. Every similarity has the potential.

BKG: The alienability question—we believe what happened with alienability is that, on the one hand, the classic locus for it is Tonga. On the other hand, we're trying to think, "Well, what's the deal with our own society?" It's the category called "art." Because of all the commodity complications of art, we had difficulty trying to understand how inalienability helps us to think about art. We had the art market, we had Chris Steiner's paper on the customs issues. We had Fred's paper on the acrylic paintings circulating in a market. The paradox of creating objects that are supposed to be beyond value, of inestimable value, incalculable value, whose value is constantly being calculated—it was a tough one. We didn't know what to do with it. What do you think?

Art

AW: Well, I was sorry there weren't a couple of papers on land. Because I think that's probably the most interesting object to consider in this kind of discussion. It doesn't move, but it does . . . I'll come back to that in a minute, but I want to talk a bit about art. I think that you have to look for these places again in the strategies that people are using. I would say off the top of my head that the place of inalienability for art is the museum. That's about as far as you can go. In time, that painting or sculpture may be deaccessioned, but it's interesting, the outcry from people when that occurs. Just recently, in Vermont, the Shelbourne Museum deaccessioned some Impressionist paintings, and there was a huge outcry from people in Vermont that they had no right to do it, that this was Vermont's property. But they needed money in order to keep the museum going. There was the same thing with the Barnes Collection, and he left it to a college or something. How were they going to get money to maintain it? They talked about deaccessioning some of the paintings, but there was again such an outcry. So they allowed them to circulate outside in shows that Barnes would never have allowed.

So that's the next step. Say a painting is deaccessioned. Where does it go? It starts another kind of cycling. Does it again end up in another museum, some place in Europe or wherever? But I think that the museum itself does exist as the repository for paintings. It does give the impression that whichever paintings get there are inalienable to this institution. They are part of its heritage, its patrimony, legacy.

How do paintings get there? I'm not sure exactly how that happens, but I don't think it just happens because there are some painters that are suddenly assumed to be great painters and their stuff automatically goes to museums. I know with Elena's work, Elena Clement [wife of Claudio Lomnitz, a participant in the seminar]—she's had a couple of shows in New York and Mexico City. Her dealer makes sure that before the show opens most of her stuff is already sold. Max [Barbara's husband, also a painter] must have this experience. And also, it really matters *who* buys it. She works very hard to make sure that a couple of her things get into museums before the show opens. So you can see how one has to work at getting an artist's work into this other place where it stands for all the great things that art should be. It matters who buys paintings, because if somebody just comes along and decides they're going to buy paintings and they're nobody—if you're the artist—does one think about that?

BKG: I think about it.

AW: Where will this painting end up? What will happen when these people die? Where will this painting go? Will it go in the trash? Will anybody recognize its value? As opposed to people who are known collectors—where you have the sense that they know what they're doing, that they will leave their paintings to an institution. There are very different kinds of collectors. And then there are the oddball collectors, like that husband and wife who were, I guess, known to the artist, but they accumulated all this very modern stuff and had it shoved under their bed and in their closets and suddenly they had this incredible collection that they left to some museum.

I think that's really important, that step between artist, dealers, collectors, and museums. If somebody like Paley [William Paley, once head of CBS and arts patron] buys a painting, it is almost as good as having it in a museum because you know it's going to be in a museum. It will get there, as opposed to somebody who is a very small collector.

BKG: I think what you're saying is particularly true for contemporary art with living artists. And it's a distinction that I think we have to make, because historical material circulates differently from contemporary material. Contemporary material is complicit with the gallery system to the point where it's often not possible to distinguish between a gallery and a museum....

AW: I want to go back for a minute to another point about art and getting into museums. Chris Steiner mentions this [in his paper], but he doesn't really go into it. What happens when an artist dies, or a member of his family dies who had a lot of his art? In the United States, the inheritance laws are such that the government wants cash; they want money. The artwork is evaluated, and then you pay the money that they ask. Often you have to sell the work in order to get the money to pay the inheritance tax.

In France, they do it in a very different way. They take part of the art for their museums, and the government comes and picks. They put a price on everything and then they select the pieces they want. You can't give them all the small pieces or something. They take the best until they've fulfilled the amount of this tax. But there is another example of inalienability where these paintings are in a museum. There's a word for it that indicates that this is a contribution of the family to this museum.

BKG: Basically, the way that artists handle it here, if they are savvy enough...is that one builds into the will the establishment of a non-profit foundation which places the work. It is to be constituted after the death and its task is to properly place the work. And when all the work has been properly placed, it dissolves. In some instances, like say with Judd or with Noguchi, they actually create the site. It becomes a permanent installation; it becomes an artist's museum. And artists' museums are very interesting in their own right. That's not the only form it can take, but it's a way to try to contend with that.

AW: It's a fascinating area to study. I read an article in the *New York Times* a couple of weeks ago about how to make something that's not worth very much into a Monet. It was about how art circulates. The interesting part of the article for me was that if you put a painting that's done by a major artist on sale at Sotheby's or Christie's and it doesn't get the price you ask and they don't auction it, they consider the painting "burned."

BKG: Actually, dealers often protect their artists by buying the paintings back. They set high reserves on them. The secondary market is critical. We tend to talk to the primary market but the secondary market is absolutely pivotal. And the other thing about these auctions—the Jacqueline Kennedy, the Camelot auction—is their almost arbitrary establishment of value: the idea that something that is so modest as an ashtray could establish an astronomical price at auction that cannot be calculated! There is no calculus that could account for why that amount of money could be paid for that object.

AW: Andy Warhol's auction was the same.

BKG: There's a real case where the connection between the person and the thing is utterly what establishes value. But it's not enough to say that, that the more important the person the more valuable the thing.

AW: No, it's just certain people.

BKG: And it also has to do with the auction as a mechanism.

FM: The auction is a mechanism that can transform monetary value enormously because you set up competitions between people. That's why they have auctions. You're creating a market of a very temporary, short—they don't want to have these things circulating all at the same time, because if you had Andy Warhol and Jackie Onassis having their things at the same time, everything would look a little different.

What you try to do, obviously, is to get people whose competitiveness with each other drives up the price.

BKG: Absolutely. The way auctions are staged, they're very interesting events for trying to understand how these things...

FM: There's a separate issue about the production of this value. Connoisseurs are critical. It's not just because Rockefeller had an object. It's not just because a painting can go in the museum, but Rockefeller bought all the other really good paintings. So you're going into a set of paintings in which he's already demonstrated his value. What we don't think about is why it's worth it for Rockefeller to do this. The symbiosis is in the fact that people are producing themselves. They're creating value in these objects at the same time they're using these objects to create value in themselves.

And any item or any set of differences can potentially become an object through which people can differentiate themselves—by acquiring it. That's why people are collecting cards. They're collecting not just aesthetic objects, but everything which is capable of differentiation and scarcity and particularity.

AW: Let me just say one thing about connoisseurship. Fred has reminded me. It's also dealership. Talk about old masters! [Joseph] Duveen, for example, was a great dealer. If you bought a Duveen, it was somehow a better painting than another Raphael that somebody else had sold you.

BKG: Sure, because it has passed through some sort of test. He was a filter.

AW: And that was another way of establishing some mark that this would be called inalienable. It was another kind of legitimization of this painting. A Duveen was far more valuable than another painting was, even by the very same artist.

FM: When we talked the other day [informally], you were talking about the relationship between those kinds of moves and *kula*—in terms of people's production of themselves.

BKG: Exchange, holding onto things, keeping them out of circulation, under what circumstances are they forced to put them back into circulation.

AW: Yes, it's not always just having a big shell or something and saying, "Okay, here it is." What happens at the very top end of *kula* is that people have these big valuables that are very well known. But as with a famous painting, you might let it circulate that you're ready to give this one up because you want a different one.

BKG: Trading up.

AW: Exactly. Because the goal is to have your name associated with every famous one that's around. So the word spreads, and maybe suddenly no one wants it. It's like being burned. Then, you have to pull that shell back and not circulate it for quite a while. That really reminded me of the similarity of these paintings with *kula*. You have to be so careful! It's not like just finally you have this great work of art. I think the basic processes are the same. This demands enormous care, enormous work. You don't just become a collector and sit with these things. You have to try to get them into catalogs. You're moving them. You're always thinking. You visit your dealer. It's a constant thing. That's what it's like in these other societies, these smaller societies where you're involved in the same way. It's enormous work to keep this stuff in the air and to keep it owned by somebody and to keep it moving, when it has to move, and to keep it hidden, when it has to be hidden. You're always thinking about it. The amount of knowledge that people have about these things. It's incredible.

FM: So [items of] material culture are forms. They're well suited to this kind of desire. It can happen at all sorts of levels, but there's some kind of desire to produce oneself that material culture allows one to do. It's a medium through which—

BKG: Absolutely. One of the things we kept coming back to is whether we could begin to specify the properties of material culture, period, and particular parts of material culture. Could we begin to specify the properties that made certain social and structural things possible? The banana bundle versus the mat versus the shell versus the painting versus the personal effects of a famous person? Not that any of the papers addressed that, but just in general.

FM: I would say that for Aboriginal art, the fact that it was turned into an easel painting was critical to its ability to [become fine art].

Making Inalienability: A Dialectical Process

AW: It's really interesting that the divide has been such an easy one between gift and commodity, but when you look at it from the perspective of inalienability, [you see] the work it takes, how difficult it is to make it happen. People want to make it happen; they try. All of those things have meaning no matter what you're looking at. In the British monarchy there are certain jewels that the queen has and she cannot give. They don't belong to her, they belong to the crown, to the monarchy. She cannot give them as gifts, she cannot alienate them. One of the things about the duchess of Windsor's auction is that the duke had given her some pieces that actually were from that patrimony.

FM: About reciprocity, the flip side is that commoditization is something that people keep trying to find an alter for. The oppositions are the gift and the commodity, and art and the commodity. And therefore, "art" and "gift" somehow have to be conflated, and they're not [the same]. The issue about "art" is actually another move in modernity. It's equivalent to the search for "reciprocity" as a trope—but it's another cultural move to try to imagine how to resist the sense that all things can be the same and can just circulate.

BKG: The paradox of art is that on the one hand it's worth more than the materials and labor that produce it. On the other hand, it is claimed that its value can't be calculated. Its value is always being calculated between those two places. It's worth more than materials and labor, but its value is beyond measure, but a price can be set. And that's what makes it a paradoxical object. I think in that way it's unlike anything we're talking about.

AW: Well, I think the notion of paradoxical objects would hold up for all of these things.

FM: If these objects are mediating two regimes of value, than their value is absolutely inestimable, incalculable.

AW: A fantasy value.

FM: Well, the fantasy is always over and against this other level. That's why the *kula* and the banana leaves are incomprehensible without each other as two systems. The image of it is the fantasy. It's like the Oscar Wilde [story of Dorian Gray] and these paintings that will last forever and the idea that people will have immortality.... I do think that you can't understand them as independent of the thing they oppose. We say "paradoxical"—that's from a different point of view. Their value, the value of art, is the way in which they contrast with these other things, which they can only do incompletely. That's why the connoisseurs are so interesting. We always were interested in Henry James's stories of the people who were trying to convert their filthy lucre into nobility.

BKG: Also, value's not a fixed quality. Value is volatile.

FM: It can be "burned."

BKG: And the trick of course is to keep on increasing the value or at least hold the value, and then the conditions for the value slips, so it's not just a matter that everything gets more value with time.

AW: In the eighties, the art market dropped. Let me just give you this last example which Nancy Munn gave me. She was just in Australia and she heard about John Kasapwaylova, a Trobriander who has great ideas, very well educated, always after something and has got some great scheme that always fails. Anyway, his uncle, who was a big chief, died. And apparently—I haven't been there since that death—he's really scheming to become really "big" [important]. He made a *kula* shell that has a carved figure in the center and then two armshells on either side of it. And according to what I heard, people are afraid to take it from him because they think there's too much sorcery involved. So talk about being "burned"!

INTERVIEW, PART 2

New York City, 24 April 1997

AW: What this reminded me of when I reread it [the transcript of our first interview], suddenly, was something I said earlier today to Fred. In all our earlier talk [the first interview], we really focused on exchange and the nature of materiality. In a sense, it's very rich because we're reversing a lot of the preconceived notions, but on the other hand, we've isolated those things. We've allowed hierarchy in because it's there, it's the potential for or the undermining of it [exchange]. But we've isolated exchange from other kinds of behaviors and systems and whatever you want to call them that involve it, contribute to it, also undermine it.

What I was telling Fred earlier today was that it suddenly seemed to me that we spent the better part of the century in anthropology clearing away a lot of ethnographic debris to get to the core of things.

So we started out in the beginning with these categories—a chapter on kinship, a chapter on magic, a chapter on the political system, a chapter on warfare. Get it all in there. But it's reduced to its discrete parts. All of these parts, then, should make up the whole of the society. And the most scraping away has obviously been structuralism, which attempted to reduce things not necessarily to their own categories but to a kind of bare bones of the brain and how it functions.

It seems to me now, at least based on my own work, that what has to occur is a reversal of that whole very positivist way of thinking about categories and a kind of building up again. You have to go back to build up these things, and it's very difficult because we're so accustomed to this reductionism. How can you not reduce? You ask questions, you get answers. Then you try to understand it, rationalize it. But now it seems as if that whole trend has to be reversed in some way, and we have to muddy the water again by building things back up on top of each other and embedding one thing in another that we used to keep separate. I think that's why it's so very difficult for people to really understand *Inalienable Possessions.* Because no matter what you say about it, what you write about it, how you define it, people bring their own thoughts to bear and their own experiences as ethnographers. And the history of exchange is so rich and so heavy and so burdened by that reduction of gift—A gives to B and B gives back to A, that sort of basic Maussian exchange or Malinowskian exchange—that it's hard to break away from that. And I think that's why people want to reduce the idea of inalienability: "Does it [inalienability] mean it never travels, does it mean…? But look! This does travel, so it can't be inalienable."

They simply don't understand. I think that problem is not so much a problem of my trying to explain it—that I wasn't clear enough. I think it's because that's how inundated we are by our past, the classical models that have worked for so long. I think the same thing with "kinship." The idea of husband and wife is where you start with kinship, the centerpiece, and then you work out from there. Because of the incest taboo, you don't start with brothers and sisters, because they're separated in some way. But they're only separated in very specific ways and often they are the core relationship in that society. Hard to make those switches.

So, all that being said and then thinking back to this, it's interesting that suddenly we came to *sorcery* at the end of our discussion last time. That reminded me of the way we've kept these categories separate. Well, Fred, I don't know if you remember, but when I came back from the Trobriands after my doctoral research, I had a lot of conversations with you. I actually didn't know what I was going to write my dissertation on because I had so much material on bundles and funerals and death. And I had as much material on magic, and these yams were driving me crazy. I didn't know where to pull the straw that said, "Okay, this is where it's going to be focused." Fred and I talked for hours about whether it should be on magic, or on these mortuary exchanges. I think that we were trapped by "magic" as well, trapped in the sense that that category, like exchange, was siphoned off at the turn of the century. And the arguments that developed around it were kind of a response to rationality, of Western thought. And this was irrationality. So most of the discussion was rationality versus irrationality, religion versus magic. It was always magic versus some Western concept. I think the same set of circumstances at the turn of the century which produced this utter reliance on "reciprocity" as its core principle also produced and separated off "magic-sorcery" as part of a different system of inquiry, and therefore not economic. Sure, there were some economics in it, obviously, when you paid people to do things for you, but that was about it.

If we're going to talk about exchange and hierarchy then, it's not just material things that contribute to it, although obviously without the material things you don't have it in the first place. But then those material things and their presence also elicit a kind of "corruption" in the system—a way to get around the formality of the system itself. I think that's where magic and sorcery and those things are located. As the means by which one can corrupt the system, can take it to your own advantage without playing the system as it should be played. Which is what John Kasapwaylova was attempting to do. I go back to these same arguments of Adam Smith: that if you have a free market people are going to corrupt it. As I said earlier, there's a lot of discussion in that literature around that same time about people who own land and how they are so much more dependable and not easily corrupted. Because land needs to be passed on for other people to care for. It has this generational quality to it, as opposed to people who are just capitalists, because they're dealing in stuff that they haven't made, that has no meaning beyond what they can make of it....

FM: I want to shift the subject because I'll forget this. But I've been talking to Annette about this particular issue for a long time. In 1982, we went to a [Wenner-Gren] conference, and you had that paper on "elementary cycling," which was about how to think about hierarchy.[4] I actually thought this was the critical paper in the movement from the Trobriand material to a more general model. You never published that paper or any part of it, right?

AW: I have to say that it received such a terrible reception at that conference that I backed away from the notion of "elementary cycling." I never backed away in terms of thinking about it, and I think it did get finally caught up in my whole notion of exchange as it attaches to kinship.

It was a very particular kind of conference, on feminism and kinship theory. I was desperately searching for some term that I could call all of this. So I thought of "elementary cycling." I didn't particularly like "cycling," because that has the connotation of things just going on and on and on. But I thought, that's really what I'm talking about, the core of how people and objects get cycled through time. I was trying to get at the core elements of that, like "bones."

FM: In fact, kinship was the problem: that kinship could be seen in relationship to objects, could be constituted in the circulation of objects.[5]

BKG: Well, this bears on your point earlier that there's been a compartmentalization of topics so that in its purest form, kinship is about social relations that may have to do with all kinds of things...

AW: With rules, mostly, to start out with, that's the core.

BKG: The idea that you would look at objects, exchange, kinship as implicated in one another, not as separate systems, and you completely reconfigure the problem so that they couldn't be imagined separately. That's what I hear.

So Fred, when you raised the elementary cycling, you mentioned that factoring objects into the discussion was one aspect. What else was there about it?

FM: The part that I thought was significant was the development of certain kinds of objects that could extend the cycle of social life beyond the reproduction of an individual's life. This was the vehicle for a transformation in the organization of social life; these objects could extend through time. It came out of the sense of adding temporality to exchange. The [previous] expectation was that the cycle of social reproduction was based on the individual. Then if you look at Hawaii or Samoa, it's not the individual's life cycle any more that is the unit of it. It is something dramatically different.

AW: What turned me on to thinking about that was the way, in the Trobriands, after someone dies, people carry the objects of the dead person around for maybe six months or a year. If a man dies, they take his basket (in which he carried his *kula* shells), and they decorate it with all the other things—his earrings, his armbands, his [clan-associated] feathers. The carrying of part of this person's identity like this, I thought, was quite incredible. For a woman, you take her skirt, and you twine her earrings and so forth into the skirt, and you carry it draped across your shoulder. It's a particular relative who does it. Then I began to think of bones as like shell. Your question, "Why stones or whatever?" But it seemed as if bones have always been universally significant. In the Trobriands, before the colonials were there, they would take the jawbone and clean it and carry that as well, if it's a really important person.

Objectification

BKG: When you say carry...?

AW: Wherever they walked, this person had to have it on their person. They attached a strap around the basket so it went around a person's neck and hung down in front of them. The skirt was carried on someone's shoulder. It was draped over the shoulder. Thus, it was always carried. And then to go to Claudio's paper again, the bones are statements of political power, of political legitimation really, more than just power. And bones have always been used historically as a way to legitimize churches, whatever.

So it seemed there was something about the nature of bones that was for all time and the most permanent sort of thing that actually had a human identity from the start. You didn't have to impose it on a piece of shell or a piece of metal. It was already there from the start. And then as cloth, somehow wrapping the bones, the significance of that, because—I said this earlier—with cloth you have all the metaphors about wrapping, tying, and weaving kin groups together, unraveling, tying...There are myths and stories that different societies have about these metaphors as they're connected to answers and regeneration, birth, death, and so forth. You could just go on and on with these examples. So I was obsessed with these two categories. And I thought that somehow kinship was really entwined in these objects.

BKG: You were talking about when somebody dies that a designated person carries around their jawbone as well as their possessions for a period of time. What do you make of this?

AW: Well, what I made of it, on the ground, was the attempt to continue the social life of the person. The person who carried these things was either from the matrilineage of the spouse of the dead person or from the matrilineage of the father of the dead person. Those were external groups that were united through marriage. So what I took from that was the extension of the social life for the lineage into which this dead person had been born, as a way of maintaining that relationship beyond the life of this person. And that's what gave me the sense of something bigger going on than just an individual. A lot is at stake for a lineage every time someone dies, focus can center on that lineage, and so again the fear of sorcery, since most people are thought to have died through sorcery—as an attack on the lineage to weaken it. The more powerful a lineage is, the more fear is generated by a death. Some of the genealogies I collected, you just see this line of women who died and people said, "Don't talk about that to anyone because somebody was after that lineage." So that again, this corruption, this magic that corrupts, enters into the system of exchange and creates real terror. By this other lineage carrying this dead person, they're going to get paid back a lot, again and again throughout any number of years that there are exchanges that take place. Sometimes these exchanges take ten years after a person dies.

BKG: You carry this person around for a number of years, then what happens?

AW: Then you're paid back a lot in the women's distribution of skirts and bundles, and then the next year, maybe if the lineage is strong, they will hold another exchange which is all taro. So you'll get a lot of that. And the next year when they hold an exchange, it's all yams. And the next year, they may hold an exchange that's all fish or pigs.

And so you're a prominent receiver in these exchanges that are all to commemorate the loss.

BKG: What happens to the stuff you're carrying around?

AW: The bones? They are kept for a very long time and then they will be buried where the person is buried.

BKG: What's interesting is when I think about the goods, whatever, of a person who has died—[I think of them as being] inherited or they are discarded. But this protocol, it doesn't sound either like inheritance nor is it discarded.

AW: Some things are inherited that have some value. Earrings are made of these special shells, or a *kula* shell can be carried, something like that certainly could be inherited, but sometimes they're hung on a little fence around the grave of the dead person after the other person no longer has to carry it. That's just the visual imagery of how the system worked.

FM: It's also exchange's extension. These bones are given as an extension of a series of exchanges.

AW: And in the hope that at some later time, maybe before this time period is over, there will be another marriage with the same group. Also there are exchanges of yams that are always going from an external group to an internal group, and those sometimes may be reconstituted. So there's a lot at stake in the sort of normal everyday series of exchanges. In the Trobriands, you want to spread out but not too much. That's another thing in terms of kinship. It's how far you are able to spread and how much you need to recoup. If you don't have too much it's more dangerous and more threatening in a sense, to spread out far, to marry far away or something like that. This may be because it's an island as opposed to Australia where people are walking in space. But I think when you've got some stuff in the system—stuff being objects—and some hierarchy in the system, then it's even more dangerous, how far you go.

FM: Well, if you have a lot of things, you can create more relationships than you can with people alone. If you think of marriage as an elementary form of being related to people, then having objects circulate, you can potentially create more multiple kinds of relationships.

Gradations of the Materiality of Exchange

BKG: When we focus our conversation on exchange of material objects, then I think to myself: well, what about exchanges that involve consumption—when whatever happens, the stuff disappears, it's used up?

FM: But there is a model. One of the models is, it is exchange. When you're feeding people it is often conceptualized as exchange and the consequence of that is a person, or growth or something.

AW: It comes back later.

BKG: What's interesting is that there's something about the durability or the consistent material presence of objects as opposed to soft areas that involve renewal. Did we talk about this the first time? That food is so interesting because it is material, but its materiality is that it's perishable, it has to be consumed, hence it has to be renewed over and over again. So the over-and-over-again aspect—it's not denying that it's material, it is absolutely, but we've been talking about bones as at one end of the durable. Bones and stones and shells are very durable, and then there are all these others which are more in that category…of perishable, soft, to be consumed, not consumed like consumption consumed but…

AW: We did talk about this, but not quite in this way. What we talked about earlier was the variation even in consumables: taro, you cut off the tops and plant [them]; there's a difference between giving a raw pig—a live pig—and pig meat, pork. A big difference in those exchanges. Also the care and feeding of a pig, the responsibility to feed it and grow it up. So all of these natural variations are played on, and they enhance and expand it. What Fred was mentioning just before, often what's consumed, what actually is consumed finally, has a big debt that's outstanding, that may only come back when somebody dies. It may be many years before that debt is actually repaid. In the Trobriands, for the father, everybody says, "Oh, that man gave me food when I was small, got firewood, caught fish." Malinowski recorded that. But what does he get back for having done that? When a person dies, [his lineage] will get the most back from the banana leaves and skirts and so forth.

BKG: It reminds me, it may not be an appropriate analogy, but of futures. There's all this speculation for objects that are on the commodities market. Expected to speculate, the stuff changes hands…. What eventually happens is eventually *X* tons of grain arrive somewhere, and that grain is five years out or ten years out, whatever it is, but there's this element of very long trajectories that involve careful bookkeeping, that are monitored...that require deferral or patience in letting them...

AW: There are things in between, of course, that have to do with yam exchanges and that sort of thing as well, but it was long term, and they're always watching what people are doing. Are they making a big enough garden, are they really sincere in this garden? So there's total accountability, strategy going on all the time. I think it's interesting; there's very little made of a marriage [in the Trobriands]. There are no formal big-time marriage exchanges, as you find elsewhere, but the bride and groom eat together and they eat publicly, which means that they are married. That's the signal, that they've eaten half a yam, they've shared a yam between them. So somehow this food, ingested, combines the biological with what's necessary in the social framework of the exchange. You've written a lot about this, Fred, in terms of "nurturing" and "growing up" and how all that's deeply connected to kinship.

FM: I used that paper you had on replacement [Weiner 1980], of separating out different kinds of exchange: one that I saw as really about producing people. Exchanges tend to be considered largely between equals, between people who are giving these objects, rather than conceiving of the whole of social life as a system built around giving and receiving. But the temporalities of that would be different. Some parts of that were focused on what Annette called "replacement," which was replacing yourself: investing your identity through activity in others. What does it mean to give somebody your identity, so that identity is a representation of a relationship produced in exchange?

But the other part of what I was going to ask you—because this leads to the other end of it—is about the social density of objects in which they can in some way summarize or stand for so much. This is where a lot of people have been interested in using the "inalienable" to stand somehow for objects that are beyond commoditization in that they are not easily exchangeable because they're so dense with meanings.

AW: In a paper I wrote [Weiner 1994], I tried to expand the notion of density. It was after my book [*Inalienable Possessions*] had come out, so I tried to lay it out a little more clearly, unencumbered by kinship and the South Pacific. My vision was the weightiness of objects, that they gained heaviness—[exemplified in] the notion that chiefs don't walk far. There's a sense that chiefs shouldn't talk. This is in many places in the Pacific.

FM: They draw things to them.

Properties of Objectifications

AW: They [chiefs] have somebody who talks *for* them. Objects take on this kind of density that relates to who owned it before, its history. It starts out with how well it's moved. The first level is always the aesthetics of it, the beauty of the object itself. Because I think you can't disguise that, in the sense of a fine mat. They all might look the same to us but actually there are these differentiations. So the really finest ones are always the ones you rank the highest. And then as those very fine mats continue to circulate, then they get attached to people who will keep them. So that all of those things allow certain objects to rise, to separate themselves out from the whole category of objects that may not be as fine, that may not have been owned by the most important people. That's what I call "density."

That density sticks to the object. I guess it separates itself, if ever, when it's in a different system. And then it does it. You don't have to ask, because then you think of Jacqueline Kennedy's auction block, and the prices that were paid for these things because she had held them and owned them, beyond what Sotheby's thought. And the same thing with the duchess of Windsor's auction of her things.

BKG: There are two themes here. One has to do with the way the person attaches to the thing, which is another theme but a very important one. This is coupled with the very particular phenomenon of "celebrity." The "celebrity" is a particular category of person, different from other ways in which a person will be important and will be attached to her thing. Although I imagine chiefs have celebrity—

AW: Of course, we're so conscious of celebrity because it's in our time right now; they're the highest ranking people around. They're world figures. But that's why I juxtaposed Jackie Kennedy and the duchess of Windsor. I was also thinking of Andy Warhol's auction, but I thought those other two were better compared. I'm not so sure. I think the major difference is that celebrityship can't be inherited. It's not like being queen of England. You don't really pass it on.

BKG: Or you do pass it on, but it weakens with each transition... The thing with celebrity is that historically in the US it emerges at the second half of the nineteenth century. People become famous for being famous, rather than famous for...

AW:—occupying a particular role that's been legitimized in some way. Maybe that is an emulation of royalty. We never had royalty in this country, but there is something about royalty that is very dramatic and dynamic. Why does England still have this queen? They keep arguing over whether they need this queen or not. And the amount of money that's taken from the British to support this monarchy.

FM: I actually see this differently.... There's a sense in which hierarchy is always potentiated in the presence of objects. Even in a commodity market where all these are mass produced to some extent, what's at work is the possibility of differentiation. And hierarchy is predicated on the possibility of differentiation, which is there. You've written about this, Annette, and Bill Mitchell [Annette's husband] has written about this: that equality is maintained through work. Equality is not intrinsic. It is not the beginning state, but it is itself maintained through the management of, the continued work to reproduce, equivalence. And there's always the possibility in any exchange of hierarchy or differentiation.

This is a perfectly good example. It is a mistake to see inalienability as the equivalent of the gift in opposition to the commodity, because commodities can easily avail themselves of this kind of possibility of hierarchicalization and exclusion. So it seems to me that the issue of the inalienable and the issue of density are linked but they're not isomorphic. They're not the same thing. In academic discourse, there's a kind of renunciation of anybody pursuing celebrity things, because it's not seen to be real value. But in fact there is an interest that people have to find some measure in the object world of something that is differentiated by whoever owned it and therefore can express yourself —can stand for the possibility of your connection to it, your distinctiveness.

People and Things

BKG: The parents and the jawbone...comparing how they walk around for months carrying these personal effects with the public auction of personal effects? It's precisely how totally alienable objects of incalculable value are. There's something about that, that their value calculated in money is astronomical beyond all belief and they are totally alienable for whatever reason, arcane... That's what to me is so totally puzzling, and what distinguishes it from the other examples.

AW: That's true, I have to think about that. It is a big difference.

FM: "Elementary cycling" actually leads to that. The model of it was [that objects are] always increasingly alienated from the individual's life cycle. But the identity that's produced in these objects is reconsumed or reproduced in people who are like that person. And when you get to the state [where] you have these heirlooms, the property, the *taonga* and whatever,[6] that only some people get—there's a kind of siphoning of value up to them that doesn't actually return except in a kind of reflected way. It is more alienated from it.

BKG: You can't imagine the crown jewels would have the same fate as Jackie Onassis's stuff, which is a measure of how weak she was. Her stuff couldn't be kept off the auction block.

AW: Well, in terms of royalty—there are jewels that the queen has that can never be given to someone as a gift, they cannot be alienated from the monarchy. They do not really belong to the queen. She wears them as a result of her being the queen, but they go back into the treasury of the British monarchy. There are people who guard those things. In the duchess of Windsor's auction, there were certain pieces of jewelry that were part of that category, those inalienable jewels, that were sold at auction. The duke of Windsor had given them to the duchess as a gift. He didn't have the right to do that at all, but he had access to them and he gave them away. There's always the possibility for draining things away.

I'm still preoccupied by the question you raised, Barbara. Because it's true, all of these things I've been using as examples are attached to some kind of identity, social identity. They are not just anybody's bones; they are the bones of certain people. The issue you raised is when part of what has created that density is removed. Another set of situations hurriedly comes in to almost patch that part up.

BKG: Who gets the proceeds? Is that part of the estate? Is it really what happens with heirs to the state?

AW: Oh, definitely. It is why—when somebody dies in this country who owns a lot of artwork—the taxes would be so great on that person's estate. If they own really substantial artwork, or if they're just wealthy, they will have to put the art (or most of it or some of it) on the market, on the auction block, because they need the money to pay the inheritance tax.

BKG: So what happens is that the auction is a way to generate revenue to pay the taxes on the estate, so that the economics of the estate actually precipitate some of these decisions that can appear to seem only in terms of the auction itself as bizarre.

FM: But it's also because these objects are insignificant, or many of them are. Jackie's children don't care if they have her lighter. They have the critical things. The principles at work are the principles through which objects get to be identified or associated with people. But they're not part of a project of social reproduction, except they are converted to money, which is part of it. But they can't embody these identities through time in the same way. The crown jewels can, but these objects, while they're valuable, don't have that kind of identity.

BKG: They belong to a category…"collectibles." And collectibles have to do with all the things you're talking about: they have to do with density, with differentiation, etc., and I think your point is really well taken. But in this case, mass-produced objects, objects that in their initial incarnation have nothing to distinguish them from hundreds of thousands of others that look exactly like them, come *through their social life* to be quite differentiated, quite distinguished. And certain marks of distinction make them more or less eligible for the category of collectible, and value gets calculated accordingly.

FM: You know where they end up. I think it's the nation in the end, or the state, because it's these museums…the only place that they can go from individuals. They have to build something that will endure. They create their own wing. They collect these things and then they give it to the Met. So I think the projects we see in these smaller-scale societies—in which people's individual identities get linked to a social project—have to link now possibly to the state or some kind of organizational entity that will endure through time. Even though the Met swore it wasn't going to keep giving personal wings, that policy only lasted fifteen years.

BKG: So in a way what's interesting is that the auction by the estate is a way in which the estate gets dispersed, becomes part of other collections. And those collections, if they don't make their way into a storehouse—a treasure house basically, a public treasure house, which starts to move it into the state idea—they actually come up on the auction block and get dispersed again...In Jackie's case, it wasn't her collection; it was her personal effects. So it had that coherence. It got dispersed, but the moment it gets dispersed, it goes into collections because when those collections get dispersed, and items circulate through that way, unless someone has the power to take an intact collection and transmit it as such to an institution who will accept it as a collection, it goes.

AW: Thinking just about art, you have collectors who hope to make a collection and give this collection to a museum. So there will be collectors who have that ability, and also have advisers. They are willing to learn, and it becomes a sort of life occupation. What will be interesting, and maybe this is the problem with the Jackie Kennedy example, is that we won't really know into the future what will happen with those things that people bought. Where will they go? What will happen to them? Will someone in the very distant future find them in an antique store, a flea market, this cheap set of pearls that went for thousands of dollars? Because it's again the guardianship. Who takes care of it?

I think maybe that has to be said about these things. Sometimes I talk about objects as if they're just moving around by themselves. Because we tend to just talk about these movements and you drop the people out because you're explaining how these things work. But I think that maybe in addition to density, there is this deep significance of guardianship—of caring for objects, of the human contact—in addition to ownership. This is beyond ownership.

FM: Stewardship, in a way.

AW: People who carry the body, that's their work. That's all they do. And so, without that, where do these things go? For example, I look around this apartment and I think, "Now, well where will they go?" Because there's nothing excruciatingly valuable. I didn't go into being a collector.

...

On 7 December 1997, Annette passed away. A few days later, her husband, Bill Mitchell, brought over her Trobriand grass skirt, which she left to Fred's daughter Samantha, a goddaughter. She left her *kula* valuables to Fred.

Notes

1. Weiner wrote a paper incorporating these concerns, titled "Sticks and Stones, Thread and Bones: What Kinship Is Made Of." It was presented at a conference on "Feminism and Kinship Theory" sponsored by the Wenner-Gren Foundation in Bellagio, Italy, in August 1982, but was never published.

2. Renne was a Ph.D. student supervised by Weiner, working on cloth in Nigeria.

3. *Churinga* is a term for a sacred object in the Arrernte language of central Australia.

4. This was "Sticks and Stones, Threads and Bones: What Kinship Is Made Of" (Weiner 1982).

5. This perspective has an obvious relationship to Daniel Miller's chapter in this volume.

6. *Taonga* are a class of Maori valuables that Annette considered in several articles and in *Inalienable Possessions.*

References

Abad y Queipo, Manuel

1964 [1810] Decreto de excomunión de los insurgentes dado por el obispo Abad y Queipo, 1810. *In* Historia Documental de México, vol. 2. Ernesto de la Torre Villar, Moisés González Navarro, and Stanley Ross, compilers. Pp. 36–40. Mexico City: UNAM.

Abu-Lughod, Lila

1991 The Romance of Resistance: Tracing Transformations of Power through Bedouin Women. American Ethnologist 17:41–55.

Adams, Laurie

1976 Art on Trial: From Whistler to Rothko. New York: Walker.

Adorno, Theodor W.

1977 Culture Industry Reconsidered. New German Critique 6(Fall):120–26.

1978 On the Fetish Character of Music and the Regression of Listening. *In* The Essential Frankfurt School Reader. Andrew Arato and Eike Gebhardt, eds. Pp. 270–300. New York: Continuum.

Afrika, Tatamkulu

1994 Against All Odds My Heart Sings. *In* South Africa April 1994. Andre Brink, ed. Pp. 9–13. Pretoria: Queillerie.

1983 [1970] Aesthetic Theory. London: Routledge and Kegan Paul.

REFERENCES

Akin, David, and Joel Robbins, eds.

1999 Money and Modernity: State and Local Currencies in Melanesia. Pittsburgh: University of Pittsburgh Press.

Alexander, Neville

1994 Robben Island Dossier: Report to the International Community. Cape Town: University of Cape Town.

Alomes, Stephen

1988 A Nation at Last? The Changing Character of Australian Nationalism 1880–1988. Sydney: Angus and Robertson.

Altman, Jon

1988 The Economic Basis for Cultural Production. *In* The Inspired Dream: Life as Art in Aboriginal Australia. Margaret West, ed. Pp. 48–55. Brisbane: Queensland Art Gallery.

Altman, Jon, Chris McGuigan, and Peter Yu

1989 The Aboriginal Arts and Crafts Industry. Report of the Review Committee, Department of Aboriginal Affairs. Canberra: Australian Government Publishing Service.

Altshuler, Bruce

1994 The Avant-Garde in Exhibition: New Art in the Twentieth Century. New York: Harry N. Abrams.

Anderson, Benedict

1991 Imagined Communities: Reflections on the Origin and Spread of Nationalism. London: Verso.

Andreotti, Margherita

1993 Brancusi's Golden Bird: A New Species of Modern Sculpture. Museum Studies (Art Institute of Chicago) 19(2):135–53.

Anonymous

1822 A Defense of Direct Taxes and of Protective Duties for the Encouragement of Manufactures. Philadelphia: Hunt.

Anonymous

1941 Art of Australia. Exhibition catalog. Carnegie Corporation.

Antze, Paul, and Michael Lambek

1996 Tense Past: Cultural Essays in Trauma and Memory. London: Routledge.

Appadurai, Arjun

1986 Introduction: Commodities and the Politics of Value. *In* The Social Life of Things: Commodities in Cultural Perspective. Arjun Appadurai, ed. Pp. 3–63. Cambridge: Cambridge University Press.

1990 Disjuncture and Difference in the Global Cultural Economy. Public Culture 2(2):1–24.

Appadurai, Arjun, ed.

1986 The Social Life of Things: Commodities in Cultural Perspective. Cambridge: Cambridge University Press.

Appiah, Kwame Anthony

1995 Why Africa? Why Art? *In* Africa: The Art of a Continent. Tom Phillips, ed. Pp. 21–26. London: Prestel.

Aronson, Lisa

1992 Ijebu Yoruba Aso Olona: A Contextual and Historical Overview. African Arts 25(3):52–63, 101–2.

Art News

1973 Conversations with Kenneth Clark: The Museum's Duty, the Uses of Art History, the Education of the Eye. 72(8):13–16.

Babcock, Barbara

1995 The Marketing of Maria. *In* Looking High and Low: Art and Cultural Identity. Brenda Bright and Liza Bakewell, eds. Pp. 124–50. Tucson: University of Arizona Press.

Badham, Herbert

1949 A Study of Australian Art. Sydney: Currawong Press.

Bailey, Martin

1995 The Art of Darkness: Plunder and Pillage in Africa. Minerva, November–December.

Bakewell, Liza

1995 Bellas Artes and Artes Populares: The Implications of Difference in the Mexico City Art World. *In* Looking High and Low: Art and Cultural Identity. Brenda Bright and Liza Bakewell, eds. Pp. 19–54. Tucson: University of Arizona Press.

Bakhtin, Mikhail

1983 The Dialogical Imagination. Austin: University of Texas Press.

Bardon, Geoffrey

1979 Aboriginal Art of the Western Desert. Sydney: Rigby.

1991 Papunya Tula Art of the Western Desert. Melbourne: McPhee Gribble.

Barnes, R. H., and R. Barnes

1989 Barter and Money in an Indonesian Village Economy. Man (n.s.) 24:399–418.

Barrett, Lindsay

1996 The Prime Minister's Christmas Card: Modernism and Politics in the Whitlam Era. Ph.D thesis, University of Technology, Sydney.

Barthes, Roland

1957 Mythologies. Paris: Éditions du Seuil.

Bataille, Georges

1988a The Accursed Share: An Essay on General Economy. Vol. 1, Consumption. Robert Hurley, trans. New York: Zone Books.

1988b The Accursed Share: An Essay on General Economy. New York: Zone Books.

References

Battaglia, Debbora

1990 On the Bones of the Serpent. Chicago: University of Chicago Press.

Baudelaire, Charles

1964 [1863] The Painter of Modern Life and Other Essays. John Mayne, trans. New York: Phaidon Press.

Baudrillard, Jean

1972 Pour une critique de l'économie politique du signe. Paris: Gallimard.

Baxandall, Michael

1988 Painting and Experience in Fifteenth-Century Italy: A Primer in the Social History of Pictorial Style. 2d edition. New York: Oxford University Press.

Beck, Ulrich, and Elizabeth Gernsheim-Beck

1995 The Normal Chaos of Love. Cambridge: Polity.

Beidelman, T. O.

1989 Agonistic Exchange: Homeric Reciprocity and the Heritage of Simmel and Mauss. Cultural Anthropology 4(3):227–59.

1997a The Cool Knife. Washington, D.C.: Smithsonian Institution Press.

1997b Promoting African Art: The Catalogue to the Exhibit of African Art at the Royal Academy of Arts, London. Anthropos 92:3–20.

Bell, Leonard

1983 Putting the Record Straight: Gordon Walters. Art New Zealand 27:42–45.

1989 Walters and Maori Art: The Nature of the Relationship? *In* Gordon Walters: Order and Intuition. Ross Simmons and Laurence Simmons, eds. Pp. 12–23. Auckland: Privately published.

Benjamin, Walter

1968a The Task of the Translator. *In* Illuminations: Essays and Reflections. Pp. 69–82. New York: Schocken Books.

1968b Theses on the Philosophy of History. *In* Illuminations: Essays and Reflections. Pp. 253–64. New York: Schocken Books.

Bennett, Tony

1995 The Birth of the Museum: History, Theory, Politics. New York: Routledge.

Berdahl, Daphne

1999 (N)ostalgie for the Present: Memory, Longing and East German Things. Ethnos 64:192–211.

Berman, P. G.

1996 The Invention of History: Julius Meiergraefe, German Modernism, and the Genealogy of Genius. Studies in the History of Art 53:91–112.

Bersani, Leo

1990 The Culture of Redemption. Cambridge, Mass.: Harvard University Press.

Bhabha, Homi K.

1990 Introduction: Narrating the Nation. *In* Nation and Narration. Homi Bhabha, ed. Pp. 1–7. New York: Routledge.

1994 The Other Question: Stereotype, Discrimination and the Discourse of Colonialism. *In* The Location of Culture. Pp. 66–84. London: Routledge.

Blake, Nigel, and Francis Frascina

1993 "Modern Practices of Art and Modernity." *In* Modernity and Modernism: French Painting in the Nineteenth Century. Nigel Blake et al., eds. Pp. 50–140. New Haven, Conn.: Yale University Press.

Bloch, Ernst, Georg Lukacs, Bertolt Brecht, Walter Benjamin, and Theodor W. Adorno

1977 Aesthetics and Politics. London: New Left Books.

Bloch, Maurice, and Jonathan Parry

1989 Introduction: Money and the Morality of Exchange. *In* Money and the Morality of Exchange. Jonathan Parry and Maurice Bloch, eds. Pp. 1–32. Cambridge: Cambridge University Press.

Bohannon, Paul

1955 Some Principles of Exchange and Investment among the Tiv. American Anthropologist 57:60–70.

Bolton, Richard, ed.

1992 Culture Wars: Documents from the Recent Controversies in the Arts. New York: New Press.

Bourdieu, Pierre

1968 Outline of a Sociological Theory of Art Perception. International Social Science Journal 20(4):589–612.

1977 Outline of a Theory of Practice. Cambridge: Cambridge University Press.

1980 The Production of Belief: Contributions to an Economy of Symbolic Goods. Media, Culture and Society 2:261–93.

1984 Distinction: A Social Critique of the Judgment of Taste. Cambridge, Mass.: Harvard University Press.

1993a The Field of Cultural Production: Essays on Art and Literature. New York: Columbia University Press.

1993b "The Production of Belief." *In* The Field of Cultural Production: Essays on Art and Literature. Pp. 74–111. New York: Columbia University Press.

Bourdieu, Pierre, and Alain Derbel, with Dominique Schnapper

1990 [1969] The Love of Art: European Art Museums and Their Public. Caroline Beattie and Nick Merriman, trans. Stanford, Calif.: Stanford University Press.

Brenner, Suzanne A.

1995 Why Women Rule the Roost: Rethinking Javanese Ideologies of Gender and Self-Control. *In* Bewitching Women, Pious Men: Gender and Body Politics in Southeast Asia. Aihwa Ong and Michael G. Peletz, eds. Pp. 19–50. Berkeley: University of California Press.

Brown, Bill

1998 How to Do Things with Things (A Toy Story). Critical Inquiry 24:935–64.

Bulnes, Francisco

1904 El verdadero Juárez: La verdad sobre la intervención y el imperio. Mexico City: Librería de la Viuda de Ch. Bouret.

Burger, Peter

1984 Theory of the Avant-Garde. Manchester: Manchester University Press.

Burn, Ian, Nigel Lendon, Charles Merewether, and Ann Stephen

1988 The Necessity of Australian Art. Sydney: Power Institute.

Butel, Elizabeth

1985 Margaret Preston: The Art of Constant Rearrangement. Ringwood, Victoria: Penguin Books.

Butler, Roger

1987 The Prints of Margaret Preston. Canberra and Melbourne: Australian National Gallery and Oxford University Press.

Cabanne, Pierre

1971 Dialogues with Marcel Duchamp. Ron Padgett, trans. London: Thames and Hudson.

Cabrera, Luis

1972 [1910] Los dos patriotismos. *In* Obras Completas, vol. 2. Pp. 47–56. Mexico City: Ediciones Oasis.

Caplow, Theodore

1984 Rule Enforcement without Visible Means: Christmas Gift Giving in Middletown. American Journal of Sociology 89:1306–23.

Carrier, David

1987 Artwriting. Amherst: University of Massachusetts Press.

Carrier, James

1995 Gifts and Commodities: Exchange and Western Capitalism since 1700. London: Routledge.

Carrier, James, ed.

1997 Meanings of the Market. Oxford: Berg.

Carrier, James, and Daniel Miller, eds.

1998 Virtualism: A New Political Economy. Oxford: Berg.

Charles, Carolle

1992 Transnationalism in the Construct of Haitian Migrants' Racial Categories of Identity in New York City. Annals of the New York Academy of Science 645:101–23.

Chatwin, Bruce

1988 Songlines. New York: Viking Press.

Cheal, David

1988 The Gift Economy. London: Routledge.

Clark, Timothy J.

1984 The Painting of Modern Life: Paris in the Art of Manet and His Followers. New York: Knopf.

Clarke, Alison

1998 Window Shopping at Home: Classifieds, Catalogs and New Consumer Skills. *In* Material Cultures: Why Some Things Matter. Daniel Miller, ed. Pp. 77–99. Chicago: University of Chicago Press.

Clifford, James

1985 Histories of the Tribal and the Modern. Art in America, April, pp. 161–77.

1986 On Ethnographic Allegory. *In* Writing Culture: The Poetics and Politics of Ethnography. James Clifford and George Marcus, eds. Pp. 98–121. Berkeley: University of California Press.

1988a "Histories of the Tribal and the Modern." *In* The Predicament of Culture. Pp. 189–214. Cambridge, Mass.: Harvard University Press.

1988b The Predicament of Culture: Twentieth-Century Ethnography, Literature, and Art. Cambridge, Mass.: Harvard University Press.

1991 Four Northwest Coast Museums: Travel Reflections. *In* Exhibiting Cultures: The Poetics and Politics of Museum Display. Ivan Karp and Steven Lavine, eds. Pp. 212–54. Washington, D.C.: Smithsonian Institution Press.

1997 Routes: Travel and Translation in the Late Twentieth Century. Cambridge, Mass.: Harvard University Press.

Cohodas, Marvin

1999 Elizabeth Hickox and Karuk Basketry: A Case Study in Debates on Innovation and Paradigms of Authenticity. *In* Unpacking Culture: Art and Commodity in Colonial and Postcolonial Worlds. Ruth B. Phillips and Christopher B. Steiner, eds. Pp. 143–61. Berkeley: University of California Press.

Comaroff, John, and Jean Comaroff

1990 Goodly Beasts, Beastly Goods: Cattle and Commodities in a South African Context. American Ethnologist 17:195–216.

Conn, Stephen

1998 Museums and American Intellectual Life, 1876–1926. Chicago: University of Chicago Press.

Coombes, Annie

1992 Inventing the "Postcolonial": Hybridity and Constituency in Contemporary Curating. New Formations 18:39–52.

1994 Reinventing Africa: Museums, Material Culture, and Popular Imagination in Late Victorian and Edwardian England. New Haven, Conn.: Yale University Press.

Corner, Lorraine

1989 East and West Nusa Tenggara: Isolation and Poverty. *In* Unity and Diversity: Regional Economic Development in Indonesia since 1970. Hal Hill, ed. Pp. 178–206. Singapore: Oxford University Press.

Coulmas, Florian

1992 Language and Economy. Oxford: Basil Blackwell.

Couvreur, A. J. L.

1914 Jaarverslag Afdeeling Soemba 1914 tevens memorie van Overgave. Typescript. Algemeen Rijksarchief, The Hague.

Cramer, Rebecca Ann

1994 Commodities, Capital, and the Confounding of Art Historical Values in the Rise and Fall of the Art Market during the 1980s. Master's thesis, Department of Art History, University of California, Los Angeles.

Crump, Thomas

1981 The Phenomenon of Money. London: Routledge and Kegan Paul.

Cutler, A.

1991 Stalking the Beast: Art-History as Asymptomatic Exercise. Word and Image 7(3):223–38.

Danto, Arthur

1964 The Artworld. Journal of Philosophy 61:571–84.

1986 The Philosophical Disenfranchisement of Art. New York: Columbia University Press.

Davis, K., John Hunter, and David Penny

1977 Papunya: History and Future Prospects. Manuscript. Australian Department of Aboriginal Affairs.

Delgado, Jaime

1953 España y México en el siglo 19. Three vols. Madrid: Instituto Gonzalo Fernández de Oviedo.

Derrida, Jacques

1992 Counterfeit Money. Chicago: University of Chicago Press.

de Vault, Marjorie

1991 Feeding the Family. Chicago: University of Chicago Press.

Douglas, Mary

1966 Purity and Danger: An Analysis of the Concepts of Pollution and Taboo. London: Routledge and Kegan Paul.

Douglas, Mary, and Baron Isherwood

1979 The World of Goods. London: Allen Lane.

Douglas, Mary, and Aaron Wildavsky

1982 Risk and Culture. Berkeley: University of California Press.

Duboff, Leonard D., ed.

1975 Art Law: Domestic and International. South Hackensack, N.J.: Fred B. Rothman.

Dunn, Michael

1983 Gordon Walters. Auckland: Auckland City Art Gallery.

Durkheim, Emile

1984 The Division of Labor in Society. Glencoe, Ill.: Free Press.
[1893]

Durkheim, Emile, and Marcel Mauss

1904 Primitive Classification. Chicago: University of Chicago Press.
[1963]

Dussart, Françoise

1988 Women's Acrylic Paintings from Yuendumu. *In* The Inspired Dream: Life as Art in Aboriginal Austalia. Margaret West, ed. Brisbane: Queensland Art Gallery.

1993 La peinture des Aborigènes d'Australie. Marseilles: Editions Parenthèses.

Edwards, Jeanette, et al.

1993 Technologies of Procreation. Manchester: Manchester University Press.

Errington, Shelley

1998 The Death of Authentic Primitive Art and Other Narratives of Progress. Berkeley: University of California Press.

Escalante Gonzalbo, Fernando

1992 Ciudadanos imaginarios. Mexico City: El Colegio de México.

Evans-Pritchard, Dierdre

1990 Tradition on Trial: How the American Legal System Handles the Concept of Tradition. Ph.D. dissertation, University of California, Los Angeles.

Fabian, Johannes

1983 Time and the Other. New York: Columbia University Press.

Fajans, Jane

1993 Introduction. *In* Exchanging Products, Producing Exchange. Jane Fajans, ed. Pp. 1–13. Oceania Monographs, vol. 43. Sydney: University of Sydney.

1997 They Make Themselves: Work and Play among the Baining of Papua New Guinea. Chicago: University of Chicago Press.

Fanon, Frantz

1967 Black Skin, White Masks. Charles Markham, trans. New York: Grove Press.

Ferguson, James

1985 The Bovine Mystique: Power, Property, and Livestock in Rural Lesotho. Man (n.s.) 20:647–74.

Fine, Ben

1995 From Political Economy to Consumption. In Acknowledging Consumption. Daniel Miller, ed. Pp. 127–63. London: Routledge.

1998 The Triumph of Economics, or, "Rationality" Can Be Dangerous to Your Reasoning. *In* Virtualism: A New Political Economy. James Carrier and Daniel Miller, eds. Pp. 49–73. Oxford: Berg.

Fisher, Philip

1991 Making and Effacing Art: Modern American Art in a Culture of Museums. New York: Oxford University Press.

Foster, Hal

1985a The "Primitive" Unconscious of Modern Art, or White Skin, Black Masks. *In* Recodings: Art, Spectacle, Cultural Politics. Pp. 181–210. Port Townsend, Wash.: Bay Press.

1985b Recodings: Art, Spectacle, Cultural Politics. Port Townsend, Wash.: Bay Press.

Foster, Hal, ed.

1983 The Anti-Aesthetic: Essays on Postmodern Culture. Port Townsend, Wash.: Bay Press.

Foster, Robert

1990 Value without Equivalence: Exchange and Replacement in a Melanesian Society. Man 25:54–69.

1998 Your Money, Our Money, The Government's Money: Finance and Fetishism in Melanesia. *In* Border Fetishisms: Material Objects in Unstable Places. Patricia Spyer, ed. Pp. 60–90. New York: Routledge.

Freund, Thatcher

1993 Objects of Desire: The Lives of Antiques and Those Who Pursue Them. New York: Pantheon.

Fried, Michael

1967 Art and Objecthood. Artforum, Summer.

1998 Art and Objecthood: Essays and Reviews. Chicago: University of Chicago Press.

Gell, Alfred

1992 Inter-tribal Commodity Barter and Reproductive Gift-Exchange in Old Melanesia. *In* Barter Exchange and Value: An Anthropological Approach. Caroline Humphrey and Stephen Hugh-Jones, eds. Pp. 142–68. Cambridge: Cambridge University Press.

George, Kenneth

1999 Introduction: Objects on the Loose. Ethnos 64:149–50.

Ginsburg, Faye

1993 Aboriginal Media and the Australian Imaginary. Public Culture 5:557–78.

Godelier, Maurice

1999 The Enigma of the Gift. Cambridge: Polity.

Goldberg-Ambrose, Carole

1994 Of Native Americans and Tribal Members: The Impact of Law on Indian Group Life. Law and Society 28(5):1123–48.

Goldthwaite, R. A.

1989 The Economic and Social World of Italian Renaissance Maiolica. Renaissance Quarterly 42(1):1–32.

Graburn, Nelson, ed.

1976 Ethnic and Tourist Arts. Berkeley: University of California Press.

Graeber, David

n.d. Theories of Value. Unpublished manuscript.

Greenberg, Clement

1961 [1939] Avant-Garde and Kitsch. *In* Art and Culture: Critical Essays. Boston: Beacon Press.

Gregory, Chris

1982 Gifts and Commodities. London: Academic Press.

1997 Savage Money. Amsterdam: Harwood Academic Press.

Grice, H. P.

1957 Meaning. Philosophical Review 64:377–88.

Gudeman, Stephen, and Alberto Rivera

1990 Conversations in Colombia. Cambridge: Cambridge University Press.

Guyer, Jane I.

1995 Introduction: The Currency Interface and Its Dynamics. *In* Money Matters: Instability, Values, and Social Payments in the Modern History of West Africa. Jane I. Guyer, ed. Pp. 1–33. Portsmouth, N.H.: Heinemann.

Hadjinicolauo, Nicolas

1978 Art History and Class Struggle. Louise Asmal, trans. London: Pluto Press.

Hamilton, Annette

1990 Fear and Desire: Aborigines, Asians and the National Imaginary. Australian Cultural History, July.

Hart, K.

1986 Heads or Tails: Two Sides of the Coin. Man (n.s.) 21:637–56.

Hartshorne, Thomas L.

1986 Modernism on Trial: *C. Brancusi v. United States* (1928). Journal of American Studies 20(1):93–104.

Hidalgo y Costilla, Miguel

1964 [1810] Manifiesto que el señor D. Miguel Hidalgo y Costilla, Generalísimo de las armas americanas, y electo por la mayor parte de los pueblos del reino para defender sus derechos y los de sus conciudadanos, hace al pueblo (1810). *In* Historia Documental de México, vol. 2. Ernesto de la Torre Villar, Moisés González Navarro, and Stanley Ross, compilers. Pp. 40–43. Mexico City: UNAM.

Himber, Alan

1983 The Letters of John Quinn to William Butler Yeats. Studies in Modern Literature, no. 28. Ann Arbor, Mich.: UMI Research Press.

Hirschman, Albert O.

1977 The Passions and the Interests: Political Arguments for Capitalism before Its Triumph. Princeton, N.J.: Princeton University Press.

Hooper-Greenhill, Eilean

1992 Museums and the Shaping of Knowledge. London: Routledge.

Hoskins, Janet

1988 The Drum Is the Shaman, the Spear Guides His Voice. Social Science and Medicine 27(8):819–28.

1993 The Play of Time: Kodi Perspectives on Calendars, History, and Exchange. Berkeley: University of California Press.

Hubert, Henri, and Marcel Mauss

1964 Sacrifice: Its Nature and Functions. Chicago: University of Chicago Press.

Hugh-Jones, Stephen

1990 Yesterday's Luxuries, Tomorrow's Necessities: Business and Barter in Northwest Amazonia. *In* Barter, Exchange, and Value: An Anthropological Approach. Caroline Humphrey and Stephen Hugh-Jones, eds. Pp. 42–74. Cambridge: Cambridge University Press.

Hutchinson, Sharon E.

1996 Nuer Dilemmas: Coping with Money, War, and the State. Berkeley: University of California Press.

Iskandar, Margaharta, and Siliwoloe Djoeroemana

1994 Kemiskinan dan Pembangunan: Kasus Kabupaten Sumba Barat. *In* Kemiskinan dan Pembangunan di Propinsi Nusa Tenggara Timur. Jakarta: Yayasan Obor Indonesia.

Jackson, Stevi, and Shaun Moores, eds.

1995 The Politics of Domestic Consumption: Critical Readings. London: Prentice Hall.

Jakobson, Roman

1960 Closing Statement: Linguistics and Poetics. *In* Style in Language. Thomas Sebeok, ed. Pp. 350–77. Cambridge, Mass.: MIT Press.

Jay, Martin

1984 Adorno. Cambridge, Mass.: Harvard University Press.

Johnson, Mark

1998 At Home and Abroad: Inalienable Wealth, Personal Consumption and Formulations of Femininity in the Southern Philippines. *In* Material Cultures: Why Some Things Matter. Daniel Miller, ed. Pp. 215–38. London: UCL Press.

Johnson, Vivien

1990 The Painted Dream. Auckland: Auckland City Art Gallery.

1994 The Art of Clifford Possum Tjapaltjarri. East Roseville: Gordon and Breach Arts International.

Jones, Phillip

1995 "Objects of Mystery and Concealment": A History of *Tjurunga* Collecting.

In Politics of the Secret. Christopher Anderson, ed. Pp. 67–96. Oceania Monographs 45. Sydney: University of Sydney.

Kahn, Joel S.

1993 Constituting the Minangkabau: Peasants, Culture, and Modernity in Colonial Indonesia. Oxford: Berg.

Kant, Immanuel

1956 [1785] Foundations of the Metaphysics of Morals. *In* Foundations of the Metaphysics of Morals and What is Enlightenment? Lewis White Beck, trans. Indianapolis: Bobbs-Merrill.

Kapferer, Bruce

1979 Introduction: Process and the Transformation of Context. Social Analysis 1:3–19.

1988 Legends of People, Myths of State: Violence, Intolerance, and Political Culture in Sri Lanka and Australia. Washington, D.C.: Smithsonian Institution Press.

Kaplan, Flora, ed.

1994 Museums and the Making of "Ourselves." London: Leicester University Press.

Karp, Ivan, and Stephen D. Lavine, eds.

1991 Exhibiting Cultures: The Poetics and Politics of Museum Display. Washington, D.C.: Smithsonian Institution Press.

Katz, Friedrich

1998 The Life and Times of Pancho Villa. Stanford: Stanford University Press.

Keane, Webb

1996 Materialism, Missionaries, and Modern Subjects in Colonial Indonesia. *In* Conversion to Modernities: The Globalization of Christianity. Peter van der Veer, ed. Pp. 137–70. New York: Routledge.

1997 Signs of Recognition: Powers and Hazards of Representation in an Indonesian Society. Berkeley: University of California Press.

1998 Calvin in the Tropics: Objects and Subjects at the Religious Frontier. *In* Border Fetishisms: Material Objects in Unstable Places. Patricia Spyer, ed. Pp. 13–34. New York: Routledge.

Kirshenblatt-Gimblett, Barbara

1991a Comments. *In* Art and National Identity: A Critics' Symposium. Art in America, September, pp. 1, 142–43.

1991b Objects of Ethnography. *In* Exhibiting Cultures: The Poetics and Politics of Museum Display. Ivan Karp and Steven D. Lavine, eds. Pp. 386–443. Washington, D.C.: Smithsonian Institution Press.

1995 Confusing Pleasures. *In* The Traffic in Culture: Refiguring Anthropology and Art. George E. Marcus and Fred R. Myers, eds. Pp. 224–55. Berkeley: University of California Press.

1998 Destination Culture. Berkeley: University of California Press.

Kopytoff, Igor

1986 The Cultural Biography of Things: Commoditization as Process. *In* The Social Life of Things. Arjun Appadurai, ed. Pp. 64–91. Cambridge: Cambridge University Press.

Kristeller, Paul Oskar

1965 The Modern System of the Arts. *In* Renaissance Thought and the Arts.
[1951] Princeton: Princeton University Press.

Kronenberg, Simeon

1995 Why Gabrielle Pizzi Has Changed Her Mind about Aboriginal Art. Art Monthly Australia 85 (Nov.):7–9.

Kuipers, Joel C.

1990 Power in Performance: The Creation of Textual Authority in Weyewa Ritual Speech. Philadelphia: University of Pennsylvania Press.

Laplanche, J., and Pontalis, J-B.

1973 The Language of Psychoanalysis. London: Hogarth Press–Institute of Psychoanalysis.

Latour, Bruno

1993 We Have Never Been Modern. Catherine Porter, trans. Cambridge, Mass.: Harvard University Press.

Lattas, Andrew

1990 Aborigines and Contemporary Australian Nationalism: Primordiality and the Cultural Politics of Otherness. Social Analysis 27:50–69.

1991 Nationalism, Aesthetic Redemption and Aboriginality. TAJA 2(3):307–324.

1992 Primitivism, Nationalism, and Popular Culture: Time, Aboriginality and Contemporary Australian Culture. *In* Power, Knowledge and Aborigines (Journal of Australian Studies, special issue). Bain Atwood and J. Arnold, eds. Pp. 45–58. Melbourne: La Trobe University Press.

Leach, Jeremy W., and Edmund Leach, eds.

1983 The Kula: New Perspectives on Massim Exchange. Cambridge: Cambridge University Press.

Lears, Jackson

1983 No Place of Grace. Chicago: University of Chicago Press.

Lévi-Strauss, Claude

1949 Les structures élémentaires de la Parenté [The elementary structures of kinship]. Paris: Presses Universitaires de France.

1962 Totemism. Chicago: University of Chicago Press.

1966 The Savage Mind. Chicago: University of Chicago Press.

1987 Introduction to the Work of Marcel Mauss. London: Routledge and Kegan Paul.

Lindfors, Bernth

1983 The "Hottentot Venus" and Other African Attractions in Nineteenth-Century England. Australian Drama Studies 1(2):83–104.

Lippard, Lucy

1991 Mixed Blessings: New Art in a Multicultural America. New York: Pantheon.

Lips, Julius

1966 [1937] The Savage Hits Back. Vincent Benson, trans. New Hyde Park: University Books.

Lomnitz, Claudio

1999 Modernidad indiana: Nueve ensayos sobre nación y mediación. Mexico City: Planeta.

Lynch, John

1992 Caudillos in Spanish America, 1800–1850. Oxford: Clarendon Press.

Lynes, Russell

1973 Good Old Modern: An Intimate Portrait of the Museum of Modern Art. New York: Atheneum.

MacMillan, Gordon, and Liz Godfrey

1993 Aboriginal and Torres Straits Islanders Arts and Crafts: Research Report. Prepared for Mingatjuta Consulting Services. Sydney: AGB McNair.

Malinowski, Bronislaw

1922 Argonauts of the Western Pacific. London: Routledge.

Malkki, Liisa H.

1994 Citizens of Humanity: Internationalism and the Imagined Community of Nations. Diaspora 3(1):41–68.

1995a Purity and Exile: Violence, Memory, and National Cosmology among Hutu Refugees in Tanzania. Chicago: University of Chicago Press.

1995b Refugees and Exile: From "Refugee Studies" to the National Order of Things. Annual Review of Anthropology 24:495–523.

Manning, Patrick

1985 Primitive Art and Modern Times. Radical History Review 33:165–81.

Marcus, George

1995 Ethnography in/of the World System: The Emergence of Multi-Sited Ethnography. Annual Review of Anthropology 24:95–117.

Marcus, George, with Peter Hall

1992 Lives in Trust: The Fortunes of Dynastic Families in Late-Twentieth-Century America. Boulder: Westview Press.

Marcus, George E., and Fred R. Myers

1995 The Traffic in Culture: An Introduction. *In* The Traffic in Culture: Refiguring Art and Anthropology. George E. Marcus and Fred R. Myers, eds. Pp. 1–51. Berkeley: University of California Press.

Marcus, George E., and Fred R. Myers, eds.
1995 The Traffic in Culture: Refiguring Art and Anthropology. Berkeley: University of California Press.

Marx, Karl
1967 [1894] Capital: A Critique of Political Economy. Vol. 3: The Process of Capitalist Production as a Whole. New York: International.
1976 [1867] Capital: A Critique of Political Economy. Vol. 1: A Critical Analysis of Capitalist Production. Ben Fowkes, trans. New York: Penguin.

Mauss, Marcel
1979 [1904] Seasonal Variations of the Eskimo: A Study in Social Morphology. James Fox, trans. London: Routledge and Kegan Paul.
1990 [1925] The Gift: The Form and Reason for Exchange in Archaic Societies. W. D. Halls, trans. New York: Norton.

Mayer Celis, Laura Leticia
1995 Estadística y comunidad científica en México, 1826–1848. Doctoral thesis, Centro de Estudios Históricos, El Colegio de México.

McChesney, Lea S.
1992 My Potteries Can Be Used in a Microwave: Indigenous Construction of American Indian Art. Museum Anthropology 16(3):25–33.

McEvilley, Thomas
1985 Doctor, Lawyer, Indian, Chief. Artforum 23(3):54–60.

McMaster, Gerald R.
1995 Border Zones: The "Injun-uity" of Aesthetic Tricks. Cultural Studies 9(1):74–90.

McNaughton, Patrick R.
1987 African Borderland Sculpture. African Arts 20(4):76–82.

McQueen, Humphrey
1979 The Black Swan of Trespass. Sydney: Alternative Publishing Cooperative.

Michaels, Eric
1988 Bad Aboriginal Art. Art and Text 28:59–73.

Miller, Daniel
1987 Material Culture and Mass Consumption. Oxford: Basil Blackwell.
1994 Modernity, an Ethnographic Approach: Dualism and Mass Consumption in Trinidad. Oxford: Berg.
1995 Consumption as the Vanguard of History. *In* Acknowledging Consumption. Daniel Miller, ed. Pp. 1–57. London: Routledge.
1997a Capitalism: An Ethnographic Approach. Oxford: Berg.
1997b How Infants Grow Mothers in North London. Theory, Culture, and Society 14:67–88.
1998 A Theory of Shopping. Cambridge and Ithaca: Polity Press and Cornell University Press.

2001 The Dialectics of Shopping. Chicago: University of Chicago Press.

Miller, Daniel, ed.

1993 Unwrapping Christmas. Oxford: Oxford University Press.

1998 Material Cultures: Why Some Things Matter. Chicago: University of Chicago Press.

Miller, Toby

1994 The Well-Tempered Self. Baltimore: Johns Hopkins University Press.

Mitchell, Timothy

1989 The World as Exhibition. Comparative Studies in Society and History 31:217–36.

Mitchell, W. J. T.

1996 What Do Pictures *Really* Want? October 77:71–82.

Moore, Sally Falk

1978 Law as Process. London: Routledge and Kegan Paul.

Moore, Sally Falk, and Barbara Myerhoff, eds.

1977 Secular Ritual. Assen, Netherlands: Van Gorcum Press.

Mora, José María Luis

1837 Obras sueltas de José María Luis Mora, ciudadano mexicano. Two vols. Paris: Librería de la Rosa.

Morelos, José María

1964 [1810] Bando de Morelos suprimiendo las castas y aboliendo la esclavitud, 17 noviembre 1810. *In* Historia Documental de México, vol. 2. Ernesto de la Torre Villar, Moisés González Navarro, and Stanley Ross, compilers. Pp. 162–63. Mexico City: UNAM.

Morphy, Howard

1977 "Too Many Meanings." Ph.D. thesis, Department of Prehistory and Anthropology, Australian National University, Canberra.

1980 The Impact of the Commercial Development of Art on Traditional Culture. *In* Preserving Indigenous Cultures. Robert Edwards and Jane Stewart, eds. Pp. 81–94. Canberra: AGPS.

1983 Aboriginal Fine Art: Creation of Audiences and the Marketing of Art. *In* Aboriginal Arts and Crafts and the Market. Peter Loveday and Peter Cooke, eds. Pp. 37–43. Darwin: ANU-NARU.

1992 Ancestral Connections. Chicago: University of Chicago Press.

1995 Aboriginal Art in a Global Context. *In* Worlds Apart. Daniel Miller, ed. Pp. 211–39. London: Routledge.

Mullin, Molly

1995 The Patronage of Difference: Making Indian Art "Art, not Ethnology." *In* The Traffic in Culture: Refiguring Anthropology and Art. George E. Marcus and Fred R. Myers, eds. Pp. 166–200. Berkeley: University of California Press.

Munn, Nancy

1970 The Transformation of Subjects into Objects in Walbiri and Pitjantjatjara Myth. *In* Australian Aboriginal Anthropology. R. Berndt, ed. Pp. 141–63. Nedlands: University of Western Australia Press.

1983 Gawan Kula: Spatiotemporal Control and the Symbolism of Influence. *In* The Kula: New Perspectives on Massim Exchange. Jeremy Leach and Edmund Leach, eds. Pp. 277–308. Cambridge: Cambridge University Press.

1986 The Fame of Gawa: A Symbolic Study of Value Transformation in a Massim Society. New York: Cambridge University Press.

Munson-Williams-Proctor Institute

1963 1913 Armory Show Fiftieth Anniversary Exhibition. New York: Henry Street Settlement.

Museum of Modern Art

1936 The United States Government and Abstract Art. Bulletin of the Museum of Modern Art 3(April):2–6.

Myers, Fred R.

1986 Pintupi Country, Pintupi Self: Sentiment, Place, and Politics among Western Desert Aborigines. Washington, D.C., and Canberra: Smithsonian Institution Press and Aboriginal Studies Press.

1988 Burning the Truck and Holding the Country: Forms of Property, Time, and the Negotiation of Identity among Pintupi Aborigines. *In* Hunter-Gatherers, vol. 2: Property, Power and Ideology. David Riches, Tim Ingold, and James Woodburn, eds. Pp. 52–74. London: Berg.

1989 Truth, Beauty and Pintupi Painting. Visual Anthropology 2:163–95.

1991 Representing Culture: The Production of Discourse(s) for Aboriginal Acrylic Paintings. Cultural Anthropology 6(3):26–62.

1993 Place, Identity, and Exchange: The Transformation of Nurturance to Social Reproduction over the Life Cycle in a Kin-Based Society. *In* Exchanging Products, Producing Exchange. Jane Fajans, ed. Pp. 33–57. Oceania Monographs 43. Sydney: University of Sydney.

1994 Culture-Making: The Performance of Aboriginality at the Asia Society Galleries. American Ethnologist 21:679–99.

1998 Uncertain Regard? Understanding an Exhibition of Aboriginal Art in France. Ethnos 63:7–47.

Nicodemus, Everlyn

1996 Art and art from Africa: The Two Sides of the Gap. Third Text, Winter 1995–96:1–40.

North, Ian, ed.

1980 The Art of Margaret Preston. Adelaide: Art Gallery Board of South Australia.

O'Doherty, Brian

1986 Inside the White Cube: The Ideology of the Gallery Space. Santa Monica, Calif.: Lapis Press.

O'Gorman, Edmundo

1977 México: El trauma de su historia. Mexico City: UNAM.

Onvlee, L.

1973 De betekenis van vee en veebezit. *In* Cultuur als Antwoord. Verhandelingen van het Koninklijk Instituut voor Taal-, Land- en Volkenkunde 66. 's-Gravenhage: Martinus Nijhoff.

Osborne, Peter

1991 Adorno and the Metaphysics of Modernism: The Problem of a Postmodern Art. *In* The Problems of Modernity: Adorno and Benjamin. Andrew Benjamin, ed. Pp. 23–45. London: Routledge.

Pannell, Sandra

1995 The Cool Memories of Tjurunga: A Symbolic History of Collecting Authenticity and the Sacred. *In* Politics of the Secret. Christopher Anderson, ed. Pp. 108–22. Oceania Monographs 45. Sydney: University of Sydney.

Pascoe, Timothy

1981 Improving Focus and Efficiency in the Marketing of Aboriginal Artefacts. Report to the Australia Council and Aboriginal Arts and Crafts Pty. Ltd. Sydney: Arts Research, Training and Support, Ltd.

Pendergrast, Mark

1993 For God, Country and Coca-Cola. London: Weidenfeld and Nicolson.

Perkins, Hetti, and Hannah Finke, eds.

2000 Papunya Tula: Genesis and Genius. Sydney: Art Gallery of New South Wales and Papunya Tula Artists.

Perry, Laurens

1978 Juárez and Díaz: Machine Politics in Mexico. Dekalb: Northern Illinois University Press.

Peterson, Nicolas

1983 Aboriginal Arts and Crafts Pty Ltd: A Brief History. *In* Aboriginal Arts and Crafts and the Market. Peter Loveday and Peter Cooke, eds. Pp. 60–65. Darwin: North Australia Research Unit.

Phillips, Ruth B.

n.d. Performing Primitivism. In Antimodernism and Artistic Experience. Lynda Jessup, ed. Toronto: University of Toronto Press. In press.

Phillips, Ruth B., and Christopher B. Steiner

1999 Art, Authenticity, and the Baggage of Cultural Encounter. *In* Unpacking Culture: Art and Commodity in Colonial and Postcolonial Worlds. Ruth B. Phillips and Christopher B. Steiner, eds. Pp. 3–19. Berkeley: University of California Press.

Phillips, Ruth B., and Christopher B. Steiner, eds.

1999 Unpacking Culture: Art and Commodity in Colonial and Postcolonial Worlds. Berkeley: University of California Press.

Pietz, William

1986 The Problem of the Fetish, I. Res 9:5–17.

1997 Death of the Deodand: Accursed Objects and the Money Value of Human Life. Res 31:97–108.

Plattner, Stuart

1996 High Art, Down Home. Chicago: University of Chicago Press.

Pointon, Marcia

1997 Pricing or Prizing Potential in the 1990s. Art Bulletin 79(1):17–20.

Polanyi, Karl

1944 The Great Transformation: The Political and Economic Origins of Our Time. Boston: Beacon Press.

Pound, Francis

1992 The Words and the Art: New Zealand Art Criticism, c. 1950–1990. *In* Headlands: Thinking Through New Zealand Art. Mary Barr, ed. Pp. 185–202. Sydney: Museum of Contemporary Art.

1994 The Space Between: Pakeha Use of Maori Motifs in Modernist New Zealand Art. Auckland: Workshop Press.

Powdermaker, Hortense

1966 Stranger and Friend. New York: W. W. Norton.

Pratt, Mary Louise

1992 Imperial Eyes: Travel Writing and Transculturation. London: Routledge.

Preston, Margaret

1925 The Indigenous Art of Australia. Art in Australia, March, unpaginated.

1930 The Application of Aboriginal Designs. Sunday Pictorial (Sydney), 6 April, p. 22.

1949 Margaret Preston's Monotypes. Sydney Ure Smith, ed. Sydney: Ure Smith.

Price, Sally

1989 Primitive Art in Civilized Places. Chicago: University of Chicago Press.

Punchon, Adeline Lobdell

1936 Dinner Table Art. Journal of Commerce (Chicago), March 14.

Quinn, John

1913 A Plea for Untaxed Contemporary Art: Memorandum in Regard to the Art Provisions of the Pending Tariff Bill. Legal brief published privately by author.

Quinn, Malcolm

1994 The Swastika. London: Routledge.

Reid, B. L.

1968 The Man from New York: John Quinn and His Friends. New York: Oxford University Press.

Richman, Claire

1982 Reading Georges Bataille: Beyond the Gift. Baltimore: Johns Hopkins University Press.

Riekerk, G. H. M.

1934 Grenregling Anakalang, Oemboe Ratoe Nggai. Typescript, no. H975 (2). Koninklijk Instituut voor Taal-, Land- en Volkenkunde, Leiden, Netherlands.

Rodó, José Enrique

1962 [1900] Ariel. Buenos Aires: Capelusz.

Root, Deborah

1996 Cannibal Culture. Boulder: Westview Press.

Roth, Michael S.

1987 Psychoanalyisis as History: Negation and Freedom in Freud. Ithaca, N.Y.: Cornell University Press.

Rovine, Victoria

1997 Bogolanfini in Bamako: The Biography of a Malian Textile. African Arts 30(1):40–41, 94–96.

Rowley, Charles D.

1972 The Destruction of Aboriginal Society. Canberra: Australian National University Press.

Rubin, Dana

1997 Fund Plans to Buy Art for Investment Sake. Houston Chronicle, 20 October, p. 2.

Rubin, William

1984 Modernist Primitivism: An Introduction. *In* "Primitivism" in Twentieth-Century Art: Affinity of the Tribal and the Modern. William Rubin, ed. Pp. 1–84. New York: Museum of Modern Art.

Rubin, William, ed.

1984 "Primitivism" in Twentieth-Century Art. New York: Museum of Modern Art.

Rycroft, Charles

1972 A Critical Dictionary of Psychoanalysis. Harmondsworth, UK: Penguin.

Sahlins, Marshall

1965 The Sociology of Primitive Exchange. *In* The Relevance of Models for Social Anthropology. Michael Banton, ed. Pp. 139–236. New York: Praeger.

1972 Stone Age Economics. Chicago: Aldine.

1976 Culture and Practical Reason. Chicago: University of Chicago Press.

Said, Edward

1978 Orientalism. New York: Pantheon.

Sánchez González, Agustín

1995 Los mejores chistes sobre presidentes. Mexico City: Planeta.

Santa Anna, Antonio López de

1988 The Eagle: An Autobiography of Santa Anna. Ann Fears Crawford, ed. Austin, Texas: State House Press.

Savage, George

1969 The Market in Art. London: Institute of Economic Affairs.

Schama, Simon

1993 Perishable Commodities: Dutch Still-Life Painting and the Empire of Things. *In* Consumption and the World of Things. J. Brewer and R. Porter, eds. Pp. 478–88. London: Routledge.

Schieffelin, Bambi, Kathryn Woolard, and Paul Kroskrity, eds.

1998 Language Ideologies: Practice and Theory. New York: Oxford University Press.

Schrift, Alan

1997 The Logic of the Gift. London: Routledge.

Sennett, Richard

1976 The Fall of Public Man. Cambridge: Cambridge University Press.

Shell, Marc

1982 Money, Language, and Thought: Literary and Philosophical Economies from the Medieval to the Modern Era. Baltimore: Johns Hopkins University Press.

Siegel, James T.

1986 Solo in the New Order: Language and Hierarchy in an Indonesian City. Princeton: Princeton University Press.

Silverstein, Michael

1979 Language Structures and Linguistic Ideology. *In* The Elements: A Parasession on Linguistic Units and Levels. P. Clyne et al., eds. Chicago: Chicago Linguistic Society.

Simmel, Georg

1990 [1907] The Philosophy of Money. Tom Bottomore and David Frisby, trans. London: Routledge.

Spivak, Gayatri Chakravorty

1989 Who Claims Alterity? *In* Remaking History. Barbara Kruger and Phil Mariani, eds. Pp. 269–92. Port Townsend, Wash.: Bay Press.

1993 The Politics of Translation. *In* Outside in the Teaching Machine. Pp. 179–201. London: Routledge.

Staniszewski, Mary Anne

1998 The Power of Display: A History of Exhibition Installations at the Museum of Modern Art. Cambridge, Mass.: MIT Press.

Steedly, Mary Margaret

1993 Hanging without a Rope: Narrative Experience in Colonial and Postcolonial Karoland. Princeton, N.J.: Princeton University Press.

Steichen, Edward

1962 *Brancusi vs. United States.* Art in America 50(1):56–57.

Steiner, Christopher B.

1994 African Art in Transit. Cambridge: Cambridge University Press.

1995 Blurred Vision: Fieldwork-on-the-Run and Anthropological Definitions of Community. Paper read at the annual meeting of the American Ethnological Society, Austin, Texas, 27 April.

Stephen, Ann

1980 Margaret Preston's Second Coming. Art Network 2:14–15.

Stephenson, P. R.

1936 The Foundations of Culture in Australia: An Essay toward National Self-Respect. Gordon, NSW: W. J. Miles.

Stocking, George

1968 Race, Culture, and Evolution. New York: Free Press.

Strathern, Marilyn

1988 The Gender of the Gift: Problems with Women and Problems with Society in Melanesia. Berkeley: University of California Press.

1996 Potential Property: Intellectual Rights in Property and Persons. Social Anthropology 4:17–32.

Sullivan, Nancy

1995 Inside Trading: Postmodernism and the Social Drama of *Sunflowers* in the 1980s Art World. *In* The Traffic in Culture: Refiguring Art and Anthropology. George E. Marcus and Fred R. Myers, eds. Pp. 256–301. Berkeley: University of California Press.

Tambiah, Stanley J.

1984 The Buddhist Saints of the Forest and the Cult of the Amulets. Cambridge: Cambridge University Press.

1985 Culture, Thought, and Social Action: An Anthropological Perspective. Cambridge, Mass.: Harvard University Press.

Tatz, Colin

1964 Aboriginal Administration. Ph.D. thesis, Australian National University, Canberra.

Te Awekotuku, Ngahuia

1986 Ngahuia Te Awekotuku in Conversation with Priscilla Pitts and Elizabeth Eastmond. Antic 1.

Thomas, Nicholas

1991 Entangled Objects: Exchange, Material Culture, and Colonialism in the Pacific. Cambridge, Mass.: Harvard University Press.

1999 Possessions: Indigenous Art/Colonial Culture. London: Thames and Hudson.

Torgovnick, Marianna

1990 Gone Primitive: Savage Intellects, Modern Lives. Chicago: University of Chicago Press.

Turner, Terence

1973 Piaget's Structuralism. American Anthropologist 75:351–73.

1989 Commentary (on T. O. Beidelman's "Agonistic Exchange"). Cultural Anthropology 4(3):260–64.

n.d. Indigenous and Culturalist Movements in the Contemporary Global Conjuncture. Unpublished manuscript.

Turner, Victor

1967 The Forest of Symbols. Ithaca, N.Y.: Cornell University Press.

1974 Dramas, Fields, and Metaphors. Ithaca, N.Y.: Cornell University Press.

United States Treasury

1916 United States Treasury Decisions, vol. 30 (January–June 1916). Washington, D.C.: US Government Printing Office.

1929 United States Treasury Decisions, vol. 54 (July–December 1928). Washington, D.C.: US Government Printing Office.

Valeri, Valerio

1985 Kingship and Sacrifice. Chicago: University of Chicago Press.

Van Gennep, Arnold

1960 The Rites of Passage. Chicago: University of Chicago Press.

Vel, Jacqueline

1994 The Uma-Economy: Indigenous Economics and Development Work in Lawonda, Sumba (Eastern Indonesia). Thesis, Agricultural University, Wageningen, Netherlands.

Verdery, Katherine

1999 The Political Lives of Dead Bodies. New York: Columbia University Press.

Versluys, J. I. N.

1941 Aanteekeningen omtrent geld- en goederenverkeer in West-Soemba. Koloniale Studiën 25:433–83.

Vickery, Amanda

1993 Women and the World of Goods: A Lancashire Consumer and Her Possessions 1751–81. *In* Consumption and the World of Things. J. Brewer and R. Porter, eds. Pp. 274–301. London: Routledge.

Villaseñor y Villaseñor, Alejandro

1962 Biografías de los héroes y caudillos de la independencia. Two vols. Mexico City: Jus.

Vogel, Susan

1988 Introduction. *In* ART/artifact: African Art in Anthropology Collections. New York: Center for African Art.

Volosinov, V. I.

1973 Marxism and the Philosophy of Language. New York: Academic Press.

Wagner, Roy

1978 Lethal Speech: Daribi Myth as Symbolic Obviation. Ithaca, N.Y.: Cornell University Press.

Wallis, Brian, ed.

1984 Art after Modernism. New York: New Museum of Contemporary Art.

Walters, Gordon

n.d. Manuscript 90/8, Archives, Museum of New Zealand Te Papa Tongarewa, Wellington.

1969 Gordon Walters: An Interview. Salient, 7 May.

Webb, Virginia-Lee

1995 Modern Times, 1935–1946: Early Tribal Exhibitions at the Museum of Modern Art in New York. Tribal Arts 2(1):30–42.

Weeks, Charles

1987 The Juárez Myth in Mexico. Birmingham: University of Alabama Press.

Weiner, Annette B.

1976 Women of Value, Men of Renown. Austin: University of Texas Press.

1980 Reproduction: A Replacement for Reciprocity. American Ethnologist 7:71–85.

1982 Sticks and Stones, Threads and Bones: What Kinship Is Made Of. Paper presented at the Wenner-Gren Foundation conference "Feminism and Kinship Theory," Bellagio, Italy.

1983 A World of Made Is Not a World of Born: Doing Kula on Kiriwina. *In* The Kula: New Perspectives on Massim Exchange. Jeremy Leach and Edmund Leach, eds. Cambridge: Cambridge University Press.

1984 From Words to Objects to Magic. *In* Dangerous Words: Language and Politics in the Pacific. Donald Brenneis and Fred Myers, eds. New York: New York University Press.

1985 Inalienable Wealth. American Ethnologist 12:52–65.

1988 The Trobrianders of Papua New Guinea. New York: Holt, Rinehart and Winston.

1992 Inalienable Possessions: The Paradox of Keeping-While-Giving. Berkeley: University of California Press.

1994 Cultural Difference and the Density of Objects. American Ethnologist 21(2):391–403.

Weiner, Annette B., and Jane Schneider, eds.

1989 Cloth and Human Experience. Washington, D.C.: Smithsonian Institution Press.

Williams, Raymond

1977 Marxism and Literature. Oxford: Oxford University Press.

1981 Culture. Harmondsworth, UK: Penguin.

Witin, Fransiska

1997 Belis dan Harga Diri Wanita. Dian, 1 August, p. 6.

Witkamp, H.

1912 Een Verkenningstocht over het Eiland Soemba. Tijdschrift van het Koninklijk Nederlandsch Aardrijkskundig Genootschap 30:484–505.

Wolfe, Tom

1976 Introduction. In Art on Trial: From Whistler to Rothko, by Laurie Adams. Pp. ix–xv. New York: Walker.

Zayas, Marius de

1996 How, When, and Why Modern Art Came to New York. Francis M. Naumann, ed. Cambridge, Mass: MIT Press.

Zelizer, Viviana A.

1994 The Social Meaning of Money. New York: Basic Books.

Ziff, Bruce, and Pratima V. Rao, eds.

1997 Borrowed Power: Essays on Cultural Appropriation. New Brunswick, N.J.: Rutgers University Press.

Zilczer, Judith

1978 "The Noble Buyer": John Quinn, Patron of the Avant-Garde. Washington, D.C.: Smithsonian Institution Press.

1985 Alfred Stieglitz and John Quinn: Allies in the American Avant-Garde. American Art Journal 17:18–33.

1990 The Dispersal of the John Quinn Collection. Journal of the Archives of American Art 30(1–4):35–40.

Index

School for Advanced Research Advanced Seminar Series

Published by SAR Press

Chaco & Hohokam: Prehistoric Regional Systems in the American Southwest
Patricia L. Crown & W. James Judge, eds.

Recapturing Anthropology: Working in the Present
Richard G. Fox, ed.

War in the Tribal Zone: Expanding States and Indigenous Warfare
R. Brian Ferguson & Neil L. Whitehead, eds.

Ideology and Pre-Columbian Civilizations
Arthur A. Demarest & Geoffrey W. Conrad, eds.

Dreaming: Anthropological and Psychological Interpretations
Barbara Tedlock, ed.

Historical Ecology: Cultural Knowledge and Changing Landscapes
Carole L. Crumley, ed.

Themes in Southwest Prehistory
George J. Gumerman, ed.

Memory, History, and Opposition under State Socialism
Rubie S. Watson, ed.

Other Intentions: Cultural Contexts and the Attribution of Inner States
Lawrence Rosen, ed.

Last Hunters–First Farmers: New Perspectives on the Prehistoric Transition to Agriculture
T. Douglas Price & Anne Birgitte Gebauer, eds.

Making Alternative Histories: The Practice of Archaeology and History in Non-Western Settings
Peter R. Schmidt & Thomas C. Patterson, eds.

Senses of Place
Steven Feld & Keith H. Basso, eds.

Cyborgs & Citadels: Anthropological Interventions in Emerging Sciences and Technologies
Gary Lee Downey & Joseph Dumit, eds.

Archaic States
Gary M. Feinman & Joyce Marcus, eds.

Critical Anthropology Now: Unexpected Contexts, Shifting Constituencies, Changing Agendas
George E. Marcus, ed.

The Origins of Language: What Nonhuman Primates Can Tell Us
Barbara J. King, ed.

Regimes of Language: Ideologies, Polities, and Identities
Paul V. Kroskrity, ed.

Biology, Brains, and Behavior: The Evolution of Human Development
Sue Taylor Parker, Jonas Langer, & Michael L. McKinney, eds.

Women & Men in the Prehispanic Southwest: Labor, Power, & Prestige
Patricia L. Crown, ed.

History in Person: Enduring Struggles, Contentious Practice, Intimate Identities
Dorothy Holland & Jean Lave, eds.

The Empire of Things: Regimes of Value and Material Culture
Fred R. Myers, ed.

Catastrophe & Culture: The Anthropology of Disaster
Susanna M. Hoffman & Anthony Oliver-Smith, eds.

Uruk Mesopotamia & Its Neighbors: Cross-Cultural Interactions in the Era of State Formation
Mitchell S. Rothman, ed.

Remaking Life & Death: Toward an Anthropology of the Biosciences
Sarah Franklin & Margaret Lock, eds.

Tikal: Dynasties, Foreigners, & Affairs of State: Advancing Maya Archaeology
Jeremy A. Sabloff, ed.

Gray Areas: Ethnographic Encounters with Nursing Home Culture
Philip B. Stafford, ed.

Pluralizing Ethnography: Comparison and Representation in Maya Cultures, Histories, and Identities
John M. Watanabe & Edward F. Fischer, eds.

Published by SAR Press

American Arrivals: Anthropology Engages the New Immigration
Nancy Foner, ed.

Violence
Neil L. Whitehead, ed.

Law & Empire in the Pacific: Fiji and Hawai'i
Sally Engle Merry & Donald Brenneis, eds.

Anthropology in the Margins of the State
Veena Das & Deborah Poole, eds.

The Archaeology of Colonial Encounters: Comparative Perspectives
Gil J. Stein, ed.

Globalization, Water, & Health: Resource Management in Times of Scarcity
Linda Whiteford & Scott Whiteford, eds.

A Catalyst for Ideas: Anthropological Archaeology and the Legacy of Douglas W. Schwartz
Vernon L. Scarborough, ed.

The Archaeology of Chaco Canyon: An Eleventh-Century Pueblo Regional Center
Stephen H. Lekson, ed.

Community Building in the Twenty-First Century
Stanley E. Hyland, ed.

Afro-Atlantic Dialogues: Anthropology in the Diaspora
Kevin A. Yelvington, ed.

Copán: The History of an Ancient Maya Kingdom
E. Wyllys Andrews & William L. Fash, eds.

The Evolution of Human Life History
Kristen Hawkes & Richard R. Paine, eds.

The Seductions of Community: Emancipations, Oppressions, Quandaries
Gerald W. Creed, ed.

The Gender of Globalization: Women Navigating Cultural and Economic Marginalities
Nandini Gunewardena & Ann Kingsolver, eds.

Imperial Formations
Ann Laura Stoler, Carole McGranahan, & Peter C. Perdue, eds.

Opening Archaeology: Repatriation's Impact on Contemporary Research and Practice
Thomas W. Killion, ed.

New Landscapes of Inequality: Neoliberalism and the Erosion of Democracy in America
Jane L. Collins, Micaela di Leonardo, & Brett Williams, eds.

Small Worlds: Method, Meaning, & Narrative in Microhistory
James F. Brooks, Christopher R. N. DeCorse, & John Walton, eds.

Memory Work: Archaeologies of Material Practices
Barbara J. Mills & William H. Walker, eds.

Figuring the Future: Globalization and the Temporalities of Children and Youth
Jennifer Cole & Deborah Durham, eds.

Timely Assets: The Politics of Resources and Their Temporalities
Elizabeth Emma Ferry & Mandana E. Limbert, eds.

Democracy: Anthropological Approaches
Julia Paley, ed.

Published by University of California Press

Writing Culture: The Poetics and Politics of Ethnography
James Clifford & George E. Marcus, eds.

Published by University of Arizona Press

The Collapse of Ancient States and Civilizations
Norman Yoffee & George L. Cowgill, eds.

PUBLISHED BY CAMBRIDGE UNIVERSITY PRESS

THE ANASAZI IN A CHANGING ENVIRONMENT
George J. Gumerman, ed.

REGIONAL PERSPECTIVES ON THE OLMEC
Robert J. Sharer & David C. Grove, eds.

THE CHEMISTRY OF PREHISTORIC HUMAN BONE
T. Douglas Price, ed.

THE EMERGENCE OF MODERN HUMANS: BIOCULTURAL ADAPTATIONS IN THE LATER PLEISTOCENE
Erik Trinkaus, ed.

THE ANTHROPOLOGY OF WAR
Jonathan Haas, ed.

THE EVOLUTION OF POLITICAL SYSTEMS
Steadman Upham, ed.

CLASSIC MAYA POLITICAL HISTORY: HIEROGLYPHIC AND ARCHAEOLOGICAL EVIDENCE
T. Patrick Culbert, ed.

TURKO-PERSIA IN HISTORICAL PERSPECTIVE
Robert L. Canfield, ed.

CHIEFDOMS: POWER, ECONOMY, AND IDEOLOGY
Timothy Earle, ed.

RECONSTRUCTING PREHISTORIC PUEBLO SOCIETIES
William A. Longacre, ed.

PUBLISHED BY UNIVERSITY OF NEW MEXICO PRESS

NEW PERSPECTIVES ON THE PUEBLOS
Alfonso Ortiz, ed.

STRUCTURE AND PROCESS IN LATIN AMERICA
Arnold Strickon & Sidney M. Greenfield, eds.

THE CLASSIC MAYA COLLAPSE
T. Patrick Culbert, ed.

METHODS AND THEORIES OF ANTHROPOLOGICAL GENETICS
M. H. Crawford & P. L. Workman, eds.

SIXTEENTH-CENTURY MEXICO: THE WORK OF SAHAGUN
Munro S. Edmonson, ed.

ANCIENT CIVILIZATION AND TRADE
Jeremy A. Sabloff & C. C. Lamberg-Karlovsky, eds.

PHOTOGRAPHY IN ARCHAEOLOGICAL RESEARCH
Elmer Harp, Jr., ed.

MEANING IN ANTHROPOLOGY
Keith H. Basso & Henry A. Selby, eds.

THE VALLEY OF MEXICO: STUDIES IN PRE-HISPANIC ECOLOGY AND SOCIETY
Eric R. Wolf, ed.

DEMOGRAPHIC ANTHROPOLOGY: QUANTITATIVE APPROACHES
Ezra B. W. Zubrow, ed.

THE ORIGINS OF MAYA CIVILIZATION
Richard E. W. Adams, ed.

EXPLANATION OF PREHISTORIC CHANGE
James N. Hill, ed.

EXPLORATIONS IN ETHNOARCHAEOLOGY
Richard A. Gould, ed.

ENTREPRENEURS IN CULTURAL CONTEXT
Sidney M. Greenfield, Arnold Strickon, & Robert T. Aubey, eds.

THE DYING COMMUNITY
Art Gallaher, Jr. & Harlan Padfield, eds.

SOUTHWESTERN INDIAN RITUAL DRAMA
Charlotte J. Frisbie, ed.

LOWLAND MAYA SETTLEMENT PATTERNS
Wendy Ashmore, ed.

SIMULATIONS IN ARCHAEOLOGY
Jeremy A. Sabloff, ed.

CHAN CHAN: ANDEAN DESERT CITY
Michael E. Moseley & Kent C. Day, eds.

SHIPWRECK ANTHROPOLOGY
Richard A. Gould, ed.

ELITES: ETHNOGRAPHIC ISSUES
George E. Marcus, ed.

THE ARCHAEOLOGY OF LOWER CENTRAL AMERICA
Frederick W. Lange & Doris Z. Stone, eds.

LATE LOWLAND MAYA CIVILIZATION: CLASSIC TO POSTCLASSIC
Jeremy A. Sabloff & E. Wyllys Andrews V, eds.

Photo by Katrina Lasko

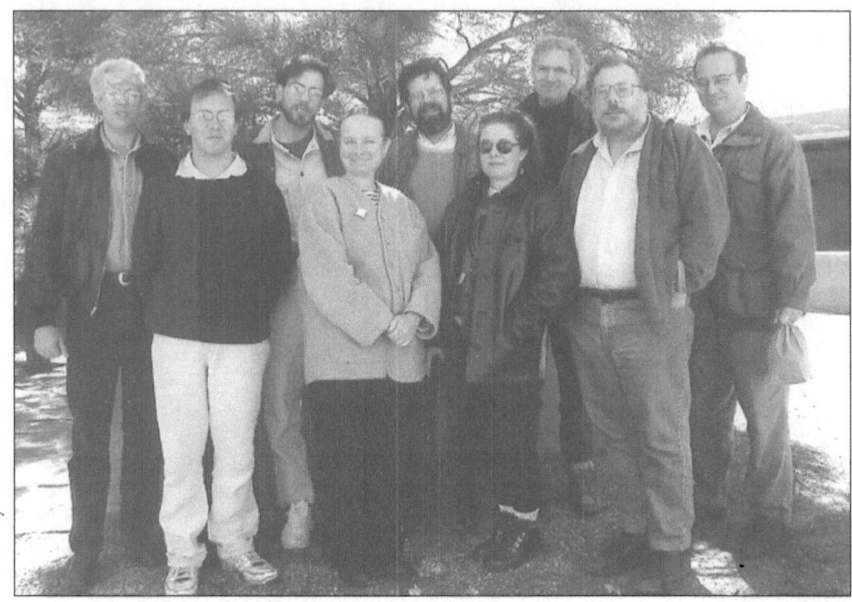

Participants in the School of American Research advanced seminar "Material Culture: Habitats and Values," Santa Fe, New Mexico, November 1996. Left to right: Fred R. Myers, Nicholas Thomas, Christopher B. Steiner, Barbara Kirshenblat-Gimblett, Daniel Miller, Annie E. Coombes, Webb Keane, Ivan Karp, Claudio Lomnitz.

www.ingramcontent.com/pod-product-compliance
Lightning Source LLC
LaVergne TN
LVHW041106080826
845145LV00007B/1702